OPERA FOR ALL

Opera for All

The Biography of Sir Peter Jonas

Julia Glesner

Translated by Edward Maltby

First published in Germany by Insel Verlag 2021

This English language paperback edition privately published in 2023

Copyright © Julia Glesner 2023

Foreword by Donna Leon. Copyright © 2020 Diogenes Verlag AG Zurich, Switzerland. All rights reserved.

Copyright in the Afterword © Daniel Barenboim 2023. All rights reserved.

Julia Glesner has asserted her right under the Copyright, Designs and Patents Act 1988 to be identified as the author of this work.

All rights reserved. No part of this publication may be reproduced, stored in a retrieval system or transmitted, in any form or by any means, without the publisher's prior permission in writing.

This book is sold subject to the condition that it shall not, by way of trade or otherwise, be lent, resold, hired out or otherwise circulated without the publisher's prior consent in any form of binding or cover other than that in which it is published and without a similar condition, including this condition, being imposed on the subsequent purchaser.

Cover image by Wilfried Hösl.

Extract from *The Complete Poems of Philip Larkin* by kind permission of Faber & Faber.

Every reasonable effort has been made to trace copyright holders of material reproduced in this book, but if any have been inadvertently overlooked the publishers would be glad to hear from them.

URLs in endnotes correct at time of writing, but subject to subsequent change.

Edited, designed and produced by Tandem Publishing
http://tandempublishing.yolasite.com/

10 9 8 7 6 5 4 3 2 1

A CIP catalogue record for this book is available from the British Library.

Proceeds from the publication will go to the John Nickson and Simon Rew Scholarship in memory of Sir Peter Jonas at the Royal College of Music.

Contents

Foreword by Donna Leon	xi
TO PORTRAY THE BEST OF PEOPLE	1
I am sort of a Glückspilz [lucky devil]	2
My life is not shaped by opera	11
A religiously musical person	17
Playing chess with death	24
The reason is always musical	29
A consummate gentleman	37
He told another cabaletta!	46
The wanderer	48
Cars, cricket and football!	52
Teaching	55
Making speeches	57
The Social Science Center in Berlin	61
CHILDHOOD AND YOUTH	
London after the Second World War	71
The Ziadie family in Jamaica	77
The Jonas family from Hamburg	80
Walter Jonas	93
Hilda May Jonas, née Ziadie	97
The Jonas family in London	100
Worth School	105
Kathryn, his destiny	113
The parents' divorce	114
Adolescence at Worth	116
STUDENT YEARS	
The experiment	122
Sussex 1965–1968	124
Kathryn's death	130
Antony Costley-White and Mark Elder	132

Chimes Music Shop	136
The summer of 1968	138
Manchester 1968–1971	142
London 1971–1973	149
Rochester 1973–1974	153
Schoenberg op 3 Variations for Orchestra	157

CHICAGO 1974–1984

Sir Georg Solti and the Chicago Symphony Orchestra	164
Simply starting	171
First tour to New York	178
Two new offers	182
The moment of diagnosis	185
Das Rheingold at the Opéra de Paris	191
Lucia Popp	194
The first leading role	199
Harry Zelzer and the Allied Arts Corporation	202
Vladimir Horowitz	207
Total trust	210
Walter Felsenstein and Wieland Wagner	215
The drama of the gifted child	217
My charming, superficial little brother	223
Innovative programming	225
Ten green bottles	229

MUNICH 1946–1947

Knocking on your own door	233
Georg Solti and Ferdinand Leitner	234
Edward Kilényi	237
Resistance to Solti	241

LONDON 1984–1993

The agony of choice	245
Lord Goodman	249
The Coliseum	252
Lord Harewood	254

Peter who?	257
End of the Harewood era	262
The ENO experience	268
Chosen enemies	271
Cuts, cuts, cuts!	279
The triumvirate: a new style of leadership	281
Creating an *ondit*	*285*
A huckster for musical theatre	288
Lesley Garrett	291
A new stage aesthetic	295
David Alden	303
Peter Palumbo	306
Pan Am flight 103	312
Innovative musical theatre marketing	314
The year 1989 and the tour to Russia	329
The 20+ season	333
Once again: Peter who?	340
The London legacy	347
Farewell in a wheelchair	351
MUNICH 1993–2006	
The dinosaur	359
People's Republic of Technology	365
21 March 1993	369
The letters of complaint	373
PJ and the Free State of Bavaria	377
David Alden's *Tannhäuser*	383
Opera and urban society	386
Each man kills the thing he loves	388
Barbara Burgdorf	389
Pierre Mendell	391
Parsifal	395
A James Bond of the opera	397
Everyday life at the opera	402
Jürgen Rose	413
Zubin Mehta and Sir Georg Solti	417

Zubin Mehta, ideal general music director	420
Criticism from the Audit Office	425
Modern music theatre management	427
The stolid and the German were shaken off	432
Programme and programme policy	436
Festspiel+	439
Opera for all	440
Music theatre as social dramaturgy	446
So shalt thou feed on death, which feeds on men	450
Footsteps in the past	453
Respect and appreciate artists!	456
Not an opera crisis, a Berlin crisis!	458
Being the one that got away	462
CODA	470
Afterword by Daniel Barenboim	487
Acknowledgements	490
About the Author & Translator	492
Picture credits	493
Notes	494

Sir Peter Jonas by Donna Leon

It is lamentably seldom these days that the formation of a friendship can be attributed to a dinosaur, but this was indeed the case with my friendship with Peter Jonas. A quarter of a century ago – just think – I saw the revelatory production of Handel's *Giulio Cesare* at the Bayerische Staatsoper in Munich – of which the dinosaur was a part – and some days later, when I was at least partially recovered from the experience, I wrote – as my Great-Aunt Gert had instructed all members of my family – a thank-you note to the person responsible, Peter Jonas.

Some weeks later, I received a response – handwritten – from Peter, the Intendant [artistic director], and thus the person responsible, who invited me, when next I was in Munich, to come along and see another performance and to stop in and say hello.

It is perhaps just as rare as a dinosaur on stage that one's first meeting with someone who will become a friend is delayed because the person to be met is busy standing on his head. But it was the lunch break when I went to visit, and I was told that Peter was in the habit of spending that time on his head. After some time, Peter returned to his feet, I went into his office, and there began the many chats and the friendship.

The link between us was, assuredly, our shared passion for the music of Handel, though his addiction was far more advanced and far more important. After all, he used – praise the Lord – his position to change the listening habits of a continent.

Before Peter put that towering dinosaur on the stage, Handel was presented in a few European festivals in a style akin to Birkenstocks worn with socks. Thump, thump, bump, a hundred voices singing the 'Hallelujah Chorus', and *Cesare* sung by a bass. Post-dinosaur and for his entire tenure as Intendant, the Staatsoper became the most famous opera house in Europe, and Handel won back his place as the leading opera composer of the day.

Today, Handel is everywhere, and he's there because of Peter and the genius of those first productions, when he pretty much grabbed the opera-going public of a continent by the ears and demanded, as Hamlet did of Gertrude, 'How like you this?' A great deal, as it turned out, and praise Peter for that, always.

I was struck at the beginning by three qualities I saw in him and that remained intact at our last meeting: intelligence, decency, and charm. He was smart, and his knowledge and understanding swept from music, to history, economics, to science and astronomy, and then back to art. He was not in the business of making moral judgment, though he had an ethical sense that disapproved of cheating and valued civility. Even with this, he never conquered his childlike wonderment at the many ways in which adults could misbehave. And he had charm. My God, the man could charm a statue from its plinth.

Over the years, then the decades, we met occasionally, corresponded intermittently, but – no matter how long the gap had been – we always picked up the conversation where it had stopped.

Peter was the Scheherazade, truth to tell. Because of the marvelous variety of his studies, travels, work, and friendships: there was always something or someone he could pick out of his memory, and there were certain stories I'd ask him to tell me again and again. I confess I had many favorites and made specific requests to hear them.

My favorite was his visit in Jamaica to his incarcerated cousins, busy running the island's drug business from the suites they maintained – with private, uniformed, and heavily armed guards – inside the prison where they were being held, one of the few places where they were safe.

Another was the story of a soprano who came into his office in a raincoat, locking the door behind her. She had come to request that he allow her to cancel her contract so that she could accept a better one in another country. When he refused, she untied her raincoat (think Ingrid Bergman in *Casablanca*) under which she wore nothing and said she'd do anything if he'd agree. The best part of the story was his acting out of his fumbling grab for the telephone, begging his secretary to come into the office immediately and save him.

He also spoke of his school days in the fifties at a Benedictine boys' school, which he described as a Gulag with a crucifix in every room. What always touched me most about his telling of the story was his nostalgia for these boys, caught at the age of first lust and with only confused ideas about what to do with it.

In all of his stories, Peter presented himself as a bumbling innocent, not at all sure what to think or do: the tone was pure slapstick, and judgment was never dragged into the telling of the tale.

Alas, there were also stories of the enemy who walked just one step behind him for most of his life: cancer. He once told me how many times he'd been diagnosed and how many operations he'd had. It would be normal, there, to write 'that he endured,' but he spoke of his medical history only with scientific interest and distance and thus spared the hearer the pain of understanding. I remember his description of the enormous cannon, many meters long, that was going to shoot a single atom into his eye, for he had so often outwitted his cancers that his eye was one of the few places left for it to attack. His real curiosity about the process was so contagious – I suspect this was Peter's desire – that the listener, too, became so intrigued by the mystery and complexity of the treatment as to be diverted from the fact that this was a deadly disease making yet another attack on a beloved friend.

Our last meeting was meant to be the first of a larkish plan we had to record him talking about his life, and then we'd somehow turn it into his autobiography. We chatted, we had lunch, more chat, and then the story of his cousins for dessert, coffee, and then off I went, delighted with the stories and his intelligence and company as well as his thoughtfulness in having had coffee ice cream for us both. And planning to continue the next time we were in the same city at the same time.

That never happened, and now he's gone. But his memory stays: he was the best storyteller I ever knew, my life was immeasurably enriched by his friendship, and I've never met a man who looked better wearing a kilt.

– Donna Leon

TO PORTRAY THE BEST OF PEOPLE

Writing a book is a long journey. Peter Jonas thought hard before giving consent to work together on this biography. He was unsure whether he would have the strength or desire. And, as a dramatist, he also questioned whether his life and what he had made of it could really be of interest to readers.

After he had given that consent, he set about it with characteristic seriousness. He was a fellow traveller on this journey, investing a lot of time in the process – in spite of his final diagnosis.

Over the course of long conversations, he immersed himself in recollections of the man he had once been. He related all that he could – or all that he wanted to – remember in the light of his experiences and learning in the years following. He spoke of many encounters with people who had accompanied him on his path. Other names he omitted. While telling the story of his life, he laughed, cried and swore. But also, again and again, silences fell. Some memories were beautiful and heartening; others proved painful.

One cannot write truthfully about a life without dredging its depths and shallows. Nor can one succeed without acknowledging that one must leave some areas untouched and some weighty questions unanswered. Beyond the image that the public had of Sir Peter, which he himself carefully cultivated, beyond the public figure of the radiant, brilliant, witty intellectual, Peter Jonas was a complex and harrowed man.

His life story takes us deep into the turmoil of the twentieth century. His life forms a chapter in its own right in the cultural history of this century. A child of immigrants, none of his achievements had been preordained from birth. His childhood was anything but carefree; at a young age he had to cope with traumatising experiences. It had not been in his character to pause or falter then. Through superhuman effort he pressed on. That made him free.

I am sort of a Glückspilz [lucky devil]

Even after his directorship of the Bavarian Staatsoper (BSO) in Munich came to an end, whenever Peter Jonas met members of the ensemble he continued to enjoy feeling part of the 'Familie'. He had received many prestigious awards for his achievements in opera, 'But the greatest reward I received for my time in Munich was not a Medaille or a Preis, but the fact that I was made an honorary member of the Bavarian Staatsoper,' Jonas recounted. 'I am so proud of this Mitarbeiterausweis [staff ID card]. You have no idea what it means to me.' Peter Jonas spoke in his typical mixture of English and German. Observers, however, knew that he spoke German much better than he pretended to.

Fig. 1: Jonas with his Mitarbeiterausweis

For theatre people, the establishment where they work often forms a cosmos unto itself. When things are going well it is their home, an anchor-point in a life characterised by wandering. To describe this special relationship, Jonas always chose the word 'family'. He stayed for at least a decade in each of the three major centres of his professional life and tried to create an atmosphere of trust and openness during each tenure. The Bavarian Staatsoper became one such 'family house' for him, and in a particular way. He always felt especially at ease there. These institutions fulfilled his need for a family, but were always far more than just a surrogate.

'Artistic institutions are our life, our heritage. They portray the best of us humans as a society,' Jonas said.

'What we have created artistically, we have to pass on.'[1] Future historians, he thought, would not judge people by their industrial feats or sales figures, but by the cultural legacy through which each generation defines itself. 'The works of art that we create, perform and interpret are the fingerprint of our civilisation. They belong to everyone and they must be accessible to everyone.'[2]

His faith in artistic institutions, in the argument for their existence, and in their powers, was unshakeable. 'The institutions make the artists, empower them, shape their talent and give them a space of freedom. Creating this space of freedom is principally the job of the artistic director.' He was firmly convinced that art and culture could hold society together, that art, a 'battlefield of tolerance', could render society's soil fertile. Jonas hoped that 'we humans never lose the need to express our most tender, dark, secret and idiosyncratic feelings through art.' No one, no government, no politician, no artistic director, he thought, should see culture as his own property. 'It is this environment that gives art its strength.' He drew a far-reaching conclusion from this: the person entrusted with responsibility for such an institution 'must obey the dictates of artistic truth and integrity'.[3]

Jonas's passion was for opera – perhaps the most 'artificial' of all art forms, for how often do we actually communicate in song? For him, opera's secret lay in how lifelike its portrayal of events on stage could be, 'although they in no way resemble what we regard as reality'.[4] The socialist in him revolted against the fact that opera enjoyed high cultural and economic capital. Peter Jonas dedicated his entire life to making opera accessible to all people: 'Opera for all' was his maxim. At the same time, he was always aware of how far he was from achieving this ultimate aim.

He was no less dedicated to the goal of breaking down clichés and prejudices about opera. With sharp obstinacy, he conducted this debate on a political level, aiming to arm the opera, which he saw as becoming a 'target for philistines from the right who would like to smash idiosyncratic culture and especially subsidised and labour-intensive culture', and at the same time to ward against accusations from the left that the opera was elitist.

Peter Jonas was one of the leading theatre figures of his generation. At the Chicago Symphony Orchestra, English National Opera and the Bavarian Staatsoper in Munich, the three major stages of his career, he achieved outstanding results. In November 1974 he joined the Chicago Symphony Orchestra (CSO) as assistant to Sir Georg Solti, and was to become the orchestra's first Artistic Administrator in January 1978. It was his first job and he was very young: twenty-eight years old. He had no idea about business and had to adapt, quickly. 'I worked very hard. And it was very hard. I worked and worked and worked. I did nothing else but work in Chicago,' Jonas said. 'I had a few love affairs, but apart from that I had nothing.'

His Chicago years were a fantastic time. He worked for one of the best conductors at one of the world's leading orchestras, encountered the most important artists of his time, immersed himself in the international art world and accompanied his partner Lucia Popp, herself one of the leading sopranos of the day, to the world's great opera houses. With the CSO, he performed several semi-staged operas annually, oversaw twenty-nine US tours, five foreign tours and over two hundred recordings for vinyl and television with the most important production companies.

Such innovations, involving as they did an increase in the orchestra's workload, required the support of the Board of

Directors. At the head of this body sat Chicago's business tycoons. Jonas met the challenge: 'a European Englishman skating on the tricky ice rink of Chicago arts politics'[5] was how he described himself. John Edwards, the orchestra's general manager, was the doyen of managers of major US orchestras. He became Jonas's mentor and taught him the business. The two were bound by a marvellous friendship and working relationship: the first of the sustaining working friendships that characterised Jonas's professional life from then on, 'a dream couple at work', as Daniel Barenboim described it.[6]

Barenboim had known Edwards since his youth. In Chicago, the three of them would often go out to dinner, and talk about music and life. 'I was very impressed by Peter's musical knowledge: it goes much deeper than those of other people who – then and now – worked or work in music administration. We could talk about music for hours without having to mention the Chicago Symphony Orchestra,' Barenboim enthused. 'It was so astonishing that a person in a position like his was so interested in music!'

It was during this time that a lifelong and precious friendship developed between Peter Jonas and Daniel Barenboim. Even at that early stage, Barenboim already admired him for his intelligence and humour. For Barenboim, these qualities were the reason why Jonas got on so well with the American mindset. The CSO with its famous guests had become the first of Jonas's 'Family Houses'. The artists who performed with the CSO – Claudio Abbado, Hildegard Behrens, Steven de Groote, Carlos Kleiber, Rafael Kubelík, Erich Leinsdorf, Charles Mackerras, Giuseppe Sinopoli and many more – were the reason that Jonas would claim: 'I am a link to a past cultural heritage.'

Jonas left Chicago in 1984 to take up his post as general manager of English National Opera. His tenure at ENO marked the beginning of the years that were to go down in British opera history as the era of the 'Power House triumvirate'. The triumvirate consisted of Jonas, Mark Elder, already music director at ENO, and their mutual friend from student days, David Pountney, who had taken over production management there. The managerial revolution in England had just begun, and the real creative impulses were then coming from the theatrical stage. With the Power House triumvirate, that was about to be overturned. Of the ten productions that a 2011 *Guardian* article counted as works that had changed the British opera world, three fell into this era: David Alden's *Mazeppa* (1984), Nicholas Hytner's *Xerxes* (1985) and David Pountney's *Rusalka* (1986).[7]

ENO was known for ensemble work and a culture of rehearsals, following the ideals of its founder Lilian Baylis, and above all for social inclusion: through low ticket prices and singing in English, ENO wanted to reach the largest possible number of people from different milieus.

To achieve this under the Thatcher government was no mean feat. From May 1979, Margaret Thatcher had been dismantling the post-war welfare state with grim determination, putting her trust in market forces. She shook the whole of British social and cultural life.[8]

When Jonas began his directorship, the Thatcher government was planning major changes in the promotion of the arts. ENO was vulnerable, as there were factions within the government and within the Arts Council, which organised cultural funding, who believed that London needed only one opera house. ENO was – and is – considered second to the Royal Opera House of Covent Garden, a ranking that, according to renowned London critic Tom Sutcliffe, only Reginald Goodall's *Ring des Nibelungen* in 1967 and the programme policy of Jonas's directorship from 1984 to 1993 ever really challenged.[9]

It was one of the great achievements of the triumvirate that, after this directorship, ENO was recognised as a 'necessary and important element of the arts in this country', as Jonas's former collaborator Maggie Sedwards put it.[10]

Jonas and his companions fought an uphill battle against the Arts Council and its chairman William Rees-Mogg, who acted without any concept of a cultural policy for opera in Britain.[11] 'We learned a lot about moral courage,' Jonas told the press. 'Mrs T. was breathing down our necks, and Rees-Mogg was hovering like some helicopter, spraying expressions of shame at every penny of public money being spent on the arts, and preaching that there was too much opera for the country to afford. The biggest load of bull ever spoken.'[12] Over the years of his directorship, the rate of Arts Council subsidy fell from 74 per cent to 49 per cent. The triumvirate reacted against the materialist spirit of the times, fought government apparatchiks and developed a radical style that made it impossible for audiences to avoid the debate. For Jonas the Catholic, it was purgatory. 'I wish there had been less politics,' he confessed. 'How much of my time there was spent on administration, finance, political issues and marketing. The whole subsidy system is so rotten and complicated.'

The triumvirate's darkest fear had been the prospect of 'opera-goer and music-lover' Prince Charles weighing in on the controversies around ENO. They worried that the Prince would 'extend his undeserved but highly influential outbursts to the subject of opera'.[13]

Their efforts paid off. ENO was an 'engine room of radical experimentation in opera production' and Jonas became the 'leading advocate for state support of the arts'[14] according to his *Guardian* obituary. Radical and dramatic productions shocked and thrilled spectators. ENO was regarded as aesthetically innovative, and it did indeed attract those new audiences.

'For the first time in the UK, a team of cultural directors, singers and musicians, and marketing and fundraising professionals, worked together to achieve common aesthetic, political, promotional and funding goals,' says John Nickson, responsible for ENO's fundraising.[15]

In the years of the Power House triumvirate, ENO was a 'Family Company', without question. Lesley Garrett, the leading soprano there, but also Jonas's partner, remembers above all the camaraderie, creativity and energy, the Ensemble's unity of purpose, and the clear quality standards.[16] For his services to opera in England, Peter Jonas was appointed 'Commander of the British Empire' by the Queen in 1999.

As for Jonas's working style, a motif began to emerge: 'In ENO

I worked from dawn to midnight. I had no life apart from that.' Of his career success he said: 'Don't be mistaken. It was all hard work.' The same would be true when he moved to Munich.

Imagine the reaction from the London press if a German artistic director (or even a female artistic director) were appointed to the top job at ENO, the Royal Opera House Covent Garden or the National Theatre.

The Free State of Bavaria took a step in a new direction when they chose Peter Jonas as the new State Director of the Bavarian Staatsoper in Munich. For Jonas, it was proof of Germany's – and indeed Bavaria's – openness: 'Might I venture to suggest,' he said in typical fashion, 'that the German-speaking world is a little more open to bridging the leadership gap in opera and theatre than the British are?'[17]

So, at the age of forty-three, Peter Jonas was appointed State Director of the Bavarian Staatsoper. He took up his post at the beginning of the 1993–94 season, catapulted into a position of responsibility for one of the largest opera companies in the world, which at that time had eight hundred and six permanent employees. Prepared tactically by Jonas's intimate knowledge of the American music scene, Bavaria succeeded in engaging the internationally acclaimed conductor Zubin Mehta as General Music Director of the Bavarian Staatsoper from the 1998–99 season onwards. Both Jonas and Mehta remained in Munich until 2006. Together they succeeded in creating 'a model of how an opera house can be run', as Daniel Barenboim described the fruit of this collaboration. Peter Jonas and Zubin Mehta were ideal partners, not least because Jonas departed from his guiding principle of treating artistic and management decisions equally, and began to shift in favour of the artists.

Whereas in England, popularity, inclusivity and accessibility are crucial values that guide the management of an opera house, and a 'bland but popular show' would always be accepted as long as it was 'what we used to call a "banker" at the box office', in Germany no opera management would be considered successful without stringent dramaturgical planning of repertoire, Jonas explained.

In Germany, audiences and critics expected a 'confrontation with a conceptual interpretation, the more radical the better', but in England a performance was expected to thrill, rather than to explore a particular concept or point of view. Jonas's assumption was that British crowds would neither forgive nor tolerate a brilliant concept, no matter what form it took, if the performances were deemed inadequate. 'In short: concept versus narrative' is how he outlined the contrast between the German and the British stance.

He discussed the differences between the two cultures, their societies and their politics often and at length, terming them 'the Anglo-German Divide.' When Jonas came to take up his directorship in Munich he was keenly aware of these differences. 'An eclectic "pick and mix" editorial policy would have led to my being crucified rather quickly as the new artistic director in Munich,' Jonas concluded.[18] 'To be considered a successful opera director in Germany and to have one's (temporary) contract extended, one has to show much more than balanced accounts and flourishing box office returns. One must at least give the impression that one's own house is adventurous, provocative and successful in order to make a name in society.'[19]

His work on the programme was extremely demanding and of the highest quality. It did much more than just trigger the Handel renaissance. It was precisely the off-beat elements he introduced, mostly shaped by his personal preferences and produced to the highest standards of modern auteur theatre, that enabled a high-quality expansion of the repertoire. Peter Jonas led the Bavarian Staatsoper in Munich into the modern age.

Even when he was still living in Chicago, visiting artists had told Jonas about the Munich National Theatre, home of the Bavarian Staatsoper (BSO). Jonas first visited the BSO in his student years, on his way back from the Bayreuth Festival. He later returned because of his partner Lucia Popp. While Jonas found the sight lines at the Vienna Opera unappealing and the audience space at the Royal Opera Covent Garden too long, he thought the Munich National Theatre, this 'replica of a ruin', was perfect: 'The Munich

National Theatre is more than a pastiche: the roots are right.'[20]

If one were to draw an axis through the stalls in the auditorium there, it would not form an angle of 180 degrees at the ramp. That's why he always felt more comfortable sitting on the right there, coincidentally where the director's box was located. At rehearsals he usually sat in the stalls in the eleventh row on the right. Later, as an honorary member, he sat in the first tier, to the right of the centre.[21] He was amused to observe that, because of the lack of a central aisle, all opera-goers in any row had to wait standing until the last latecomer had found his or her seat. He loved living in Munich. He lauded the city for its advantages over the metropolises of the world, especially Chicago and London. As an 'Alpine Oxford' and 'Athens of the North', it combined the best of both cities for him: despite its small size, there was an abundance of world-class cultural institutions, great restaurants, the local shops and cinemas, not to mention its beautiful natural setting. He would rattle all this off to anyone who asked.[22]

Jonas was proud to have managed 'three big jobs' in his life – apart from student jobs as a labourer on the London docks or as a dancer in *West Side Story*. Above all, he was proud of never having been fired. 'I feel very privileged that these opportunities have fallen into my lap, without any application letters at all,' he kept emphasising. 'I am very aware of that.'

Careers like his are no longer possible: the business runs differently. It saddened Jonas to see young talents who had just started a job looking over shoulders when greeting someone at the party, scanning the room for someone more important, constantly searching for their next role as soon as they had landed their current contract. 'I am sort of a Glückspilz. I did what I did and it didn't turn out so bad,' Jonas mused. 'I can't complain with anything that happened in my career. I never wrote a CV.'

This was probably the reason he would often mix up dates when talking about his own life, while at the same time be able to pinpoint with absolute precision other events.

My life is not shaped by opera

Jonas thought he had been given unique opportunities far too early. 'I had to do it my way. I tend to get from A to B following a curved path, I am not talented enough to go in a straight line.' Jonas was speaking in earnest when he said: 'My whole professional life has been one of shoelaces – this is serious!' Jonas claimed he was never able to tie his shoelaces 'normally', because his nanny had always tied his shoes as a child and no one had ever shown him how to do it at boarding school, which is why – in order to avoid beatings – he only ever managed a messy knot under pressure. 'That's why I always much preferred trainers without laces,' confessed Jonas, who was wearing an eye-catching pair that day, adorned with imitation laces that served no practical function.

It would be wrong to try to understand Peter Jonas purely in terms of the stages of his professional life. Behind his supposed problem with shoelaces lies a question, which for a long time he found hard to tackle, of what influence his parents' double-migrant background had on his life.

John Peter Jonas was born on 14 October 1946 in London, to immigrant parents. His mother came from a renowned but poor Lebanese family who had emigrated to Jamaica. His father was the son of secularised Jews from Hamburg. To escape the National Socialists, he had moved to London in 1933. The pressing question for Jonas was this: how had a child of migrant parents from Jamaica and Germany risen to the top? How had this boy, schooled at an ostensibly excellent but in reality rather limited Benedictine boarding school, and who could draw upon no family networks of his own, and who hailed from an unfashionable part of south London, managed to make it to the Munich Staatsoper? 'I came out of nowhere. I didn't deserve it, I was not qualified. At least that's how it feels to me.' This was the Catholic in him speaking.

When Jonas was eight, his parents had sent him off to a Benedictine boarding school, which resulted in lifelong trauma. And that would not be the only trauma he would face.

His parents separated and his father died a few years later. As a child, a teenager, Jonas lost any feeling of being at home. 'I am a fraud. And tomorrow everyone will find out!' His origins were a handicap, he was convinced of that at a young age. 'I am a blended person,' was how Jonas described his identity. 'I had a confused idea of who I was. At school I was teased mercilessly either for being German or Jewish.'[23] It was the writer W. G. Sebald, whom he met during his later studies, who was able to point him in a possible new direction. 'Your heritage will be your most important asset,' Sebald told him. This prediction was to prove accurate.

But there is another reason why any understanding of Jonas that looks only at his professional life would necessarily be inadequate. At the age of twenty-nine, in May 1976, just as he had established himself as Solti's assistant in Chicago, he fell ill with cancer. His doctors told him to put his affairs in order, telling him that he had only a year to live. Jonas was diagnosed with Hodgkin's lymphoma, a malignant disease of the lymphatic system. The survival rate was very low.

Hodgkin's lymphoma does not affect a single organ; it usually starts in a single, swollen lymph node and spreads through the lymph vessels to the entire body. The course of the illness is divided into stages. At the moment of diagnosis, Jonas was in an advanced stage, 3b: the tumour had already affected several organs. In addition, it was hidden behind his breastbone, where his final cancer was diagnosed in 2018. This is called a mediastinal tumour.[24]

'My life is not shaped by opera. I am convinced that I would not be who I am, that I would not have achieved what I have achieved, if I had not had to endure this illness with all its consequences,' said Jonas. 'Endure' is perhaps not the right word. It was about surviving, literally.

Since Thomas Hodgkin first described the symptoms of this tumour in 1932, scientific knowledge of the condition has come on substantially, and many new treatments have been developed. Survival rates have increased greatly. Until chemotherapy became an established part of cancer therapy in the 1970s, Hodgkin's lymphoma was considered incurable. This new treatment inspired high hopes in Jonas. Initially, cancer patients had been treated by surgery alone, but soon disciplines such as pathology and radiology grew more important. At the beginning of the 1980s, a paradigm shift was clearly underway. The likelihood of a cure had greatly increased, and some oncologists now even regard cancer as a chronic disease. Comprehensive treatment involving all different specialists now allows patients to live with cancer.[25]

Peter Jonas tracked all these phases of medical science, starting with his first chemotherapy and radiation treatments in 1976–77. His biography involves the progression of an illness and a dying process that spans almost half a century and several continents, because just as these medical debates were international, so was the team that treated him. He himself was the object of medical history, an object, of course, who was able to tell his own story.

Jonas repeatedly overcame life-threatening situations. 'The first time I witnessed it, we were running to the train on our way home from a hike in England when Peter suddenly started having breathing problems,' recalled his wife Barbara Burgdorf. 'Later he was given a stent. We had hiked for days before. He could have dropped dead on the spot on the platform.'[26]

After a stay in hospital, Jonas usually returned to work immediately. He could not let his work suffer, and he preferred not to let his colleagues know about it. His discipline, including yoga and Pilates, provided a coping framework, which at certain points simply became a form of emotional repression. He was characterised by 'his presence in the here and now', said Jutta Allmendinger, President of the WZB, Berlin's Social Science Center, a non-university research institution that conducts problem-oriented research in the field of social and political sciences; Jonas worked there after retirement. She continued: 'His carpe diem. Nothing was postponed. Quite different from people who are not confronted with the finite nature of their existence.'[27]

At the second congress of the European Organisation for Research and Treatment of Cancer in Brussels in 2016, he was invited, as a cancer survivor, to give the opening lecture and to talk about the challenges faced by people with cancer whose immediate treatment has ended and who now want to return to everyday life. He gave a striking account of how difficult it was for him to even be able to take out health insurance in the various countries in which he lived. In his lecture, he called openly on health insurance companies to change the way they do business and recognise the reality of cancer survivors.[28] He must have taken particular satisfaction when, after his lecture, an elderly gentleman approached and introduced himself as the Chicago resident who, in 1976, had typed up the report containing the prognosis that Jonas would live only a year.

In the moment of diagnosis Jonas, a healthy, vigorous, handsome young man, became a sick, disabled, still-young person with an uncertain future. From that moment of transition he could no longer suppress the knowledge of inevitable death. 'I have developed as a person, but cancer has also changed me a lot physically, from the naïve sunny boy my sister used to call me, to … someone rather grey, gaunt, kind of spooky, half dead. At times I have looked like a ghost.'

But Jonas had a very particular mindset: he was calibrated differently from others. For him, contact with death sharpened his will to live, his hunger for life. His diagnosis lent his innate curiosity a driving force that grew exponentially stronger in combination with his discipline and will. He loved life, the world; he quoted the words of his friend, the graphic designer Pierre Mendell: 'I like it here.' This gave him hope, even as he struggled with the after-effects of the initial treatments. He was able to overcome the typical symptoms of cancer, such as chronic fatigue, exhaustion and weakness, almost without breaking his stride, especially during his professional years. He was powerless in the face of his infertility, a direct result of his initial treatments; he was conscious of it ever since.

Peter Jonas's ability to cope with this excessive, unbearable challenge was due in part to how his innermost Chicago circle – Lucia Popp, Georg Solti and John Edwards – dealt with it. Popp cancelled performances in Europe to be at his bedside. Her care aided his recovery. Solti tried to make his everyday life bearable, offering him all manner of comforts, but above all this: Edwards and Solti believed in Jonas and in his future in the music business. After the fatal prognosis, giving Jonas one year to live, had been revised and Jonas was to resume employment, they offered him his first leadership position, a sign of confidence in his powers and skills. He was always aware of what his illness meant for the people who loved him.

In conversation with his doctors, he resolutely demanded his freedom: he wanted to be 'a bearer of freedom'. Despite his obviously dependent condition, he wanted to retain autonomy. He could not stand the idea that his doctors might spare him the truth, or hide the full extent of their diagnoses. He demanded of his doctors – often people who loved music and opera and who became his friends – something that had long been an exception rather than a rule for cancer patients: open, clear and truthful communication.[29]

For his part, he spoke in exactly the same way – openly, clearly and truthfully – about his illness. His appearance at the Cancer Congress in 2016 was just as much a part of this as a letter written in summer 2018 in which he informed friends, acquaintances and the media about his latest, and now probably final, diagnosis: 'A large fast-growing malignant tumour in my chest (at the site of my first HD lymphoma in 1976!) … If nothing is heard from me, it only means that, immodest and greedy as I am, I am battling. I don't want to wind up my expiring lease on this earth … yet!'[30] Jonas did not go into unnecessary detail, especially in professional contexts, but if during a meeting he needed to go and sit shivering by a radiator he would not hide it. He spoke about his fears with a select group of people: he did not conceal them. He was acutely aware of these fears, but would not let them make his decisions for him. When friends like Mark Elder described him as absolutely dauntless, it was this freedom from fear in his decision-making that they referred to.[31]

Jonas suffered the consequences of his first cancer treatment all his life. Again and again, he was confronted with new cancer diagnoses and other life-threatening developments. Death sat on his shoulder, it was his constant companion. 'Near-death experiences may pass, but with each new life-threatening situation they awaken once more. That doesn't make it any easier,' said Jonas, who spent years of his life dominated by his body and by treatment regimes. He was constantly robbed of his bodily integrity: infusion needles, blood collection syringes, medication, catheters, pain, nausea, fatigue, digestive problems, problems with eating, skin and hair changes. And yet, as an old man, he let himself be used as a subject by Barbara Luisi for a photography series: AKT – Ageless Beauty. The result was images of great intimacy and honesty, which though wordless allow him to tell his story. He described the portraits as 'pictorial life stories of nature and humanity in their inevitable but beautiful decline'.[32]

In the 1970s, when cancer research began to look at the causes of the disease, everything from chemical substances, radiation, injuries, trauma, parasites, viral diseases, stimulants to psychological dispositions and emotions were discussed as possible triggering factors. For a long time, it was considered a proven fact that negative feelings that persist over a long period could trigger cancer. The concept of a 'cancer personality', and the metaphorical use of the term cancer in general, were common. Jonas refused this line of thinking: his tumour was too concrete.

He would have agreed with Susan Sontag on this point. However, he had never read her book *Illness as Metaphor*, although it was published in 1977 at the height of his illness.[33] Contrary to doctors' predictions, Sontag had also survived cancer. In her essay, she vehemently opposed heaping metaphors onto cancer. For Sontag, the healthiest way to be ill with cancer was to detach oneself as much as possible from metaphorical thinking.[34] Jonas did not pursue this aim. The language of battle and war was what came naturally to him as a means of talking about his condition. 'Obviously, I have the talent to grow cancers,' he explained succinctly. 'Why? Nobody can explain.'

Why he had been hit again and again with The Big C – he alluded to the title of the US show, which as an avid viewer of television he had of course seen – was a question that he could never get past. He knew that he would not be able to beat cancer without destroying himself. He had to find a way to deal with this existential threat, this lifelong insecurity.[35]

It was not the only burden Jonas carried. In addition to the traumas of childhood – the move to boarding school, his parents' divorce, the death of his father – he had also not come to terms with the death of his sister.

A religiously musical person

When Kathryn Jonas died at the age of twenty-five, her mother and brother Peter found a will among her papers. Only a short while before her death, Kathryn had moved to Spain to work as a lecturer. She had made the will just a few months before she moved.

News of his sister's accidental death reached Jonas while he was studying for his first degree at Sussex. Jonas and his mother had to have his sister's body brought over from Spain. Although her mother and brother were familiar with her serious, religious and ascetic nature, the discovery of the will unsettled them deeply. Jonas could only interpret his sister's decision to make a will as a sign that this brilliant woman suspected her imminent death.

Fig. 2: Kathryn Jonas

Jonas had a close relationship with his sister, five years his senior. He adored her beyond measure. His faith in her was boundless. Even as an old man, tears came to his eyes when he talked about her and her importance in his life. Whenever he spoke of his own death, the idea of being reunited with her always resonated. Her death was one of the most fateful moments in his life. With her departure, he lost his moral compass. He continued his studies, bottling up the experience for years. His mother also never recovered from this tragedy.

Outwardly, Jonas's life seemed to be going well. After surviving his first chemotherapy and radiation treatments in 1978, he took up his post as artistic director of the CSO. But inwardly, Jonas had to admit that his soul was not in a good way.

In 1979 he underwent psychoanalysis in Chicago. He and his analyst discussed a crucial question: why was he never satisfied by any of his achievements? Why did he have to keep setting the goalposts higher and higher, like in show-jumping? Was it because his father had openly derided him as 'good for nothing'? Was it because the father had preferred Kathryn, whom Jonas envied for her intelligence? Was that a reason for Jonas to keep setting his goals higher and higher, in pursuit of the unattainable? 'Is it true? After all, in matters of upbringing, what is the truth?' Jonas reflected later. 'But who else might I want to impress if not my father or my sister?' He realised during his analysis that finding the answer to this question would not help him: because in the end, he would still want to achieve the unattainable. This dissatisfaction with himself, this inferiority complex, the compulsion to perform beyond his own capabilities, combined with a strict Catholic upbringing, created feelings of guilt that persisted throughout his life. The fact that a Jewish heritage from his father's family was largely concealed exacerbated the problem.

In her will, Kathryn had stipulated that she wanted to be buried in a secluded, quiet graveyard near an old church in Sussex, a beautiful place with tall, old trees and moss-covered headstones. Kathryn had also chosen the epitaph to adorn her gravestone, which was set apart from the older, crumbling graves by its unassuming design. The epitaph was set in a modern typeface: 'Happy the man who fails to stifle his vision'.

The line comes from the autobiographical essay 'Le Milieu Mystique', written by the French Jesuit Pierre Teilhard de Chardin in 1917, when serving as a medic in the First World War. The essay did not appear until 1956, one year after Teilhard's death. Kathryn read Teilhard after the first rejection of his writings by the Curia in 1957, and probably even after the monitum that the Catholic Church issued in 1962. The Holy Office had published this reprimand on the grounds that it would 'protect the souls – especially of young people – from the dangers contained in the works of Teilhard de Chardin and his followers'.[36] To the Catholic Church, Teilhard's unorthodox thinking seemed incompatible with doctrine.

But as is so often the case, this rebuke only increased the appeal. Many artists and intellectuals were inspired, and Teilhard had an enormous impact on the educated middle classes. The first English translations of Teilhard's texts appeared around the same time as the Curia condemned them. The original, which the linguistically gifted Kathryn would surely have understood, reads: 'Heureux celui qui n'aura pas réussi à étouffer sa vision.' In his essay, Teilhard outlines his personal journey to God as a movement of the soul towards the divine. Vision, for Teilhard, is the contemplation of God as the goal of human life. The passage continues: '… sous prétexte qu'il est absurde de trouver le Monde intéressant à partir du cercle, où, pour la majorité des humains, il cesse de devenir perceptiple.' 'Happy the man who fails to stifle his vision under the pretext that it is absurd to find the world interesting once one has reached the circle in which it ceases to be perceptible to the majority of human beings.'

For Teilhard, the mystical journey towards God proceeds through circles. Happy, then, is the person who has not arrested their journey towards the divine on the grounds that other people could no longer perceive the divine. Mystical happiness is achieved only by those who are prepared to maintain their vision in the face of the doubts of the majority.

For Jonas, this quote became his life's watchword. He committed himself to Kathryn's aspirations.

To call Jonas an observant Catholic would be an understatement. Jonas didn't like to be asked what he thought of religion. 'I am Catholic. I believe in art, art is Catholic. It's not Protestant,' Jonas would use this terse remark, summing up several centuries of church history, iconoclasm and controversy over images, as a means of deflection.

Peter Jonas was a profoundly religiously musical person. This metaphor – or rather the metaphor of the religiously unmusical man – was coined by Max Weber in his letters to Ferdinand Tönnies, written in 1909. In them, Weber draws an analogy between religious and musical practice. Weber understands both music and religion as human aptitudes, or as talents that can be developed through technique and practice.[37]

Jonas's Catholic upbringing in a family that tried to brush away his father's German-Jewish heritage, and whose religion put them in a minority in Britain, had a decisive influence on him, as did his education in a Benedictine boarding school. For better or worse, he had grown up in an environment that was highly conducive to the development of such faculties.

His first religious experiences were closely connected with the experience of art, and especially with the experience of music. His family life was structured around the church calendar, and through his sister's piano playing he became familiar with sacred music. He even adopted the Benedictine principle of 'ora et labora', with the less well-known addition: '… et lege'. This triad of prayer, work and reading defines the priorities of Benedictine life. The boarders lived by the monks' routines. Their education centred on the history of Christianity and on the Christian worldview. Jonas loved to stand by the abbey organist after mass and listen to him playing music by Bach and others.

The young man's fascination with the composer, impresario and manager Handel and his works began in the monastery library. 'I don't think I'm particularly gifted. I've always been a strange mixture of deliberate sloth and diligence,' the aged Peter Jonas once remarked. He was superstitious in a very simple way, which fitted in well with the many little rites that surround the life of the stage. He was no longer the little boy who walked the halls of Worth thinking to himself: 'If I break this rule now and commit a sin, God will surely punish me.' He had experienced too much, he knew that no divine retribution would strike. And yet the thought remained: 'If I put one foot wrong, he'll get me.' Decades later, lost in thought, he would still write the letters AMDG on his papers: Ad Maiorem Dei Gloriam, for the greater glory of God.

Worth Abbey in Sussex was Jonas's home for ten years, and its aesthetics had a decisive influence. Certainly those years had a hand in the development of his love for the paintings of the Old Masters, which he would later collect, as well as a general aspiration to consciously shape his own behaviour and speech.[38] He organised his collection of paintings based on his own particular set of rules: 'the works are connected by my own aesthetic, a little tough, monastic. Otherwise, my dwellings are rather pure temples.'

Jonas had an open mind towards the ultimate questions. 'Peter Jonas has a special relationship with God,' Daniel Barenboim has said. 'He doesn't like the Church, but he is somewhat attracted to religion. We have often talked about his Jewish roots.'

But the Jewish religion takes the view that the mother determines one's religion, because one can be certain only of her. Jonas's relationship to the Catholic Church, on the other hand, was clear: 'What I loved about the Church was the rituals.' The aesthete in him loved the form, if not necessarily the content, of the Latin mass.

After the Second Vatican Council, which ran from 1962 to 1965, the Catholic Church introduced the new liturgy in vernacular languages: 'It made me angry when the Church abandoned the Latin mass. What I loved about the Church was the fact that if you hitchhiked across Europe, you could go into any Catholic church and hear a language you understood. Even people who could not understand Latin had learned the liturgy. I missed that, I was quite militantly against it.'

Peter Jonas could rant hard and persistently about the failings of the Catholic Church. When he moved to Munich, he decided to leave the Church. 'Peter hung a big sign around his neck saying that he had resigned,' said his wife Barbara Burgdorf with a smile. 'But it was impossible for him, a Catholic, to go to a Protestant church. At Christmas he either wanted to go to mass or nothing at all.' Jonas fought against his Catholic upbringing, but his self-flagellation when he failed to achieve some goal, his feelings of guilt – 'I do feel guilty all the same' – were a part of his DNA. Peter Jonas was a deeply spiritual person. Right to the end, he retained a powerful vision of what art can and should do. He did not let outside voices dissuade him from his belief in the power of art. In this, he was following the guiding principle that his sister had chosen: 'Happy is the man who fails to stifle his vision.'

The things that guided Jonas in his behaviour, and moved him as a religiously musical person, seem also to bear, at some deep or even subconscious level, the imprint of the Benedictine Rule. The Rule says: 'Idleness is the enemy of the soul' (Leonard J. Doyle's translation). There could be no better guiding principle for Jonas, who – although he was sometimes called an ascetic – knew how to enjoy the finer things in life, but who nevertheless always struggled with feelings of guilt. The Benedictine Order understands humility as a process of self-knowledge and self-acceptance, an 'existential movement' that does not exclude setbacks. It would certainly be going too far to attribute to Jonas a search for a life of humility in the Benedictine sense. But his willingness to acknowledge and accept his illness as his own reality, to withstand this burden and to bear it to the end, were marked by unmistakable traits of this attitude to life. 'The way he talks about his illness and enduring the ordeals that now have to be endured,' said Jutta Allmendinger, who worked with him intensively during a bout of illness, 'it seems to be about a higher being who has ordered him to endure these sufferings.'

There are also conspicuous similarities between his conception of the role of a director and the Benedictine Rule. 'The truly humble person serves willingly and out of conviction,'[39] said the nun Michaela Puzicha, who emphasised not only willingness to serve but also self-sacrifice in the exercise of one's ministry, the acceptance of responsibility, and loyalty. For Jonas, the central activity of an artistic director was to serve the arts and the artists. That is what he geared his actions towards; that is what he demanded of those around him. But just as he drew a clear line by leaving the Church, he was certainly not religious in the sense that he organised everything in his life around that idea.

Jonas once confessed to thinking a lot about his tendency to make life difficult for himself through love. He had no intention of sparing himself 'these sufferings bordering on delirium' which occur 'when two people who are attracted to each other still cannot get together'. In his darker moments, he wondered what love was good for.[40] 'I have not lived the life of a saint. It would be foolish to say that,' Jonas confessed about his relationships with women. 'I have lived a completely normal life with many adventures. I am not afraid to talk about these adventures. It's just, the moment I start going into detail, I hurt someone.' As he said this, he was leaning against the radiator in his wife's kitchen, warming himself. The chemotherapy had made his body cold: he was constantly freezing. 'So many of my partners have either come from the industry or have inspired me in other ways. I had a classless love life, with ladies from all social classes: scientists, singers, doctors, waitresses and cleaners. So many of them only lasted a few years.' He fell silent. 'Only with Barbara has it been different. Her sense of freedom, her dedication to a third person, her violin, makes all the difference.'

Playing chess with death

For Jonas, who knew both God and the world, one film took on existential significance: Ingmar Bergman's *The Seventh Seal*. His sister had included it on one of her 'holiday lists'. Kathryn wrote lists of books and films for her brother to read or watch during each holiday. He accepted this without question, and benefited from her choices, which were a far cry from the canonical works taught at his school.

'This film tells the story of my religion. It is a symbol of my life,' Jonas explained. 'The knight who plays chess with death, that's me.' In Bergman's 1957 film Max von Sydow plays the knight Antonius Block who, together with his squire, returns to his Swedish homeland disillusioned and exhausted from the Crusades: he is the image of the intellectual in search of God. On the final stages of his return to his castle, the Knight sees a country emaciated by the plague, and fearful people firmly in the grip of the Catholic Church. As early as the opening scene, Antonius Block encounters Death.

> KNIGHT: Who are you?
> DEATH: I am death.
> KNIGHT: Have you come for me?
> DEATH: I have been walking by your side for a long time.

KNIGHT: That I know.
DEATH: Are you prepared?
KNIGHT: My body is frightened, but I am not.
DEATH: Well, there is no shame in that.

Fig. 3: Death and the Knight play chess

'DEATH opens his cloak to place it around the KNIGHT's shoulders,' Bergman's script went on: but the knight manages to persuade Death to play a game of chess, the duration of which is supposed to give him a final reprieve. The idea for the film came to him while looking at motifs in medieval paintings, Bergman wrote in the preface to his screenplay. He, the Swedish pastor's son, only ever half-listened to his father's sermons. Instead, he devoted his 'interest to the church's mysterious world of low arches, thick walls, the smell of eternity, the coloured sunlight quivering above the strangest vegetation of medieval paintings and carved figures on ceilings and walls ... the jugglers, the plague, the flagellants, Death playing chess, the funeral pyres for the witch burnings and the Crusades.'[41] A fresco of Death playing chess with a knight in a forest was on the wall of one of the village churches where his father took him. Bergman described his film as an 'allegory with a very simple theme: man, his eternal search for God and death as his only certainty'.[42]

'This film does not pretend to be a realistic picture of Sweden in the Middle Ages. It is an attempt at modern poetry, which translates the life experiences of a modern man into a form that deals very freely with the medieval setting.'[43]

Bergman, as a modern man raised in the Lutheran tradition, formulated an existentialist attitude in his film that is neither Christian nor atheistic, noted film critic Jacques Siclier.[44] 'My intention has been to paint in the same way as the medieval church painter, with the same objective interest, with the same tenderness and joy,'[45] Bergman explained. He created a 'panorama of worlds, bursting with details, events and characters, multiple plots and complex modalities of representation',[46] as the literary scholar Christian Kiening put it. Bergman shows people who are driven by feelings of guilt and fear of death.

The knight's search for knowledge, for the meaning of life, chimed with the pressing questions, the burdensome fears and feelings of guilt of the young Peter Jonas, who was sixteen years old when he first saw the film. 'For a Catholic boy, that scene in the confessional when the knight is betrayed by Death, who appears as a priest, is a really tough scene,' Jonas confessed. 'But it was no coincidence that my sister kept telling me that I should watch the film. Again, again! Until you know every line! It is my life story.' He also saw himself reflected in the characters' feelings of fear and guilt, their rituals, sometimes good, sometimes evil: 'A lot of what the Church passed on to us during my school years was fear – fear of hell,' says Jonas, for whom the Knight's questions were also his own: Why does God 'hide in a haze of half-promises and invisible miracles ... Why can I not kill God in me? Why does he live on in me in such a painful and humiliating way, although I curse him and want to tear him out of my heart?'[47]

When he fell ill, the film took on a very real meaning. It seemed that he was cheating death. 'For forty-four years I have been playing a kind of chess game with death. I always feel like I'm cheating a little bit.' He fell silent, only to start again a few moments later. 'It can't be that I am so talented at chess that I can beat him. I can't, nobody can.'

The voice of Death quotes from Revelation, the last book of the New Testament, at the beginning of the film: 'And when he had opened the seventh seal, there was silence in heaven about the space of half an hour.' (Rev. 8:1.) Bergman's film is interpreted as a visualisation of this 'half hour' in which preparations are made for the final revelation.[48] 'The film not only shows, it is the respite that death allows,'[49] according to Kiening, whereby the opening of the seventh seal in the Bible reveals 'not secrets of life and death, but God's judgement on humanity,'[50] as Siclier has it.

Jonas left the Church when he went to Munich. However, anyone who observed him at the artists' Ash Wednesday service in the Frauenkirche in Munich would have thought they were watching a practising Catholic. On 1 March 1995 he preached the Ash Wednesday sermon there, 'fifty years after the bombardment of the city of Dresden, the liberation of the concentration and extermination camps in Germany and Poland, the Yalta Conference and the end of the Second World War'.[51] He began with the paradox that art is 'indispensable to human existence, but not necessary in the strict sense'. Fifty years after the end of the Second World War, it is unthinkable to reflect on the significance of art without facing the fact that 'civilised man is capable of destroying culture, morality and even life itself with the tools of the technology and bureaucracy that he has created.' Even if art often fails to achieve its utopian goals, there can be no mistaking the truth of its mission. 'The fundamental integrity of any artistic endeavour always reinforces its fragile result because, along with religious conviction, the integrity of culture is one of the few things that supports the idea that our continuing existence as a community has real meaning and moral content.'[52]

Without God, exclaims Antonius Block in *The Seventh Seal*, 'life is an outrageous horror. No one can live in the face of death, knowing that all is nothingness.'[53] Essentially influenced by the Catholic Church, but alienated from it by a painful Benedictine upbringing, Jonas remained religiously musical. Jonas continued his sermon, saying that he saw a direct connection between the performing arts and collective prayer, through the origin of theatre in ritual and the need of every society to share its collective feelings. Whereas in religious rituals society tests its relationship to God, in the profane ritual of theatre it tests its relationship to itself: 'In opera, you have a conversation with your soul.'

Jonas saw today's society as weakened because too few people still participated in religious rituals. This imposed a 'burden' on the profane rituals of the stage that it could hardly bear. Because of its liturgical origins, opera occupies a unique position among the arts. It has a special power to probe 'the deeper mysteries of the religious'. The 'act of becoming aware of, hearing and listening to the inner voice, carried out in a community, is a profound social experience for the whole individual, much like communal and individual prayer.'[54]

One of the poems that Jonas often recited was Sonnet 146 by Shakespeare. In it, the lyrical 'I' addresses his own soul, 'Poor soul, the centre of my sinful earth.' It takes the form of a dialogue between soul and body, a format that was familiar as far back as the Middle Ages. 'Why so large cost, having so short a lease,/Dost thou upon thy fading mansion spend?'

It seems Jonas had these lines in mind when he spoke of his 'lease', his tenancy, on this earth not yet expiring. Shakespeare gave the sonnet a religious tenor: it seems like a psalm. 'Shall worms, inheritors of this excess,/Eat up thy charge? Is this thy body's end?' But for all that, it resists classification within any particular religious tradition. Here, spiritual content finds expression through an artistic medium, poetry – or music. That was the way Jonas expressed his religiosity, his spirituality.

The reason is always musical

For Jonas, the opening of Busoni's *Faust* is one of the most magical moments in all of opera. His fascination with this work was mixed with a conviction that he himself had made a Faustian pact with the devil: playing chess for his own life.

But *Faust* also touched on his German heritage, to which his father had always barred the way. 'Ferruccio Busoni was a German composer.' Jonas continued, 'He was Italian, but essentially a composer in the German tradition. When you sit in the darkened theatre and listen to the opening of this piece, you hear the most incredible, evocative sound painting of the German struggle with one's own soul, the Germans' hunt for answers. I have always felt that.'

When he was a student, he listened to a newly released first record twenty times. Late one evening, Jonas was talking about Busoni in his Zurich flat. The bells of the nearby Oberstrass church rang. 'Busoni is not accessible in an unmediated way. But he almost is.'

Jonas paused again. 'If there is an opera that illustrates the German problem, it is *Faust*. It is this deep, collective depression and introspection about the intellectual and emotional meaning of why we are here. Germany is very much preoccupied with this. The attraction of Germany and German culture, the darkness, there is no better expression of it than in the broad brushstrokes of the music during the opening of Busoni's *Faust*.' He searched for a long time that evening for a recording that would meet his requirements, and then broke off the meeting.

The broad brushstrokes of opera: Jonas first used this image in 1992 with his colleagues Mark Elder and David Pountney in a publication about the Power House years at ENO: 'Opera is a very clumsy medium for the expression of political ideologies – its brush is too broad for all those sub-clauses and selective hatreds. Yet political feeling, rather than ideology, is at the heart of all great opera. Its massed forces instinctively address the unspoken areas of emotional politics that are, in the long run, more fundamental. In so doing, it also illuminates the politics of personal relations: the vital fabric of social life that exists in the silence between people – exactly that space which is filled by music.'[55] Music gives expression to the inner voice. The collective act of harkening to this inner voice of ours is a crucial social experience.

During a conversation a few weeks before his death, Jonas wanted to clarify what really matters in opera. Each word emerged only with great effort. He often gasped and could not continue. He was lying on the sofa with an oxygen device at the ready. 'The reason is always a musical one. I stand by it: when I hear Daniel Barenboim play a piano sonata by Beethoven, that is the origin of drama in music! I make no apologies to my ur-dramaturgischen Freunden [primordially dramaturgical friends], David Alden and other compatriots. The drama and what the director makes of it originally comes from the score, from what Monteverdi or Cavalli or whoever wrote. The original energy of these works always comes from a musical thought.' Even the most pragmatic decision, the composition of the small building blocks of a production, stems from this primordial musical substrate. 'We do not learn from history, we do not honour history. It was important for me to be aware of history. This is very important for the reinterpretation of older works. Not just taking a fresh approach, but through an understanding of history. A strict inner dramaturgy. That's what's stopping me from going to the opera in England now. The death of dramaturgy.' Jonas sank back, exhausted. After he had regained his strength, he started to rail against that type of Bayreuth pilgrim who 'with his old evening dress, the dinner jacket not quite a good fit anymore because the Franconian beer was too nice, the bratwurst too tasty' attends the Festival performance only to 'rant about so-and-so's *Ring*. It's not so-and-so's *Ring*! It's Wagner's *Ring*!' For Jonas, music always came first, as did service to artists. 'That's what I really wanted to say.'

When Jonas was invited as a keynote speaker to mark Andreas Homoki's farewell at the Komische Oper Berlin in July 2012, he set out some of his fundamental ideas, in a witty but also moving philippic on music theatre. Opera, the 'most irrational art form';[56] 'the most complex and all-encompassing art form of humanity',[57] according to Jonas, is immensely important in a 'society with a flourishing culture of discussion', because it is one of the most important zones of freedom of thought and expression. It is 'a zone in which we can exercise our duty of civil disobedience and mistrust towards the state. Creativity in the interpretation of operatic works that refuse all realism and naturalism thrives on Walt Whitman's maxim: "resist much, obey little". As history teaches us, when organs of civil society grow, governmental apparatuses retreat, selfishly using our resources for things we do not approve of, and hoards for itself ever more power, military force and instruments for disciplining society. This may sound like liberal nonsense, but the fact is: for the past hundred and fifty years, the state has been responsible for most of our nightmares, and nowhere is that more evident than in the city where this theatre is located.'

He was convinced that a society is less healthy if it is not aware of the arts. He understood this notion at the individual level, but not in the sense that everyone has to be an expert on Shakespeare, Molière or Goethe. Instead, each and every individual should engage in the arts according to their means. 'Some kind of artistic life in a nation is essential for the health of the nation. It is also essential when it comes to communicating to people what they are afraid of, what they love or what they want to resist.' At the same time, he kept emphasising the proletarian nature of the life of an opera house. The amount of manual work that is done there is often underestimated. Moreover, people from all social classes work there, all of whom share a love of opera. He was painfully aware of the limitations of his own work. His labours had made opera more accessible but only up to a certain point. There were some parts of society that remained out of his reach. Conceptually, he also defended certain limits of accessibility: going to the opera should not be made as easy as going to a sauna. A certain preparatory education – education, education, education! – was a necessary precondition.

When discussing this idea, Jonas liked to refer to Preston Sturges's 1941 film *Sullivan's Travels*, at the end of which the hero realises that only humour can save the world.[58] During the thirty-five years Jonas worked as an artistic director, he was often asked about the most important quality for his work. He had often replied to the effect that 'most of us in this profession' were there by accident. He described himself as an 'accidental Intendant [artistic director]': 'Today, with hindsight, I would say: the most important qualities a director must have or acquire and develop are: the urge to SERVE with moral courage; the ability to listen (though not necessarily to follow); and reckless-naïve bravery.'[59]

He concluded with one of his recurrent remarks: 'I have often said, and not only in jest, that I only took on this post after my time as director of ENO because I was never offered the job at the Komische Oper Berlin.'[60] He referred to the house run by Walter Felsenstein and Harry Kupfer, whose profile is so similar to that of ENO. In conversation, he added that he believed he could not have survived in Berlin. He was, he said, not as tough a negotiator as Daniel Barenboim.

In 2013, Jonas published an essay in *Opera Magazine* on the state of the German-language opera world. In it, he said that 'the art form must be dramaturgically-led and form part of a larger social and intellectual concept if it is to be accepted.'[61] In passing, he attacked the pamphlet *Der Kulturinfarkt*, which had appeared a few months earlier. Delighting in his own flights of rhetoric, he accused the authors of the latter, from his Thatcher-tortured perspective, of being 'devil's advocates', of undermining their undoubted talents as analysts through their own arrogance: 'pointing to what they see as a narrowing of culture's coronary artery, caused by a calcification of the walls through the elevated fat content of its blood supply'.[62] He flatly rejected the authors' thesis that the closure of 50 per cent of all publicly funded cultural enterprises would lead to innovation. For him, it was grist to the mill of both left- and right-wing anti-opera ideology. 'Because opera is, in the best sense of the word, gloriously elitist and at the same time, with its intellectual and financial accessibility, highly alluring and popular, it tends to provoke the poisonous arrows of the extreme right and left of the political spectrum, who would prefer to either cut off popular culture altogether or make it a plaything for the rich – under the banner of "necessary alignment with market forces".'[63]

Jonas was always keenly aware of these accusations, which he saw as ideological. Against the right, he insisted on freedom of art, and would strongly defend every production, even the failures, to the end. Against the left, he pursued his vision of an opera house that was not defined by being exclusive. 'I do believe opera is for interpreting and not representing,'[64] was his attitude.

In his role as director, Jonas was only too aware that, as Horkheimer and Adorno had it, all cultural products also have the character of a commodity; he had worked in the USA for a decade; he had successfully led ENO through the Thatcher years; he knew that the Munich box office figures had to be right.

As director, however, he also saw it as being very much his own job to counter prejudices of the left and right at the political level, not only with words, but with his entire appearance, his habitus. Barenboim thought that Jonas had been predestined for a leading position in the classical music world. And this was why Jonas, who instinctively opposed the establishment, said also that he was a traditionalist. Jonas had always wanted to have it both ways, that was the 'key to his personality', as Daniel Barenboim put it at Jonas's farewell in Munich: 'He wants to be part of the establishment to fight what he dislikes. He manages the balancing act of belonging to the establishment without conforming. For this he is admired by many, but he also provokes hostility.'[65]

Jonas rejected that type of German artistic director who would see any obligation to serve the audience as an insult to artistic integrity. He considered it a suicide mission when such colleagues flew 'so low (or high)' that they paid no attention to income, attendance figures or even labour-law obligations, and rejected any hint of innocent enjoyment as an expression of an unsophisticated, boring, safe, petit-bourgeois attitude.[66] On the other hand, he held in the highest regard the type of person who did not place himself in the foreground 'except as a figurehead and defender. As one who makes things possible!' He radically rejected directing himself, describing himself as a 'non-playing captain', because in directing a particular production an artistic director would lose objectivity.

From his own experience, he knew that as such a figurehead one becomes by turn a whipping boy and an object of adulation, because the public fully identified this person with all artistic and administrative processes.[67]

'I would rather see a director who says yes to everything and supports everything that comes out of the company than a director who imposes his own will. Of course, I also wanted things to run in a certain way and match my own tastes. Which conductors and directors you choose is an instinctive decision. You're not always right about that, but one has to have an affinity for it,' Jonas explained. 'I know many directors whose work I have liked, but I could not work with them. It's a question of wavelength.'

Jonas was a great admirer of the German theatre system and no wonder, after his experiences in Chicago and London. He was aware that the city's prosperity, its history and the mindset of its politicians as well as its inhabitants had proved decisive for his success in Munich. When asked for advice on what could help a small opera house in an economically depressed town, he honestly admitted that he was often unable to offer any. 'Have you looked at the city, how the people live there? Have you tried to learn their language or dialect? All these different factors are terribly important.'

But what mattered to him first and foremost, regardless of what opera house it was under discussion, was human chemistry: 'First find out whether two people fit together. Ansonsten [otherwise] it isn't going to work anyway.' He rejected collective leadership, saying 'there has to be someone with the ultimate say at the top.'[68] With regard to the question of what significance an artistic directorship wields, he was extremely sober. 'Theatre and opera are about the now, not the past. A former artistic director should have no further significance beyond the years of his or her directorship.

When those are over, they are over, just like a performance. They live on only in memory. You did your best, whether it worked or not. You stimulated people's imagination and seduced them – or not. You have entertained people – or not. And then it's over.'

Peter Jonas's professional career came to an end in his sixtieth year, a decision made five years in advance. He'd been planning ever since taking up office in Munich in 1993. In 1996 he had announced his intention to retire at the age of fifty-seven.[69] He considered ten, or perhaps thirteen or fifteen years, the ideal period for a directorship. He didn't want to defy the ephemerality of such a role: 'You are ultimately a person of your time. The style of an Intendanz [directorship] is determined by its times. When switching between opera houses, you cannot survive the changes indefinitely. You start getting older, and younger people don't have to like your ideas.'

Jonas followed the #MeToo debate in a state of dismay and shock. He could not recall any incident that took place at his opera companies that might have prompted him to act. The years he spent at the helm of the Bavarian Staatsoper had been another era: thresholds of perception were different then.

Many did not believe Jonas when he announced his departure. He knew his wife supported his decision. But he also struggled with it, and as retirement approached he was not always at peace with it. Back in London he had said of his departure that everyone had a shelf life, and that it was time to go. 'That is probably why so many directorships end rather unhappily. Many do not retire soon enough. God knows, there are enough old people in the world today who hang on to their jobs and their official cars because they can't live without privileges.'

Institutions like an opera house are 'a bit Navy-like' in their hierarchy, 'a kind of democratic autocracy, a kind of liberal military structure'.[70] Here he followed his mentor Solti, who had described an opera house as a 'military operation'.[71] Or perhaps it would be better to use a different metaphor: 'An opera house is as difficult to run as a football club. There are big egos and prima donnas. Only, in the opera house, you have a game every day and you have to win it every day. If you lose, if the singer doesn't hit the note, the audience will be just as ruthless as the fans in the stadium.'[72] Efforts at democratising decision-making processes in the company, or leadership models in which management positions might be filled by teams of people, had no place in his outlook.

For many colleagues, operating outside this 'liberal military structure' would be immensely difficult. Jonas himself found intolerable the idea that one day he might find himself forgetting that he no longer had a chauffeur and climbing into the wrong door of his car. He didn't want to lose traction, or to have to find out for himself how Uber worked.

The official version was that he took his leave because of 'poor health', as he put it. 'That was also true.' Being an artistic director was not only sapping his strength: 'it is costing my life'.[73] But Jonas was always much more than just a man of the opera. He had so many interests, and wanted finally to have enough time to pursue them. 'A third phase of life. I was told that I would not have one. I feel it is a bonus. I have no regrets.' Indeed, he said that he was proud of his choices – and yet in the same breath he described this pride as hubris.

Of course, job offers promptly rolled in – he had already turned down an offer from La Scala in Milan during his tenure. But even the Metropolitan Opera no longer interested him. He knew only too well the 'insoluble' problem that plagued his business. It was – and still is – the high wage costs and the astronomically high fees of the singers. With four thousand seats, it was particularly difficult for the Met to achieve a sell-out. He would not have been able to pursue his favoured demanding repertoire there, either. To spend all his energy again to convince a Board and sponsors of the virtues of his programme, and to establish permanent financing of the Met – that was not his thing. 'The Met can't go on as it is,' Jonas had told the *New York Times* in 2006.

He also turned down an offer from the Salzburg Festival. He had never wanted to work for a festival, and he didn't want to plan the whole year: that wasn't in his nature. He loved repertory theatre, the atmosphere of an opera house and his daily schedule.

'I am quite lazy. I need my daily deadline, my daily injection of adrenaline,' he said, banging his knuckles on the table. 'Ich bin ziemlich proletarisch [I am rather proletarian]. I am a journeyman opera director.'[74]

Peter Jonas was a 'gutter rat' of the opera business, as he put it.[75] 'I observe with great suspicion what our industry thinks about its own importance. I wonder if I had any significance at all, in a way. Maybe most people will forget my work. Maybe I will be forgotten.'

A consummate gentleman

Since taking the helm of English National Opera, Jonas had been meticulous about promoting a certain reading of his life. In all major portraits and interviews, more or less the same statements about his life come forth time and time again. He had spoken openly about his family, his life and his profession – and yet left many things untouched. Over the decades, various anecdotes were recycled – absurdly. His London number plate, ENO-1, forgotten by colleagues up until his obituaries, was presented as evidence of vanity.[76] Various errors of fact have been perpetrated: his paternal grandfather did not commit suicide to avoid imminent arrest by the Gestapo;[77] neither did he shoot himself and his wife.[78] His father was not a doctor.[79] He was never married to Lucia Popp.[80] Jonas did have Scottish ancestors through his maternal grandmother, but so distant that he himself did not know the degree of separation. He wore a kilt for the sheer pleasure of provoking and entertaining his guests. He did not go to boarding school at the age of five. His wife did not become his concert manager at the Munich Staatsoper, because she was already in post there before he took up his directorship. She didn't move to Zurich with him.[81] No article written during his lifetime ever included the tale of his avoiding an assassination attempt by accident, thanks to an air crash.

'I have had a God-blessed life. Only my appreciation of myself is a bit flawed,' Jonas stated when, after careful consideration and inner struggle, he agreed to work on this biography. This deep discrepancy between his perception of himself and the perceptions of others is striking. But the key to his success lay precisely in this delta, in his Sisyphean willingness to raise the bar again and again in order to meet the demands he placed upon himself. 'To achieve the good, you have to want the better. The urge to do better is an essential ingredient,' was the interpretation offered by Steffen Huck, who became his friend through their work together at the WZB. 'There are leaders who are not troubled by such thoughts. Without these ingredients, his directorship would never have been such a success.'[82] John Nickson, who worked with Jonas in London, had this to say: 'Leaders like Peter are rare. They have a clear vision. They are willing to take risks to make their vision a reality. They have extraordinary charm and high emotional intelligence. They are persuaders and they make connections. Their power increases by being given away and by empowering others to take action.'

The obituaries for Peter Jonas unanimously acknowledged his influence on opera in the twenty-first century. This influence was partly a product of his ability to combine artistic and administrative qualities, his visionary power, his courage, his humour and his coolness. 'For decades, he shaped musical theatre and concert life with courage, originality, energy and an irrepressible desire to take risks,' his successor Nikolaus Bachler said in a eulogy delivered on behalf of the Bavarian Staatsoper. 'He completely redefined the audience's feeling and understanding of opera and far beyond Munich; he found this art form a place within twenty-first-century society.'[83] Anthony Tommasini of the *New York Times* emphasised his achievement in transforming the opera houses where he had worked 'into influential hotbeds of innovation'.[84]

At the end of his directorship, the Bavarian Staatsoper had developed into a standard-bearer for a forward-looking, courageous and at the same time accessible concept of opera, wrote Klaus Lederer and Georg Vierthaler for the Berlin Opera Foundation.[85] For Wolfgang Schreiber of the *Süddeutsche Zeitung*, Peter Jonas was a 'consummate gentleman', not a German cultural official and certainly not a shrewd opera manager.[86] Zubin Mehta saw the artistic zenith of his life as the eight years he spent in tandem with Peter Jonas at the Bavarian Staatsoper; he had lost a 'wonderful colleague and true friend'. 'One of the noblest, most humorous, most original, kindest people that music and theatre people can recognise as one of their own' was how the composer Jörg Widmann paid tribute to him.[87] David Alden told the *New York Times* that it was the 'extraordinary combination of political savvy and financial daring' that made Jonas so successful, as well as an 'ultimate lightness of being (very unusual in German theatre), which all combined were unbeatable.'[88] Lady Valerie Solti managed to sum up all this and more in her tribute to him and his life's work: 'Peter Jonas led a Helden life,' she wrote, alluding to Richard Strauss' symphonic poem *Ein Heldenleben*. 'He was a very special, amazing, and highly talented man – very disciplined, very dedicated, highly intellectual, and quick witted – as was shown by his incredible career. Peter was a legend and a luminary in the world of international opera, and no one had a more thorough knowledge of the repertoire and who should be performing it. There was an extraordinary brilliance about him, as an administrator and as a human being, and despite his health challenges, Peter kept going, never complained, and never gave up.'[89]

Peter Jonas was an impressive figure. Even before his illness, his wavy brown hair, reminding some of the German hero Siegfried in Lang's film *Die Nibelungen*, had turned white. He had been absurdly tall and an athletic, muscular man until cancer struck. But after his illness began, he was still striking. He was lean, with penetrating blue eyes, if not always 'invariably dapper in his attire,'[90] as *The Times* wrote in its obituary – the writer seems unaware of his casual dress in his latter years. In professional life he was always impeccably dressed for official appointments, often sporting tailor-made suits and shoes. He criticised the Germans for their bad shoes. Otherwise, he loved jeans, turtlenecks and a leather jacket.

In Munich he also cultivated the image of the quirky Brit and liked to pair red socks with his dinner jacket. It might also have been a political statement. In later years 'P' or 'PJ', as he had been known in his school days, stretched the boundaries of convention willingly and generously. 'He came in a shirt and a flutter scarf without making a statement, without setting himself apart,' wrote Jutta Allmendinger in her obituary. 'He would often just stand there, tall, thin and laughing.'[91]

Even in his London days, his striking appearance had provided material for caricatures, including his left ear, which he tended to hide. When deep in thought, his tongue would protrude. When he wanted to underline a point, he poked the air with his long index finger. If something was exercising him, he would tap on a surface with the back of his hand. He liked to let a bunch of keys on a yellow ribbon swing through the air, very occasionally banging into the table.

Peter Jonas was a humanist, imbued with values he lived by and expected others to live by in equal measure. He pursued an unconditional demand for quality, was uncompromisingly professional and completely loyal to the artists he worked with. He would never speak ill of them: 'I have always acted entirely on instinct. If I see someone working and I love the work, I support the person. I had a good chemical reaction to good work.'

He was honest and upright and liberal, a cosmopolitan and a democrat. He could also be extremely charming. 'Peter could charm the birds out of the trees!' was how his close friend Lesley Garrett described him.[92] He had the manners of a gentleman and radiated class. However, his bravery, his tenacious will to survive and an almost endless lust for life and for beauty meant that he would rarely rest. 'This, combined with astute intelligence and an exceptionally generous spirit, makes him an outstanding, powerful, inspirational and charismatic leader,' commented John Nickson.

Many observers wondered how Jonas found the energy to collaborate directly with so many different people in large organisations. But anyone who spent time with him felt that they were important. 'Peter Jonas was able to look very directly at people he liked and to dispense with all role-playing in such moments,' described Christine Lemke-Matwey, who first observed him as a journalist and then accompanied him as a friend.[93] 'Peter inspired and fascinated. He was stylistically confident, eloquent and charismatic, a breaker of taboos and a perfectionist. He mastered the art of seduction, and was all too happy to seduce others into thinking new things and, like himself, to venture down new paths again and again,' wrote Steffen Huck of the WZB in his obituary.[94]

Jonas was also a gifted communicator. 'He really had the gift of the gab! He could talk people into wanting the things he wanted,' Lesley Garrett said. His will was unwavering, he was witty, funny, focused and committed, sometimes melancholic. But his true weapons were irony, charm and elegance. His 'courage, this tremendous will to survive, combined with very northern German discipline, shaped his character and was also the prerequisite for his astonishing professional development'[95] is how Daniel Barenboim put it, underlining Jonas's refreshingly youthful curiosity, his dramaturgical understanding, his unshakeable pragmatism and his ability to motivate.[96]

Peter Jonas was self-confident, even arrogant, and ambitious. He inspired his peers and 'passionately promoted artists who, like him, were passionately serious but did not take themselves too seriously', according to David Pountney, who also emphasised Jonas's rigour and inflexibility, his extraordinary stubbornness, his consistency, his determination and his unerring sense of style.[97]

Jonas was intellectually brilliant and able to react rationally even in threatening situations and crises. He was not devoid of fears, but he did not let them rule him. And he did not assume that he was brilliant. 'Don't be under any illusion. Es war alles harte Arbeit. [It was all hard work.] I am not a brilliant person,' he would often say. He knew too well all the things that he had to do for success, all the things he had not achieved and all the things he had renounced. 'Learning new things about the world was something that he set great importance upon,' says Steffen Huck. 'He took things to the extreme; he had a certain uncompromising quality about his own actions. For him it was important intellectually, but also emotionally, to know that I am really giving my all. That was certainly a guiding principle for him. And of course his sense of duty was immense.'

But for everything that connected him to the world, he was always moving onwards. Egbert Tholl chose an appropriate metaphor in his obituary when he termed Jonas 'a wanderer'.[98]

Jonas also had a remarkable memory for every detail – except faces. He was a perfectionist and a control freak, and always wanted to keep full control over everything in his opera house. 'All my life I have had a rather stupid sense of accuracy and detail. I meticulously prepared all the appointments with interview notes, which helped. This was not learned: it was part of my personality.'

Of course, Peter Jonas did not only have good sides. He was an unusual person, highly sensitive, full of contradictions, a tremendously complicated personality with many facets, not all attractive. He also had a dark side not to be underestimated. He could at times be brutal, ruthless and selfish. He hurt many through his rigidity, even when his criticism was justified. He was an eccentric who always had to take things to the limit. And when he did so, it didn't matter at all what anyone thought about his behaviour.

Jonas liked to say things that no one wanted to hear at a given moment. He could make people cry. 'When he needed or wanted to criticise people, he could be really fierce,' Daniel Barenboim observed. 'Often, however, he used his humour to regain control of a situation, making it acceptable even to those who might criticise him.' David Pountney claimed in his obituary that Jonas was 'a driven man, a very complex personality who did not shy away from playing confusing games with people'.[99] Peter Jonas was therefore not free from – as the Benedictines might have put it – the mortal sin of *Superbia*; not in the sense that he overestimated his value and rank, but in his flashes of vanity and narcissism. He had himself photographed in the Munich National Theatre for a Bavarian manufacturer of made-to-measure suits.

He was skilled at concealing arrogance under a thin veneer. Peter Jonas was superior to many people. 'If you have the trait of being strong, that goes with it,' Lesley Garrett said. 'He is the most ambitious man I have ever met. But he does not realise it! He has many qualities that he does not recognise. This is because he has lived with them all his life. He's very competitive, especially with himself.'

Criticism of his human frailties should not obscure what it meant for a person like him to be confronted with stupidity, laziness and despondency, things he found difficult to bear when they impinged upon the things to which he had dedicated his life. 'He was, deep down, a solitary soul,' Norman Lebrecht wrote after his death.[100]

Jonas was one of the most generous people in the opera world. He was very free with dinner invitations, though if someone issued an unsanctioned invitation on his behalf, he did not like it. He generously supported other theatres, like the Zurich Opera House. He loved postcards, often from museum shops.

Jonas did a lot to keep fit. He had become addicted to Pilates in his London days. Later he went on to practise yoga intensively, doing headstands in his office, even during a tour of Japan. At certain points he took to performing an 8am ballet with certain members of the ensemble in the auditorium of the Staatsoper. He went power-walking in Nymphenburg Palace Park with his wife. He also went on yoga and Pilates retreats.

After performances, he liked to go to late showings at the cinema, always with a Diet Coke and popcorn, 'aber nur salzig! [but salted only!].' He liked to drink Augustiner Edelstoff and 'Sanbitter with Pellegrino all the time!', a non-alcoholic aperitif. In his final years, he smelled Arabian: amber wood, resin and vanilla, his favourite aftershave being Ambre Sultan by Serge Lutens. He had been wearing his Omega for many years, a signet ring on his little finger and bands around his wrist.

He was an actor, a player, a person who kept returning to the imagery of the stage when he spoke – 'Zurück zum Stück! [Back to the play!]', he would shout when he wanted to return to the topic at hand.

When Peter Jonas was appointed Director of the Bavarian Staatsoper, his good contacts in the industry had been an important criterion.[101] In his Chicago days, this network had already allowed him to call James Levine at the Metropolitan Opera in New York at night to ask him for help. Jonas, however, had never conceived of these contacts as merely professional. Long-standing friendships developed with many colleagues, even though some of them were not privy to his whole story.

He repeatedly made friends with his doctors. Some friends said he would never have stayed alive so long otherwise. For John Nickson, loyalty was one of his outstanding qualities: 'loyalty and the gift of his friendship'. For decades before the advent of the calendar function on smartphones, no one had a better memory for birthdays than Jonas. Jonas said that his greatest friendships were not with *conductors*, but rather with Daniel Barenboim, Zubin Mehta and Mark Elder. Barenboim and Mehta had known each other since they took part in a conducting course in 1956 at the ages of fourteen and twenty. Jonas met Elder in 1968 at the age of twenty-two. These friendships, forged very young, carried him through his life.

Peter Jonas had a great sense of humour. He could hold court at dinner parties and conduct long conversations without once becoming remotely serious. And many of his friends would say: Thank God! Provoking laughter allowed him to break social rules, to express his distaste for the rules. He loved a serious joke, the cognitive shift, the rapid switch in thoughts and feelings involved in a good joke, and he relished holding up the tragic, the gross and the macabre alongside the humorous. It was something that tickled Jonas at an intellectual level.

Humour also offered a distraction when matters took a more serious turn: in particular, when he received yet more bad news about his health and nothing could be done except detach himself emotionally and let it be funny rather than tragic. He could dispel tension or a dark mood with a humorous remark. 'Die laughing. It's the ultimate comic relief.'[102] This was the kind of comic relief that Jonas liked.

His was a black, British humour, and he could put it to very rude use. He could deploy it to create distance, to keep something at bay, but also to establish a position of conscious superiority, and some of his companions have called that arrogance. 'He loves to get a rise out of people'[103] as the *New York Times* said of him. Early on, at a reception of the Friends and Patrons of the Munich National Theatre in 1998, he tipped his hand to his audience: 'British humour, meine Damen und Herren, is unyielding and all-encompassing. It is our hard Panzer that crushes every unruly emotion, every dissenting feeling. It is used as a weapon to keep people at a distance from one other and to admonish them to stay in their place. It is the perfect camouflage and it reflects a need to express no emotions at all. It is, if you like, the darker side of the often-admired quality of "understatement". Hide your feelings under Geist und Witz [esprit and wit] and never speak of ethereal things!'[104]

He went one better. If this audience sometimes found him too angular and uncomfortable, they would simply have to get used to it: the only real difference between British and German humour, he said, came after the Thirty Years' War, when the Germans developed the concept of the state out of a need for structure – 'with the result that today, three hundred and fifty years later, the British laugh at authority and the Germans respect authority.'[105] On another occasion, at the Munich Press Club, he confessed that he generally got away with his wisecracks, but that irony was often tricky to pull off.[106]

And how he liked to use the mask of the Englishman to get his way! His act of speaking only broken German allowed him to address subjects that would have been more ticklish for a German to broach. Jonas, though, could speak more freely. 'Peter knows exactly how well he can speak German,' says Barenboim. 'But every now and then he deliberately puts on the mask of the Englishman and hides behind it by speaking wretched German.' Eccentricity is so alien to Germans and permitted only for artists; they came up against Jonas, with 'that peculiar English talent for extravagant, way-out, eccentric or even just odd dressing habits'.[107] The signet ring on his little finger was part of it, as was his kilt, the colourful socks and sneakers, his scarves, the bands on his right wrist, and generally the very casual style of dress adopted after his departure from the Bavarian Staatsoper. That, and the cartoons, especially those from the *New Yorker*, which he sent to his acquaintances and friends. The journal had been a weekly must-read since 1973. He loved carrying the paper edition around, taking it on the plane, although he would also read it on his iPad.

His eccentricity also extended to his eating habits. Marmite was a favourite breakfast staple for quite a while. In later years, he also liked to eat Tunnock's teacakes: 'ganz anders [quite different]! It is like a cake that promotes digestion. In England, something like that is completely normal, in Germany it wouldn't work.'

He told another cabaletta!

Peter Jonas was known for telling fabulous stories – you never really knew how much truth they contained, but the rendition was always spellbinding. 'His ability to not always quite tell the truth is incredible. He tells porkies. He just makes things up. You can never be completely sure,' as his oldest friend Mark Elder told us.[108]

His circle of friends had known of this habit for a long time. During one holiday together, the music lovers had been chatting about the 'cabaletta', an aria form of mysterious origins. Without hesitation, Peter put them right: 'You don't know about that? I've known for years!' And he talked uninterrupted for four minutes, fluently and brilliantly, until Mark Elder stepped in: 'You made that up!' Jonas laughed and admitted he had just invented it all for the sheer pleasure of the telling. From that moment, whenever they caught him out in another tall tale, his friends would exclaim, 'He's told another cabaletta!'

As chairman of the Deutschen Opernkonferenz, he once indulged in a rather high-stakes cabaletta. The Lord Mayor of the City of Frankfurt addressed the conference in the Kaisersaal at the Römer; Jonas, returning her greeting, said there could be no more suitable place for their meeting than Frankfurt, because in the days of Konrad III – of whom a painting hangs in the Kaisersaal – when the mendicant friars crossed the Alps and brought opera with them from Italy, Frankfurt became an important place for the art form. Mayor Roth was astonished, as she had been unaware that her city had enjoyed such historic significance. Some of Jonas's colleagues saw in this a cavalier attitude that bordered on impertinence. The Konrad story was just one among many.

Jonas's friend David Alden found himself on the receiving end of a cabaletta; browing in a bookshop, he found a study of opera directors and, curious, opened the chapter concerning himself. He was rather surprised to read that he was, apparently, a practising Buddhist[109] – news to him. Alden later learned the source of this fiction when he related the story to Jonas. Peter then revealed all: the author had interviewed him, and 'I just wanted to tell him something crazy.'[110]

'Many of his stories featured the idea that something-or-other in European history was in fact all down to the arrival of syphilis,' recounted Steffen Huck. 'Because in Schubert's, Mozart's or Beethoven's time, this disease was one of the biggest unsolved medical problems and almost every family had to suffer some consequences.' Huck conducted workshops with Jonas in which scientists, intellectuals and television producers worked in collaboration. In the first of these, Huck opened up a discussion about *Lohengrin*, specifically the issue of *why* Elsa asks the unknown hero his name and origins, despite the prohibition on her asking questions. 'Peter interrupted and said that one could really understand *Lohengrin* only if one looked at Wagner's skin diseases. Then followed an excursus on Wagner and silk, which seemed historically accurate. He delivered this in a tone of such seriousness, as if his comments were based on decades of research. Years later I was still being told how interesting Peter's explanations had been.' Huck's own take on the question had been quite forgotten. Later, when they had become friends, Huck asked Jonas if he had in fact made it all up. Jonas confirmed that, yes indeed, he had plucked it out of the air.

'Peter was someone who could embellish beautifully. He was someone who could keep hold of the truth, and also add some things that I could never have thought up or put together.'[111] This view was shared by Peter's cousin Monica Melamid, to whom he had also told many such stories.

The wanderer

When Sir Peter Jonas said of himself, 'I wanted to be the one who got away,'[112] he was speaking in deadly earnest.

'I was wondering: When can I fulfil my dreams? I have so many projects, so many interests, the visual arts, yoga, hiking, cinema. When will I get around to hiking from Northern Scotland to Palermo? I want to discover this Europe that shapes us all. And I need time to do that. So, as Joseph Volpe, now-retired chief of the Met, put it: I want my life back. This life I gave up when I was twenty-seven or twenty-eight.'[113] Once again, Jonas set the bar very high: a mere long-distance hike would not do. It had to be the whole of Europe. When he set his mind on something, he set it right. He followed up this announcement with action, although he was not able to realise completely the great project of a European peregrination.

He had learned to love hiking in step with wife Barbara Burgdorf. In the summer of 1998, Peter and Barbara had taken their first long-distance walking holiday together. They had decided to travel from Munich to Prague, or almost: they skipped the Isar Valley. Eastern European countries had not yet been really opened up for tourism, and Jonas and Burgdorf were often the only guests in hostels that had all the charm of holiday camps. They were completely alone in corridors of twenty-five rooms.

The few staff they encountered were rarely sober. They all ate together in the kitchen, wine and fried potatoes being the safest option. The atmosphere was clammy, and at night they pushed the wardrobe against the door to their room. 'Everything was adventurous and very easy,' says Burgdorf: 'our first hike with backpacks was a real adventure. Peter had no idea that you could holiday like this.'

Their backpacks were – rookie mistake – much too heavy. The first day of hiking was almost the end of the entire holiday, twenty-eight kilometres with an eight-hundred-metre climb, which was absolutely exhausting.

'But fortunately, and quite by chance, we fell upon some good accommodation in Finsterau with an even better restaurant and a magnificent wine cellar, which made us forget the hardships of the day.' These shared hikes became a favourite habit, a real escape from the exceedingly harsh demands that each season placed on Jonas as artistic director and Burgdorf as concertmaster: 'The biggest thing for us was always to plan the next stage of our hike. It was our anchor: so and so many weeks we have to hold out, then we'll be on holiday. It was our elixir of life.'

During the great north–south hike from Inverness to Palermo that Barbara and Peter undertook together, Barbara got to know her husband's homeland in a special way: 'England is a walking country par excellence, you always get to talk to people there. Especially when you have such a multilingual companion as Peter, who is never shy. We had an incredible number of interesting encounters and it was really nice to have so much time just to ourselves.

Fig. 4: Barbara Burgdorf and Peter Jonas, Sicily, 2006

'Together we were able to trace European history, to follow the Roman roads across Europe. After many years and individual stages, we finally walked from Inverness in Scotland to Palermo in Sicily. It was awesome, it was the realisation of our life's dream, a unique experience.'

Jonas undertook one of the stages of the Inverness–Palermo hike near Andernach on the Rhine alone; Barbara had had to return to Munich for work. In his luggage he had Geert Mak's opus *In Europe*, a survey of Europe's history over the previous one hundred and fifty years, structured by location. This hypnotised him. He had the book in hardcover for reading at home – alongside Jacques Le Goff's *Old Europe and the Modern World* – and a paperback copy for the walk. He tore out the pages he had read as he went… What sounds like an act of vandalism becomes understandable when one realises that the paperback edition alone weighed 1850 grams and was 4.5 centimetres thick. 'My backpack weighed eleven, twelve kilograms. It was all right on my back,' he said, defending his choice, 'although I was fitter back then.'

It was March, it was cold and the wonderful landscape lay deserted. When he reached Andernach, he needed a place to stay. Browsing online, he discovered a bed and breakfast that seemed to be reasonably nearby, a little bit south of the centre of town, which would offer a convenient starting point for the following day. It was 5:30pm, he was terribly tired at the end of a typically German grey overcast March day, a 'Garnichts-Tag': neither rainy nor sunny.

But as he approached, the bed and breakfast was nowhere to be found. Jonas found out why when he called. It was in fact an old people's home that was taking in overnight visitors only because it was not fully occupied. Not fully occupied? It turned out that it was completely empty. He could shower, sleep and have breakfast there, but he could not expect dinner. He was given the key to the garden gate so that he could get back that evening.

On the path down to the Rhine, he spotted a sign pointing to a Lebanese restaurant. 'How could that be there, in such a deserted place? I found it eerie,' says Jonas. A decent restaurant awaited him with Lebanese food and even Lebanese wines on the menu. One particular vintage was a real rarity. Jonas got into a conversation with the waiter, naturally curious why this stranger was so familiar with Lebanese food and drink. When the waiter realised that Jonas, like himself, was a scion of the Ziadie family, he hugged him, exclaiming, 'My friend, my brother, my brother!'

At this point, one ought not to get carried away. The Ziadies were and remain a large family with many branches. Jonas guessed that he had around two hundred cousins worldwide.

It turned out to be a long, long evening. After Jonas had staggered back to the old people's home in the dark, he found the place firmly locked, with not a soul to be seen, 'not even ghosts. It was like an American horror film: no one can see, and suddenly you're murdered.' He used the key and found his room. Not trusting the silence, he wedged a chair under the doorhandle.

Cars, cricket and football!

The ringing of bells sounded from across the street, and people flocked to lunch in the Glockenbachviertel. Jonas was breathing heavily as he walked along Pestalozzistrasse to the Old South Cemetery, 'one of my favourite places in Munich'. But nevertheless, he used every moment to talk about his enthusiasm for cars. 'Look, cars!' he began. 'I'm a petrolhead, ein Autofreak.'

Jonas had been passionate about design from a young age. He had invested in Apple shares just because he thought the devices looked good. But for many years he was unable to use one. 'I can't tell you how many machines and phones I've owned that I couldn't get to work properly. But I liked their design.'

This applied to cars as well: when Jonas saw a model that he thought looked beautiful, he would admire it adoringly. The engine noise, the design of the machine: everything appealed.

Fig. 5: Peter Jonas in his Ferrari, Zurich, 2015

He went through periods of collecting car magazines, and had a phase when he loved certain German models: 'VW Käfer: I used to love Beetles.' Another classic, the 3-series BMW Coupé in dark green, also briefly stole his heart.

'BMW has lost its direction today: they are interested only in sales. And I never liked Mercedes,' he commented disparagingly, 'but Italian cars: always! No Lamborghinis, but Fiats, Alfa Romeos and Ferraris.' For daily use, Jonas drove an Alfa Romeo, a blue Giulia Veloce. 'Absolutely fantastic!' he enthused, 'it's reliable, it's beautiful, it's fast and easy to drive.' One might add that the car was immaculately clean; spotless inside and out.

Fig. 6: Peter Jonas plays cricket

Jonas also owned a small treasure, as he put it: a Ferrari, not a modern, low-slung one, but one of the old-fashioned Grand Tourer models, each of which had been individually customised. 'Maybe I'll sell the Ferrari … but Barbara has forbidden me…' Jonas thought aloud as he looked for a bench in the cemetery. 'Sometimes I think that as soon as I sell my Ferrari, I'll have given up on myself.'

He also liked to fulminate about how people, especially Germans, bought their cars. He had fun imitating a sales pitch in a thick German accent with comments about the horsepower and the engine, all things that cost a lot but were hardly needed: 'It is so rare to be able to admire such a combination of industrial and product design, especially when, as we're seeing now with the combustion engine, there is a struggle to bring about a revolution through new design. It's like the old-fashioned conventions of the eighteenth- and nineteenth-century proscenium stage that need a new perspective.'

Neither Peter Jonas nor Zubin Mehta could imagine a life without cricket. 'The countless hours I spent sitting in front of the TV with Zubin Mehta and Peter Jonas watching cricket!' Natalia Ritzkowsky, Mehta's personal assistant, chuckled as she recalled. 'But that was when you could get a decision about something: they were totally distracted.' While Mehta liked to have a friend update him on the score over the phone when he was travelling, Jonas continued to play intensively for quite a while as a member of the Munich Cricket Club. When trying to explain the laws of the game to their staff, both failed.

Jonas was also a true football fan, albeit a one-club man: Crystal Palace, the Premier League club from his home patch of south London. He was often asked to comment on the latest happenings in the football world, especially the English national side.

As a young boy, Jonas had decided that he wanted to play for Crystal Palace, although this was complicated by the fact that his boarding school refused to allow him to play football. 'At that time, society was snobbish,' he explained.

'Football was considered a gentleman's game played by non-gentlemen. Rugby, on the other hand, was not a gentleman's game, but it was played by gentlemen.' His then-girlfriend Rosalind, a die-hard Manchester City fan, took him to his first football match while he was at university. She understood the movement of the players, and taught him to have fun playing. In his Zurich flat he could receive the BBC, which was probably the key factor in his decision to move in there: 'Ah, the line-up!' He interrupted everything for the latest news about Crystal Palace. He put the fixture list in his calendar. After his death, his widow received a message of condolence signed by all the players.

Teaching

Even though Jonas visited the opera much less frequently in the years after retirement, he continued to engage in other ways. From 2009 to 2018 he worked on the supervisory Board of the Netherlands Opera. Together with former colleague Maurice Lausberg, owner of a Munich-based cultural consultancy and professor at the University of Music and Theatre in Munich, he took on consulting work for opera houses. 'Sometimes even the talented staff of such houses need a moment to remove their watches and ask people like me to tell them what time it is,' said Jonas.

While still a director in Munich, Jonas had begun teaching in 2003, first at the University of St Gallen, where he became a member of the university council in 2012, as he had done in Lucerne in 2007. More significant for the opera sector, however, was the Executive Master in Arts Administration programme at the University of Zurich, which he initiated as President of the German Opera Directors' Conference, together with Alexander Pereira and Klaus Zehelein, during his directorship in Munich. While in Basel he taught undergraduate students in compulsory courses; they were 'young, fresh, fixed, but not necessarily interested'. The Executive Master is aimed at people who have already completed their first degree and gained their first professional experience. This more demanding Master's level teaching was more satisfying for Jonas. Through this work he met figures such as Christian Berner and Sophie de Lint ('an absolutely dedicated born Intendant [artistic director]'); he often stayed in touch with students after graduation and frequently became friends.

Peter Jonas taught modules on artistic freedom, designing playbills and conflict management. There were no slides, handouts or summaries, but there were intensive discussions. 'The lessons were actually chit-chat sessions,' Christian Berner, who now works as commercial director at Zurich Opera, told me. 'Jonas shared from his vast wealth of experience how to run a company, solve problems, settle conflicts, in general, how to get so many hundreds of people rowing in the same direction. That was exciting because he was a charismatic person.' In one lesson, Jonas asked exactly that question: what constitutes charisma. 'That was important to him because for him art always has the aura of something special and it has a high value. It was a pleasure to talk to him about it.'[114]

For Jonas, the concept of service was central. 'If you want to understand how the arts work, how creativity comes about, you have to forget the conventional understanding of management,' he proposed. 'If you think of yourself as a servant, you have a chance to be successful in the classical sense, to survive, to flourish, to do something new.' Jonas underlined this with an example from *Downton Abbey*. The maid is asked to serve the guests a soufflé and has to walk two floors to do so. It is a long way, and she burns her hands and complains to the butler. But he views her sacrifice as nothing more than what is expected. 'My dear, your hands will recover, but the soufflé, once it collapses, is of no use.' Jonas demanded that level of personal sacrifice of himself, but he also expected it from the executives he worked with at the opera. When people start working in an opera, they often just want to be successful, he explained. They do not understand that their work consists of service. 'You are a servant. If you can accept that, it makes life so much easier.' So many of the arguments and disputes that come about in theatres, he pointed out, are rooted in the fact that the artistic director, who should be an enabler, does not accept that they are a servant, and so cannot gain the artists' trust. If an artist feels the artistic director wants to support the creative process and not interfere with it, then they will respond appropriately. 'To the young people in these courses I have always said: being an artistic director is not a glamorous job. If you put power out of your mind and have no ambition except to serve the artists, people will take you into their confidence.'

Jonas also drummed in one central tenet of his personal credo to students: 'When you get a job like this, never feel secure.' His teaching style was easy-going and sympathetic, but he adopted a more critical tone as he approached the heart of the subject matter. 'That was exciting, because ultimately that's what running a theatre is all about: leadership, responsibility and control. Those were his themes,' says Berner. The modules were taught in groups of around twenty-five people and lasted three days. In this charged atmosphere, conversation naturally became more intense, especially at the communal meals; Jonas enjoyed these, showing off his humour and wit.

Jonas had an eye for who stood for what, who wanted to go where. For Christian Berner, he was 'a mentor who became a friend. He inspired me, he was my role model, both personally and professionally. It meant a lot to me to have been on friendly terms with Sir Peter: it greatly enriched my life.'

Making speeches

Sir Peter was a well-regarded orator, especially at the Munich Film Festival, where he gave one of his most acclaimed speeches on the occasion of the presentation of the Bernhard Wicki Film Prize to Marc Rothemund for his film *Sophie Scholl – The Last Days* in 2005. He told the story of his own family, and of his grandfather's 1939 suicide. He quoted Verdi, saying that it was the 'force of destiny' that had brought him, in 1993, to this former 'capital of the Nazi movement' – to his family's horror. Rothemund, he said, had created a 'quiet film' that dispensed with 'guard dogs and Nazi uniforms', but offered an impressive argument for tolerance and civil courage.[115] The film asks why people are so easily led astray. It was still incomprehensible to him how one of the most civilised and educated countries in Europe had allowed itself to be manipulated in this way.[116] 'It is rare for an orator to receive so much applause, even Sir Peter Jonas, who is used to the limelight. For whole minutes, the spotlight in the Carl Orff Saal remained focused on the tall director of the Staatsoper',[117] the *Süddeutsche Zeitung* said in its assessment of Jonas's speech. 'The Laudatio he offered the award-winner struck a chord because film people are not used to hearing serious, substantial speeches. There was political knowledge behind it,' says Barbara Burgdorf.

When Nike Wagner and the Wieland branch of the Wagner family asked Sir Peter to deliver the speech at the ceremony marking the centenary of Wieland Wagner's birth in July 2017, they knew what to expect. Jonas had criticised the German government for linking its small subsidy for the Bayreuth Festival to what he saw as a set of 'bean counting' conditions.[118] In 2011 in the *Frankfurter Allgemeine Zeitung* he had also published eleven wishes for the future of Bayreuth – which he had not attended in the past decade because it had become too boring. Bayreuth deserved better than the current festival, he had written: 'It doesn't have that fancy-pants, black-money-laundering aspect that Salzburg has.' If he were the good Lord, he would not only establish a forum for new music theatre, as Klaus Zehelein had done in Stuttgart, but also a singers' academy; and he would actively recruit the best conductors and directors in the world to Bayreuth. He would put *Die Feen*, *Rienzi* and *Das Liebesverbot* on the programme. He wanted to rejuvenate the audience through a particularly drastic intervention in the social structure of the festival. He would sell the five front rows reserved for celebrities to people under twenty-five for ten euros a seat. The shortfall in revenue would be made up by a sponsor:

'The established audience would certainly be outraged at first to see people in jeans sitting in front of them in the better seats. I can only tell them: Sorry, but Bayreuth is not a social club for the established German middle class.'[119]

This would also disrupt 'the eternal, identical ritualised applause': 'The singers come and there are bravos without end, and then the director comes and gets thousands of boos, no matter what it was like.' Jonas didn't stop there: he would take orchestral arrangements from Wagner's operas and hand them over to leading choreographers: 'An experimental Tanzzentrum [dance centre] in

Bayreuth, I would definitely do that if I were the good Lord.'

He kept hammering on the subject of politics and economy: 'Bayreuth is a piddling little trifle in the state's budget. This debate about money is over-done. And the most effective way of doing sponsorship is to use a spot of blackmail. Example: Audi is in the immediate vicinity. Why is Audi much more visible as a sponsor in Salzburg than in Bayreuth? If I were the Bavarian state government, I would say to Audi: "Children, excuse me, but we want you to support Bayreuth." Pure blackmail. Only then can sponsorship be relied upon.'

He saved his sharpest dart for the end of the essay, where he inveighed against the festival's opening ceremony: 'the most embarrassing thing ever to exist in Germany'. Although Germany had spent all its energies on 'denazification' after the Second World War, 'of all things, this highly symbolic opening ceremony' had remained untouched: 'I would say to the politicians: "Children, you may keep your privileges. But you get a complimentary ticket for a seminar or a production of the Forum Neues Musiktheater, or you must come to the final performance." This opening is not harmless.' He ended on a conciliatory note: 'Wagnerians, relax: I am not the good Lord.'

The celebratory address at Wieland Wagner's centenary would be one of his more important speeches. 'He put more work into this speech than into any other,' said Barbara Burgdorf. 'He read and researched an incredible amount. He knew it was a sensitive issue. Talking about someone with such an ambiguous past was necessarily a balancing act. At that time he asked many people for advice and had the speech proof-read.'

One of these people was Egbert Tholl. In Tholl's obituary of Peter Jonas, he described how the pair worked 'like a couple of rascals' to insert a particularly good joke into this speech.[120] The manuscript in fact reads quite dryly. It was his charisma, his authority, that gave power to edgier transitions and to metaphors that didn't quite fit. Jonas opened on a note meant to activate his audience's imagination – 'imagine'[121] – before moving onto the subject of the Wagner dynasty via Vincenzo Bellini, whom Wagner called the 'gentle Sicilian'. 'With all the dark history and with all the quarrels and stories of deceit and fraud – let us be grateful that this dynasty was at least born out of culture and stands for artistic values. In view of this fact, one can certainly generously forgive a lot of the other things.' With his first thesis, Jonas was then able to open up his biggest theme, about the responsibility that the Federal Republic of Germany has towards Europe: the Bayreuth Festival is the 'weathervane that shows how Germany is getting over the horrors of the past, especially those of the middle 20th century; and reflects its present as a new beacon of hope for Europe's future'. In broad brushstrokes, he touched on Wieland Wagner's childhood and youth, described his relationship with 'Uncle Wolf', and then addressed the 'break that must have sent shock waves through his psyche': in 1944, Wieland Wagner was taken away from active military service at the front and transferred to a Bayreuth subcamp of the Flossenbürg concentration camp. Wieland Wagner is said to have suddenly changed, to have entered a period of inward flight, Jonas said, using this image to invoke current horrors – 'Brexit, Trump, Orbán's cultural revolution': 'manifestations of extreme danger'. Jonas ventured a look into the future: 'how many of us will remain silent then?'

Wieland's 'youth among demons', which had left him marked and scarred, helped shape him into the man and the artist that he later became. The productions of 'New Bayreuth' made a lasting impression on Peter Jonas. This was his personal view of European cultural history in the making. As one of the leading theatrical figures of his time, he made an assessment of the influence that the Bayreuth Festival had on the European youth of the 1960s, on himself, and on his friends. He offered a charming, witty description of his first pilgrimage to Bayreuth. The anecdote culminated with Wieland Wagner's production of *Tristan und Isolde*. After that, he was determined 'never again to accept opera performances that were not prepared to brutally interrogate the work in question. Our theatre world would not have developed as we know it today, so rich, so free and so progressive, without the achievements of Wieland Wagner, especially here on this stage, at this Festival.' Jonas quoted Barrie Kosky, whose production of *Die Meistersinger von Nürnberg* opened the 2017 Festival: 'Auschwitz is horror, Bayreuth is comedy – but a jet-black comedy!' A truer word had never been spoken, said Jonas.

'Comedy, as we all know, is not an easy exercise and in particular it is not free of pain. Comedy is tragic, as the clown's tears show, and it can cause conflict, doubt and moral turmoil.'

Jonas concluded with an appeal to his audience: 'He has achieved that cathartic goal of musical theatre in its purest form: not only to search the soul, but to touch it. We owe it to his legacy: to sweep our past under the carpet no more, never again, and never again to be silent.' Jonas's speech was fabulously well received, according to Egbert Tholl.[122] The sell-out crowd answered his oration with a minutes-long standing ovation.

The Social Science Center in Berlin

Barbara Burgdorf noticed that, in his latter years, opera played a lesser role in Jonas's life: 'These are creeping transitions. Now he's experiencing other things that are taking him in other directions mentally.' How easy it would have been for Jonas to simply join the opera jet-set after 2006. But during these years he went to the opera comparatively little, by his standards at least. 'Sometimes going to the opera is a frightful bore. *Sometimes*,' he said with a laugh.

One new focus of his energies was his work at the WZB Berlin Social Science Center. Maurice Lausberg organised Jonas's involvement, at a time when Lausberg was responsible for development and sponsors at the Munich Staatsoper. Lausberg had been approached by Steffen Huck, Professor of Economics at University College London (UCL). Huck had already put in place funding for a particular study related to opera, but it had to be spent quickly. Leading British opera houses and orchestras turned down the opera lover's approach because of the short turnaround, and so he turned to Lausberg. They ran through the basics of Huck's plan during an interval in *Norma*. Lausberg signed up on the spot.

Around that time, Steffen Huck had co-authored an essay on *Tannhäuser* with fellow economists. This piece used economically oriented game theory as an interpretive framework for the plot of the opera. The authors investigated why Tannhäuser in the second act confesses to having been in the Venusberg. The authors' approach was to investigate Tannhäuser as an individual and to ask what alternative options he might have chosen. They posed counterfactual scenarios, investigating how the opera might have developed had he made a different choice. As a particularly talented singer, he could have tried to win the competition. He could also have purposely sung badly. Neither would have been good strategies. Had he won, he might have chosen Elisabeth as his prize, but this would have been a direct path to hell – for he would have entered into the marriage wracked with guilt. Had he lost, he would have lost Elisabeth too. He solves the dilemma through the path chosen, sabotages the competition and wins Elisabeth, albeit only in heaven.[123]

After this study received a lively response from scholars in the humanities, Huck organised an interdisciplinary workshop on the topic of rationality, drama and fiction in May 2007. He told Maurice Lausberg about these plans at a dinner in 2006, whereupon the latter spontaneously suggested inviting Jonas, who accepted.

It was only later, when Huck and Jonas had already become friends, that Peter confessed (shortly before the workshop took place) that he no longer wanted to take part: 'Sitting in a stuffy little room at UCL with some nutters for two days… But of course he drove over, dutiful man that he is,' said Huck. Jonas, however, had found something of a way out. Of the two dinners that framed the workshop, both supplied with ample and good wine, he attended only one. 'He minimised the risk for himself a little bit,' Huck grinned.

Jonas enjoyed the workshop a lot. As someone who came from the field and was not privy to the jargon of any of the disciplines involved, he played an important mediating role and fuelled the discussions. 'People love to listen to him, we know that: he's fantastic at storytelling and he can take interesting contributions and make them fascinating. In other words, he took this workshop to another level.' Other workshops followed, including one on game theory and opera, which Jonas had already formally co-organised. Both men experimented with the juxtaposition of scholars from the social sciences with students of the humanities and with creative practitioners. Neither saw a primacy of science over the arts or of one discipline over the other, Jutta Allmendinger recalled. They hit it off right away, given that they were both petrolheads, opera lovers and art collectors. 'We talked a lot about making life beautiful, from buying art to cars,' Huck recalls. Above all, however, they were addicted to television series. Retirement allowed Jonas to pursue his passion for series – 'the art form of our time', as he always emphasised to his students. Sometimes he would watch four or five hours a day and could tell Steffen Huck about new releases.

Huck continued to run his events with the WZB. The first workshop there took place in November 2011, which Steffen Huck and Peter Jonas titled 'The Anglo-German Divide', a topic of great preoccupation for Jonas. He was very concerned about developments in his home country: 'my opinion is that Boris Johnson is just a more sympathetic and a bit more intelligent edition of Donald Trump – and just as cynical.'[124] 'Wir Briten sind ein spezieller Fall [We Brits are a special case]. Because they live on an island, they feel independent and think that across the water there is only chaos and darkness. We do things differently. We are not special at all! The British cannot imagine that everyone else is rather special.'

Brexit, then looming, worried him greatly and, once completed, infuriated him. Jonas described it as a collective suicide. He had remained loyal to Anderson & Sheppard, the company that had produced his first ever tailored suit, for decades. But when he saw that they also made suits for Jacob Rees-Mogg, one of the leaders of the Brexiteers and the son of William Rees-Mogg, who had harried Jonas as a representative of the Arts Council, Jonas ditched the brand and got rid of all their clothing.

The workshop at the WZB began by examining the differences between British and German theatrical aesthetics and the role played by narrative in the British system and that played by concept in the German system. Huck and Jonas wanted to find out whether there was a connection between these differences and the fact that academic economics in England is predominantly empirical, whereas in Germany it is theoretical, and what the reasons for this might be. This event was Jonas's first visit to the WZB; neither of them had expected to have more dealings with the organisation.

But when Huck became Director of the WZB's 'Economics of Change' department in 2012, he was able to launch a new series of events entitled 'TV, Economics and Society' in summer 2013. This series saw a real coup: both men were 'totale Fans [huge fans]' of *Breaking Bad* and had actually managed to persuade Vince Gilligan, the show's creator and producer, to come and do a workshop at WZB.[125] When Jonas went to the 2017 CineMeritAwards in Munich, he wore a T-shirt with Bryan Cranston's face printed on it.

Huck saw *Breaking Bad* as a social science laboratory in which social relations, economic conditions, individual decisions and moral change were all negotiated. 'Chemistry teacher Walter White, who after his cancer diagnosis decides to secure his family's economic future by going into drug production, undergoes a dramatic transformation,'[126] he explained in his introduction. The video of the discussion with Vince Gilligan is still the most popular on WZB's YouTube channel:

'Peter Jonas radiates an incredible brilliance and lightness to the outside world. This mixture of spontaneity and depth, only a few can do that, that is brilliance,' said an effusive Huck. 'It's easy to overlook how much work goes into it. I saw in how much detail, how precisely he prepared for his evening with Vince Gilligan! He is insanely diligent. On the outside, however, nothing seems rehearsed.'

Fig. 7: Peter Jonas with Diana Iljine and Bryan Cranston

Vince Gilligan's visit and the video of the event helped attract other top TV makers to collaborate with the WZB. Tom Fontana, who had produced the HBO series *Oz*, accepted an invitation. Huck's and Jonas's work with WZB was gaining recognition and credibility. The pair were creating spaces where things could happen that were otherwise not possible. A highlight of a recent workshop was the lecture 'Surprise and Suspense' by the technically and mathematically focused economist Jeff Ely, who discussed the question of how to construct a machine, a programme, that could tell stories with an ideal mix of suspense and surprise. Among other things, he explained that this optimal machine would have to tell dull stories every now and then, because if you come to expect a plot twist at every turn, that would become boring in itself. These notions, from an economics-oriented game theorist, were a revelation for screenwriters who attended the session. 'A light bulb came on for them. These were people who would never meet in real life. Peter always liked that a lot. And as an artistic director, he had created spaces where people could make something extraordinary.' The fact that they were both having a lot of fun with this work was a pleasant side effect of their friendship.

'He was incredibly pleased and honoured to be involved with the WZB,' his wife agreed. 'There, he brought all his ingenuity and global interest and knowledge to bear.' His involvement at the WZB gradually increased. In 2015 Jonas joined the Board of Trustees of the WZB, which took his admission as an opportunity to amend the statutes. Public figures would now be explicitly permitted to be members of the Board of Trustees. 'Working at the WZB was pleasure for me, pure intellectual pleasure,' Jonas recounted. 'The workshops with Steffen were like a hobby.' But it was through them that he became interested in the WZB's work. For the first time, he realised that he was interested in economics and social sciences. 'I am fascinated by what pure mathematics can resolve in combination with economics and social sciences. I would have laughed to hear that in the past, but not any more: everything has a formula. Every instinctive decision has a formula. I learned that the hard way. If you analyse decisions after the fact, if you have enough knowledge and discipline, you can find out why such decisions came about.'

While sitting on the Board of Trustees of the WZB, he got to know people who could understand such decisions in a formal, arithmetical sense. 'Knowing this, I could have managed a lot of things better as a director. Why people behave in a certain way, react to something in a certain way. Why you make certain aesthetic choices and what that means to the people you serve as a director. The logic behind certain things. If I could just have the knowledge and interest I have now and go back in time and apply them – maybe the results wouldn't be better or worse, but different.'

Jonas's sense of duty and meticulousness were also on display in the meetings of the Board of Trustees. 'Be prepared,' was already his watchword when speaking to dramaturgists in the theatre. 'Before a Board of Trustees meeting, you get hundreds of pages of social science stuff to read. I really always prepare. I really do read all the papers. But there is another aspect, too: as an Englishman who can speak German, who has German roots, I can make certain points in meetings that a German would not dare to say.' He also sometimes formulated contexts differently, thought completely outside the box. That was good for the discussion, Huck recalled. 'We did not offer him any special liberties because he is not a professional or because he is not a scientist. Or because he is from Britain. It tends to be the case that few people in academia are able to think outside the box and to take liberties,' said WZB President Jutta Allmendinger. Jonas also permitted himself a few very fine performances. Allmendinger reports on one: 'In the Board of Trustees he also pointed out things that did not matter to us. I will give you an example: Wolfgang Merkel, a well-known democracy researcher, presented his research at a meeting of the Board. SPJ spoke first and said: this voice is incredible, this baritone! This makes a wide-reaching impact. That's what you need.' This was a completely unexpected intervention. We looked at each other. He was really enjoying himself! SPJ was also a prankster. He tested us.'

Jonas gave active and committed support to the WZB during a 2018 assessment with the Leibniz Association. Speaking as the coordinator of the collaboration, he delivered an impassioned polemic in defence of the WZB, underscoring the importance of the organisation's interdisciplinary work. The speech is said to have impressed the panel, who made a positive assessment.

'Him and the WZB: that's the story of an incredible commitment. He took things on himself that were anything but straightforward,' Huck said, underlining Jonas's importance to the project. 'From the very beginning, the WZB was always about more than the fulfilment of duty for him; it gave him genuine pleasure.'

His special qualities as a mediator came into play during preparations for the celebration of the WZB's fiftieth anniversary, which took place on 19 June 2019 under the heading 'Europe: Myth and Vision', in cooperation with the Barenboim-Said Akademie, in the Boulez Hall. Jonas set up a meeting between Jutta Allmendinger and Daniel Barenboim and travelled to attend himself. He did the WZB an incredible service by curating the event at Barenboim's suggestion, said Huck.

'The special quality of his work at the WZB was that he allowed no limitations, from beginning to end. He demanded that we all think without limits. That doesn't happen often,' Allmendinger said.

'Most people move in the space of the possible. In this space, certain things are unthinkable: the Boulez Hall as the venue for the WZB event, the presence of Daniel Barenboim, his speech on Europe. The first performance of Jörg Widmann's work. The opening up of the academy to the public. The urban society, pupils as guests. He always addressed the seemingly impossible, without hesitation, with seriousness. And woe betide anyone who thought that something was impossible.'

But this ethic also had its downsides. During the preparations for the ceremony, Jonas fell seriously ill. 'He managed his appointments with his last ounce of strength: without him they would never have put together such a dazzling, multi-faceted celebration,' Barbara Burgdorf explained. Even when he was really unwell, he attended all his appointments with discipline. 'He would never have cancelled projects which he had given his word to carry through,' says Huck. And the ceremony was indeed extraordinarily unusual for an institution like the WZB.

The intensity of this work can also be felt in the way Jutta Allmendinger and Steffen Huck remember Peter Jonas. 'He empowered people to be less conformist, to behave less in the way you think things should be done.' Allmendinger saw him as a person who was utterly himself:

'His flutter scarf represented this attitude. Outwardly, he was not interested in status symbols. He looked behind what was happening in a series, behind what music represented, behind what science wanted to say at its core. Behind organisational principles, behind relationships between people. For me, that is his legacy.' Allmendinger sees his special quality as a mediator as lying in the fact 'that he didn't just say any old thing. He did not claim anything without verification or use empty phrases. He worked his way through biographies, assignments, projects. He stood on solid ground. Then he began to mediate. His second very special quality I would call humanity, a very, very great love for people. He approaches people with good courage: he is open, friendly and optimistic. He does not approach them with stereotypes, reservations, limitations. This basic attitude explains a lot of his charisma.'

Steffen Huck knows few people 'who were more youthful than him, with this insane openness to new things, to rethinking things, to changing life. That's quite a gift, especially when you're at your absolute peak in your profession.'

At the end of 2019, Sir Peter was named the first 'Honorary Fellow' of the WZB. He was proud of the accolade.

CHILDHOOD AND YOUTH

London after the Second World War

'My first memory of my sister is of her playing the preludes and fugues by Bach, Beethoven, or from Mozart sonatas. In the morning I would be asleep in my room, and I would wake up slowly and listen to her practising the piano.' Peter Jonas fell silent again and reflected on his memories. The singing of the sparrows, finches, but also of the swifts, which nested very close to his flat in Zurich, came through the open windows.

His sister Kathryn was born in London in September 1941, in the middle of the Second World War. 'She looked very cute with her long plaits. She may not have been a dream child, but she was an exceptionally talented pianist.'

'Either Kathryn was practising the piano – I don't mean *Für Elise*, I mean Beethoven's later sonatas – or she was reading a book. She was incredibly serious. She used to call me "my charming superficial brother". She had brains. Das sagt viel aus [That says a lot].' He couldn't stifle a laugh and looked out of the window of his living room over the roofs of the old Unterstrass district, so quiet on this spring morning. Kathryn was much more than just a big sister to Peter. He looked up to her all his life. She was his mentor, his fixed point, an unreachable, gently shining star. 'I would love to meet her now. I really love my sister very much. I really miss her.' His voice broke. 'I thought she was the most wonderful person. I wanted to be like her.'

Fig. 8: Peter and his sister Kathryn

His parents Hilda May Ziadie and Walter Jonas lived in St John's Wood near Regent's Park in central London at the start of the war. In late 1940, Hilda May became pregnant with Kathryn, out of wedlock. Hilda May was expecting her first child while the Blitz raged outside. In the first months of her pregnancy, the Germans and the Italians dropped around two hundred bombs over the city every single night. By August 1941, 43,000 civilians had died, and one million houses had been destroyed. Hilda May must have longed for her Jamaican home more than ever. And as if all that were not enough, Walter was considered an enemy alien and was interned for six months. He was released only on condition that he agreed to work for the secret service of the British army. His son never found out quite what this work consisted of.

Fig. 9: Hilda May Ziadie and Walter Jonas, London 1939/40

In 1942–43, it appears that Walter was tasked with finding National Socialists in Germany who were guilty of economic crimes. It was not until 1951 that he received permission to leave the secret service.

Even though the war years had undermined many conventions, in England as elsewhere marriage was considered an unquestionable norm. What landlord would have rented his flat to an unmarried couple? Until the 1950s, illegitimate births were exceptional.[1]

At the age of twenty-nine, Hilda May was already relatively old for her first pregnancy, but her Jamaica-based father Tewfik's reaction would have been harder to bear than the social stigma of pregnancy out of wedlock.

His reaction was not difficult to imagine: to this strict Catholic, an illegitimate child would have been simply unacceptable. Walter and Hilda May married. To protect themselves, they went to

Purley in the far south of London. But – bitter irony – a stray German bomb destroyed the roof of their house. So they moved back to central London and waited with their baby for the war to end.

Finally came 8 May 1945, VE Day, 'Victory in Europe'. People regained hope. Hilda May and Walter were now among the lucky ones. Not only had they survived: they had a whole life ahead of them.

And yet it is inconceivable that they escaped the horrors of the war unscathed. Neither Hilda May nor Walter could have survived the war years in London without developing post-traumatic reactions. Both carried these traumas with them throughout their lives. Hilda May's children felt this, even if they could neither name it nor understand it.

The situation was particularly hard for those returning from the war. Their demobilisation often took a long time; the war-weary population no longer wanted to celebrate them as heroes; and they had lost their jobs. The end of the war had long been yearned for, but the prosaic reality of the post-war period was hard to bear. The British Empire was on the brink of insolvency, inflation was running high. It was only with great difficulty that the British were able to meet the costs of occupying Germany.

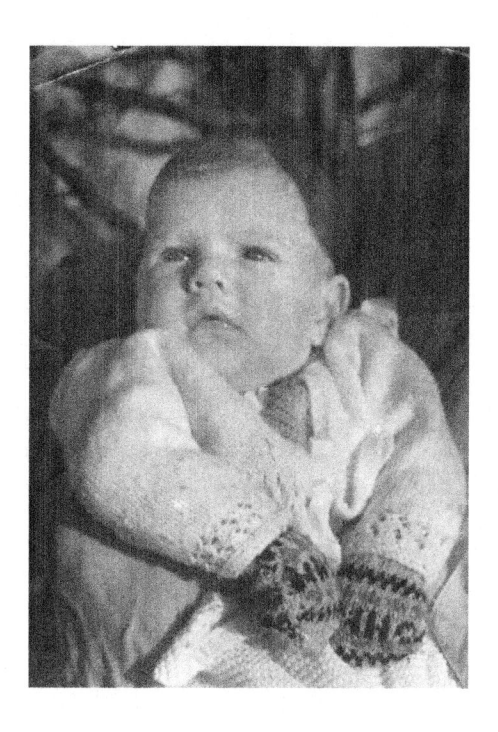

Fig. 10: Peter Jonas, early 1947

Despite all the adverse circumstances, the dance halls and cinemas in post-war London were packed. But Walter and Hilda May were preoccupied with taking care of their daughter. Hilda May, now thirty-four, was expecting her second child during these months. He was born on 14 October 1946 and was christened Jens Peter after his paternal uncle. His name was later changed to John Peter. From then on, the boy was called by his second name: Peter.

The winter of 1946–47 was the worst for half a century, with vicious winds whistling through the destroyed city, frost penetrating the devastated houses. The Thames froze over, there were frequent power cuts and electric light was a rarity.[2]

After Peter's birth, the young parents bought a house at 24 Glebe Hyrst, Sanderstead. At that time, it was located in one of the southern suburbs of London. Today, as then, the properties on this street are carefully maintained. Peter's parents were able to afford the property only with the help of Hilda May's father Tewfik Ziadie. But the house did not satisfy Hilda May, who was used to more spacious living quarters in Jamaica.

Her sentiment contrasted with the situation that many Britons found themselves in, as they struggled to find any housing at all. More than half of the couples who married between 1947 and 1955 lived with relatives at the beginning of their marriage.[3] Having hot water was far from the norm, and the same went for indoor toilets. Many middle-class people like Hilda May found the 'austerity years', as the British historian David Kynaston termed the post-war period, harder to bear than did other social classes.[4]

Most British people were preoccupied with finding a safe home, building a secure family life and getting enough food. Their discontent focused mainly on the lack of bread, which had always been plentiful during the war years. In 1947, an opinion research institute had asked how the British imagined their dream meal if money were no object. 'Their lovingly detailed responses – sherry, tomato soup, sole, roast chicken and coffee – belonged in large part to the realm of fantasy.'[5]

People's everyday resentments were directed against Germany, whose reconstruction was supported from 1948 to 1952 with funds from the Marshall Plan 'For European Recovery'. Even though the UK had received far more funds from the Marshall Plan than had Germany, the British were dependent on food ration cards for longer than the Germans were. Peter Jonas remembered sarcastic remarks by his mother, who would exclaim indignantly from time to time: 'Why do we have to have powdered milk? Because we sent our milk to the Germans!' Parts of the population were opposed to this aid. Kynaston quotes typical reactions: 'I'd be against it, myself. It's Germany's turn to go without … I wouldn't care what happened to the Germans – they've asked for it.'[6]

That is the image of Germany Peter Jonas grew up with. The fact that his father was German, the reasons for his emigration, the fate of relatives in Germany, none of this played a role in the lives of the Jonas family. It was only through his father's half-sister, his beloved Aunt Elizabeth, that Jonas learned of his Jewish heritage.

The Ziadie family in Jamaica

On his mother's side, Peter Jonas descends from the Jamaican Ziadie family, one of Lebanon's old Christian families. The story of the arrival of the first Ziadies in Jamaica revolves around two brothers, Michael and Tewfik, who would become Peter Jonas's grandfather. Tewfik came to Jamaica with an important job to do for his family: he was supposed to be bringing a bride from Beirut for his older brother Michael, who had emigrated there on a ship in the early twentieth century.

Like many other Christian Lebanese, the Ziadies were Maronites who recognised the Pope and belonged to the Catholic Church, but separated themselves from local Catholic communities. Because of the religiously motivated repression by the Muslim Turks who controlled what was then called the Mount Lebanon province in Syria, Michael, like many other Lebanese, decided to emigrate.

Since the migration movement had begun in the nineteenth century, the Lebanese diaspora worldwide grew larger than the population of the home country itself. Many of them, like Michael and his younger brother Tewfik, went to Jamaica. The Great Exhibition, which took place in in Jamaica's capital Kingston in 1891, had attracted more than 300,000 visitors over four months. This was the first time many Lebanese people had heard of Jamaica. 'Jamaica was, in many ways, an inspired choice,' said Lady Colin Campbell, second cousin of Peter Jonas. 'About the size of Lebanon, Jamaica has a comparable climate, albeit without a winter, and is reminiscent of home with its lush Caribbean coastline and magnificent blue mountains.'[7]

When Tewfik arrived in Jamaica, he had no intention of settling there permanently. Like so many other new arrivals, Tewfik found a vibrant market awaiting his arrival in Kingston harbour. Jamaican workers in cream-coloured 'Jippi Jappa' straw hats, businessmen in fine suits or Indians in loincloths were all busy haggling over prices. Elegantly dressed ladies used horse-drawn carriages; others had to resort to cheaper mules. Electricity and running drinking water were standard. Kingston was booming.[8]

Tewfik's brother Michael had already become wealthy by working hard in the import-export business. He now helped Tewfik to set up his own business.

Some of the richest families in the world have a Christian Lebanese background. Their success in business, politics and entertainment is attributed to a family network that spans several countries and continents. As a Christian minority, they had had to assert themselves in Lebanon and could now draw on this experience in their new lives abroad.

Tewfik was extremely successful in plying his trade. But his true passion was racing. He founded a stable which started out with twenty racehorses and they enjoyed great success. Today, the Ziadie family belongs to the upper class of Jamaica and is one of the big names in commerce and horse racing. No race meeting in the 1940s was complete without several Ziadie horses running, as Lady Colin Campbell put it.[9] Thanks to this, and the ubiquitous family name displayed above their shops, the family enjoyed a high profile.

Fig. 11: Hilda May Ziadie, Jamaica, c. 1930

Tewfik married Hilda Tingling, Peter Jonas's grandmother. Time and again, newspaper reports spoke of his having a Scottish mother or grandmother. He never corrected such statements, but they were wrong. There were Scottish ancestors in his mother's line. However, they were at least three times removed: he himself did not know the exact degree of distance.[10]

Tewfik and Hilda had fifteen children, and adopted two more. On 10 February 1912, their second child, Hilda May, was born. Jonas described his mother as being 'in a coolish way beautiful. Very exotic. She was a dark, sultry beauty. Her beauty and attractive qualities attracted men. In those days, women in the Caribbean could make a career out of being a woman, a feminine woman. They could shape their lives around their beauty. If you had good ankles and a good figure you could get a very long way.' So Jonas tried to see something positive in these narrow conventions. He never rejected the word 'exotic'. The discourse surrounding the pejorative or racist connotations of this term never had a lot of meaning for him. It was a different time.

Without question, Hilda May would have been able to chart a path as a 'feminine woman'. When she became a young woman, her parents had to consider who she should marry. The answer was simple: whoever her father chose – and he already had a distant relative in mind. But Tewfik made his calculation without counting on his daughter, who her son still admires today. 'My mother was very, very stubborn. She decided to run away. How she ran away, I don't know exactly. I admire her and give her credit for that. She got money from the family, boarded a ship and came to Europe.'

When Hilda May arrived in Europe in 1936, she was twenty-three years old. For a short time she modelled in Paris, but then moved to London. She modelled there, too, and sometime around 1939–40 she met the thirty-year-old Walter Jonas; for as long as she lived she never discussed the circumstances of their meeting with her son. The Second World War was casting its long shadow. Walter was a Jewish refugee from Germany. His parents were dead, his siblings had left Germany. Jonas described Walter when asked: 'Quite attractive, a bit heavy built, not overweight and shorter than me'.

In September 1939, the Second World War began. Britain, having declared war on Germany together with France, was a party to the war from the very beginning. In September 1940, a year before Kathryn was born, London was bombed by the Germans for the first time. It was around this time, at the very latest, that the pair became lovers. Both were emigrants, still young, both largely penniless.

The Jonas family from Hamburg

The Jewish roots of Peter Jonas's family on his father's side – his German roots – lie in Hamburg, in the still-chic Altona suburb of

Othmarschen, on the Elbe. As one walks from the S-Bahn station, the path to the former home of the Jonas family at Walderseestraße 48 leads through quiet, green streets, although motorways have brought the big city closer. Today, Walderseestraße has four lanes and a green strip separates the two sides of the road. Signs at the entrances of the houses rarely reveal the names of their inhabitants. Magnificent villas and genteel townhouses stand on lushly landscaped grounds. The brick-built house at No. 48 is hidden behind a wall that is no longer quite white, with tall bushes protecting it from view. Only those who peer down the driveway will recognise the conservatory at the south of the property, on top of which a terrace has been built. Moss pushes through between the flagstones of the path; the parking space for the car was a late addition. How many passers-by in Walderseestraße will be aware of the small, ground-level brass plaques that sit by the garden gate? These so-called Stolpersteine, or stumbling blocks, are not placed there to trip up visitors. The slabs embedded in the footpath commemorate the victims of National Socialist violence. This one memorialises Peter Jonas's grandfather and his second wife: Julius and Julie Jonas. Their story takes us to Jewish Hamburg.[11]

Fig. 12: Stolpersteine for Julius and Julie Jonas

In 1910, Walter Adolf Jonas, Peter Jonas's father, became the second child born to Julius Jonas and his first wife Käthe. While there are many traces of the respected lawyer Julius, the available sources do not provide a clear picture of Käthe, a daughter of assimilated Jews from a wealthy family.

Käthe's family, originally from Lodz in Poland, had settled in Hamburg during the ninth century and achieved great prosperity.[12] Käthe's great-grandfather Jussuf the Elder settled in Hamburg around 1820, the year in which the Orthodox Jewish community accepted him. Although he had learned the fur-dyeing trade, he worked as a haulier in Hamburg.

He achieved his first success when the Chevra Kadisha, the Jewish community's funeral organisation, assigned him the job of transporting corpses. While his first son, Jussuf the Younger, was born in Poland, Veitl, who would later rename himself Theodor upon baptism, was born on March 1823 in Hamburg. Both sons helped with their father's business. Theodor was soon considered the 'king of the coachmen', but his true destiny was the opera stage. In his *Biographical Dictionary of the German Stage in the Nineteenth Century*, the author Ludwig Eisenberg reports the decisive turn that took place in this young man's life: how he was driven to the theatre again and again by his great passion for opera and song. Since Veitl-Theodor attached great importance to the 'nobility of his team' and is said to have had a 'fashionable appearance' himself, he received many commissions from 'distinguished families and well-to-do young people'.[13] When he returned from a tour in 1838 at the age of fifteen – 'without a passenger', Eisenberg adds – and himself singing alone on the coach box, the wine merchant Gerstenkorn discovered him. He financed Theodor's singing training, which he completed in the evenings alongside his paid work. After his debut in Hamburg with the 'Portrait Aria' from *The Magic Flute*, he was able to establish himself first in Germany and then internationally – in London, Paris and the USA – as the 'king of tenors', 'reaping laurels and gold everywhere in abundance', as Eisenberg writes. His star role was as Postillon in Adolphe Adam's *Le Postillon de Lonjumeau*, which he sang over a thousand times. 'Audiences everywhere could not get enough of the funny Chapelou and could not demand the obligatory "Wachtelschlag" [quail's call, a musical term but also a play on Wachtel's name] with the whip often enough, da capo.'[14]

Theodor Wachtel died on 8 March 1893. His three sons also worked as singers with varying degrees of success. Eisenberg writes nothing of their mother.

It fell to Jussuf the Younger to take over his father's haulage business. He acquired two fur-dyeing factories and was able to expand his father's wealth. Although he turned to the Reform community and thus advanced the process of his family's assimilation, he was later buried in the Jewish cemetery in Ottensen.

In 1854, his son was born. Samuel Joseph was able to add to his father's wealth, and married Selma, née Sonnersberg. They lived in a villa at Mittelweg 87, and owned a country house in Baron-Voght-Straße and two estates near Lübeck.

Selma Wachtel was an educated and above all artistically engaged figure, and it was in her salon that Hamburg's high society met. The Wachtel family no longer identified with Judaism, even though Selma did not get baptised. She was buried in an urn at the Christian cemetery Stiller Weg in Groß Flottbek – something that did not go unnoticed either by the Christian community or by the National Socialists. Her daughter Käthe, Peter Jonas's grandmother, was also buried there after her early death at the age of thirty-four.

Käthe, also spelled Katchew, was born in 1884, the third of the six children of Samuel Joseph and Selma Wachtel. Her parents' wealth meant that she could be educated by private tutors. She is also said to have been very beautiful. At a young age – the exact year is not known – she married Julius Jonas, Peter Jonas's grandfather, who was on his way to becoming a respected criminal lawyer.

Julius Jonas was born on 15 December 1874 in Itzehoe, Schleswig-Holstein, the child of merchant Adolf Wolf and Jenny, née Horwitz.[15] Like his four sisters, who later became teachers, he studied in Kiel and Göttingen and received his doctorate in 1897 with a 58-page thesis on 'The Concept and Significance of Bona

Fides in Acquisition and Limitation of Actions' at the University of Erlangen.[16] He dedicated the thesis to his parents. At the end of the account we find his curriculum vitae, which provides information in particular about his years of study in Munich, Kiel and Berlin, and his military service in Kiel. He passed the first state examination in 1897 and completed his dissertation during a stint as a legal clerk at the Schönberg district court. From 1898 Julius Jonas lived in Hamburg, where he was admitted to the bar in 1902 at the local and regional court in Altona. He founded his own law firm at Fischmarkt 26/27, later a second one in Altonaer Königstraße, and was an honorary Board member of the German Bar Association.[17] From 21 December 1919 until his dismissal by the National Socialists on 8 June 1933, he also worked as a notary.

His daughter Annemarie was born in 1909, Walter Adolf, the father of Peter Jonas, in 1910 and their youngest child Jens Peter in 1914, shortly before the start of the First World War.

Peter Jonas would be baptised with the name of his uncle Jens Peter. Since 1912, the family had lived in their house at Walderseestraße 48, a villa that Julius Jonas had had built in the Dutch style.[18] Like many other German citizens of Jewish descent, Julius Jonas had taken part in the First World War as a soldier and had been awarded the Iron Cross. Käthe died in 1918 during the flu epidemic, leaving behind three children aged four, eight and nine.

When Julius Jonas married Julie Oppenheimer, twenty-one years his junior, on 27 March 1920, two years after the death of his first wife, he was already a recognised lawyer. His business partner Otto Siems would state, during a reparations hearing in 1964, that 'Dr Jonas was respected as a criminal defence lawyer, especially at court'.[19]

Like his first wife, Julius was born into an assimilated Jewish family, but he still felt part of the Jewish community and worked for a time on the Board of the Altona Synagogue Association.[20] Julie, who was born in Hamburg on 3 November 1895, came from the rabbinical Hess family on her mother's side, but no longer considered herself a member of the Jewish community. According to Peter Jonas, she was extremely assimilated. Julie gave birth to her daughter Elizabeth – Peter Jonas's beloved Auntie Elizabeth – on 13 April 1921 and to her second daughter Margarethe the following year, on 7 August 1922. Julius Jonas was now the father of five children. Annemarie, Walter and Jens Peter also lived in Walderseestraße. Elli Salewski assisted the couple as a nanny and housekeeper. She remained with the family even after she was no longer officially allowed to work in this Jewish household.

Fig. 13: Dr Julius Jonas, circa 1930

On 30 January 1933, the Weimar Republic ended – and with it there disappeared German Jews' civil rights. On 28 March 1933, the Nazi Party called on all party offices to boycott Jewish businesses, goods, doctors and lawyers in an appeal personally drafted by Adolf Hitler. A few days later, on 31 March, the Prussian Minister of Justice ordered all Jewish lawyers to submit applications for leave. Jewish lawyers were allowed to appear in court only in numbers that corresponded to the ratio of the Jewish population to the total population. After an agreement with the president of the Altona Regional Court, Heinrich Berthold, only Dr Julius Jonas and his colleague Dr Rudolf Warburg were granted this right.[21] On 7 April 1933, the Law for the Restoration of the Professional Civil Service, which aimed to exclude political oppositionists from the civil service, and above all 'civil servants of non-Aryan descent' was passed. As a result of these new rules, Dr Julius Jonas was dismissed as notary on 8 June 1933 and thus also lost his income.

In addition to these threats to his professional life, Julius also had to cope with the emigration of his sons from his first marriage. First, in 1933, Walter departed for England. Walter had last worked in Leipzig as a fur dyer in a relative's factory, where he also learned the trade of a chemical worker. His father and stepmother visited him on Christmas Day 1937 to celebrate his birthday on Boxing Day. The option of never returning to Germany and simply staying on in England may have also motivated them to make the trip, but Julius loved his homeland, and the German language, too much.[22]

One year after Walter, in 1934, Jens Peter also left.

He emigrated to Tel Aviv at the age of twenty and worked on a chicken farm. He later took up a post in the Ministry of Agriculture.[23] In the first Six-Day War in June 1967, he lost both legs. As a war-wounded veteran, he took on office work for the Israeli Intelligence Service. Peter Jonas remembered his uncle's prosthetic legs lying around the flat during later visits to London. After marrying an Israeli woman, Jens Peter became the father of two sons, cousins to Peter Jonas. Jonathan died in a bomb attack, David became a successful pharmaceutical entrepreneur in the USA.

By late 1933, of all the five children from Julius's first marriage, only his daughter Annemarie was still in Germany. 'She seemed a bit wild,' Peter Jonas said of her. In Berlin, she attended a school for Jewish children at Auguststraße 11–13 for one year. Today there is a restaurant there, the Pauly Saal, where Jonas liked to eat. Until the National Socialists forbade her to do so, Annemarie studied medicine at the Humboldt University. Following paths that Jonas was unable to reconstruct exactly, she came with her husband and child first to Lisbon, and later to Peru. The son died in 1972 as a passenger on Air Force Flight 571 of the Fuerza Aérea Uruguaya that crashed in the Andes.

While the National Socialists used the Olympic Games of 1936 – in winter in Garmisch-Partenkirchen, in summer in Berlin – as an opportunity for propaganda, Julius Jonas had to dissolve the offices in which he ran his law firms. On 27 September 1938 – the Anschluss (annexation) of Austria already in effect – the Fifth Decree on the Reich Citizenship Act came into force.

The bar excluded Dr Julius Jonas as a Jew on 30 November 1938, and in December he was provisionally admitted as a 'consultant', as the Jewish lawyers who were allowed to work exclusively for 'non-Aryans' were called.[24] Previously, the district court director Dr Schwarz had emphasised Jonas's 'extensive criminal practice' in his statement. 'His outstanding knowledge in the field of criminal law deserves mention.'[25] After his death, 'lawyer – without profession' was noted in the cemetery register.[26] Peter Jonas still knew the story of a Gestapo officer whom Julius had successfully defended against an accusation of rape: during one of the interrogations Julius had to undergo, the officer recognised him and helped him. During the third interrogation, however, he allegedly told him clearly that the family had to leave Germany. If he could not escape, he had better kill himself. Julius suffered a nervous breakdown from which he tried to recover in a sanatorium in Badenweiler near Freiburg im Breisgau. Elli Salewski, their housekeeper, who brought up the children, now had to leave the family; she was no longer allowed to work in a Jewish household.[27]

The daughters Elizabeth and Margarethe had attended the Bertha Lyceum in Othmarschen, but were both now excluded from taking the Abitur exam. At her father's request, Elizabeth briefly attended a higher commercial school in Switzerland and completed training at the Swedish Institute for Therapeutic Gymnastics. In her US identification papers, she would later list 'physiotherapist' as her profession. Elizabeth last attended the Talmud Torah School in Hamburg's Grindel Quarter in 1938. Elizabeth and Margarethe also left their home in Walderseestraße for good. With growing concern for their daughters' wellbeing, the parents had used their influence in the Jewish community to get Elizabeth to London in November 1938 on the first Kindertransport organised by the Jewish Relief Society. At the age of seventeen, she had already exceeded the prescribed age limit. One month later, on 1 December, her sixteen-year-old sister Margarethe also left Germany.

The moment the girls left, an intense and deeply sad correspondence developed, which ended only with their parents' suicide. Their farewell letter would be the last document in this correspondence. The letters and the postcards sent almost daily by the parents have been preserved under their daughter's later name as the Elizabeth Melamid Collection at the Leo Baeck Institute in New York. Elizabeth had jotted down 'Mutti & Pappis Briefe 21.10.43' on the first sheet of the collection. Mostly the cards and letters were in her mother's handwriting. Julius added only a few words. Julie wrote to her 'beloved pair', her 'beloved noodle dogs', her 'beloved, good children'. Elizabeth was her 'Wänzlein', Margarethe called her 'Nenna', and she addressed them both together as 'Schnuddels'. Julie repeatedly asked her daughters to write to her completely honestly about how they were doing in England with the Rosenbaum family, as she herself aimed to write honestly about how she and their father were feeling.

And Julie did write honestly, although not to the end. Her domestic help Gertrud Wrangel later reported that the couple had been thinking about the possibility of suicide for some time. The restlessness and the waiting were wearing on Julie. The children's father had become depressed again despite his stay at the Sanatorium. Her nerves were on edge. Julie herself was 'furiously broken'. 'I have such a longing for you again that I almost can't stand it any more.' On the day before Christmas Eve 1938, the couple received a letter from their health insurance company saying that they no longer had health insurance. Julie asked if the children still played the violin.

The couple spent the turn of the year 1938–39 largely alone. On

New Year's Eve Julie noted at 6:30pm:

'Daddy and I are alone and will go to bed very early with Phanodorm to avoid all the thinking and brooding that comes with such a day.' Her handwriting is becoming increasingly difficult to read. 'It is growing cooler every day and so are we.' Her letters are hard to bear. They paint a picture of two people who love each other, who are in poor health and whom the National Socialists have robbed of all possibilities.

Their only remaining hope was emigration, and for a long time they staked everything on that. They had handed in the emigration questionnaire and had been informed by the Hamburg-Altona tax office that they would have to pay RM 39,000 in 'Reich flight tax' in the event of a so-called 'flight abroad'. Since 2 January 1939, the Chief Finance President had placed their entire assets under a 'security order': the Walderseestraße property, a credit balance and securities at various banks, as well as gold and silver items. They had RM 2,500 per month at their disposal, out of which they still had to pay taxes and duties. They hoped to be reunited in England in five months, on Elisabeth's birthday in April, and the pair learned English. Julie wrote to her daughters about finding and cleaning out the old baby baskets in the attic with Gertrud Wrangel:

'Whatever the case, I want to keep things in order.'[28] Because of the rules around obtaining a residence permit, the couple was dependent upon Julie's sister Paula and her husband, who were already living in England. Julie fervently hoped that the sister would take her in. When her sister refused her request, she was paralysed. In her cards to her daughters, Julie fearfully asked about her sister's reactions and asked the children to behave moderately towards their aunt. It reads as if Paula's refusal prevented the couple's emigration.

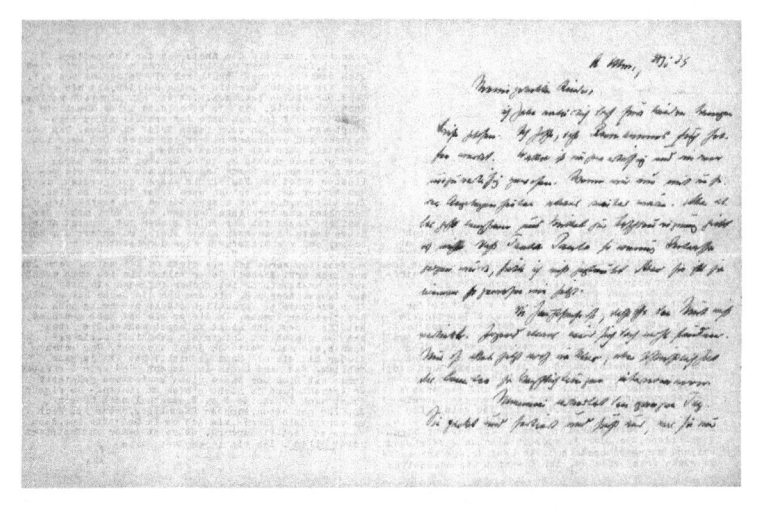

Fig. 14: Farewell letter from Julius Jonas

A single letter from Julius has survived, probably dating from 28 January 1939. It deserves to be reproduced in its entirety. The handwriting is barely decipherable. When read as a whole, the author's peculiar style becomes clear. This transcription mirrors the original line-by-line to enable a better comparison with the original.

H Altona, 28 January 1939
My beloved children,
I have, of course, read both of your long letters. I hope that Rosenbaums will help you. Walter is unreliable and has always been unreliable. If only we were a little further along in our affairs. But everything is going slowly and there are no means of speeding things up. I would never have believed that Aunt Paula would show so little interest. But she has always been like this.
The main thing is that you do not lose heart. Surely something will turn up. Only everything is still unclear now, but after all, the committee has made commitments.
Mummy works all day. She packs and sorts and picks out what she can and has only one wish to be with you. Hopefully it will come true soon. It all happened so quickly. So don't lose heart. We must not lose heart either.

The letter hid the fact that Julius had meanwhile arrived 'in his gruesome state of depression'. Nevertheless, in January 1939, Dr Julius Jonas still took on the task of representing Mr and Mrs Rosenstern in Amsterdam and other relatives whose assets or payments had been confiscated. Hugo Möller, the consultant and guardian of the estate, later recorded:

'The deceased were in the process of emigration, had paid the Jewish tax and the Reich flight tax, had already given away some of their belongings for transport, had placed others in storage: in short, they had made all the preparations for emigration.'[29] The 'clearance certificate', indispensable for leaving the country, had been issued on 25 February 1939. The house at Walderseestraße 48 was for sale, and there was a buyer, one Birgit Gewehr.[30]

The day before the house sale was notarised, the couple took their own lives together. Julius Jonas died on the evening of 4 March 1939 after taking a sleeping pill, and Julie Jonas died on 6 March 1939. They had saved up the Veronal in the bedside cabinet. Julie began her farewell letter (preserved in the files of the police authority) to Elizabeth and Margarethe with the words:

My beloved beloved children. Our nerves have given up and Vati and I can't take any more. I know we are making you terribly unhappy, but it can't go on any longer. You should know that the decision to make you so horribly unhappy makes it terribly difficult for us, but you will and must try to become good and capable people in memory of us. You have no idea how much we love you until our last breath and how much we have suffered from being separated from you. This letter is also to Walter. He should continue to be good to you. I think of nothing but you, even though I cause you this terrible pain. May God grant that you can overcome it. Your Mum
Greetings to Jens Peter and Annemarie.

There was no word from Julius, to Julie's daughters or to Käthe's children. His silence must have left deep wounds in all five of them. Walter would later do likewise, ceasing to speak to his son Peter.

Fig. 15: Grave of Julie and Julius Jonas

Julie and Julius Jonas were buried on 9 March 1939 at the Jewish cemetery Bornkampsweg in Bahrenfeld. As one of the few Jewish cemeteries in Hamburg, it survived the Nazi era unscathed.[31] Elli Junge, née Salewski, travelled to England to deliver the news to Elizabeth and Margarethe personally. It is not known how Walter learned of their deaths.

Walter Jonas

For a long time, Peter Jonas was far more aware of his mother's lineage than his father's Jewish-German one. Walter was a middle child sandwiched between an older sister and a younger brother: he was neither the firstborn nor the baby. He belonged to the generation that survived both world wars: he lived through the First World War as a small child in a well-off, assimilated-Jewish home. His parents' prosperity largely saved him and his siblings from having to go hungry when food stamps and bread rationing were introduced in Hamburg from 1915 onwards as a consequence of the British naval blockade. From 1916 onwards, there was a shortage of basic foodstuffs such as bread and fat in Altona, and the famine in the workers' districts also affected Altona, Bahrenfeld and Ottensen in February 1917. By then, even wealthy families were having to cut back.

At the end of the war, he became a half-orphan. He was eight years old and must have missed his mother bitterly. Together with his siblings and half-sisters, he grew up in a wealthy, respectable household. As a young man, he had the courage to flee his homeland in the face of terror against Jews, to a country where he had only a rudimentary command of the language. He was penniless, and had no networks to draw on.

A passport of his issued by the German Embassy in London has survived, dated 5 August 1939 – roughly the period in which he met Hilda May Ziadie. His name is given with the additional middle name as 'Walter Israel Jonas', as had been obligatory for

Jews since August 1938; he is travelling 'unaccompanied', the passport notes, and his profession was 'chemist'.

Fig. 16: Passport photo of Walter Jonas

The photo shows a serious-looking young man in a checked suit and a dotted tie, his face clean-shaven. 'Shape: medium/Face: oval/Colour of eyes: blue/Colour of hair: black-greying/Special characteristics: none'. He had a strikingly curved upper lip, which Peter Jonas inherited from his father – although he didn't like it.

Peter Jonas's memoirs and the surviving documents do not provide a clear picture of his father Walter Jonas. Walter continued to work for the British Home Service until at least 1951, and had to travel around Europe a lot. An Occupational Force Travel Permit issued in his name has been recovered through strange means and preserved. More on this later. Document No. 1176965 also authorised him, in French and Russian, for the period 28 February to 8 March 1952 to travel via Kitzbühel to Vienna. The paperwork stipulated that he had to journey by train. His wife stayed alone with the children in London during his travels. A few months after the birth of her son Peter, Hilda May decided to visit her homeland Jamaica together with the children.

His father had refused to speak German ever again after the war. Germany was the defeated enemy. 'Me a German? I was shocked!'[32] Jonas exclaimed in an interview. Wanting to confront these roots and search for his own history had been a weighty factor in his decision to accept the appointment as State Director in Munich. His father, however, remained a stranger to him throughout his life. The relationship was distant: in fact, it was bad.

Jonas knew that the man, who had died young, had been the black sheep of the family; but he could never really tell why. 'Cars, business, action,' Peter Jonas commented laconically: 'and girlfriends,' he added.

Even after many years, it is still depressing to read how harshly Julius judged his son Walter in his letter: 'Walter is unreliable and has always been unreliable.' Was that Julius's judgement of his son? Did Walter pass this contempt down to his own son? His stepmother Julie had mentioned him several times in correspondence with her daughters: she was happy that Walter was taking care of the girls. He brought the young women's clothes to the cleaners and often sent them parcels with sweets. Walter also seemed to annoy his half-sisters at times. 'Look, I don't think Walter is such a beast as you always say when he sends you a package … He's an old slob, but still a good sort at heart.' The events preceding these remarks remained unclear in all the correspondence: 'Walter has always been a moody fellow!'

But also: 'I'm sure there's a good lad in there somewhere.' Just once was enough for Julie: 'I don't think Walter being there with his girlfriend seemed quite right.'

Julie and Julius remembered his birthday and mentioned letters that had arrived from him in England, which they found encouraging – but they also wrote that they were waiting for letters, for news from him. Walter had grown up in Julie and Julius's household. Even if Julie was not as familiar, loving and intimate with him as she was with her biological children, it is inconceivable that he grew up in a truly cold environment. But why did he insist later, in the 1950s, that his own son address him formally as 'sir'? That remains unexplained.

In a letter from Walter dated 21 January 1939 he wrote to the sisters, giving his new address in London: 77 Hillsborough Court, Mortimer Crescent, in South Hampstead, north-west London, 'a much nicer room'. He thanked the sisters for their letter and complained that he had not received any news from Hamburg. He also admonished his sisters to get on well with their Aunt Paula and asked what the young women were up to with their lives. He himself was on the verge of opening a sheepfold: '(two hundred lambs, all two months old) We have already built a sheepfold.' What became of this project is not known. His letter also mentioned that he had not seen a certain Judith, whom the sisters seemed to know, for a fortnight, because he had left her at home. Another letter makes it clear that he discussed the sale of the furniture from the house in Walderseestraße with his stepmother, but could not help her.

When Walter met his future wife shortly before the start of the Second World War, his father had only recently died by suicide. His young sisters, who were still minors, were living in the same country. None of them had anyone who could help them in an emergency. They were on their own. Hilda May, on the other hand, had fled from Jamaica to London to escape her father's restrictions in an otherwise existentially unfraught, privileged life. Her family was alive and would continue to support her.

So why should Hilda May have stayed in bombed-out, grey London when Walter was forced to travel for the secret service, given that in Jamaica she could have enjoyed family, prosperity and security, and been wonderfully well-provided for? Looking back, Peter Jonas wondered whether the first disagreements between his parents had already started to arise at that time. Or maybe it had been the other way round: the completely understandable decision to escape the deprivation of London and the longing for her own family contributed to the couple's drifting apart. Only the pair of them could know the truth of the matter, but Hilda May resisted deeper questions from her son throughout her life. It is inconceivable that the children did not sorely miss their father.

Hilda May Jonas, née Ziadie

The first memory of his mother takes Peter Jonas back to Jamaica: 'I vaguely remember being in Jamaica and everyone smelled so good. Because in this warm, humid climate, they always wore white linen or cotton that was freshly laundered.' Labour was still cheap in Jamaica in the late 1940s. Servants also worked in the Ziadies' household, and one of their daily tasks was to keep the family's clothes fresh. 'My mother, a rather cool, beautiful, elegant being in freshly washed and ironed linen clothes. That's the earliest memory I have.' Jonas paused and looked out the window of his living room. The bells of the Oberstrass church were striking noon. In his memory, the smell of freshly ironed linen was joined by the taste of mango. 'The better the mango was, the more I loved it. If anything remains of my exotic origins, it's the mango.' In many interviews, Peter Jonas discussed his family's maternal line in such terms, untroubled by those anti-racist discourses which see this term as a Eurocentric aestheticisation of some 'exotic' other.

Born in 1949, Lady Colin Campbell is the granddaughter of Michael Ziadie. She achieved dubious fame in England with her books about Princess Diana and the royal family; her nickname is 'Lady Poison Pen'. Her accounts of the lives of the Ziadies in the 1950s were vivid and full of colour: how warm and cordial the 'army of servants' was towards them, the children, in contrast to their own parents who always demanded that they should remain discreet and inconspicuous. 'For us children, they were also a source of continuous warmth, care and affection.' She described the pain of parting that the children had to go through every time a loved one left the parental household: 'At least we learned at an early age how transient life can be.'[33] Peter would also experience this pain of separation, when in Jamaica Hilda May sought out a nanny for him and his sister. Her smell, the smell of the woman and her uniform of starched linen, now competed with the smell of the mother. 'The smell of my Nanny is one of the earliest memories I have.' Together with Hilda May and the children, she travelled to England in 1948.

The ship the four were travelling on was the HMT *Empire Windrush*. In the 1930s, the Germans had used the ship under the name *Monte Rosa*, first as a cruise liner and then for military purposes during the Second World War. The British took it over as a war reparation in May 1945. In June 1948, the *Windrush* brought the first eight hundred or so immigrants from Jamaica to England. This marked the beginning of the first large-scale economic migration from the non-white Commonwealth.[34]

For the reconstruction of their country, the British government urgently needed cheap labour. Whitehall placed advertisements in Jamaica to promote passage on the *Windrush* to England. Under the British Nationality Act of 1948, all members of the British colonies were entitled to 'Citizenship of the United Kingdom and Colonies' status. The passengers of the *Windrush* thus had the right to stay in England indefinitely without any further conditions. It was not until 1962 that England introduced immigration controls.

Fig. 17: Kathryn and Peter with their nanny, Jamaica, c. 1948

The entire cohort of people who emigrated to England before 1971 were named for this ship: they became 'the *Windrush* generation'.³⁵ They became bus drivers, train drivers, construction workers, nurses and hospital workers and played a decisive role in the reconstruction of the country. For them, the discrimination and racism faced by dark-skinned immigrants was ultimately a lesser evil. After all, they were able to earn a living in this country, despite its horrible weather.

The Home Office's approach posed an existential problem for this generation: not only had the immigration authorities issued no entry papers to the passengers of the *Windrush*, but they also destroyed all their landing cards, i.e. all the paperwork that could document their arrival in England, in 2010.³⁶

This was to have fatal consequences. Following changes to the Immigration Act, members of the *Windrush* generation – even before the Brexit vote in 2016 – were asked to identify themselves in order to continue receiving free care on the National Health Service, pensions and other benefits. For Nanny's generation, this was a real danger. For some of these people, their very right to stay in England at all was thrown into question. Some of them awaited deportation in internment camps.

The *Windrush* generation had worked hard to rebuild England and often had no contacts left in their home countries. Now the *Windrush* scandal threatened to divide the country. In April 2018, Prime Minister Theresa May had to apologise to representatives of twelve Caribbean Commonwealth countries for her government's actions. Peter Jonas was outraged by this affair, as well as about the imminent exit of his home country from the European Union.

The Jonas family in London

The Jonas family household in Sanderstead in the late 1940s included representatives of the two major waves of immigration into England in the twentieth century: Walter belonged to the group of survivors and descendants of the European refugee population from the Second World War[37] who were 'invisible' because of their skin colour. Of this group, Jewish refugees from Germany in particular had an influence on British academia and publishing, especially in the arts.

Paul Hamlyn, André Deutsch, Peter Owen and Max Reinhardt were exemplary representatives of this group of refugees, which was anything but homogeneous.[38] The same applied to Hilda May and the nanny, both representatives of the second wave of immigration in the middle of the twentieth century. While Nanny belonged to the working class, Hilda May represented a status-conscious group of Jamaican emigrants whose numbers were steadily increasing in the London diaspora. This 'Jamaican diaspora aristocracy', as Peter Jonas called them, were very conscious of their families' lineage. The Ziadies also saw themselves as one of these old Lebanese families. 'At that time it was about status, about family. You know the phrase: "She comes from a good family." Those were very important things.' And they all became immigrants, in London, New York or elsewhere. Peter Jonas was born into this family on 14 October 1946 and, although living in London, grew up more aware of his Lebanese-Jamaican side than his German side. His parents were neither particularly cultured nor academically educated. In accordance with the conventions of her family, Hilda May could ride a horse, play the piano – in short, knew how to move around on all social occasions, but had no real schooling to speak of. 'She knew how to behave at a dinner party, how to flirt. She was a model, she could wear dresses,' her son outlined the pattern that young women from these families grew into.

But his words also revealed an inner distance from his mother that Jonas had not yet overcome, even in his old age. It seemed as if he could not forgive her for her failure to overcome her own traumas. His cousin Monica, the daughter of Elizabeth Melamid, who was born in 1954, had just as intimate a relationship with her Aunt Hilda May as Jonas had with Monica's mother, his Aunt Elizabeth. 'Aunt May was as charismatic as Peter. She was the epitome of femininity: she was gorgeous, beautiful!' Monica Melamid's view of Hilda May is consistently positive, yet more nuanced than Jonas's. 'Aunt May was the perfect housewife. She could cook. She could charm anyone. She was not an intellectual, even though she enjoyed art.' Because Monica's mother dealt more actively with her own experience of emigration, her children were also able to grow up with a more stable understanding of their family: 'We are not a family that embraces family – because we lost family,' Monica said. 'The joke was: family is a picture that you hang on the wall.'[39]

Unlike his mother, Jonas's father came from an educated middle-class family, even though Walter was considered the black sheep. Peter Jonas's first memory of his father was associated with the smell of pomade. It was also linked with the odour of cigarette smoke, naturally (even if the children never took much notice of it at the time), because in those days people smoked everywhere and always, even when eating in restaurants.

Trained as an industrial chemist, Walter had worked in a Leipzig dye works and later as a factory director. Jonas described Walter as a restless man whose many affairs alienated him from his wife. Walter, for his part, had been moulded by his own father, a member of the educated bourgeoisie who judged him harshly from a young age. The latter's suicide forever prevented any settling of accounts. Walter passed this silence on to Peter.

Despite having come to England at the age of twenty-three, Walter spoke astonishingly clear, unaccented English. At home, Walter would not tolerate a single word of German. For Peter, he was a distant character. Kathryn, on the other hand, managed to build up a close relationship with her father. She was extraordinarily gifted. 'She was brilliant at everything, even the subjects I couldn't do, Latin and stuff,' Jonas grinned. He admired her for her talents; in his eyes she succeeded in everything, the adults loved her for it.

He himself was wholly ordinary. Each had their own room in the house in Sanderstead. Peter was fascinated by model making and collected boats, trains and aeroplanes. He learned to read at an early age, even before he started school – and he loved reading, even if he received only selected literature from his mother, such as *Lamb's Tales from Shakespeare*, a collection of Shakespeare's comedies and tragedies edited by Mary and Charles Lamb in 1807. They were prepared in a child-friendly way, but were based on the words of the poet and were intended to introduce young readers to the study of his works and to teach them 'the effect of the beautiful English tongue'[40] as the Lambs put it. Then there was *Tales of Chivalry*: whimsical tales of travelling knights and other characters from the Middle Ages.

As he sucked his thumb, his father gave him *Struwwelpeter* to read. 'The tailor's scissors in *Struwwelpeter* hunting for a thumb was a more or less undisguised castration metaphor from which I hid under the duvet at night.'[41]

According to Jonas, his mother displayed an almost 'religious zeal'[42] to provide her children with the best possible education in the humanities. On his tenth birthday, he was allowed into the

National Theatre for the first time. The family sat on the wooden benches in the gallery, where the knees of the spectators in the row behind pressed into their backs.

Jonas grew up in an England that had not yet joined the European Community and whose currency was based on the duodecimal system. In Jonas's youth and student days, there were pounds, shillings and pence. Everything was calculated in twelves. For Kathryn and him, as for many other children, there was 'no escape from the tough, tender, purifying embrace of family Britain'.[43] The nanny organised the children's everyday life. As in other European countries, the role of women in Britain in the 1950s was largely determined by their function as wives and mothers, caring for the emotional development of their children.[44] In Jamaica, however, employing a nanny was standard even among the middle classes. 'My nanny was a very nice black woman from Jamaica. She did everything for me. I worshipped her, she worshipped me.'

Curiously, she also tied his shoelaces whenever necessary; a disastrous kindness, as it would turn out for the little boy when he entered boarding school. But although they developed a close, intimate bond, Peter never learned her name. He was not allowed to know it. For him, she was her role: Nanny. She addressed him as 'Master': 'Master Peter, I can't tell you my name.' Their close bond would render him very vulnerable a little while later.

Hilda May looked after the family's religious life. Raised strictly Catholic, she passed on her faith to her children, had them baptised, and thus fulfilled the role of the British mother in post-war England. His father was a Jewish-born atheist, on the other hand, and was not interested in religion at all, no matter the form. Britain was traditionally a deeply religious country. Going to church permeated everyday life, and strict rules set narrow limits on individual behaviour. British women, who made up the majority of church-goers, still shaped religious life in their families.[45]

The church year also structured the life of the Jonas family. Hilda May went to church with her children and chose the best Catholic schools for them. Her first choice was the prestigious St

Anne's Convent, which both children attended at pre-school age. There Peter learned to read fluently from an early age, making everyone very proud of him. But then his mother received some frightening news, Peter Jonas recalled. She was asked to attend a parents' meeting one day: Peter had stood in front of the class and said that he no longer knew how to read. She was asked to take the boy to an ophthalmologist. This caused great consternation at home. Hilda May made an appointment with a doctor, who was a good doctor because a wise man. He thoroughly examined Peter, only to ask if he had a good friend at school. Did this friend wear glasses? With that, the solution was found. It was Ian, with whom Peter had a deep friendship. But unlike Peter, Ian could not yet read; Peter wanted to be like him and had therefore pretended not to be able to read. Peter Jonas did get his glasses in the end, just a little later in life.

Fig. 18: Jonas family

At the beginning of the 1950s, a piece of America entered the family, a car: 'a revolutionary car. It was called an Austin Metropolitan,' Jonas enthused. It was a gift from his father, now successful in business, to the children's mother. While all other British cars in the post-war years were black and grey, Jonas's father had chosen an Austin Metropolitan painted in turquoise and white. The parents had not announced the spectacular purchase to the children. No wonder that the first time his mother picked him up in this dream car remains a key memory for Peter Jonas: 'This car seemed so impressive to me, so beautiful. I'm terribly interested in cars. I love the smell of cars, the smell of leather, the smell of petrol and oil.'

Worth School

As for so many other children in England, buying his first school uniform was a rite of passage for Jonas. He had to go to Harrod's with his mother, as that was the only place where the uniform could be got. It was all very difficult, Jonas explained. For the first time he had to wear stiff black shoes. Later, he needed a separate stiff collar. The list was incredibly long. It included his sports kit.[46]

While Kathryn transferred to St Mary's Convent in Ascot, Peter, aged just eight, in September 1954 went to Worth School, which, along with Ampleforth College and Downside, is still considered one of England's leading private, elite Roman Catholic boarding schools.

The school is located around thirty miles south of London near Crawley in West Sussex, in the grounds of the Benedictine Worth Abbey. 'That was my Waterloo, the big mistake,' Peter Jonas said even at an advanced age. 'Don't be afraid,' his mother had told him as she stopped on the country road, still a short distance from the school gates. His father had not come along.

Even in the last stage of his life, it was not easy for Peter Jonas to talk about this trip, about his first day, the first years and his many worries and injuries. He kept breaking off. Why did he have to go there, he had asked his mother in tears. 'It is better for you,' came her reply. His memories of meeting a monk for the first time in his life were blotted out by his constant weeping. 'I was scared to death when I saw this tall, thin monk. The tallest man I had ever seen, in black robes and with this hood. I thought he was a skyscraper. It was a very brutal moment, a big shock for me.'

Later, Peter Jonas spoke repeatedly of being sent to Worth shortly before his sixth birthday.[47] The traumatic memory of the tall, darkly dressed monks, into whose care his mother had handed him without further explanation, must have been so overpowering for him that in his memory he pictured himself as being younger than he actually was.

Peter had it a little easier than other boys who were only a year or two older than him and were housed in the 'Monkey House', a huge dormitory with around thirty other boys. He shared his dorm room with just one classmate, Christopher Brutton. When mother and son visited the room and the two boys were introduced to each other, Peter, still in tears, discovered something on Christopher's bed that until then had been completely unknown to him and which immediately and completely captivated him: it was a comic – a special comic. On Christopher's bed lay the boys' magazine *Eagle*, with its colourfully-illustrated stories about the spaceship captain 'Dan Dare, Pilot of the Future', his companion Digby and the adversary Mekon, after whom the British band The Mekons later named themselves. There had never been anything like this in his parents' house in Sanderstead: it would have been unthinkable! For a moment, little Peter sank into the pictures and forgot the world around him.

His mother took advantage and left without saying goodbye. This little boy, barely eight, 'born with a sunny nature', as his mother described him, was now alone in the elite Benedictine boarding school, 'in a kind of jungle, a completely different society. Anything could happen to you. You knew danger was around the corner: discipline, corporate discipline. We were beaten … die ganze Zeit [all the time].'

Fig. 19: Peter Jonas reads the *Eagle*

In order to be able to talk about these dark moments in Worth, Peter Jonas chose impersonal language, as if he were not speaking about himself. He was still weighed down by these terrible experiences. He knew nothing about his parents' motivation for sending him to boarding school. How did his mother feel about it? Was she, who had no education herself, merely following conventions and trying to give him the best education she could? Was she capable of bringing up her children well, after her experiences in the war?

His parents were not alone in their decision to send Peter to boarding school, financed by a scholarship. Three quarters of public-school pupils boarded at this time, mostly in secluded locations in the south of England.[48]

Worth Abbey must have been an ideal choice for Peter's mother – his father thought it was a waste of money – as the boarding school aimed and still aims at a triad of academic excellence, moral orientation towards Benedictine teachings, and social responsibility. The abbey and its school settled in Somerset in the south-west of England in 1884, and in the 1930s founded a second community in West Sussex, where Worth School still stands today.[49] Among the founders was Dom Maurice, who directed the school from 1940 to 1959, during Peter's attendance, and increased its number of pupils from sixty to two hundred and fifty.[50] Worth Preparatory School, where Peter first arrived, no longer exists today.

Ora et labora – et lege: Pray and work – and read. The Benedictines live by this motto. Little Peter passed his first test to the greatest satisfaction of the monks: he had to read – and he could do it fluently. As a consequence, he was placed one year higher than he otherwise would. That meant that he was living and learning with boys who had already been at Worth for a year and had already absorbed the system and its hard spoken and unspoken rules.

Unlike them, Peter knew neither Latin nor Greek. Because he could not translate the Gallic War from Latin, he was beaten on his second day at Worth. 'My first years at school were very difficult, unlike my sister's,' Peter Jonas summed up. 'A lot of things were very, very hard for me.' Now the world was taking revenge for his nanny's tender care. He still could not tie his shoes. What sounds like something small became a real problem for him, a 'catastrophe: I walked around boarding school with loose shoelaces. The monks summoned me for a beating. But I just didn't learn and was endlessly punished for not tying my shoelaces. Why? Because my nanny used to tie them up for me.'[51]

For the rest of his life, Jonas had his own system of dealing with laces and therefore liked to choose shoes without them. That he retained that preference until the end gives an inkling of how severely this experience had affected him. Unfortunately, this was not the last such trial: he faced what he called 'the Nanny thing' when he came home for the first school holidays. Looking forward to having his nanny around again, Peter arrived in Sanderstead to find that she no longer lived with them. 'That was one of the greatest traumas of my life. Probably on a psychological level it caused a lot of disruption in my relationships with people – the vanishing nanny, the nanny who disappeared.' His parents had dismissed her without talking to the boy about it or allowing him to say goodbye to this person whom he loved above all else.

While talking about it, Jonas kept rapping his knuckles on his chair. 'My parents were probably right to decide that I was old enough. Nanny was Nanny, and then Nanny wasn't there. That was it.'

In later years, whenever Peter Jonas wanted to ask his mother about this decision, what he called her 'iron curtain' came down. His mother seemed to have sensed the drama of this event. 'It hurt me deeply. I have never forgiven my parents.' And as always, when something really got to him, he added: 'I can tell you.'

The writer W. G. Sebald would lead Peter Jonas on the trail of his German family a few years later. During his student years in Manchester, Peter had lived together with Max, as Sebald was called by friends, and his wife Ute in a shared flat.

Even at that time, Sebald, who was working as an assistant at a university, felt driven to seek out personal accounts from emigrants. Every now and then Max told stories from his life and those of other people, unrecognisably mixed with figments of his own imagination, as would later do in his books.

With the memories Peter recounted, probably over the summer of 1966, Sebald would create his character of Jacques Austerlitz, who feels like a 'stranger among men': Jacques grows up with foster parents and is sent to a public school at the age of twelve. 'Like most educational establishments, Stower Grange was the most unsuitable place imaginable for an adolescent,'[52] Sebald wrote. But as for the headmaster, although he was a 'remarkably kindly man', whenever he had 'to chastise one of us in his office for some reason which had been brought to his notice, you could easily have gained the impression that the victim was temporarily granting the headmaster who inflicted the punishment a privilege due in fact only to him, the boy who had reported to take it.'[53] Life in Jacques's school was characterised 'through customs and traditions, some of them positively oriental in character, going back over many generations of pupils.' In the novel, as in real life, the intrigues that the boys spin serve to expand their own position of power. 'There were all kinds of forms of major tyranny and minor despotism, forced labour, enslavement, serfdom, the bestowal and withdrawal of privileges, hero-worship, ostracism, the imposition of penalties and the granting of reprieves, and by dint of these the pupils, without any supervision, governed themselves and indeed the entire school, not excluding the masters.'[54]

Like Jacques, Peter would realise a few years later what potential his education in Worth had offered him. 'However, unlike poor Robinson, said Austerlitz, I myself found my years at Stower Grange not a time of imprisonment but of liberation. … From the very first week, I realised that for all the adversities of the school it was my only escape route, and I immediately did all I could to find my way around its strange jumble of countless unwritten rules, and the often carnivalesque lawlessness that prevailed.'[55]

Peter would also find his way. Fortunately, despite all the discipline and strictness with which the monks regulated the boys' daily lives, they did not manage to drive the childishness out of them. Making 'apple-pie beds' was a popular prank. The beds, which had to be made to a strict military standard, were secretly rearranged for this purpose. From the outside they still looked perfect, but underneath the sheets were so knotted up that the classmates could not slip under the blanket quickly enough during the evening roll-call, so that their legs were left hanging out: the unfortunate boy would be punished if a monk deemed him too slow at getting into bed. The students did not play tricks on the monks; the punishments were too draconian and were carried out for trivial reasons, and often without cause.

For Peter, art classes were the best time of the week. There he was allowed to paint aeroplanes and battleships. 'The art teacher was always late, and in the meantime a few boys were running around. The teacher extended his index finger: "You, you and you!" and those he indicated were then battered. I was always there, and I was the quietest. "That's not fair!" I shouted, to which he only replied: "Life is not fair, boy!" These rude educational methods are more commonly associated with Wilhelmine Germany. England was the master of it.'[56]

In another interview, Peter Jonas recalled Dom Fabian's verdict, delivered during a sermon: 'Jonas uses shampoo and listens to music by Mahler and Wagner on the gramophone. This is seductive corruption. He might as well kill himself!'[57] He read the biography of Georg Friderich Handel in his dorm room, secretly, with a torch under the sheets.[58] This made a lasting impression on him. He became obsessed with learning more about Handel's life: his ever-changing existence as an emigrant and immigrant; how he used the harpsichord as a composer; his work as a designer, manager and impresario: 'God knows why.'

Throughout his life, he was most moved by Handel's music. 'The Concerti Grossi op. 3, not op. 6! For me it is perfect music.' Jonas drew a thread from his nightly reading of Handel's biography to the Munich production of *Giulio Cesare in Egitto* in his first Munich season in 1993–94. It was no wonder that he was able to convince conductor Ivor Bolton to play the first movement of the Concerti Grossi op. 3 as an entr'acte after the second interval, to summon the audience back into the auditorium.

Some of Peter's happiest moments were at the end of the services, when he was allowed to stand next to organist Dom Theodore, listen to him and watch him. The masses themselves moved him little, but these times, when Dom Theodore played a prelude, toccata or fugue by Bach or Buxtehude, aroused strong emotions in Peter.

As an older pupil, he was allowed to go to the music room and listen to the few records that were available in Worth. Gradually, the pupils were given more and more personal freedom. In the Senior School from September 1960, he lived in his own room and owned a small Bush gramophone on which he listened to the classical music records he had bought during the holidays, over and over. He no longer collected model aeroplanes or model ships, but music. He had to listen to records only three or maybe four times before he could memorise the pieces. Jonas attributed his excellent musical memory to this phase of his life. The virus of music had infected him.

His choice was music by Mahler and Wagner, which at Worth was tantamount to heresy. It was only during his studies that Peter

Jonas realised that, for the monks, the world came to an end with Henry VIII, Martin Luther and the Reformation. Everything after that was blasphemous as far as the monks were concerned. The historical, cultural, social and aesthetic developments from the sixteenth century onwards did not feature in the otherwise excellent monastic curriculum. The focus was on the Catholic liturgy and its significance for the aesthetics of the Old Masters, and the church architecture of the Gothic and Baroque periods.

Once a week, the young men received basic military training, which they completed in uniform and with weapons. This was to enable them to take an officer's rank right away when they had to complete National Service. An older schoolmate, later a publisher, David Bell, spoke of his father: 'Your father is German!' Even after the war, they were still the enemy. A day later, Bell came again and added another epithet: 'Jonas, your father is Jewish!' The accusations, the accusatory atmosphere in general, deeply confused Jonas. He could not explain how his classmate even knew about his family background.

'I grew up kind of innocent,' Peter Jonas described himself as a schoolboy between the ages of ten and fifteen. 'I could not imagine anything higher than the worlds of Bach. It was a happy school life in a way.' The privilege of being taught individually and in small groups at the Senior School was something Jonas also appreciated in his later education. He was not good at Latin, Greek or maths. Here his friends helped him, one of whom was Angelo Hornak, who became a well-known architectural photographer. Angelo wrote many essays for Peter when the latter was unwilling or unable to do so. Students read William Shakespeare, Christopher Marlowe or Geoffrey Chaucer's famous fourteenth-century *Canterbury Tales*, which brought vernacular Middle English into literature. The famous authors of British Romanticism, however – William Wordsworth, Mary Shelley, John Keats or George Byron – had no place in the classroom. The pupils knew Monteverdi, Bach, Handel and Buxtehude, they lived with them, but Brahms, Beethoven, Schubert, Wagner, Mahler and Bruckner were denied them. Their peers at other – Anglican – schools were educated completely differently. Peter did not feel very well-prepared for the world outside.

Kathryn, his destiny

It was his sister Kathryn who revealed a new world to him – the world according to Bach and Handel – when he heard her play Beethoven, a composer who was completely absent from Worth. During the holidays, she taught him how to behave, what books to read and what films to watch. Whenever he came home in the hope of free time and idleness – 'I am a marvellous expert in doing nothing, I love doing nothing' – she greeted him with a reading list, which he accepted because he admired his sister, and even spoke of idolising her. The two were exceptionally close.

Kathryn attended the renowned Catholic St Mary's Convent in Ascot, whose prominent former pupils included Caroline of Hanover and Lady Amelia Windsor.[59] Kathryn studied under the famous headmistress Mother Bridget Geoffrey-Smith, who ran the convent from 1956 to 1976. Mother Bridget hot housed Kathryn intensively.

Through her influence, Kathryn was allowed to attend a finishing school in Rome for a year after school and only then took up further studies. Kathryn took her daily reading of *The Times* very seriously. In her eyes, this was the only way to be passably well-informed. In London, parents rarely took their children to museums or the theatre. It was Kathryn who organised the family's trips abroad. They travelled by car to Florence, Siena, Assisi or to Spain. When Jonas was fifteen, Kathryn gave him a small wooden crucifix from Assisi. Jonas kept it on his desk in Zurich. He was convinced that it was protecting him.

The family only saw each other during the few short days of the holidays. Her brother's memories focused on Kathryn's great musical talent, her ability to penetrate music and her extraordinary intellectual gifts. 'Beyond her age, she had a strange maturity, a strange moral and intellectual rigour. The word "rigour" really comes to mind when I think of my sister. I'm not saying she wasn't lovable or that she didn't have charm. She was very strict and serious. She thought I was very superficial, also very "dilettantisch". Kathryn was not a dilettante at all, she not at all concerned with form, but only with substance.' Thomas Mann, Alberto Moravia, Fyodor Dostoevsky, Lev Tolstoy, D. H. Lawrence, Franz Kafka and Stendhal – Peter met all these authors for the first time in the lists his sister prepared for him. Interestingly, she omitted Goethe and Schiller. In his view, she focused on him because he was good at reading. And he was. Because he adored her. She was the 'sister figure', as he aptly summed up her significance in his life.

The parents' divorce

In the mid-1950s, Hilda May found there was something she could no longer overlook: Walter had too many mistresses, and the pair had grown distant. Hilda May and Walter separated; he moved out of the house in Sanderstead, and later, after Hilda May had long opposed it, they also divorced. Along the way they fought a gruelling battle, and Peter accepted Hilda May's account as the truth. Father and son were now, from the end of the 1950s, completely – and definitively – estranged. In many respects, Hilda May deviated from the pattern of the middle-class British woman who takes care of the household and raises children. She had household staff and her children did not live with her.

But in terms of the separation she was very much in step with the times: the number of divorces in England had quadrupled since the end of the war.[60] As in other European countries, legislation paved the way to make divorce easier: the basis for granting a separation changed from 'facts proven' to 'irretrievable breakdown'. From the end of the 1960s, a divorce could granted by mutual consent.[61]

Hilda May continued to live in her house in Sanderstead after her separation from Walter, until she moved in with a partner in central London some years later. Peter's father married 'the wicked woman mistress', as Peter's mother dubbed her. Walter had met Pauline years earlier as a colleague in the intelligence service. She, too, was a German émigré and had first been interned under suspicion of being a spy. After the war, Pauline had married a wealthy South African and had two daughters. The two couples were friends with each other. 'Long before they started a physical affair, Pauline had a soft spot for my father – and he for her,' Jonas knew. He remembered how it had irritated him at parties when he was fourteen to notice his father's hand on Pauline's body.

It was only decades later, when he was already living in Munich, that a lucky coincidence – no, Peter's ex-girlfriend! – brought him and Pauline's daughters together. From them, Peter learned what made Pauline and Walter's marriage 'a tremendous relationship of total harmony – sexually and emotionally.'

Walter had lost weight and looked healthier. Hilda May, who had demonised Pauline to Kathryn and Peter, prevented her children from learning what drove Pauline and made her a fascinating woman: life in the post-war country was bitter and full of privation. But besides butter or eggs, women had been deprived of their menfolk. So many of them had died in the war, or were mutilated or brought illnesses home. But for a short time during the war, when every day began with the thought that one could be dead tomorrow, moral inhibitions had fallen away. These years had shaped Pauline and liberated her sexually. Now she saw how even young women had no chance to meet men. First, Pauline wrote a column for a magazine in which she advocated a more tolerant sexual morality. But then she went a step further and founded a kind of subscription club where women and men could meet to socialise, but also to have sex. Pauline believed that it would lead to enormous problems if people had to repress their sexuality.

In England in the 1950s, women's magazines spoke of sex as an 'important part of marriage', of 'physical lovemaking' or 'intimate lovemaking'[62] so as to avoid using the word 'sex' itself. Behind this silence was a profound ignorance of sexual issues that led to unhappy marriages, unwanted pregnancies and abortions. Pauline's idea struck a nerve. It was bold and revolutionary. Although she drew harsh criticism, she stuck to her position. She was a 'semi-official social worker, a trailblazer, a modern woman', Jonas judged. It is not surprising that Peter's mother could not understand what motivated Pauline.

How Kathryn and Peter experienced their parents' divorce was irrelevant to Hilda May and Walter. Divorce itself was still so much the exception that the psychological burden on the children of divorce remained considerable.[63] Nobody considered talking to the children about the separation. They had to cope with their pain alone.

Walter died on 26 December 1962, his birthday. His son attended the funeral but later on found that he could hardly remember that day. The trials and tribulations of his adolescence, however, were still clear in his mind.

Adolescence at Worth

Jonas was a gawky, slightly overweight boy when he entered the Senior School. Then his body stretched out; he lost weight and he became athletic. Peter played cricket and rugby, and became a true sportsman: the most important quality a boy could have at a British boarding school. In those schools, aptitude for sports meant social status; the boys were quite indifferent to academic brilliance. Peter played rugby for the school, an honourable role. 'For me, entering puberty meant becoming part of the social structure within the school. I was happy. That's how simply these schools work.'

W. G. Sebald later incorporated this, too, into his Jacques Austerlitz character:

> ... it was a great advantage that I soon began to distinguish myself on the rugby field, perhaps because a dull pain always

present within me, although I was unaware of it at the time, enabled me to lower my head and make my way through ranks of opponents better than any of my fellow pupils. The fearlessness I displayed in rugger matches, as I remember them always played under a cold winter sky or in pouring rain, very soon gave me special status without my having to try for it by other means, such as recruiting vassals or enslaving weaker boys. Another crucial factor in my good progress at school was the fact that I never found reading and studying a burden.[64]

Whole generations of pubescent boys at Worth had had to navigate this closed male world and its strict, Catholic rules. For Peter's year, however, there was an attraction. The son of the Spanish ambassador Marqués de Villaverde attended the school and for this reason many Spanish maids also worked there. The boys' fantasies revolved around them. They were objects of desire.

Once a semester there was an old-fashioned dance evening. Chasing the few girls the boys got to see was a common preoccupation. 'There was an undercurrent of sexual explosivity all the time,' Jonas said, outlining the mood. It was around this time that Peter got his first bespoke suit, from Anderson & Sheppard on Savile Row.

Once, the boys, who had little family life of their own, were allowed to go on a skiing holiday in the Tyrol with Father Kevin, and Jonas discovered how much he enjoyed this sport. But he also discovered his affinity for the German language, which was not taught in Worth. Jonas reported nothing of the stay itself, or what the boys experienced there. His focus was on the few hours the troupe had in Innsbruck before the return journey, time they used to visit a brothel. The monk withdrew discreetly and left his charges alone, led by the older boys. With a basic democratic attitude, everyone pooled their remaining pocket money. A suitcase porter received one Schilling. However, going to the brothel cost thirty Schillings. Why should no one be allowed to go just because there was not enough money? Better to pool it! 'Only a few were allowed – or had to,' Jonas revealed. 'The rest of us waited in the basement. There was a register book on a large desk in which the prostitutes wrote down how many customers they had received. When we could, we looked inside. The fattest one had the most!' Moving his arms in big gestures he illustrated what the little boys had seen. 'I have never been lucky. Maybe that was my luck.'

At that age, the boys were still forbidden to smoke. Anyone caught by a monk was usually punished severely. But if that same student then went to a one-on-one tuition session, perhaps even on the very same day, it was possible that the same monk would offer him a cigarette during the supervision.

Peter acted in the school theatre, but above all he was a 'champion debater', the debates serving to prepare the students for a future in Parliament. Peter was often approached by schoolmates when they needed an advocate against the monks. This talent also contributed to his status. 'They came and asked: "P, could you argue my case?"' Just *P*, that's how he was known, even then. At the end of his school years, he became a prefect; not head boy, he emphasised, 'just somebody'. In this way, Worth established a hierarchy within the student body and extended the monks' reach into boarding Houses. This was perhaps the only moment when leadership qualities could be demonstrated during school years.

The Benedictine boarding school functioned as a society unto itself. For Jonas, it seemed obvious to compare the boarding school with an opera house: 'You had to distinguish yourself, be good at something, excel at something. If you weren't good at anything, you had to survive. In this sense, it was a good preparation for society. Man musste seinen Weg gehen [You had to go your own way].'

When Peter Jonas spoke about his time in Worth, he was in the middle of a busy week of travelling. From his flat in Zurich, he had first been to Munich to visit his wife and was now staying in Berlin. An important trip to Los Angeles was scheduled, where he would visit his ill friend Zubin Mehta. 'I feel at home in all those places. I don't feel more at home in Zurich or in Munich. I feel at home wherever I am at that particular moment. Which is a good thing in some ways, but also a very restless thing. I am sure that goes back to all that.'

When he continued to speak that afternoon, after moments of silence, he could only speak of the little boy he had been in the third person. 'On the one hand, this strange little boy had been spoiled, on the other hand, he came from an exotic, large but fragmented family: from two worlds so far apart – from well-to-do Hamburg and the Lebanese diaspora in Jamaica. And yet, apart from his relationship with his sister and his nanny who had left, he was very much alone, you know. In this confusing system of the boarding school with its long aesthetic and intellectual tradition, he developed a quality that saved him: Dass er nirgendwo zu Hause war [that he was at home precisely nowhere]. From what should have been his home, he moved to what should have been his boarding school. He built his own little world, a world born of loneliness and the imagination that reading stimulated in him… The older I get, the more I am convinced that these very confused parental circumstances had a great influence on everything I have done in life, but also on everything I have not done. And on everything I missed.'

Peter was seventeen years old when, in the middle of the academic year, he scored highly enough in his A-levels in various subjects that he was able to go to university. How he managed to get so far so quickly was not clear to him. He did not pass the aptitude test for Cambridge, where everyone saw him going but where he did not necessarily want to study. He had set his mind on the renowned Trinity College in Dublin. This aspiration had nothing to do with the excellent reputation of the university, but with Jane Monahan, the beautiful daughter of James Monahan, who worked as a ballet critic for the *Sunday Times* and lived with his family of 'upper middle-class arty people' in a Georgian-style house in Chelsea. Like her older sister Judy, Jane went to Trinity College. But she was not the only reason: in Ireland, a degree took four years instead of three as in England. If he were accepted and received a scholarship, a whole year more freedom awaited him, Peter calculated.

But he had not reckoned with the headmaster, Dom Dominic Gaisford, with whom he got into a terrible confrontation. The Benedictines did not approve of sending a Catholic boy to a Protestant university in a Catholic country. Dom Dominic flatly refused to make the necessary recommendation.

Peter was – 'How do you say it in German? – stinksauer [pissed off]': his sense of justice was deeply offended. Benedictine logic would have allowed Peter to be sent to St Andrews University, the oldest Scottish university, because it was a Catholic university in a Protestant country: but it would not allow him to study at a Protestant university in a Catholic country. Instead, they officially supported his application to the newly founded Sussex University, which was non-denominational. His farewell to Worth, in early 1964, was unspectacular. There was no official ceremony. Peter got drunk with his rugby team.

STUDENT YEARS

The experiment

After the University of Cambridge rejected Jonas's application, the same response came from the University of Sussex. His sister Kathryn intervened on his behalf. She asked a tutor for help, who explained the procedure to her: the abbot's letter of recommendation had made an unfavourable impression; he had not supported Jonas after all. Kathryn obtained permission for him to appear for an interview. By the beginning of 1965, it was finally certain: Peter would be studying at the newly established Sussex University from October. 'Kathryn pushed my enrolment through by hook or by crook,' he quipped nonchalantly afterwards.

But before that happened, he had 'nine months to burn', for which he initially had no plan. This changed after his parish, Croydon Council, awarded him a scholarship to attend a French course at the Institut Catholique de Paris in May 1965. A stroke of luck? No!

'It was a big waste of time, I can tell you that.' He went only to clubs and bars. Young Jonas was not interested in anything that had to do with culture there. 'Hormonally disadvantaged,' is how Peter Jonas described the eighteen-year-old he had been. Outside the monastery walls for the first time, unsupervised by his own family and in Paris in the 1960s – need one hear any more to hazard a guess what he was like on his travels? He wanted to go to Monte Carlo with friends in a Beetle, but the trip ended in an accident.

Peter Jonas later spoke of this time with some hesitation. He mourned the lost opportunities. 'If I had been my father, I would have been shocked. I lived like a bum.'

It seemed that all was not well with him in those months when he was partying in Paris. Kathryn, however, knew her brother too well not to have noticed his condition. 'She smelled a rat. My sister – God bless her! – noticed that something was wrong. She travelled from Sussex to save me.' One must imagine the effort Kathryn had to make to travel from remote Brighton to Paris – just to pick up her little brother. She took him to her place in Sussex.

There she was living with two other students in an apartment, which Peter now moved into. Kathryn didn't mind because she was having an affair with one of her professors: she wasn't using her room. Peter was relieved, in a way. His sister's authority helped him find his feet again. He worked through her reading list.

But he only had a few weeks to do this, because Kathryn had soon hatched a new idea: she had persuaded her mother to allow Peter to go to Jamaica. And so he took the boat from London to Kingston, travelling from there to Miami to visit one of his favourite aunts, Lorna Antonia, and from there, via Mexico City, to New York.

Everywhere he went, he stayed with members of his far-flung family. He had met his cousin Monica Melamid, daughter of Elizabeth, before, but only during these weeks of his visit did they get to know each other more closely. It was to be the foundation of an intimate relationship of trust that each carried throughout their lives. For decades they spoke on the phone almost daily and stood by each other's side. But the relationship could well have developed differently: the first thing Peter did when he came to Monica's home was to chase her around, trying to shoot her with a BB gun. For his cousin, Peter was a bogeyman.

But all the relatives had been briefed by Peter's mother. So, much to Peter's chagrin, 'Uncle Jo' in Kingston and all the family knew of his escapades in Paris, and so kept him on a short leash. All except Aunt Lorna Antonia, known as Tony. Just fourteen years older than Peter, she was the youngest of his mother's fifteen siblings – a seductive woman in Peter's eyes. She had been on Jamaica's Olympic swimming team and had later worked in Hollywood as a swimming double for movie stars until she met and married the vice-president of an airline. With her, Peter learned a little of her savoir-vivre, a world full of joie de vivre, lightness and sensual intoxication. Together they went to bars and parties, and attended 'real orgies'.

A true Bildungsbürger, Peter's 'experiment', as he called his Grand Tour, would have been a failure had he not met an Argentine actress, Mirtha, through Aunt Tony. Mirtha was ten years older than him and, of course, beautiful beyond measure. To make matters worse, Mirtha also taught him 'what women like'. When he told me about this, Jonas's voice was filled with pride, but also with a hint of indulgence towards the young man he had been then.

When he met Mirtha a second time, the evening after their first night together, she was in company. He wanted to be cool, and he acted completely neutrally towards her. He ignored her: a mistake that proved difficult to correct. Aunt Tony and Mirtha asked him to talk. 'Auntie Tony was unequivocal,' Jonas later recalled. 'She said: "If you sleep with a woman, you have to show her respect. When you see her later, you have to kiss her hand and her lips and tell her how much you adore her, whether you feel it or not." It was a different universe: gallantry was of the utmost importance.' But for Aunt Tony and Mirtha, this lesson was not yet enough: '"Sexual passion is not the same as love. A relationship between two people weighs more heavily than any kind of sexual passion. If you want to live a life without bitterness, you must learn to show your affection and cultivate friendship. If passion prevails, there is no reason not to keep the friendship. To achieve that, you have to respect people." I think that was a wise piece of advice from two women of the world.'

Sussex 1965–1968

Thus educated and refreshed, and equipped with a full government grant for the three years of his studies, Peter Jonas started at Sussex in the autumn of 1965. He felt rich because he could afford a pack of cigarettes every day, thanks to his scholarship grant. He also assumed that he would not have to work during the years of his studies. He later claimed that, throughout the three years of his studies at Sussex, he had not attended a single lecture. Could this claim be true?

The novel reform ideas for which the University of Sussex became famous permitted a completely new form of study. The university was founded in 1960 as one of the first universities to be created in the 'years of plenty',[1] the years of abundance after the Second World War. Sussex quickly came to be regarded as a radical, left-leaning and hip university in the tradition of Berkeley. This reputation was what attracted Peter Jonas. By the end of the 1960s, Sussex had a reputation as a rock 'n' roll university: Jimi Hendrix and Pink Floyd appeared there at the invitation of the Students' Union.[2] Given total freedom over how to structure the university, the founding members chose an approach that later became famous: in one of the 'Schools of Studies', students chose a major subject to study on an interdisciplinary basis, alongside the school's other disciplines.[3] Peter Jonas chose English at the School of English and American Studies.

The intellectual traditions, working styles and viewpoints of the 'core discipline' were to be enriched by this broader study.[4] Around fifty students enrolled in the first year, many of them women.[5] In 1958, the proportion of women in British universities was only 24 per cent.[6] This rate was higher at Sussex. Kathryn was one of those who enrolled, and Peter wanted to follow. The first cohort lived in two Victorian buildings in Brighton, which reminded some of life in a Kibbutz, but the campus – a term the founders adopted from the Americans – was built swiftly thereafter, to the north-east of Brighton, where the landscape is characterised more by lush flowering meadows than by the modernist teaching buildings. Sussex was gentle country, with ancient farms, cottages, barns and wind and water mills. Animals were the main actors in this picture: at the start of the twentieth century, the famous black Sussex oxen with their white horns, the last of their kind, were still ploughing the thick, boggy soil into which horses would have sunk. The oxen also pulled the farmers on their final journey to the graveyard. The meat on the sheep absorbed the taste of the nearby sea, but also that of the fine, sweet grass.

The people of Sussex were very attached to their homeland; they were rather alienated by teaching and the many young people.[7] The university must have felt like an invading alien being. For the locals, the very idea of taking a trip was unusual, and the notion of leaving home beyond imagining. In her portrait of Sussex County, Esther Meynell tells of a man who embodied one particular outlook of people there: when he left home for the first time and travelled – only fifteen miles – he returned satisfied and said he did not care for foreign lands, and that Old England was good enough for him.[8] For a long time it was difficult to travel by train across the county. To the people there, London seemed infinitely distant.

The year 1963 marked the beginning of the Swinging Sixties. It was the *Annus Mirabilis*, as Philip Larkin entitled his famous poem:

> Sexual intercourse began
> In nineteen sixty-three
> (which was rather late for me) –
> Between the end of the 'Chatterley' ban
> And the Beatles' first LP.
>
> Up to then there'd only been
> A sort of bargaining,
> A wrangle for the ring,
> A shame that started at sixteen
> And spread to everything.
>
> Then all at once the quarrel sank:
> Everyone felt the same,
> And every life became
> A brilliant breaking of the bank,
> A quite unlosable game.

> So life was never better than
> In nineteen sixty-three
> (Though just too late for me) –
> Between the end of the 'Chatterley' ban
> And the Beatles' first LP.

When Peter Jonas moved onto campus among the first years in the early autumn of 1965, the Beatles had just released their fifth studio album *Help!* It immediately reached number one in the charts. Those were the years in which adult life also began for Peter Jonas. And he, too, took off – albeit in his own way.

At Sussex, he was primarily taught in the tutorial format, which encouraged independent study. Margaret McGowan, a professor at the School of European Studies, valued the openness and flexibility of mind that the format fostered; the willingness to ask questions; the skill of weighing material sensibly and, above all, the temperamental independence that emerged from the exchange of arguments.[9] Ideally, tutorials were meant to foster the development of mature personalities. Of course, McGowan pointed out, such a mode of teaching requires a lot of initiative and presupposes a strong sense of independence, especially from students who, at least in the humanities, have to spend many hours in the library if they want to make the most of what is on offer.[10]

Even though Jonas did not rate his own initiative very highly, he seemed to have internalised this principle. 'I often sat in the library and read,' he recalled. 'I learned a little. My tutor Reginald Mutter was very nice.' Peter and Sean Linehan, an Irish tutorial partner, met Reginald once a week. Sean was a wild young man, Jonas recalled. He took a clear stand in the anti-Vietnam movement in 1968. Fifty years later, Linehan described his 'colourful protest': the 'lies' told by the representative of the US Embassy during an event on campus enraged him so much that he attacked the man with paint as he was leaving the hall.[11] From then on, he was no longer allowed on campus, although he was allowed to take his exams. The student revolts did not play a big role for Peter. He mentioned them, but they never drove him.

Sean and Peter would drink sherry every now and then with their tutor, who was only a little older than themselves. 'He would give us a play or a project and we had to write some essay or other about it.' So they took the *Oxford Companion to English Literature* and used its summaries. 'When we were really naughty, we didn't even write the essay. We took a blank sheet and improvised the text. That was a skill we acquired very quickly.' Naturally, they did this to leave more time for going to parties, Jonas added. He would never have dreamed that he would still be making use of this improvisational ability on his seventieth birthday.

This was not quite what David Daiches, one of Sussex's first professors of English literature, had hoped for his students – but nevertheless he did not want to present them with an orthodox reading list, a conception that ran counter to the canonical thinking Peter knew from his sister.[12] Sussex's approach broke radically with traditional university schemas: after the students studied the literature of an era, they became acquainted with the social and intellectual movements of the period. They studied the 'texture of a culture',[13] according to Daiches. For these purposes, the 'minor writers' are often of greater importance because they reflect the tastes and prejudices of a time more reliably.

Fig. 20: Peter Jonas on stage, c. 1966

However, Peter Jonas seems to have missed the second important building block in the Sussex experiment: students of the humanities and the natural sciences had to take courses in other disciplines in order to broaden their horizons.

Instead, he befriended Mary Ann Goodbody, a girl of the same age, whom everyone called Buzz. Buzz Goodbody had already succeeded in taking over the university's theatre in her first year as an undergraduate. Without any training in the field, as artistic director she staged plays to the highest quality. Under her direction, Peter experienced professional theatre for the first time. He played Sergius in George Bernard Shaw's *Arms and the Man*. The production was staged at the Theatre Royal in Brighton and his mother also came to one of the performances.

In her final project, Buzz Goodbody dramatised Dostoevsky's novel *Notes from Underground*. The production won a prize at the National Student Drama Festival and had a short run at the Garrick Theatre in London's West End.[14] Peter even played the lead role in an adaptation of John Steinbeck's *The Pearl*, commissioned by Goodbody. Goodbody joined the Royal Shakespeare Company after graduating and became its first female director.

While Peter worked with Buzz Goodbody, he dreamed of a future in acting. Looking back, Jonas seemed dissatisfied with his performance as an actor. He thought he was just too big for the stage. Moreover, his sister had told him that in her view, his talent was somewhat lacking. And her judgement counted for a lot with him.

Kathryn's death

Fig. 21: Kathryn's gravestone

On that Saturday morning in April 2018, all was quiet in Peter Jonas's flat. It was the weekend of the Sechseläuten in Zurich. The 'Sechselaüten' is a traditional early spring festival at which the figure of a snowman, the 'Böögg', is burned as a symbol of the end of winter. Many families in the Kreis 6 neighbourhood, where Jonas lived, had gone away for the long weekend. Unlike the many visitors to the festival, they did not care how long it took for the head of the Böögg to explode when the fireworks placed within caught light. Jonas was silent, but he did not hesitate long before he started to tell the story of his sister's death. He seemed to have decided that it had to be done now.

While Peter was finding his way to music, Kathryn had completed her studies in classical languages at the School of European Studies with excellent results. She then taught at a private boarding school for girls in Sussex, before taking up a post as a lecturer in classical languages at the University of Madrid in 1964. She was fascinated by her father's family history and wanted to follow the traces of the Sephardic Jews in the south of Spain.

A short time later, in 1966, she received an offer from the University of Córdoba, which she was only too happy to accept. Her boyfriend at the time helped her move. He steered the car through the hilly landscape as darkness slowly fell…

He was not responsible for the accident. He could scarcely have seen the lorry, which had been at a standstill under a bridge. Kathryn's boyfriend survived, and she herself was taken to Córdoba hospital, where she succumbed to her injuries.

The news reached Peter at university. Together with his mother, he flew to Spain to identify the body. 'That created a lot of trauma. My mother had severe mental problems afterwards and until her death. It was a great shock to her.' Barely five years earlier she had been confronted with the death of her first husband. She would never be able to get over Kathryn's death. 'It was a big shock for me too. She was my mentor.' He fell silent.

Through his long life, Peter Jonas had been forced to deal with many terrible, tragic events. He was able to speak calmly about all of them during the interviews for this biography; and of course he controlled the extent and the intensity of the discussions, but he always remained calm. Except when it came to Kathryn or her accident. He fought back tears every time he spoke about her.

Immediately after her death, he did not mourn. He merely functioned. He had to find a way into what his life would be from now on. And her absence would always be a part of it.

Antony Costley-White and Mark Elder

After Kathryn's funeral, Jonas returned to university. Two more years of his first degree lay ahead of him. Peter knew for sure by now that for him, the only path would be a musical life. During his first summer holidays, he listened through the symphonic repertoire from 1750 to 1860. After all his academic work, this was a breath of fresh air. But opera still played no role in his life.

That changed when he met physics student Antony Costley-White. Ant, as his friends called him, didn't want to stay on campus any longer. From second year onwards, students had the right to live out. And so he suggested to Peter they rent a rather dilapidated farmhouse together. It belonged to a professor who had gone to Kenya for two years. The house was in a tiny village in the middle of nowhere. That was no real problem for the two men: Ant drove a sports car and Peter his Mini Cooper. Peter agreed to Antony's proposal and so they both moved into the farmhouse. Of course, they stuck out in the new neighbourhood like a sore thumb. The residents had no idea of the life that the students lived between the university campus and London. 'Oh London, I have never been to London' was a phrase they heard a lot – spoken in the broad Sussex dialect, which is increasingly rare nowadays.

The handsome Antony had a lot of success with women. He also played the cello brilliantly and loved opera. He couldn't abide Peter's lack of familiarity with the opera. In 1967, he chose the *Flying Dutchman* at the Royal Opera Covent Garden for Peter's initiation. Sir Colin Davis conducted. When he related the story of this experience, Peter Jonas paused for a moment: 'I remember it like it was yesterday. I was so thrilled.' The choral scene, 'Steuermann! Laß die Wacht!' gripped him most of all. Later that night, they walked through the old market, humming this melody and dancing to it. After that, Peter Jonas was insatiable.

Antony and Peter became 'Young Friends': they purchased the subscription that the Royal Opera offered together with Sadler's Wells Opera, which would later become English National Opera.

From then on they paid about ten shillings for a ticket in the top tier. But that was not all. They were subsequently reimbursed 80 per cent of the ticket price and 50 per cent of the travel costs. They either went by train from Brighton or in one of their cars. The more people in the van, the more they could account for, and everything ended up being done quite practically by sending forms in the post. 'It was pretty socialist,' Jonas said, looking back.

At that time, it was quite easy to park directly in front of Covent Garden. Of course they had to use the back entrances, as they only had tickets for the top tier. But this also released them from the strict dress code. They watched all – literally all – the productions.

Peter Jonas also took up the challenge of learning to sing during his student years at Sussex. By then, he had already made the decision to go on to study music after his first degree. Staff from Glyndebourne (see later) had recommended the Royal Northern College of Music in Manchester, where he would receive the proper training. Peter didn't want to arrive there unprepared; he was already wrestling with music theory. The mother of a fellow student was an opera singer and was able to help him. He also told her that he badly wanted to travel to Vienna before his studies in Manchester, in order to see performances at the Staatsoper. His singing teacher arranged for him to stay with singing students, and train tickets were cheap. So he travelled overnight in a sleeper from Dover via Calais to Vienna.

His accommodation was in the Annagasse in the First Bezirk, right next to the Staatsoper. His host showed him around Vienna, but most importantly, he explained how to queue for tickets in the standing-room-only section: you had to go to a certain door, wait two hours, and then there was another door and another after that, until at some point you found yourself in the auditorium and marked your place with a handkerchief on the balustrade. Then one could go home to change. Jonas had brought his tie and jacket in his luggage. The singing student also introduced him to the deeper secrets of going to the opera in Vienna. This included eating a certain sausage with mustard on a slice of bread before going to a performance.

Jonas was especially interested in performances in which a particular singer appeared. He admired her very fiercely, but only from a distance. She was Lucia Popp. In the afternoon he had bought a photograph in a bookshop near the Staatsoper House. It showed Lucia Popp as Sophie in *Der Rosenkavalier*, holding the silver rose against her cheek with a gentle smile. He saw her in this role that same evening. 'I was in a rush of happiness!' he would remember. 'I went to the performance, I was absolutely swept off my feet. I was completely and utterly smitten with her and with the *Rosenkavalier*.'[15]

Antony had another new idea for the summer. He wanted them to work at the Glyndebourne Opera Festival. Every year the Festival would look for stagehands, extras and ushers and the friends from the farmhouse drove the quarter of an hour down to the Festival site.

The Festival at Glyndebourne had a reputation for providing the highest quality for an audience that was prepared to accept different operas and styles than their usual fare.[16] However, after John Christie, who had founded the festival, died in April 1962, it experienced turbulent times. Although the Glyndebourne Arts Trust secured continued funding for the otherwise completely privately-financed programme,[17] Harold Rosenthal wrote in the renowned magazine *Opera* in 1965 that Glyndebourne, as a major international festival, needed a truly firm, dictatorial musical and artistic leadership and that this was precisely what was currently lacking.[18]

This didn't put off our two young opera fans one bit. In his very first year, Jonas joined the company as an extra and stagehand. They were well-paid by the standards of the time: five shillings per rehearsal, seventeen shillings and sixpence per performance. In one week, this came to about ten pounds. This corresponded to the price of about twenty opera tickets in London if bought via their subscription, which in today's money – calculated in the most important currency, i.e. how much opera tickets cost – would be about four hundred pounds per week.

Antony also had a crucial insider tip: in Glyndebourne there was a production manager who had an eye for young men. Antony was not only handsome – 'all the English boys were good looking,' Peter Jonas claimed – but he was also athletic. He was sure he would get a job as an usher. Together with John Abulafia, whom Peter knew from Goodbody's troupe, Peter went to the audition – and got the gig.

La Bohème, which opened the 1967 season, was directed by Michael Redgrave. Promoters were shocked by this decision, because Puccini was considered a lightweight, even vulgar, at the time.[19] After his *Werther*, great things were expected from Redgrave. But this time he disappointed. His health was said to have already been in decline; others say he had been drinking.[20] One of his ideas was to introduce a new character, the 'Beautiful young man – or BYM': because he flirts with Mimi, Rodolfo gets angry. Peter was given the role of an extra in this critically-panned production and got into trouble with the production manager: Peter would have been wiser not to have accepted his invitation to dinner in Brighton – after all, there's no such thing as a free lunch. Peter did not want to fulfil his colleague's request to extend their date late into the night.

In Glyndebourne, Peter got a swift education in the nature of the opera business. He understood the technical procedures and the mentalities of singers and, above all, he dug into the repertoire at the highest level. He was employed as a stagehand in the Mozart cycle, which the director Franco Enriquez worked on together with the stage designer Emanuele Luzzati and which the audience adored. The time he spent at Glyndebourne surely made Peter happy.

One day, Antony invited his best friend, a young man who studied musicology at Cambridge and played the bassoon, to the farmhouse for the weekend. It was Mark Elder, who was to become Peter Jonas's friend for life, and one of his most important artistic companions during his time at English National Opera. On this first weekend together, the three young men toasted the opera. On an old, terribly out-of-tune piano, Elder played pieces from various operas, and the others sang along. They drank a case of champagne that someone had organised from somewhere. The weekend established a lifelong artistic friendship.

Chimes Music Shop

Between a satisfying summer at Glyndebourne and the start of the upcoming term, Peter still had five weeks free. And he always needed money. He was looking for a job again, and this time he found it in London. His mother was living with another man by this time. Dickie Michaels, a film producer, owned one of the old mews houses in Devonshire Close near the Royal Academy of Music. Originally used as stables in the eighteenth and nineteenth centuries, today these small houses are mostly lovingly restored and correspondingly expensive.

Peter was able to live there, and nearby was Marylebone High Street, where Anne Knight had opened the famous Chimes Music Shop in 1951. This is where the students of the Royal Academy, as well as the musicians of the London orchestras, bought their scores, records and other necessities. Peter simply went to the store, introduced himself to the strict, upper-class lady there, claimed to know a lot about music, and asked for a job. And, as sometimes happens in life, the lady was planning to go on holiday and was looking for a replacement. But why should she believe this young man, whom she had never met before? She quizzed him on conductors, recordings and current productions, found that he was able to answer all her questions flawlessly – and she had him start there the next day.

For four weeks Jonas ran the shop alone. His salary was quite low, but in return he was allowed to listen to all the records. And he really did play them all. In the shop were two very precious recordings, copies of the very recent and later legendary recordings of Wagner's *Ring des Nibelungen*, which Solti had recorded together with Decca production manager John Culshaw between 1958 and 1965. This set Peter Jonas on what he called his Wagner odyssey. He played the records over and over again, storing every single note in his memory.

Later, when recounting this episode, he paused for a moment to recall the famous Swiss character tenor Hugues Cuénod, whom he had met in the canteen at Glyndebourne. Laughing loudly, Cuénod had prophesied: '"You'll suddenly realise that it wouldn't be Wagner you'd take to a desert island. It would be Verdi and Monteverdi. The two Verdis, they will give you comfort, consolation and support. Wagner's drink is powerful now, it will be weaker later," and Cuénod was right. Wise words.'

Very gradually, his London network also developed, and he got to know a lot of musicians. Amelia Freedman, who founded the 'Nash Ensemble', was one of them, and so was Sir Colin Davis, who bought his scores from him. Neither of them could have known that Jonas would later engage him for the Chicago Symphony Orchestra and the Bavarian Staatsoper.

After closing time at seven o'clock, Jonas would take the Tube to South Kensington and join the queue of people hoping to get tickets for the Proms, the summer concerts at the Royal Albert Hall. Jonas had already heard the CBS recording of Bruckner's 7th Symphony, conducted by Bruno Walter, in the shop 'a thousand times'. The recording was a rarity, especially as the work was too long for a single vinyl record. And on one particular evening, Bernard Haitink conducted Bruckner's 7th, which was rarely played at the time. Jonas got a ticket. Stormy applause started after the final chords were played. 'Haitink, however, did not bow, but instead just held up the Eulenburg score,' Jonas's eyes shone as he spoke of it. A conducting score of the work did not exist at that time. The Scherzo from the 7th Symphony was known to the British public from a trailer, but the work itself was largely unheard. The concert made a deep impression on Jonas. 'Mmmm, memories. I learnt a lot.'

But he still had to complete his third and final year at Sussex. At the end of his first year, he had taken the 'preliminary exams', which were the same for all students in the School of English Studies. After that, Sussex students needed to sit only the final examination, which was identical for all – regardless of whether they had chosen English literature, philosophy or history as their main subject: conditions today's students could only dream of.

But how was Peter supposed to pass it? Whenever he could, he was either working at the Chimes Music Store or going to see opera performances.

Antony Costley-White was the same, preferring to go to the opera and party rather than prepare for the exams. Antony suggested that they continue living in their habitual manner until two weeks before the exam. Then they could go to his mother's country house to study together. They spent most of their time hiking in the rain over the hills, sitting down to excellent meals and good wine in the evenings, and so they came into the exams wonderfully relaxed but completely unprepared. Peter graduated on 9 July 1968 with a 'Bachelor of Arts (with Honours) Second Class' in English Literature. His tutor Reginald Mutter commented dryly: 'Peter would prefer all novels scored instead of written.'

How true. Antony and he both graduated with Second Class degrees, and were very relieved. 'It shows you are not as stupid as you thought you were,' his tutor later wrote on a postcard to Peter. 'That was the end of that,' Jonas said, concluding his recollections of Sussex. But there was just one addendum: in 1994 his alma mater awarded him an honorary doctorate. Certainly not because of his grades.[21]

The summer of 1968

Mark Elder is one of the few friends who knew Jonas in his student years. 'Physically, he was incredibly striking, powerful, magnetic,' Elder emphasised. 'His hair turned white before he was twenty. It was extraordinary, always silver-grey. Peter was physically big. We would say in English, like a rugby player, a second row forward, a really big man.'²²

Mark Elder and Peter Jonas spent the summer of 1968 together. 'Peter and I, day in, day out. We got to know each other intensively. We shared an enormous amount with each other, even though we were very different,' Elder later said of their friendship. They both took part in the production of *Anna Bolena* that month, also a rarity in the programme, as the opera had last been performed in England seventy-three years prior. Looking back, Mark Elder liked the fact that Peter had played the captain of the guard and Mark a sheriff, which seemed like a charming anticipation of their work at ENO, when Peter became director general and Mark director of music.

Directly after rehearsals, Elder and Jonas often went to Covent Garden to see performances. 'He always said he didn't like Covent Garden as a theatre, that he didn't want to work there, but that's where we went as students, for the singers and the conductors,' Elder recalled. 'It was a great experience for us to hear these great artists.'

In July 1968 Jonas learned that Lucia Popp, his 'goddess from Vienna', was to perform as Despina at Covent Garden. The new production of *Così fan tutte* was conducted by Georg Solti. Peter drove to London and waited for Lucia Popp at the stage door. Finally she came, 'a smallish, blonde girl'. He gathered all his courage, approached her and introduced himself. 'I am your biggest fan. You are the most beautiful and wonderful woman in the world and a great singer,' at least that's how he later acted out the scene. And he asked for an autograph on the photo. 'How sweet!' is her reported reply. Jonas kept the photograph for the rest of his life.

This period marked the beginning of the careers of Jonas and his friends. 'There were a number of operas that we adored, an interesting catalogue,' Elder reported. '*Les Pêcheurs de Perles* by Bizet, *Die Frau ohne Schatten* and *Der Rosenkavalier* by Richard Strauss, *Tristan und Isolde* by Wagner and Puccini's *La Rondine*, all such different pieces! We were obsessed and played them all the time.'

Even then, Jonas admired what ENO stood for: accessibility. Mark and Peter loved the atmosphere and the sound, which was so different from Covent Garden. 'Covent Garden is basically an Italian house, the Coliseum has a much richer acoustic. Listening to Reggie…' – as Mark Elder calls the conductor Reginald Goodall – 'conducting the *Ring*, the *Meistersinger von Nürnberg*, was amazing! It played a big role in our youth. His knowledge of the pieces was immense. It was very exciting when he started playing the *Ring*. It was the first time we heard an orchestra play with that kind of sonority.' They decided that an opera house was the best place in the world to work after hearing *Die Meistersinger von Nürnberg* conducted by Reginald Goodall.

Together with his friends, Jonas also went to the Bayreuth Festival for the first time. There was not enough money for a train ticket, so they hitchhiked. Jonas described his first visit to Bayreuth in his speech at the ceremony marking the centenary of Wieland Wagner's birth:

> There were more of my kind – Wagner fanatics with little knowledge and even less money. If we could afford it, we ate in the relatively good and cheap station restaurant: otherwise we hung around the stage entrance of the Festspielhaus during the day and tried to get a ticket by any means – no matter what seat, no matter what price – and if it was an expensive one that we got hold of, we traded until we got one for the cheapest corner of the house that was appropriate for our wallet. The Maisel beer was good and affordable. The Franconian girls were approachable, friendly and, above all, helpful; they had a lot of tips and tricks up their sleeves on how we could see the performances even without successfully hunting for tickets. The best of these was to climb over the outside wall of the artists' canteen, which was quite doable for a limber eighteen-year-old. There you met someone who knew the ropes and who then led you to the lighting bridge above the stage. How many evenings I spent there during that happy time, when there was no mention of 'Arbeitsschutz' or 'health and safety' yet! The biggest thrill for

us young opera fans was when Wieland or Wolfgang appeared at the stage door. They were happy to take their time and were not too proud to exchange a few words with all us sweaty and badly-dressed youths. Not that we could have said much (my German was non-existent at the time; British schools, please don't be surprised, didn't teach that language for a while after the war) – but for us, the best thing of all was knowing we were accepted.[23]

Over the following six years, Jonas returned to Bayreuth again and again. His personal moment of greatest happiness was when Wolfgang Wagner personally gave him a ticket for a seat in the back of a box for a *Lohengrin* with Jess Thomas. 'I lived off the experience for years afterwards,' he confessed in retrospect.

Peter Jonas was a graduate in the summer of 1968, a young man of barely twenty-two. 'What the fuck should I do?' England was struggling with inflation, a low export rate and high unemployment. The Cuban Missile Crisis and the Vietnam War dominated international politics. The UK had been a nuclear power since 1952, and the anti-nuclear movement was getting underway. London was full of young people, a consequence of the baby boom of the 1950s. In April 1966, *The Times* had declared the city's standard of living to be the best in the world: London became The Swinging City. *The Times* published a map with the city's hotspots. Of the rest of England, the piece mentioned only Liverpool, the home of the Beatles.[24] 'In a decade dominated by youth, London has flourished. It swings; it's the scene,'[25] noted *The Times*.

On 3 July 1966, Geoff Hurst achieved the unbelievable: a World-Cup-winning goal in the 101st minute, completing his hat-trick. England won the World Cup against West Germany, 'possibly the definitive confirmation of the Swinging Sixties and its metropolis'.[26]

However, neither Carnaby Street, Twiggy, Mary Quant's miniskirt, nor contraception, nor sexual liberation could disguise the fact that the Swinging Sixties were primarily a middle-class phenomenon in London's West End. The rest of the English stuck to what they knew.[27]

Peter Jonas was one of these confident young people thirsting for life – and he wanted to study music history, a choice that was 'out of the question' as far as his mother was concerned. He had to be tactically astute and applied for a scholarship from the Croydon parish, which covered his mother's residence. During the interview, he was asked where he wanted to study. Peter already had an offer from the Northern School of Music in Manchester. With this, he convinced the lady who was conducting the interview. He said thank you and went home with a full scholarship for further studies. His mother was deeply indignant.

With the first instalment of his scholarship, Peter bought himself an orange Beetle. This purchase was vital: without it, how could he possibly get from Manchester to London to the opera? The train was far too expensive! Besides, he could repair a Beetle himself if necessary. 'So, I went up to Manchester.'

Manchester 1968–1971

'Before I started my studies in Manchester, I had never been north of London,' Jonas confessed as he started his story of his years in the distant north. There are only about three hundred kilometres between the capital and the economic heart of the north-west of England, but as a young graduate Peter did not yet know the north of the country. In fact, this was typical of that era, and of Londoners who tended to look south rather than north. In those days, people travelled much less; but there was also a greater difference in how people spoke back then. Every few kilometres the dialect changed, even if southerners did not necessarily notice the subtle differences.

Manchester had been one of England's economic centres since the beginning of the Industrial Revolution. 'Take Lancashire and all it stands for from Britain and at once we become an unimportant, storm-bound island lost in the mists of the north',[28] wrote the novelist Walter Greenwood in the early 1950s. Peter arrived there in the final days of heavy industry. The originally red brick buildings were covered with black dirt. In his memory, everything was grey and dark.

The cotton industry had experienced an economic boom in the eighteenth century, triggering much growth. In the Pennines, England's spine, there are many streams whose water power was used to drive the cotton mills. These mills meant jobs and income for many people in the area. When discussing them, Jonas quoted William Blake's famous poem: 'And was Jerusalem builded here / Among these dark Satanic Mills? … In England's green & pleasant Land.'

These 'dark Satanic mills', in which children and adults worked in terrible conditions, brought wealth to Lancashire. There is a lot of rain west of the Pennines. The humid air was ideal for spinning cotton. The nearby port of Liverpool opened the region to international trade.

For a London boy, the North was another country.

'When I saw these dark Satanic mills, it was a total shock to me,' Jonas recalled. 'They were run-down and poor areas that had not been rebuilt. The weather was terrible.' A friend from Manchester had prepared Peter: in January, there would be an average of only five hours of sunshine per day, but there was a silver lining to this cloudy outlook.

'Everybody fucks,' he said, introducing Peter to his new life in Manchester. 'You will have a great time, too. All these Lancashire women have the most beautiful skin. Their fresh, soft skin is famous.'

What sounds like a young man's fantasy was actually confirmed by local writer Walter Greenwood – with a hint of pathos: 'Lancashire women are extraordinary. Those in the towns live under a permanent canopy of filthy smoke that ceaselessly deposits its soot on everything.'[29] Peter's friend went one better: 'Everybody has an incredible romantic and sex life in Lancashire.'

His prophecy certainly came true for Peter. Jonas emphasised the enormous warmth of the people in Manchester, without a hint of irony. Less formal than the Londoners, they were instead curious, open and tolerant.

But his first impressions of Manchester were certainly rather depressing. He rented a room in Demesne Road in Whalley Range for thirty shillings a week, exactly the sum of his weekly stipend. The neighbourhood had been particularly popular in the Victorian era, but by the end of the 1960s it had become quite run-down. Many single people lived there. When the crowds cheered in the nearby football stadium, the whole house shook. There was a brothel on the ground floor.

At the end of the corridor was the bathroom, shared by all the residents of the floor. Gas heating, which was common at the time, was coin-operated. If Peter didn't have any coins to hand, then his room stayed cold. To make himself a little bit more comfortable, Peter painted his room white. It didn't help: he felt uncomfortable there and deeply depressed.

He kept up his habit of roaming the neighbourhoods in his free time. Whether by chance or providence, one of these walks in search of beauty led him to people who were to gain special significance in his life. He was particularly taken with the tree-lined streets of Didsbury to the south. Close to Fletcher Moss Park was Kingston Road, a beautiful, pleasant street similar to those in north London. Peter was walking along this path on a wonderfully sunny day when his eyes fell on number 26 and he immediately wanted to live there. The house had been freshly renovated and divided into individual flats. There was a small bay window under the roof, and a mighty chestnut tree stood in front of the house.

That day he went back to his musty room in Whalley Range without having achieved anything. But a few days later, when he was wandering through Didsbury again, he saw a young woman come out of the house. Peter approached her and told her how much he would like to live there.

Margaret was an art student who also worked as a model. She gave Peter the address and telephone number of the owners and advised him to contact them, because one of the rooms in a shared flat was free at the moment. He did so immediately and so he met Dorothy Parker – 'with the most wonderful eyes!' Parker first questioned him intensively about his background and then showed him the room: it was indeed the bay window room with a view of the chestnut tree! The rent was twice as high as in Whalley Range, but Peter took the risk.

Here he had to share the bathroom only with his flatmates. And these flatmates were none other than W. G. Sebald and his wife Ute, who had emigrated to England. Sebald was only two years older than Peter, but the couple seemed to Peter to be far more mature than he felt he was himself. Even his first encounter with Sebald, working as a lecturer at the University of Manchester, was impressive for Jonas. Sebald sat in the only armchair in the flat, Peter cross-legged on the floor in front, while Ute cooked spaghetti bolognese for everyone, which Peter ate happily, still cross-legged on the floor.

Sebald rejected his first names Winfried and Georg as National-Socialist-inspired and had friends call him by his third name, 'Max'. That was how Peter was to address him, too. The Sebalds became like a family to Peter, something he had bitterly missed. Together they went on weekend tours of the surrounding area in Peter's Mini. Ute was regularly shocked to see Peter come home with a new girl. The libertarian lifestyle of the 1960s was alien to her.

Even at that time, Sebald was already intensively occupied with the stories of emigrants and listened attentively to what they had to say. In conversation with Peter, Sebald sat in his armchair like a kind confessor: sage, curious and utterly attentive to Peter, noting down everything Peter said in his notebook. This was how Sebald would collect material from talking with people and fuse it with his own memories to make his novels. The story of Hilda May and Walter quickly became the focus of his interest. Sebald's questions about his parents made Peter see his own family in a new light. He arrived at an understanding about his German descent and his parents' emigration. They also spoke about his time at Worth Abbey: about the cold, the punishments, the pressure and the fears, both at night and during the day; and about the feeling of being rejected by one's parents. Through these discussions, Peter inspired Sebald's figure of Jacques Austerlitz. And Sebald opened a path to Jonas's past. 'Through the fate of this walk, I got to be known and friends with one of Germany's most important minds, somebody who has helped me understand what it was to be an emigrant,' Jonas said of Sebald's importance in his life.

Peter only realised that the house at number 26 Kingston Road was a kind of German diaspora house when Sebald also drew his attention to the story of Dorothy's husband Peter Jordan. The latter had become known as the architect of the tenements in Manchester. In 1939, at the age of fifteen, he had been sent to England by his Jewish parents. They themselves remained in Munich, were deported by the Nazis in 1941 and shot in Lithuania. It is one of history's strange coincidences that the first Stolpersteine were laid in Munich for that pair, Siegfried Fritz and Paula Jordan, in 2004 – and removed again the next day. The city of Munich had not approved their installation, and a scandal ensued.

At that time Peter Jonas was working as the artistic director of the Bavarian Staatsoper. He met the Parker-Jordans again when he was squeezing past the guests to his seat in the seventh row at the opening night of the *Incoronazione di Poppea*. He was embarrassed to be upsetting everyone, but he had had something to settle backstage. Right next to him there sat an older couple who seemed very familiar. It was Dorothy Parker and Peter Jordan.

Thanks to her somewhat chaotic nature, Dorothy had once put Peter in quite a serious predicament: she had thrown him into debt. Peter had handed Dorothy a cheque for the rent every month. But she put the cheques in a drawer, forgot them, and then added the new cheques on top, until one day, many months later, she cashed them all at once at the bank. Peter, however, was also not giving this matter his full attention: he had only ever looked at the account balance on his statements and was pleased to find that he had money left over at the end of each month. And what money he had left over, naturally, he spent.

What happened next was inevitable. England is a small country, and, 'horror of horrors', the bank told his mother. By now Peter owed seventy pounds. He was in desperate need of a job. Between terms, he worked for a security company in London, guarding the BBC building. His shift ran from eight in the evening to eight in the morning. During the day he transported money for department stores on Oxford Street. He and his colleagues wore protective masks because criminals had started throwing acid in the faces of security guards on cash transports. They carried the money in cases chained to their wrists. 'Not a very nice job,' as Jonas put it later in his rather British way.

Peter often took his girlfriend Rosalind with him in his orange VW Beetle. 'I loved her very much. It was not a relationship I can explain. I was passionate about her,' Jonas said later. She had originally wanted to become a ballet dancer, but then came to Manchester to train as a piano teacher. As they were driving home in the rain together after a party, the car overturned. Both were taken to hospital with serious injuries. The car was a write-off. Later, Peter replaced it with a blue Beetle.

But the accident did not diminish their love: on the contrary. In his last year in Manchester, they put a Union Jack on the bonnet, packed a tent in the car and drove to London for a short stopover at Peter's mother's place, then took the ferry and drove to Moscow via Berlin and Warsaw. 'As young Brits, we could do that!' Jonas recalled with enthusiasm. 'Rosalind wore hot pants and knee-high boots; I was an unkempt hippie.' They spent a wonderful summer in Russia and visited – of course! – the Stanislavsky Theatre, the Bolshoi Theatre and saw as many opera performances as they could. 'It was a great, formative experience.' The blue Beetle survived the trip to Russia, and Rosalind later worked as a piano teacher at an elite boarding school for girls in Salisbury. But – how would Jonas put it? – 'zurück zum Stück!'

His studies in opera and music history at the Royal Northern College of Music brought him forward significantly, especially in terms of practical skills. The progressive orientation of the University of Sussex had opened Peter's intellectual horizons to developments in cultural history and aesthetics that had taken place after the Reformation: in short, to everything that did not belong at Worth School, things he knew about, if at all, only through his sister's recommendations. But the years at Sussex had meant more to him than that. During those days, he had been able to see himself as an adult, to lead a life that was genuinely self-determined, including in terms of love affairs. Above all, however, this phase established his love of opera. His studies at the Royal Northern College of Music in turn taught him the craft of music making.

The history of the conservatoire dates back to the nineteenth century, when Sir Charles Hallé, after whom the city's current orchestra is named, founded the predecessor institution, the Royal Manchester College of Music. When Peter studied there, the college was about to merge with the Northern School of Music, founded in 1920, which had traditionally trained teachers. The result was the Royal Northern College of Music.[30] Peter was already taking courses at both schools. Students were expected to master the mechanics of music making and music history. Intellectual concepts were not in the foreground. 'In Manchester, they insisted that I should not only study music history, but that I should also master instruments – the piano, and another instrument. I didn't want to start playing violin in my 20s. The simplest instrument for me was singing.'

He didn't have a bad voice and he received excellent singing lessons, Jonas said in retrospect. The singing lessons allowed him – or forced him, as he put it – to work with fellow students who were striving for a career as singers, to get to know and understand their worries and hardships, but also their singing techniques. Memorising the parts helped him develop his memory, which benefited him enormously later. A college production of *Nabucco* was to be his trial by fire, and his powers were sorely tested.

Jonas also received dance lessons: he appreciated them because they kept him physically fit. In general, he emphasised the excellent practical education that the Royal Northern College of Music offered. He had a special advantage over his fellow students.

He had already received his academic training from Sussex, which meant that he passed all his music history exams without any effort – or as he puts it: 'I could very, very easily blag my way through the examinations. He spent three extremely happy years in Manchester. 'I enjoyed my time there very much. I had close friends and a love life.'

At the end of his time in Manchester, Peter still felt terribly young. Despite his academic training in English and music, he had no idea what to do next. He applied for a postgraduate course and the unbelievable happened: the prestigious Royal College of Music in London accepted his application to study singing.

'To my astonishment, I was accepted. And to my even greater astonishment, the City of London said: two more years! My entire education was to be state-funded!'

London 1971–1973

The venerable, traditional conservatoire is located in Kensington opposite the Royal Albert Hall. It was founded in 1882 by the Prince of Wales, later Edward VII, and produced many renowned graduates with artists such as Vaughan Williams, Colin Davis, Benjamin Britten and Joan Sutherland. From 1960 to 1974, the bass baritone Sir Keith Falkner led the Royal College. It expanded under his leadership: Falkner introduced many innovations. In 1967, the first lessons took place in an electronic studio, the first courses in Dalcroze's ideas of eurythmics and in music therapy were offered; and in 1968 the college introduced its first tutorials.[31]

While the economic instability of the time presented Falkner with some difficulties in financing the college, the student unrest of the late 1960s and early 1970s had little impact within its walls; possibly because the aspiring musicians simply had too much practising to do.[32]

In his final address, Falkner looked back on his time at the Royal

College of Music, an era in which he had mentored five generations of future musicians, including Jonas. He painted an accurate, because vivid and honest, picture of how the Royal College had to respond to the new lifestyles of the 1960s generation. Falkner had seen fashions come and go: they were little more than mayflies to him. In his speech, he was having fun bringing them all back to life: unruly bell-bottoms for women, miniskirts in bright colours, short, peppy hairstyles like Twiggy's. Over the years, these changes inspired many discussions, but also much amusement. The college had responded decisively: students who were unpunctual had to pay fines. Falkner spoke of education as a lifelong task; of how methods and systems can have no value without good teaching; of an artist's need to entertain; of drugs and sex; of excellence and of discipline, discipline and discipline again.[33]

Peter became completely absorbed in this world, its lifestyle and its values. He had found a room near the college and spent two happy years with a school friend and his sister from September 1971 to July 1973, when he immersed himself deeply in his studies, but also in the cultural life of London. First of all, he was impressed by the magnificent library of the Royal College, which was infinitely better equipped than the library he had known in Manchester. Even then, the Royal College library had an impressive number of records, as well as some fifteen listening booths equipped with the latest technology. Jonas could finally give himself over to his desire to listen to music for hours. Starting with the Baroque, he systematically listened through the stock of records in every free moment.

Then he took on the British canon: Ralph Vaughan Williams, William Walton, Edward Elgar, George Butterworth and Hubert Parry. Finally, the Russian and French composers followed. 'That was heaven for me,' Jonas beamed, looking back. 'I had an excellent memory and I could hoover up the repertoire. I felt really encouraged at the Royal College.'

From his time at Glyndebourne, Jonas already knew a lot about how opera was made. But at the Royal College Opera Institute he learned the craft from scratch. The Opera Institute at the Royal

College had a small theatre. His dance teacher awakened his interest in modern dance. She was very fond of him and bequeathed him an enchanting statuette after her death, which stood on the coffee table in his Zurich apartment until his own death.

His feeling that he was in the right place at last deepened when he learned that Peter Morrison, a wealthy man, had made a special donation to the Royal College: two front-row seats were available to students for each performance in Covent Garden. They were the A21 and A22 seats, which Jonas would later come to know well. From then on, he always had a soft spot for aisle seats, not least because of his long legs.

Morrison had bought the tickets for these two seats for each performance, and made them available to the college. It was an insider tip among the students, but hardly anyone knew about it. Peter had heard it from one of the younger staff members in the library. All you had to do was fill out a form and hand it in to the head of the library, 'a stern dragon', in the morning. Peter planned which performances he wanted to see at the beginning of each week and then waited patiently until the dragon had decided. He had always been one of the first in the queue, with only a few other students waiting with him: sometimes six, maybe eight. If he came away empty-handed, he bought tickets for the gallery, because once he had chosen a performance, he meant to see it. To be able to sit directly in front of the stage (and free of charge) for the first time was a dream! He savoured it. He saw all nine performances of *Don Carlos* directed by Luchino Visconti. Jonas named the performance numbers exactly and laconically commented of the piece: 'completely mad'. But he also came to a very central realisation: he knew the entire opera repertoire.

On 11 November 1971 Jonas attended a performance in Covent Garden with Mark Elder. One of the works they revered the most was on the programme: *Rosenkavalier*. It was a special evening, as Lucia Popp was to make her London debut as Sophie. After the second act, something happened that Mark Elder later remembered vividly. Jonas turned to him and announced: 'I'm going to marry this woman!' – 'It was incredible, strange, because in a certain sense he did marry her later. It was like a' – Elder thrust his fist into the air – 'like a big bang! I have held onto this memory all my life! It was so extraordinary and something I could never have said.'

But it wasn't all music and opera with Jonas. There was also cricket.

At the Royal College of Music, Peter was not alone in his passion for cricket; he had support from the very top. Headmaster Falkner was not only a passionate lover of the sport, but also a talented player himself. In the inner courtyard of the college, he had a net set up for batting practice. Peter often took advantage of this. He was able to play with a 'straight bat', which immediately caught Falkner's eye and which he naturally valued highly. He wanted to know who this music student was who had such a gift for cricket. This was their first contact, and it would prove decisive for Peter's career. 'The fact that I could play with a straight bat was more important for my career than many other things. It's how I managed to be Intendant at the Bayerische Staatsoper,' he opined. Jonas was firmly convinced that, if he hadn't caught Falkner's eye while practising, he would never have been summoned to Falkner's in his first year (naturally, Jonas overlooked the accolades he won at the Royal College). He jovially imitated Falkner's nonchalant voice: 'What are we going to do with you? You are not a good instrumentalist, not a good singer, but you know so much. I have an idea. I think you should apply for a scholarship to go to the Eastman School of Rochester in New York.'

The scholarship was a dream. For one academic year, one student from Rochester came to London, and the following year London sent one student to Rochester through the Francis Toye Memorial Scholarship. There were no guidelines at all. The scholarship holders were free to do whatever they wanted: listen to recordings, take classes, dance, write a book, learn an instrument – anything at all. The scholarship covered all costs, from flights and accommodation to living expenses.

Peter faced the selection process among the six students chosen by Falkner – and was accepted for the academic year 1973–74.

For him, the scholarship meant the gift of another year before he would have to face the world of work.

Before he could leave for the USA, he still had to submit his thesis. Jonas prepared a new translation of Carl Orff's *Comoedia de Christi Resurrectione*, which was performed for the first time in England on 4 March 1973 by an ensemble of the Royal College (he later proudly notes in his curriculum vitae: 'International copyright reserved'). 'And off I went.'

For a moment on this afternoon of the Sechseläuten weekend, Jonas's gaze lingered on the delicate sculpture that stood on the coffee table in his living room that his dance teacher had given him; from then on, it had accompanied him through all the stages of his journey. 'When you realise how much it costs to study, it's so amazing!' Peter had managed to finance his entire academic education through scholarships. 'My mother felt that I was wasting my time. Peter, the perpetual student. Looked at objectively, maybe she was right. Someone who has studied for so long without showing any real results: what chances does he have? She did not understand. It was all very complicated.' And once again he missed Kathryn, his sister. She could have convinced her mother that Peter had found his way.

Rochester 1973–1974

The Eastman School of Music at the University of Rochester was then – and still is today – one of the leading music colleges in the world. It was established as a foundation in 1921 by the philanthropist George Eastman, owner of the Eastman Kodak company, himself a music lover. The showpiece of the Eastman School is its theatre, which opened in 1922 and was described by critics at the time of its opening as either 'the world's greatest experiment in attempting to exchange money for culture' or 'the most beautiful and costliest picture palace in the world.'[34]

The Eastman Theatre is a traditionally built proscenium theatre with a fully equipped opera stage. Red and gold dominate the interior; in the background of the stage one can see replicas of Greek columns; large-scale murals decorate the auditorium with its two tiers, and the mighty chandelier towers above everything. This building is all about opulence. Originally, the theatre had 3,352 seats and was the most important venue for the Rochester Philharmonic Orchestra. The students of the Eastman School regularly performed there. 'I thought it was the most wonderful paid holiday. I could not take it seriously, I have to say.'

Peter Jonas had experienced only rote-learning and chastisement with the Benedictines: he could not really grasp the idea of learning for himself, even if it involved only a very little joy and pleasure. But surely he did learn in Rochester. Once again, he immersed himself completely, soaking it all up. This was his preferred form of learning, he called it osmosis.

In Rochester, he met female and male students with 'raw talent', as Jonas put it. 'There is no substitute for raw talent. No amount of skill and intelligence can replace raw talent. A raw talent is hard to discover, it needs an ambassador.' In meeting his highly talented fellow students, Peter felt for the first time that this could be his vocation: to be such an ambassador for artists. It was also in Rochester that the thought first occurred to him that he could direct an orchestra or perhaps even an opera house. But he did not talk to anyone about it yet.

His professors impressed him deeply. Robert Spillman had just started his apprenticeship at the Eastman School. Peter took classes in song repertoire and chamber music with the pianist and musicologist, which inspired him. Spillman also accompanied the famous mezzo-soprano Jan DeGaetani, whose interpretations of modern music were influential. With her, Peter experienced a completely new form of teaching that made a lasting impression on him. The professor of singing taught classes in breathing and relaxation techniques. 'DeGaetani showed me that I was not really breathing. She was incredibly nice to me and supportive.'

On that April afternoon, the memory of how intense his time in Rochester had been, how deeply the encounters had shaped him, carried Jonas away. He broke off the conversation and looked for a very specific recording by Jan DeGaetani, one in which she performed songs by Charles Ives. For a while he listened, absorbed in the music. He enjoyed DeGaetani's fine technique, her perfect diction and the delicate spirit of her interpretation.

Eastman School students were triple-cast in the opera productions at the Eastman Theatre. So Peter had to take on the task of singing *Don Giovanni* in a production. His laconic comment afterwards: 'The role is not that difficult.' But he did encounter some challenges. At the end of each academic year, the advanced students were given a special opportunity to prove their skills. The Chautauqua Institution in south-western New York State hosted an extensive cultural programme for nine weeks each summer.

The non-profit educational institution is part of the Protestant tradition, with roots dating back to the second half of the nineteenth century. Originally founded as a Sunday school, after a successful start it expanded its programme. Music came to play an increasingly important role. At first, a concert series was added to the programme, and then in 1929 the Chautauqua Symphony Orchestra and the Chautauqua Opera Company were founded. The main venue is the open-air amphitheatre, whose stage and auditorium are protected from rain and sun, but whose sides are open.[35]

In 1968 Chautauqua established the Young Artist Program.[36] 'A summer camp for middle-class people who wanted to spend their summer in a kind of outdoor environment with cultural offerings. Very bizarre,' Jonas described the atmosphere. 'Eastman and the other music schools would supply cannon fodder to form the staff for the productions. No irony!'

Peter was clearly an advanced student, and his teachers encouraged him to apply for a production. What followed was a 'great summer of 1974, a great learning curve' for him.

Fig. 22: Peter Jonas in *West Side Story*, Chautauqua/New York, 1974

Peter auditioned for *West Side Story*. They were looking for dancers who could also sing reasonably well. That seemed to be a good fit. And so he played Gee-Tar, one of the Jets who consider New York's West Side to be their territory. To do it, he completed an unexpectedly tough training course. He had to get really fit for the role in a short time. 'It was incredibly enjoyable. I didn't really have a performing bug, I wasn't really a committed performer, but I enjoyed the piece, enjoyed doing it, the physical exhaustion. I enjoyed being fit, the discipline, that you have to be doing it every third night.'

This is what an older Jonas had to say about himself at the age of twenty-seven, about a young man at the height of his powers – and shortly before he learned of his cancer. The photograph of Peter Jonas as Gee-Tar in *West Side Story* is precious. Only a few years later, the record of pictures showing him full of life and bursting with strength would dry up.

In his second role, that of Doctor Grenvil in *La Traviata*, he shared the stage with the legendary Karan Armstrong in the role of Violetta. And of course her husband Götz Friedrich also attended the performances. Alongside him, Jonas would fight the closure of one of Berlin's three opera houses twenty-six years later, just weeks before Friedrich's death. Together with the couple, Peter and his girlfriend Patricia Ann Richards went on excursions into the countryside.

Clearly, his scholarship at the Eastman School helped him build his international network. But this time also came to an end. 'I realised that the endless paid study leave was coming to an end. There can't be more free lunches.'

His visa expired, and so Peter returned to England at the end of August 1973 together with Patricia. His girlfriend wanted to follow Peter's example and study at the Royal College. Both first came to live with his mother, who still kept up the family's former residence in Sanderstead. There, something unusual happened: his mother rejected Patricia immediately, profoundly and irrevocably. Peter had never seen her react to someone like that, aside from Pauline, with whom her husband had started an affair during their marriage. So Peter had to leave home early and seek alternative accommodation for himself and Patricia in London. To enable her to get a visa in England, the two got married.

Schönberg op 31 Variations for Orchestra

What now? 'I didn't know what the hell to do,' Jonas said in retrospect, summing up his situation as a highly qualified young professional in London's cultural life. It was clear that to complete his scholarship, which he had officially ended with a Licentiate in Singing in July 1973, he had to go to a final interview with the Director of the Royal College of Music. As before, Keith Falkner held Peter in high regard. Of course, Falkner first wanted to find out what Peter had experienced and learned during the months in Rochester. But he would not have been the conscientious and devoted director his companions described him if he had not also taken an interest in Peter's future. Jonas acted out their conversation: 'Well, what are you going to do with this great education?' Falkner asked him. The implicit instruction that he should make something of his training was clear. For the first time, albeit in the disguise of Falkner's words, Jonas was letting slip how damn good his training had really been. And he, the young professional, had had the chutzpah to answer his director: 'I want to run an orchestra or an opera house.'

Falkner kept his composure and replied to him: 'Well, Peter, I wonder if you are aware that things are a bit more complicated.'

'A bit more complicated' – a quintessentially British way of expressing in four words that Peter hoped for something presumptuous, impossible, even. Peter countered by listing the places where he had already worked, which singers and directors he had seen; in short, that he knew how a theatre is run.

'I was so naïve,' Jonas judged himself as a young graduate. When he prepared for the interview, he had applied the exclusion principle: that he could not become a singer, a dancer or a musician was clear. So what was left? For him, with his in-depth knowledge of the repertoire and inner workings of these institutions?

He now felt like a prisoner who no longer felt comfortable living on the outside. 'I feel comfortable in institutions. I like their rules and structures. That there is a building. I felt like that at boarding school. I never wanted to be a freelancer. Once I was offered the directorship of the Salzburg Festival. That's not for me.' He produced a violent choking noise to express how alien the festival business was to him. 'A festival en plus on top of regular business, gladly! I like the prison of the institution, of repertory. Later I became a great advocate of repertory theatre. To work within the rules, das hat mich interessiert.'

During his conversation with Falkner, Peter had no idea just how soon he would find himself having to function in a business of that kind. Falkner answered him: 'I can help you with this, just a little bit. I am very friendly with the director of the Royal

Opera House Covent Garden, John Tooley. At least, we can get your foot in the door. You are a clever student, you have done well, even if you are an odd case. I will tell him he should see you for an hour. But it will take time.' That was a promising prospect, but the question of how he should earn a living was still not settled.

In September 1974 he applied to Lord Harewood at English National Opera, whom he would succeed ten years later. 'Dear Lord Harewood, I am writing to ask if I could possibly have an interview with you to seek your advice,' Jonas wrote rather awkwardly on 16 September 1974. 'My ambition is to work in opera administration. I am fully aware that there are few openings in this field and that one has to knock on as many doors as possible; therefore, I would be very grateful if I could see you; even if you know of no openings at present.' Quite logically, Harewood's assistant offered him a job, albeit in the choir, as Jonas had a degree in singing. His application for a job in management was not considered.

Peter decided to start as a substitute teacher. At that time, university graduates could take on positions like that in the state school system without further teacher training. But it was a hard gig. He was sent to Croydon, to one of the roughest schools in one of the roughest areas of London. Officially, he was supposed to be teaching, but in reality it was to prevent the students from killing each other, he claimed. There were constant fights, some involving knives. 'It was so rough I can't tell you. I wasn't prepared for that. One day a girl raised her hand and asked to go to the toilet. When she didn't come back after five minutes, I had to ask a second girl to bring her back. The second girl found the first on the floor of the school corridor, covered in blood. She had given birth to a child in the meantime. No one had known she was pregnant!'

Not even the dangerous jobs he took during his studies in Manchester to pay off his debts could compare. He claimed that he had never been so exhausted at the end of a day, but he could no longer remember which subject he was supposed to be teaching. It was probably English.

After months of waiting, the longed-for call finally came from

John Tooley's secretary, who invited Peter to Covent Garden for an interview. After intensive questioning, Tooley offered Peter the chance to start as an apprentice at Covent Garden. Peter would first work in ticket sales, then in accounting, and later in stage management, gradually working his way through all the departments. But Peter would have to wait for that, because there was no money at the moment as the budget had been cut. 'But you are definitely on the list.'

So Peter waited for a second call. Once again he was asked to talk. There was still no money to hire him. Instead, Tooley asked him if he knew the Chicago Symphony Orchestra? Did Jonas know Solti? What a question!

From 1961 to 1971 Georg Solti had been Music Director of the Royal Opera Covent Garden. Peter had regularly attended performances under his direction, back when he was regularly travelling to London with Antony and Max Sebald. Georg Solti had a legendary assistant: Enid Blech. Peter Jonas described her as a 'sophisticated woman' who impressed him not only with her work for Solti – 'She knew everyone, everyone knew her' – but also because she drove a Peugeot 504 sports coupé, a convertible, silver, with red leather upholstery: what more need be said? Peter vaguely knew her son Robin: he had been at boarding school with Antony Costley-White and Mark Elder.

Like Solti, Enid Blech was of Jewish descent. She created a family atmosphere around Solti, which Norman Lebrecht described in his study of the Royal Opera House. 'Enid held court in Solti's antechamber,' Lady Valerie Solti said of her husband's assistant. 'She smoked cheroots, made excellent black coffee and spoke fluent Italian, so artists from the continent were always hanging around her.'[37]

Above all, Enid Blech tried to keep all troubles and turbulence away from Solti. She is said to have distracted Schönberg's widow from Solti with shopping trips in London. Another time, during a performance of *Siegfried*, a visitor is said to have disturbed Solti by coughing. The visitor had dropped the sweet that Solti had given him after the first act and coughed on – until Enid Blech offered him her seat in a more distant row during the next interval.[38]

In 1969, when Solti became Chief Conductor of the Chicago Symphony Orchestra, he asked Enid Blech, who was married to conductor Harry Blech, to continue working for him there as well. But in 1973, she fell seriously ill. Solti looked for a replacement for the next three months, but could not find an adequate person in Chicago. Perhaps he, a native Hungarian, had not wanted to find anyone there either. Jonas suspected that Solti wanted to fill this position with a European.

Together with the general manager of the Chicago Symphony Orchestra John Edwards, Solti had in any case turned to John Tooley and asked for help. Tooley could not spare any staff, but mentioned Peter's name, not without pointing out that this excellently trained and presentable young man had one flaw: he had no experience at management level at all.

Solti thought about it for two long days before he invited Peter to his home for tea. The two talked for an hour and a half until Solti bid Peter farewell with the promise that he would receive news from John Tooley by the following evening.

Peter had gone home with a good impression of the conversation. Solti had been extremely friendly towards him. Peter had become acquainted for the first time with what he would dub Solti's 'Hungarian manners'. As promised, Tooley contacted Peter. Solti might like Peter, Tooley explained, but he wasn't sure yet. Solti was expecting Edwards to visit London, and Peter was to meet them both at Solti's house in two days: 'I wanted a job. I was excited. Remember how naïve I was. I thought it was a great chance.'

'A great chance' seems to have been Jonas's way of saying that he was really taking something seriously. Two days later he went to Solti's house again. John Edwards had already arrived, 'a legend! He was a strange-looking man, as broad as he was tall. Monstrously fat and small with a broad smile. Because he was so round, he was completely immobile.' They talked for a long time until Edwards had to leave. When Solti sent Peter off, the all-important question arose, the moment of decision: 'Everyone praises you for your knowledge of music. What do you know about Schönberg's op. 31 Variations for Orchestra?' And Peter told what little he knew about Schönberg's first orchestral work composed following a purely dodecaphonic technique.

Solti promised that he would get back to him within twenty-four hours. He did. Georg Solti opted for Peter Jonas. The offer was conveyed to him by John Tooley: Jonas was to be given a three-month contract to replace Enid Blech. Departure in four days. 'I said: "Sure." And off I went.'

His wife Patricia stayed in London. Things were not going well in their marriage.

Enid Blech was never to resume her work with Solti. She died in 1977. The Chicago Symphony Orchestra commemorated her with a memorial concert on 10 July 1977.

CHICAGO 1974–1984

Sir Georg Solti and the Chicago Symphony Orchestra

In November 1974, Peter Jonas flew to Chicago for the first time in his life. 'I got on the plane with a suitcase that had a suit and a pair of jeans, nothing else.' For the short duration of his contract with the Chicago Symphony Orchestra (CSO), he was planning to keep up his flat in London. His wife Patricia was staying there.

His year in Rochester had prepared Jonas for the American way of life. His beloved cousin Monica lived in New York, so he was not completely adrift in a foreign land. But when he saw Chicago for the first time in the clear light of that sunny day, he was overwhelmed: 'It was breathtaking. I was not prepared for this beauty. The architecture of classical modernism struck me like an aesthetic lightning bolt. The administration got me two rooms in a hotel on East Delaware Place, nice, not too expensive. This was a beautiful street right on Lake Michigan, centrally located in one of the finest areas of Chicago.' Not far away was Orchestra Hall. His later love of architecture stemmed in large part from these early impressions of Chicago: 'you can't not be impressed. Every morning when I went to work, I stood in Delaware Place in front of the John Hancock Center. I was thrilled, totally thrilled.'

Chicago's skyline was indeed imposing: the Skidmore, Owings & Merrill skyscraper, completed in 1968, with its one hundred floors, was the second tallest building in the world at the time. A year before Jonas's arrival in Chicago, in 1973, the Sears Tower had been opened, which, at 442 metres, was to remain the tallest building in the world for three decades.

At that time, Chicago was the most populous city in the USA after New York, with around 3.6 million inhabitants. Affluent people moved into the newly created suburbs during this period, and social segregation and structural discrimination were increasingly afflicting disadvantaged groups, the African American population in particular. When Jonas arrived in Chicago in 1974, the city was suffering from structural change in industry: many people lost their jobs during the steel crisis in the recession years 1973 to 1975. Poverty and crime were on the rise, and the violent events surrounding the Democratic National Convention of August 1968, when anti-Vietnam demonstrators and other protest groups had fought the police for eight days, were far from a settled matter.

So Peter Jonas was among the privileged part of Chicago when he took his first job with one of the most renowned orchestras in the United States. 'On my first day at work, I was very excited,' Jonas recalled. 'I arrived an hour before rehearsals started and had to find my office very quickly. Everyone was nice and friendly, and of course a bit curious: who is this new guy? What experience does he have? Can he even speak English? And then Solti arrived twenty minutes before rehearsal began. I remember the scene very clearly!'

Solti usually appeared in the company of his second wife Valerie, whom Jonas had already met in London. 'Valerie came to me and asked me: "Have you ever really heard them? Before you start working, you simply have to listen to them. Just sit down in the hall."'

The first piece that the CSO rehearsed that day was Tchaikovsky's *Fifth Symphony*. 'I remember it so vividly. I entered the hall, and the members of the orchestra looked at me so strangely: "Who is this new person?"'

Finally, Solti also entered the hall and greeted the orchestra, which he had not seen for several months. Then he introduced Jonas: 'Oh, by the way: don't worry about him. He's just my temporary assistant.' Jonas's position in the orchestra was clearly defined: he may have been Solti's assistant and thus endowed with certain privileges, but for only a limited time.

The rehearsal began: 'I was completely taken aback. The orchestra and its brass made a hell of a noise, but with a precision I was not used to. The sound was very impressive, although a little too direct. When the orchestra played forte' – Jonas imitated the violinists while remembering and hummed the theme from Tchaikovsky's *Fifth Symphony* – 'when the cellos played in unison, I felt minimised, I had become a tiny little person, hidden away in the violin. Someone was playing the violin, and I was inside it: the only person in the hall. I will never forget this experience on my first day.'

On top of all this, a troubling detail. When the suburban and underground trains passed near Orchestra Hall, the entire hall shook. 'You also have this effect in London, but I only really felt it in Chicago, on the very first day of work. The strings played as if possessed, in einem fantastischen Unisono [in fantastic unison], and every now and then the lines of the S-Bahn and the U-Bahn crossed under the hall and made this venerable, beautiful concert hall shudder.'

The rest of his first day was a nightmare, Jonas said by way of summary. 'I didn't know what to do, I had no idea what the hell I was doing there. I was so naïve, but I just loved the sound of the orchestra. I was completely captivated by it.'

The reputation of the CSO was legendary even then. Its story began in 1889 when Theodore Thomas, one of the leading conductors in America, was invited by Chicago businessman Charles Norman Fay to found a symphony orchestra in Chicago. Thomas gave his first concerts in 1889 and served as music director until his death in 1905. He died just three weeks after the inauguration of Orchestra Hall, the home of the CSO, which was designed by Daniel Burnham. Theodore Thomas was followed by Frederick Stock, Désiré Defauw, Artur Rodzinski, Rafael Kubelík, Fritz Reiner, whose recordings with the CSO are still considered legendary, and also by Jean Martinon. They were all extraordinarily successful conductors.

But Sir Georg Solti's stint as their musical director proved one of the CSO's most fruitful musical partnerships. Under his direction in the years from 1969 to 1991, the orchestra consolidated its position as one of the 'Big Five', the five leading orchestras in the

United States. Donald Peck, principal flute of the CSO, described the collaboration between Solti and the orchestra as an exceptional bond: 'Solti made use of the orchestra's greatness to advance his own world reputation, but at the same time took the orchestra with him in this venture, thereby making it an internationally recognized icon'.[1] In 1970, the orchestra made its first tour under Solti's direction, down the East Coast. The performance of Mahler's *Fifth Symphony*, Peck said, was hailed as the musical event of the year. It marked the moment when the combination of 'Solti' and 'Chicago' became unbeatable.[2] Eighteen months after Solti started in the role, the orchestra embarked on its first European tour. Audiences were ecstatic. Further tours to Europe, Japan and, naturally, New York followed. Numerous award-winning recordings were made, which received a total of twenty-five Grammys.[3]

The organisational structure of American cultural institutions differs from those in many other countries, but its difference from German norms is particularly deep. The structure of the CSO results from the way the orchestra finances itself. The orchestra is subordinated to a Board of Trustees, which was founded in 1890 and is known at the CSO as the Orchestral Association of Chicago. The Orchestral Association assumes the function of a supervisory council and also acts as a patron for the orchestra: it aims to finance the orchestra itself or else to raise financial support for it. The city of Chicago only offers a small subsidy to the body. That means that the Orchestral Association also assumes all financial risks. It is also responsible for the orchestra's different departments.

When Peter Jonas took office, this included the music department, the Civic Orchestra of Chicago training orchestra, the Orchestra Hall building, the Chicago Symphony Chorus and the administration. John Edwards, born in 1912, was the Executive Vice President and general manager. He had previously worked at the Pittsburgh Symphony Orchestra and the National Symphony Orchestra in Washington and was considered the doyen of artistic directors of American symphony orchestras. He took over operational management from 1967 until his death in 1984. Jonas worked directly under him. 'Any orchestra that ends their season with a surplus is doing something wrong,'[4] was his battle-tested credo. He was alluding to the then-common practice of general managers informing the Board at the end of the year about what was basically a planned deficit. They justified the deficit to the Board and received a cheque to make up the shortfall. 'Those days were over when I came to Chicago,' Jonas recalled. 'No one was pulling out the chequebook any more when there was trouble.'

Fig. 23: Peter Jonas and John Edwards

Edwards was an exceptional talent among music managers. He was universally respected. Colleagues such as Donald Peck praised Edwards as an excellent person and music lover. Georg Solti, in turn, honoured John Edwards after his death as a person 'with infinite wisdom to whom I often turned. And his advice, not always what I wanted to hear, was in the long term always right.'[5] Edwards and Jonas surely had a wonderful working relationship and friendship, although Edwards was first a supervisor and mentor to Jonas, and taught the younger man his craft. 'Peter

Jonas and John Edwards shared the work beautifully,' said Daniel Barenboim, who performed regularly in Chicago. 'When it seemed to make more sense for John to take on a task, then Peter let him do it. But if he felt he had to do the task himself, he simply took it on. They were always perfectly coordinated, a dream team at work!'[6]

Edwards was appointed CSO by the legendary Louis Sudler. Sudler was President of the Board of Trustees and Chairman of the Orchestral Association from 1966 to 1976 and played a decisive role in Solti's appointment. From 1976 to 1992, Sudler served as so-called Chairman Emeritus. He was a Chicago real estate magnate and philanthropist who had previously worked as a singer with the Civic Opera House of Chicago. His company operated out of the John Hancock Center on East Delaware Place, which Jonas looked at every morning on his way to work. 'He was a WASP,' Jonas told me with undisguised mirth. 'A White Anglo-Saxon Protestant. He was a powerful businessman in Chicago, a patriarchal figure in public life.'

Jonas met him shortly after his arrival, when the powerful Sudler suddenly walked into his tiny office unannounced and explained the laws of the Chicago cultural world to him. Of course, Sudler was interested in getting to know Solti's assistant, no matter how briefly the young man was to stay. For all that Jonas was still a lightweight, he now finally had an influential position in the music director's inner circle: 'I had the privileges of a gatekeeper. I shielded Solti and selectively passed on information and requests to him.' In Jonas's memory, Sudler was a tall man with white hair and a good figure 'for his age'. 'I had been warned to be exceedingly polite.' Sudler asked about Jonas's background, but not really in detail, as they chatted. Jonas spoke of how deeply he admired the institution, the orchestra itself, Solti and Edwards. He explained to Sudler that the short while he had spent there so far had already made a great impression on him. Sudler listened quietly.

Finally Sudler looked him straight in the eye and began to speak: 'There is something very important I have to tell you.

This is not advice. This is just a simple explanation of how things stand here. It is very simple. Catholics work in the administration and management. In the orchestra, they are all Jews. We, the Orchestra Association, we keep the whole thing going. We are all Protestants.' That explained the world and its rules. Jonas had to fit into the entrenched, hierarchical structure of Chicago society. Had Solti – consciously or unconsciously – taken care to conform to this scheme when he chose the Catholic Peter Jonas? 'This had to be a kind of coincidence,' Jonas believed. This 'coincidence' revealed an implicit rule that more or less corresponded to reality in the USA at the time, a rule that the powerful wanted to uphold.

Jonas also recalled the efforts of a wealthy, influential African American who wanted to become a member of the 'club', as Jonas called the Board of Trustees: 'It just didn't happen. That's the point.' This structure did later begin to disintegrate. But when Peter Jonas arrived in Chicago, the old-fashioned values of the 1950s still prevailed there. 'I cannot emphasise enough how naïve I was. I was so naïve! The profession, the level of the Chicago Symphony, Solti. The musical pinnacle of this institution! I was well trained, I knew that. But I had no idea how a business like this worked. Why had they chosen me?'

There was no false modesty here. He would later express his amazement that as a young man he had been given this totally unexpected opportunity to stand in for an ailing Enid Blech at the CSO, for just three months.[7] These three months became eleven years. Jonas saw himself as a late developer: in his view, these eleven years were the formative, decisive time for his professional life. Jonas met famous conductors and artists, later negotiated their fees and contracts, expanded his international networks and tried out innovative concert programmes. He was still benefiting from this deep knowledge of the US music world during his tenure at the Bavarian Staatsoper: 'In Chicago I learned my profession, its practical side. The Chicago Symphony is not an opera house, but the working method of how to run the institution as a cultural enterprise is identical.'

Simply starting

In Chicago, Jonas would work a seven-day week. The orchestra gave concerts from Thursday to Saturday, and rehearsed on Mondays and Tuesdays. On Sundays, the Orchestral Association hosted other music events in the concert hall. Rehearsals lasted two and a half hours with a twenty-five-minute break. The rehearsal rules had to be published one week in advance and could not be changed after that. 'I had no chance at all to talk to Enid Blech, whom I was supposed to represent: no chance to have her explain what I had to do,' Jonas reflected on his inner turmoil at the outset of the job. 'I was totally confused. But over the course of the next few days, it became clear what was really important.' Very clear, in fact: anything that involved Solti took the highest priority. When Solti arrived in Chicago in 1969, he found the city in an enchanted slumber. The boom of the post-war years had evaporated. The city was somewhat isolated from America's eastern seaboard, and indeed from the rest of the world, Solti recalled in his memoirs. European newspapers usually arrived days late. The Chicago Orchestra was like a beloved but neglected piece of furniture, Solti wrote. It was clear that this role would be the one of which Solti felt proudest. Under his leadership, the orchestra's international reputation rose to the highest level, the people of Chicago were finally proud of their orchestra, and the musicians were financially secure. For Solti, his years with the CSO were the happiest time of his professional life. 'Being in charge of the Chicago Symphony was the fulfilment of my dreams, but at the same time it was a new learning experience for me, a masterclass in musical directorship.'

Solti was artistically responsible for the CSO: he was its figurehead. He came from the European tradition. His path from Munich via Frankfurt to London had been made up of work in institutions where the experts knew their roles inside out before they started.

Fig. 24: Peter Jonas and Sir Georg Solti

As his assistant, one of Jonas's main tasks was to translate Solti's concerns, whether artistic or logistical, into terms that fit with the administration's traditional ways of thinking and working. In London, Solti had grown used to having his requests carried out promptly. In Chicago, things were different. The administration was organised like a business school. Everyone was terribly polite to one another, but everything was also a bit slow, Jonas recalled: 'Solti, with his Hungarian temperament, was used to only having to snap his fingers: We shall do this, this and this! In Europe, all the staff knew what that meant. In Chicago, however, many in the administration reacted with a polite: 'Oh, yes, Maestro! Very nice. We will see to it,' but nothing happened. I had to make sure that his commands got through to these people and that they reacted as quickly as he acted.'

Solti had been known in London for his insistence on high professional standards. He is said to have swept through the Royal Opera House like a whirlwind, 'a hum of cosmic energy that brooked no resistance',[8] according to Norman Lebrecht. Donald Peck also confirmed this in his memoirs: Solti was constantly looking for new ways of doing things. He was never satisfied with what had gone before.[9] In Chicago, Solti, Sudler and Edwards created a completely different atmosphere at the Orchestra Hall, Peck reported.[10] In Louis Sudler, who had brought Solti to the CSO, he saw a man of vision.[11] Edwards was a bachelor and a bon vivant, enormously well read. He loved people, going to parties and talking about the orchestra. Solti compared him to Mr Pickwick, the character from Charles Dickens's novel. On the evenings of performances, Edwards stood in the entrance hall of Orchestra Hall and welcomed the guests. The orchestra was his whole life, and his office on the seventh floor of Orchestra Hall was as much his home as his workplace.[12] 'We were the joint parents of a large family,' Solti wrote, 'and whatever else we may or may not have achieved, we gave the orchestra the feeling of being a family.'[13]

Like Jonas later, Solti also preferred the atmosphere of 'family houses', orchestras and opera houses where people share more than just work; institutions where all employees create a whole life together, through common work and annual rhythms.

For Jonas, the fact that Solti's commands took time to filter through to Chicago staff was also a result of Solti's English: he spoke the British English of a Hungarian who had worked in Germany and now spoke to Americans: 'My dear everybody' is how Solti is said to have greeted the orchestra.

Jonas also got to feel the different mentalities. 'I arrived in the morning, ready to start work, and was greeted with a "Hi, Peter, how are you today? Let's have a cup of coffee. How is it going?"' Jonas spoke slowly and ever-so-softly. It was a pleasure for him to imitate his former colleagues, and he liked to stage re-enactments of old conversations, probably always a mixture of fiction and truth.

In Chicago, the beat was different than in Europe, colleagues did not regard Solti's ideas as being as urgent as Jonas thought. 'The people who worked in the arts in America also saw it as a job in business, not as a burning artistic mission. So it was very different from what I had imagined. I quickly got used to it.'

Jonas offered a list of examples that vividly illustrate just how many different things he had to learn, quickly and independently.

Right at the start of his career in Chicago, there was a performance of *Salomé*, which was also to be performed during the tour in New York with Birgit Nilsson in the leading role. This was new material for the CSO. The orchestra was not used to opera. Thanks to their skill, professionalism and discipline, Solti and the orchestra managed to prepare the opera over the course of four days of rehearsals. During one of these rehearsals, Solti was dissatisfied with five performers and demanded a separate rehearsal for them. Jonas was to take over: what might not sound like a big deal became a real problem for Jonas. 'I never rehearsed an ensemble!' How was the time of the rehearsal to be fixed, how should he find a room, who would play the piano, how would the singers be kept informed? It wasn't so much that that these tasks were too demanding in themselves – they were clear enough, but how should he carry them out at the CSO?

British tenor John Lanigan recognised Jonas's distress and showed him how to lead the rehearsal: decide the time and place, inform everyone, draw up a schedule, drive the whole thing with a steady hand. Jonas managed it by the skin of his teeth. It was an enormously good learning experience, was his later taciturn comment.

Jonas immediately understood that in many cases he was the only one who could implement Solti's needs, because he had Solti's trust, subliminally at least. On one occasion, Solti approached him with a request to assist him in writing an extremely important, confidential letter concerning a recording contract. Solti did not want to entrust the text to anyone else. 'To be honest, yes, I knew how to formulate the letter. Solti had given me precise instructions. But I couldn't type! I had learned an incredible amount at all those elite schools, but how to write with a typewriter, how to format a letter, I hadn't learned that.'

Fig. 25: A dedicated door sign for Peter Jonas

In the evening, when everyone else had left, he had no choice but to sit down at his desk – equipped with a typewriter, of course – and slowly and systematically work his way through all the tasks. 'In my own, slightly autistic way, I was working out my own little system.' Only in this way, with diligence, discipline and working through the night, was he able to make his way through his list of near-disasters, as he called them. Jonas was not alone during his long nights at the typewriter. One of the security guards watched over him, checked in on him from time to time and asked how he was doing. And Tom Mulligan, who had just started his own limousine service and looked after the conductors of the Chicago Symphony, would also help him out. Jonas could ask him anything, because Mulligan knew the business inside out.

'Slowly I found my feet. But what still amazes me is that everyone assumed I had experience. They didn't know that I had none at all! Everything I had done before, working in the music shop, in Glyndebourne, all those things were easy compared to what I had to deal with at the CSO. This was not only my first or second day at the Chicago Symphony, but my first or second day of work ever! It was an incredibly hard start, very scary.'

The Rosenthal Archives of the CSO contain numerous memoranda and letters by Peter Jonas from this period: Jonas often spent pages summarising conversations with partners and working out the most important content for his next meeting with Solti and Edwards. He drew up the agenda for their meetings: 'GS/JSE/PHVienna 13/16 1977'.[14] In these papers the reader finds little idiosyncrasies of Jonas's: the first item on the agenda at this meeting was 'Sir Georg Solti personal situation viz (sic) CSO'.[15] Jonas had also put Solti's residency status in the USA, the new contract for Solti and the Japan tour on the list. Last: 'Peter Jonas … future situation'.[16] The archival documents show that Jonas neatly jotted down all the points and added comments, but even then he allowed himself little idiosyncrasies. He writes 'viz', talks about 'kiddies' in the mediation programme, signs sometimes with 'Pedro', sometimes with 'Petrus' and an elaborate cross and always puts lots of dots, exclamation marks and even more question marks. In one document, the item 'Next meeting' is followed by twenty-five question marks.[17] His ample annotations ended only when Linda Dominguez started working for him as an assistant and he could dictate his texts to her.

The correspondence preserved in the archive paints an eloquent picture of how Jonas's professional network developed. He was in contact with all the artists who worked with the orchestra, but also their agencies: with Rafael Kubelík, André Previn, Charles Mackerras, Brigitte Hohmann, Vladimir Ashkenazy, János Ferencsik, Wolfgang Rennert, Erich Leinsdorf, Claudio Abbado, Kazuhiro Koizumi, Evgeny Svetlanov, Edo de Waart, Carlos Kleiber, Barbara Hendricks, Alexis Weissenberg, Christa Ludwig, Giuseppe Sinopoli, Steven de Groote and many others.[18] He sent out contracts; his cover letters began with the usual formulas such as 'I have the greatest of pleasure' or 'This is to confirm to you'.[19] He wrote welcome letters to Kiri Te Kanawa and Bernd Weikl – 'Welcome to the windy city of Chicago' – which were delivered directly to the Palmer House Hotel next door or even to the Ritz Carlton.[20]

He would write identical thank-you letters, sometimes in

Italian, and he negotiated with agents such as David Schiffmann, HarrisonParrott, Marie di Anders and, most importantly of all, with Ann Colbert, who was one of Solti's closest advisors. Many letters and telegrams also went back and forth between him and Eva Wagner-Pasquier, who worked on the films with Solti at Unitel. He had the authority to set engagements and rehearsal schedules and he recorded the level of fees he had agreed with Edwards. Handwritten lists showed the fees of the artists under contract. Jonas worked with them daily.[21]

His intimate knowledge of the fees helped him enormously later, during the discussions with Zubin Mehta before he took up his post at the Staatsoper. This knowledge offered a basis for him to successfully negotiate with Mehta's lawyer.

The correspondence also reveals who ceased to be 'just' a colleague. The tone of Jonas's letters to Carlos Kleiber became increasingly friendly over the years: 'Chicago at the moment is an endless vision of snow and more snow and "cabin fever" seems to have gripped everybody to an unusual degree.'[22]

In this letter, sent in February 1978, Jonas also told of Lucia Popp, his great love, of reading the latest novels by Iris Murdoch – it must have been *The Sea, The Sea* – whose unique English prose he had begun to admire, so distinct from the normal run of contemporary literature. And Jonas confessed: 'I miss Europe so much and only count the days until I can return. I feel like an exile here who goes through a period of oblivion before he can return to his native land, but a talent for oblivion is after all a talent for survival (a Murdoch-inspired phrase).'[23]

Both the friendship with Claudio Abbado and the decades-long, intense friendship with Daniel Barenboim began in Chicago; 'Dear Danny',[24] Jonas wrote in a letter from December 1984. By this time, he had already slept at Barenboim's place after a party in his flat. 'When my first wife fell ill, it was very, very hard for me. Peter was an incredible support for me,' Barenboim reported.

In 1987 Barenboim's first wife, the cellist Jacqueline du Pré, passed away. Jonas was one of the few people Barenboim let near him during this time.

First tour to New York

When John Edwards discussed the concert programme for the coming weeks and the upcoming tour to New York with Jonas shortly after he had started work, the young man came to realise the extent of the organisational tasks that lay before him. The insight left Jonas rather disillusioned. He would have little to do with artistic or dramaturgical questions. His hopes of finding a long-term home in the music or opera business still seemed remote. So he busied himself about his tasks and did what he had to do. He organised the logistics of the tour to New York, prepared the payment of the daily allowances to the singers and discussed with his colleagues in New York how Carnegie Hall should be set up for the concerts. There were complications every day, and like many others, he found that the experience of dealing with them helped him grow.

The tour to New York turned out to be a huge adventure, and also a shock – but an inspiring, enticing shock. First of all, Jonas was amazed by the sheer number of people, around one hundred and fifty, who travelled to New York in December. 'We set off like a circus troupe or medieval army' as Solti put it, 'with orchestra members accompanied by their families, from small babies to grandparents, and some of the trustees and supporters.'[25]

Peter Jonas was overwhelmed by the reaction of the New York audience. The reason was not only the musical excellence of the orchestra, but also the extremely clever public relations work, masterminded by Kenneth Utz. Jonas described him as always being relaxed, and never getting excited: someone who liked to lean back in his office chair and put his feet up on the table. He is said never to have spoken quickly or been seen to be in a rush, which is hard to imagine today. After months of work, Utz had managed the incredible coup of getting Sir Georg on the cover of *Time* magazine in May 1973. 'Solti on the cover, you can't overstate how valuable that was! Ken arbeitete extrem effektiv [worked most effectively],' Jonas enthused as he retold the story.[26]

The cover shows Solti in the middle of a downstroke, with his impressive, highly concentrated face and its dark eyes directed into the distance, probably at a musician, his eyebrows raised, his brow furrowed, his collar turned up and, in his right hand, his baton painted yellow and pointing emphatically up into the corner of the cover. The headline, also in yellow, read: 'The Fastest Baton in the West' and 'Chicago's Georg Solti', a soup of consonants in which the names of the conductor, the city and the orchestra all seem to merge into one.

'When I saw the impact his work had, I understood why Kenneth had worked so hard for that cover. It was a massive thing, on everyone's lips.'

For Solti, the cover piece offered a different kind of satisfaction. Five years earlier, *Time* magazine had already honoured Zubin Mehta, who was a full twenty-four years younger than Solti, with a cover picture: 'The Baton is passed to Youth.' This had offended Solti, who had spent years locked in a legal battle with Dorothy Chandler of the Board of the Los Angeles Philharmonic Orchestra. The subject of the lawsuit was the contract Chandler had signed with Zubin Mehta without seeking Solti's prior agreement as the orchestra's designated general music director. The steps Jonas took to get Mehta to perform with the CSO, despite this feud, led more than two decades later to Mehta being selected for the post of General Music Director of the Bavarian Staatsoper.

For New Yorkers, the CSO visit traditionally marked the high point of the musical season. The orchestra's concerts at Carnegie Hall were always eagerly awaited. Sumptuous evening events followed the Chicagoans' performances. An eminent figure in the midst of all this was Terence McEwen, the American head of London Records, the classical music division of Decca Records. McEwen, who would later become artistic director of the San Francisco Opera, was once described as an enormously charming, self-indulgent and fun-loving person who invited people to glittering parties at Trader Vic's, the legendary mid-town bar, 'where they served Polynesian food and Mai Tais, which were still quite exotic at the time'.

Terence McEwen hosted one of these parties after the performance of *Salomé* on 18 December 1974. Still horribly inexperienced, Jonas left his wallet with important papers, including his driving licence, in his room at the Sheraton Hotel. He had assumed he would not need these things at the party. That was true, but what he didn't know was that, at that time, rooms at the Sheraton were frequently being robbed. When he returned late at night, his valuables had disappeared. This happened to him only once. Mark Elder, Peter's friend from his student years and later music director at English National Opera, also lost his wallet once when he worked with Solti at the Royal Opera Covent Garden. Solti generously reimbursed him for all the money lost.[27] It is not clear whether Jonas received similar help: possibly he concealed the incident from Solti.

From his time at the CSO; from seeing the way Solti put together the programme with Edwards and other colleagues; from hearing how they discussed the demands of the press and marketing, Jonas became acquainted with a way of thinking and working that he would reproduce as artistic director at English National Opera, and perfect at the Bavarian Staatsoper.

Solti had first encountered the Chicago press in 1969, a few months before he took office. He had given an interview to the *Chicago Tribune* in which he expressed his displeasure about the orchestra's age structure. He found himself dogged by the consequences of this piece for some time thereafter.[28]

Claudia Cassidy, one of the most influential critics of her time, also wrote for the *Tribune*. She is said to have hated mediocrity of any kind and she was known for the caustic tone of her reviews when a performance disappointed her. This had earned her the nickname 'Acidy Cassidy'. Jonas was thinking of Cassidy's power when he and his female collaborators at ENO dealt with the London press.

Solti was deeply concerned that his concerts should not only be successful in terms of ticket sales, but also in terms of press. He did not like the subscription structure that the CSO had offered at the beginning of his tenure. In particular, he wanted to change the subscription arrangements for Friday afternoons, which he saw as a concession to the wives of rich patrons. The lukewarm, restrained applause he perceived in his early years irked him. He preferred to be booed, he wrote in his memoirs. He did not want his concerts to represent the fulfilment of some social convention: he thought that each concert should be a unique musical experience.[29]

Solti did not only pursue his vision in terms of the music. He consulted what he called his 'brains trust', an informal body of employees who enjoyed his confidence. These included John Edwards, Peter Jonas, Ann Colbert with her artists' agency and Edgar Vincent, the legendary PR agent who has worked with many giants of the opera world, including Plácido Domingo and Birgit Nilsson. The CSO had appointed Vincent to handle press relations in New York: 'It had to be done by a local expert, no matter how well known you were,' Jonas explained. 'New York still works like that. All previews and portraits in the major newspapers are arranged by press agents on behalf of the artists.'

The work of the 'brains trust' fascinated Jonas. For him it became like a university of marketing. Box-set aficionado that he was, Jonas naturally thought of *Mad Men* and its unhinged marketing executives. Jonas would bring this expertise with him to Europe. 'Credit for Georg Solti,' Jonas would later say by way of homage to his first boss, who also became his mentor. This lesson – that one ought always to address programming and marketing together at once – was not the only piece of wisdom Solti would impart.

Ann Colbert, the fourth member of the gang, had come over from Germany in 1936, and in 1948 she and her husband Henry had founded the company Colbert Artists Management Inc., which still represents some of the most renowned artists of their day. With her and the rest of his 'brains trust', Solti would discuss which concert programmes suited the CSO's new image and its 'Corporate Marketing Policy'. They combined sure-fire crowd-pleasers with lesser-known and riskier numbers, and sold both together in their subscription series. Together with the coverage that Edgar Vincent was generating, they managed to win a name for themselves: they created an 'ondit' – they became a topic of discussion on the cultural scene. Jonas loved this expression, derived from the French '*on dit*'; an atmosphere, a pressure that heightens the drama of the concert experience. The whole world knew how hard it was to get tickets for Solti's CSO concerts. It was better to buy tickets for the whole run.

Two new offers

After Jonas returned from his first tour in New York in December 1974, he had decisions to make about his professional future. His contract had only one month left, and the holidays and the New Year were looming. He only had two and a half weeks of work ahead of him until he would have to return to London.

At the time, Solti was recording Tchaikovsky at the Medina Temple and Jonas was helping him. Suddenly, Jonas received a call from Edwards. As so often, Peter Jonas re-enacted these fateful moments as a dialogue: would Peter be so kind as to come to Solti's hotel to speak with Edwards? As cheerfully as Edwards had made the request, it made Jonas nervous. Had he done something wrong? What was he to expect?

He was greeted in Solti's suite by his housekeeper, a friendly person who accompanied Solti everywhere – and who on this day, 'as always', according to Jonas, wore no shoes. She led him into Solti's study, where Edwards was already waiting. When the two men started talking, Jonas realised that he had in fact survived his 'suicide mission' at the CSO quite successfully: they were impressed by his work, by how he had immersed himself in the orchestra and its way of working. 'Everybody likes you!' opened Edwards. 'Terry McEwen is crazy about you.' And what was more, Kurt Herbert Adler wanted to engage Jonas as his personal speaker.

At the party at Trader Vic's, during which Jonas's s wallet had been stolen from the hotel, McEwen, the head of Solti's record company, had introduced Peter to his friend Kurt Herbert Adler. The Austrian conductor had come to the USA in 1938 following

Austria's *Anschluss* with Germany, which had also radically interrupted Solti's life. Jonas knew the man's story. He knew that after an engagement at the Chicago Civic Opera, Adler had gone to the San Francisco Opera, where he had since been appointed general director. Jonas knew him as the editor of *The Most Important Arias*, a widely used compendium that summarises arias for aspiring singers of each voice type.

Jonas, however, had no idea about Adler's reputation on the scene. He was considered a brilliant director, legendary in fact, but merciless and hard on the people who worked for him. Jonas knew nothing of Adler's darker side. During the party, the two had talked animatedly. Jonas felt wonderful when he returned to the hotel – until he discovered the theft. And now Adler's offer was on the table. It had rather the feel of an offer you can't refuse. Edwards informed Jonas that the San Francisco Opera would arrange a green card for him. Besides, Jonas would earn three times as much as he was making with the CSO. 'I was twenty-eight years old. I was flattered. I thanked him and just said: "Sure. Fine. I will do it."'

Later that afternoon, Edwards called him again. There was still one little aspect to discuss. Could he come back to Solti's hotel tomorrow at ten o'clock? 'What the fuck was going on?', Jonas asked himself during a sleepless night. The next morning he was greeted by the housekeeper, still barefoot. Once again Edwards and Solti were waiting for him in his study. 'We have been thinking,' Edwards opened the conversation. 'I spoke to Enid Blech yesterday. Her illness is worse than expected. The prognosis is poor. We thought we should say this to you. You'll have to decide for yourself. We think you'll have no trouble doing the job. But in light of the news about Enid Blech, we wanted to tell you that we'd love for you to stay in Chicago. Enid is by no means certain that she will be able to return.' Finally, Jonas understood: he was being offered Enid Blech's job! 'This offer from Kurt Adler … on the surface it's a better position,' Edwards followed up. 'More money. But if you would stay in Chicago, we would be very happy. Don't worry about Kurt, we'll sort it out with him.'

The music world, like everywhere else, was full of manipulators. Peter Jonas had sensed this, but he still accepted the offer. 'I don't need change for the sake of change. That's how I came to the Chicago Symphony Orchestra. It was as simple as that.'

Looking back, Jonas reflected that he might just as easily have wound up back at the job centre in London, or working as a schoolteacher. 'I am a kind of an accident, a nice sort of accident,' was how he sought to explain the early steps of his career. But this account didn't seem to satisfy him a great deal, either. 'There are no coincidences. People who are given a chance, take the initiative, learn quickly and then demonstrate their skills. So the accident is in fact the test. When you're younger, you don't understand that. I was very lucky.'

Clearly, this offer from Edwards and Solti meant that he would have to continue to work hard. As Solti's assistant, Jonas also accompanied him on recordings for his record company Decca.

In 1975 Solti recorded the *Meistersinger von Nürnberg* in Vienna and Jonas 'invented' a new singer along the way. In Jonas's recollection, the story went like this:

Decca's operations office had forgotten to hire a singer for the role of the Nachtwächter, the Nightwatchman. It was only when everyone else had turned up for the recording that the omission was noticed. Bernd Weikl, who sang the role of Hans Sachs, convinced Kurt Moll – who himself sang the role of Veit Pogner – to share the short part. Moll sang the first appearance, Weikl the second. But what should their new colleague be called? It was Peter Jonas who suggested rearranging the letters of both their names a little, and so 'Werner Klumlikboldt' eventually appeared on the cast list. It's a charming little story, but the real significance of these recording sessions lay in the experiences they afforded Jonas. He saw these recordings as the beginning of his exploration of the unique sound of an orchestra: 'I began to understand how important it is to uphold tradition. How an orchestra sounds, the scores with which it feels at home, is not simply a question of style. It has to do with the personality of the orchestra. It was only in Munich that I really appreciated this. It's so difficult to explain what it is that marks out an orchestra's particular sound.'

The moment of diagnosis

In May 1976, everything changed for Peter Jonas. While the CSO was rehearsing for a concert performance of *The Flying Dutchman*, which was to be performed in New York with Norman Bailey in the lead role, the company doctor Bernard Levin asked him to come in for a routine check-up. The CSO had excellent health insurance coverage for all employees. Normally, the examination was scheduled before the start of the contract, but in Jonas's case it had been forgotten about up until then.

The orchestra had just appointed Bernard Levin from the University of Chicago as its company doctor. Music lover Levin had jumped at the chance. He also volunteered to accompany the orchestra on its tours. Levine had thoroughly examined the files and discovered that Jonas had not undergone the mandatory entry examination upon joining the company's policy.

A few months earlier, Jonas had felt really ill for the first time in his life. He was suffering from the symptoms of flu and had a fever. By phone, he had contacted his GP in London, who had prescribed a course of penicillin that had seemed to work. Jonas had already forgotten about the illness but now and then at night he suffered from bad sweats. Otherwise he was physically fit.

Levin examined Jonas at the University of Chicago Hospital. It was a Tuesday, Jonas recalled. Levin ordered a blood test and a chest X-ray to rule out TB: 'Nothing more sophisticated.'

The following day, however, Jonas received another call from Levin. The blood test was fine, but he wanted a second X-ray. 'There is something that we find concerning,' Levin revealed. Jonas's X-ray had the wrong patient number. Because of the ongoing orchestra rehearsals, the second examination did not take place until Saturday. 'I should have been suspicious,' Jonas said, looking back on that warm, sunny Saturday in May, when he had a date lined up in the evening with a choir singer. 'Why were the doctors willing to repeat the examination at the *weekend*?'

A technician oversaw the test and then asked him to wait outside the changing room. The hospital seemed deserted that day. No one came to help Jonas. He was sitting in a long corridor with other passages branching off down its length. He waited. Then Levin, in his white coat, stepped around a corner with a group of other doctors. Levin was holding an X-ray in his hand and the group was discussing it. No one paid any attention to Jonas. 'I saw those doctors, the X-ray. I thought: uh, oh. Suddenly Bernard spotted me and came towards me: "We have to talk to you. There is a problem."'

Together with his colleagues, they went into a meeting room. 'The X-ray shows a very large shadow here, in the mediastinum, in the middle of your chest,' Levin started. 'Because of the wrong patient number on the first picture, we had hoped that it belonged to some other patient. The shadow is the size of an orange. We don't know what it is, but we can see that it is growing. It can be either a tumour or myasthenia gravis, a neurological disease. Or, it could be benign, but that's unlikely because it's so big.'

The probability that it was myasthenia gravis was also very low, Levin explained to him. This seemed to be good news, because Levin had added that there was no treatment for that illness, and that a patient with it would have to spend the rest of his life in hospital. 'Don't worry, we need to talk to other colleagues and do some more tests.'

The way Jonas reacted to this announcement showed his complete inexperience in medical matters: he didn't want to do the examinations until the beginning of June, when the recordings and the tour to New York would be finished. Jonas acted out their conversation for me:

Bernard: 'What we are talking about is Monday. This needs to be taken right now. Tomorrow is Sunday, we can't do the tests. Monday.'

Jonas: 'Bernard, you must be joking.'

Bernard: 'Monday morning at 8 o 'clock.'
Jonas: 'How long will it take?'
Bernard: 'To be honest with you, I do not know.'

Jonas was devastated. He informed Edwards and Solti, and both were horrified. Solti asked Jonas to visit him on Sunday. He thought that Jonas ought not to be alone. He sent Jonas his driver and offered him words of encouragement. Jonas spent the rest of the weekend in a trance. 'From the moment I entered the hospital, I felt like I was in prison. I was given one test after the other. In the evening, Levin came to me and told me that I would have to have an operation the next day.'

The situation was very serious. What was growing inside him had to be removed immediately: that was the only way of telling what tumour it was. The next day saw the first of countless operations that Peter Jonas was to undergo. It lasted five hours. Using a cardiopulmonary bypass machine, the doctors opened his sternum and removed the tumour. Or, in Jonas's succinct version: 'They cut me open, then the operation was over.'

The evening after the operation, Levin came to see him. Again, Jonas offered a dramatic interpretation of this dialogue, with moments of Shakespearean comic relief.

Levin: 'The operation was successful. We know what it is.'
Jonas: 'What?'
Levin: 'It is very advanced Hodgkin's disease.'
Jonas: 'But Bernard, I am not shaking!'
Levin: 'No, my dear. That's Parkinson's disease. You got the wrong disease.'
Jonas: 'Thank god you got it out.'
Levin: 'I am terribly sorry to tell you. But that's not the end of it. It's a systemic cancer. It affects the blood stream, the whole lymphatic system.'

Cancer? Jonas didn't really know what this diagnosis meant. He knew that people were afraid of it. Levin had diagnosed him with

Hodgkin's lymphoma, a malignant tumour of the lymphatic system, in an advanced stage – 3b. 'Stage 3' meant that two or more areas of lymph nodes were affected by the tumour: that the tumour had progressed. The 'b' in turn indicated the accompanying symptoms, i.e. fever, night sweats or weight loss.[30]

Jonas stayed in hospital to recover from the operation. Ten days later, he underwent a second operation to remove samples of his organs to find out which ones were already affected by Hodgkin's lymphoma. The stay at the hospital was fine, he said. He had quite decent neighbours: in the next room, there was a man who had killed his wife and three children and then tried to burn himself to death. Further down the corridor, a serial killer was lying under police surveillance.

The nurses liked Jonas. One nurse in particular was fond of him: she loved to smoke marijuana. She also thought that he should get out of the hospital. Once she took him in a wheelchair, simply pushed him out the front door, put him in her car and drove him to Meigs Field Airport, a small airfield with spacious grassy areas. At that time, such sites were not yet guarded. He lay in her arms, they both smoked, watched the planes and got 'completely high'. Then, in the car, he found he was suddenly ravenous. He could hardly walk, but she took him to a pizzeria and then brought him back to the hospital: 'a nice experience'.

A few days later, the result of the second operation brought certainty and confirmed the diagnosis: the lymphoma had spread, and it was definitely stage 3b. His doctor John Ultmann predicted that he had only one year to live.

The diagnosis shook Peter Jonas to the core. He had never been remotely seriously ill before. As a child, he had the typical complaints now and then, nothing more. He first spoke to his aunt Elizabeth Melamid in New York, and finally informed his mother. Their relationship was strained at the time because Jonas was divorcing his first wife Patricia.

His mother, who had not got over the death of her daughter, could hardly bear the diagnosis. His ignorance of medicine and its powers made Jonas confident that he would pull through. What he really wanted, what drove him, was to keep his job.

The orchestra finished recording and took off for New York. Jonas was distraught not to be able to come. He was missing the party. When the orchestra returned, Jonas learned that Solti and Edwards, who normally got along well, had quarrelled in New York. Solti also mentioned such incidents in his memoirs: Edwards had been a close friend, but their relationship became strained now and again, whenever Solti tried to change Edwards's way of working. There were a few minor storms between them, but these never lasted long.[31] One after the other, Edwards and Solti visited him in hospital and each gave him their version of events.

When they met at his bedside, they got into an argument over a planning issue in Jonas's presence. Jonas was able to mediate the dispute and he felt honoured that the two confided in him about their worries and their quarrels.

As the season drew to a close, there was no one in Chicago to see Jonas through his treatments. Levin, who would become a close friend over the years, recommended that he seek treatment in London.

Forty-three years later, in July 2009, at the age of seventy-two, Peter Jonas was warming himself at the radiator in his wife Barbara's apartment and recounting the weeks in which cancer became a part of his life forever. He was about to undergo his next operation, this time at the Klinikum rechts der Isar. 'Mir ist schwindlig [I feel dizzy]. Even I have my limits. Ich habe Angst [I am afraid],' he confessed quietly. Then he went on with his story.

His Chicago doctor Ultmann told Jonas that after he recovered from the operation, three months of radiation treatment and six months of chemotherapy, either in Chicago or London, would follow. This treatment method had been known for barely a year at the time. Only after Jonas had undergone this treatment did his doctors revise their view about his life expectancy. Ultmann, however, prepared him for the fact that his body would have difficulty withstanding the treatment: he would change completely. Jonas would lose weight, his hair would fall out, he would be permanently exhausted. Ultmann therefore recommended that he return to his mother in London. He put him in touch with Michael Peckham, head of lymphoma oncology at the Royal Marsden Cancer Centre in south London.

After about four weeks in hospital in Chicago, Jonas, now in a wheelchair for the first time in his life, was taken to live with his aunt Elizabeth Melamid in New York, where she cared for him for a few days. He was then flown to London, back to his former flat in Bloomsbury, where his wife Patricia still lived. Although their relationship was strained and divorce was pending, he did not want to move in with his mother.

Jonas introduced himself to his new doctor, Michael Peckham. The latter was not only a well-known oncologist, but also a renowned painter who exhibited in London. Jonas later acquired some of his works. Peckham was one of the many music-loving doctors who accompanied Jonas through his darkest times. Under Peckham's care, Jonas underwent the first of many radiotherapy sessions. Even before the treatment began, he was only a shadow of his former self. The radiation was not targeted at individual organs, as is done today: it hit his entire body from his neck to his thighs. Jonas knew that this was going to be demanding. And it was. Every day, five days a week. For twelve weeks. Jonas drove to the treatments in his own car. 'The radiation burned all the skin on my body. It was like a fire, it came off completely. But I was also burning up inside. I felt so sick. Usually three quarters of an hour after the treatment. I was given marijuana so that the urge to vomit didn't become too strong. I kept hoping that there would be less traffic on the way back to downtown London. But if the journey took longer, I had to pull over and vomit on the road.'

1976 saw the second hottest summer in the UK since temperatures were recorded. The heat intensified the pain caused by the burns. His mother could not cope with his illness: they remained distant from one another. But all the same, he drove to her now and then – and threw up there. 'Somehow I survived the radiation. In the end, I was still alive. We had achieved good results.'

From then on, however, Jonas also lived with the knowledge

that he would never be able to become a father.

Das Rheingold *at the Opéra de Paris*

After the radiation, Jonas wanted to resume his work immediately. In autumn 1976, Solti was working with Peter Stein on a new production of *Rheingold* at the Opéra de Paris. Solti suggested Jonas go to Paris with him as his musical assistant. Edwards agreed.

Jonas's doctors Peckham and Ultmann had organised treatment for him at the oncology institute in Villejuif. Every morning Jonas got up at five o'clock to drive to Villejuif in Solti's Volvo, receive an infusion in a horrible treatment room, drive back to the Palais Garnier and start his labours with Solti at ten o'clock. 'I must have been bloody crazy,' Jonas commented on the young, pathologically ambitious man he once was. 'When I think of it! No wonder I almost killed myself with it. But um alles in der Welt [for anything in the world], I didn't want to miss working at the Opéra de Paris! It was my first major opera production at a European opera house.'

The previous time that the Paris Opéra had staged a complete *Ring* was in 1911. Hans Knappertsbusch had conducted Wagner there in 1955. Now, the artistic director of the Opéra, the Swiss composer Rolf Liebermann, had decided not to produce the *Rheingold* until the end of the celebrations marking the centenary of the opera's première. He also wanted to produce the *Ring* successively, with two different directors.

Liebermann had chosen Peter Stein with Karl-Ernst Herrmann as stage designer for *Rheingold* and *Siegfried*. The second director was to be Klaus Michael Grüber for *Walküre* and *Götterdämmerung*, with pictures by Eduardo Arroyo and costumes by Moidele Bickel.[32] Liebermann did not complete his plan, however. He stopped the *Ring* after the production of *Walküre*.

While working in Paris, Jonas also met Hugues Gall, who was Liebermann's deputy at the time and later became the artistic director of first the Grand Théâtre de Genève and then the Opéra de Paris. Solti was assisted by Edward Downes, who conducted the performances after the première. Jonas's task was merely to annotate the score.

'I loved noting Solti's cues in the score, even if the work was mindless in some ways. I learned so much about aesthetics, about stage design, the complexities of how to make things work when nothing works. Because nothing worked at the Paris opera!'

And for the first time, he experienced clashes with trade unions. The orchestra's representative had approached Solti to say that the orchestra's trumpeter was the official instrumentalist but could not perform the part. Solti's reaction was straightforward: they would just have to find someone who could do it! Yes, but he would also have to be paid, and so on. They repeatedly ran into such impasses, problems for which no one seemed able to find a solution. Jonas compared the rehearsal work at the Paris Opéra to Federico Fellini's film *Prova d'orchestra* from 1979: chaotic conditions, nothing worked.

Time and again, the ones in charge – Gall, Grüber, Stein, Solti, Downes 'and little me' – arrived at Liebermann's office around noon for a crisis meeting – and waited for Liebermann, because he had never arrived at work so early in the day. 'Then Liebermann walked in, and I was so impressed! Through the windows of his office you could watch him arrive in the courtyard in his limousine.' Liebermann would get out, 'looking absolutely perfect, grey flannel shirt, impeccably dressed', open the door for his wife and see her off for her walk into town, and then turn to his task: which was to calm down his agitated colleagues. 'What I learned from Liebermann is to neutralise hysteria. When everyone thinks nothing can work, you have to shut everyone down.'

Jonas saw some absurd decisions first-hand. The fee for the second trumpeter had only been the beginning. Liebermann and Solti had urgently sought a singer who could master the role of Siegfried. Solti was enthusiastic about a British tenor he knew from English National Opera. But this youthful *Heldentenor* was known for being unable to learn foreign languages. Liebermann and Solti agreed to offer this singer a salaried post for a year: officially, this was to be chalked up as an administrative role. Only instead of working in administration, he was to spend that year learning the role of Siegfried. A deal was reached: but the singer insisted on being paid his salary for the first two months in cash. This they also granted to him. 'Unbelievable,' Jonas commented looking back. The quick-witted singer put the money to good use and bought a Jaguar, but he did not learn the part of Siegfried, or at least not in German. But such work would have been in vain anyway, because the Opéra later cancelled the production.

Peter Jonas was deeply impressed by the way Peter Stein worked, and the way the singers and the orchestra responded to him. 'The aesthetic world they created was so completely different from the one I was used to. Regietheater [directorial theatre] was still a thing of the future. Director Stein and set designer Herrmann created a metaphorical world that most people could never have understood. But this metaphorical world excited me. Sick as a dog, I came back from Villejuif every morning feeling like microwaved shit. Suddenly then this world opened up before me on stage, and it seemed so wide, so infinite…'

The German-language press described the production as 'stage magic with fantasy and tangible realism'[33] and lauded its magnificent images: 'This constant oscillation between a profound theatre of allusion, in which small gestures and seemingly insignificant details conceal dense interpretative work, and the gleefully amusing, bubble-bursting mechanisms of illusion and identification; the movement between allusive symbolism and the mysticism of signifiers, and a pure theatricality which is sufficient unto itself … which deployed the technical apparatus of the opera stage (in the course of which Stein became so annoyed by technical imperfections that he disappeared back to Berlin after the dress rehearsal) – it is this ambivalence of a techno-romantic style that defines Stein's first part of the Paris production of the *Ring*.'[34]

On the afternoon that Jonas spoke about his time at the Opéra de Paris, he looked out the window of his living room into the Zurich rain. In passing he mentioned 'I got friendly with Gwyneth Jones' and then fell silent for a while before continuing again. Grüber had often been drunk. 'I remember Christa Ludwig coming up to him during a rehearsal and saying: "Mr Grüber, everything you want me to do is shit, but I'll do it because I'm getting paid." I was thrilled by it, absolutely thrilled.' At the joint lunches, the crew met – without Stein – and everyone grumbled about everything. It was obvious that Jonas was in a bad way. He was often invited to these lunches out of pity, but he could barely keep any food down.

After the première he was completely exhausted and happy to be able to leave Paris.

'Now it seems such a vague memory. It is painful to remember all of that. The experience as such was so painful.'

Jonas only spent a few seconds reliving that experience. Now he wanted to tell the story of Lucia Popp.

Lucia Popp

'When I was physically at my worst, I once again met my first and greatest love, the soprano Lucia Popp,' Peter Jonas said in a letter sent a year and a half after the production at the Opéra, on 1 May 1978. The letter was sent to the Penguin publisher Eunice Kemp. 'We are now firmly together. I hope we are even destined to be together forever.'[35]

Born in 1939, Lucia Popp arrived at the peak of her thirty-year career in 1978. She began as a coloratura soprano in 1963 at 'her' establishment, the Vienna Staatsoper, before joining the ensemble of the Cologne Opera until 1977. She performed at all the major opera houses around the world. Her exemplary career included individual stand-out roles such as Sophie from *Der Rosenkavalier*, for which she was celebrated in the 1970s, and also an extensive and widely admired repertoire, courtesy of her well-developed vocal talent.[36] In addition to Sophie, she became known for her performances as Marschallin, Susanna, Contessa, Despina, Fiordiligi and Pamina.

Popp had an extraordinary memory; she had to practise very little for recordings of roles, Jonas said. Lucia Popp described herself as a 'theatre cat'.

For the opera critic Helena Matheopolous, she was an exceptional talent: Lucia Popp, she said, was a meticulous, conscientious craftswoman, passionately dedicated to patient, analytical and detailed work to refine what had been a natural talent.[37]

Finally, in Chicago in the early summer of 1977, Lucia Popp knocked on Peter Jonas's office door and walked into his life: 'within a week, we were lovers.' Lucia Popp had travelled here for a concert with the CSO, where *Vier letzte Lieder* by Richard Strauss was to be performed under Solti's direction.

The cycle, which was not intended to be presented as such by Strauss, is often interpreted as the composer's final testament. These are his last works, in which he used poems by Joseph von Eichendorff and Hermann Hesse. The compositions speak of a 'sense of a farewell and the awareness that everything in this world is finite'.[38] They reflect the situation in which Strauss and his wife Pauline, herself a soprano, found themselves: looking back on their shared path at the sunset of their lives.

> Wir sind durch Not und Freude
> gegangen Hand in Hand;
> vom Wandern ruhen wir (beide)
> nun überm stillen Land.

> We have gone through joy and hardship
> hand in hand;
> we (both)[39] rest now from walking
> over the silent land.

The fact that these songs, of all things, gave artistic expression to the beginning of the love between Peter Jonas and Lucia Popp seemed like an anticipation of both of their fates, especially of Lucia Popp's death: she succumbed to an inoperable brain tumour in 1993 at the age of just fifty-four. Jonas was friends with her until her death.

Excerpts of Lucia Popp's interpretation of these works are available on the DVD produced by Decca *Sir Georg Solti: The Maestro*. Most importantly, a photograph has survived that captured the couple with the concert programme in an intimate, quiet moment. The photograph hung in the office of Jonas's collaborator Martha Gilmer, née Schmeling, for decades afterward, until she became president of the San Diego Symphony Orchestra and gave it to Frank Villella, director of the Rosenthal Archives, where it is now preserved, along with the programme for *Vier letzte Lieder*.

'I must honestly admit: I don't think I could have done it in one piece without her,' Jonas wrote to Kemp about their first year together. 'Lucia loves me so much and I love her so much. This process of giving and receiving from each other is something very unusual and wonderful for me.'[40]

In January 1978, Jonas was to return to his old job in Chicago, alone: he did not feel ready to do this and talked with Georg Solti and John Edwards. Neither wanted to let him go and instead offered to create a new position for him, that of Artistic Administrator. He would thus be responsible for the artistic development of the orchestra and the Artistic Administration Department, which was also founded in 1977.

As generous and promising as this offer seemed to Jonas, it did nothing to allay his fears. The job would be the fulfilment of his dreams, but he would probably not be able to cope with its physical demands, he told them. Solti and Edwards insisted that he should just give it a go. But they had one condition: he would have to give up his flat in London and move to Chicago for good. Jonas accepted.

Fig. 26: Lucia Popp and Peter Jonas, Abbey Road Studios, 1982

Peter Jonas was physically diminished. There was nothing left in the 31-year-old of his former strength. He finished his first course of chemotherapy in 1977, with a month's break over the 1977–78 festive season, which he spent with Popp in Munich and Berchtesgaden. 'We had a wonderful month and both of us recovered tremendously well,'[41] Jonas wrote in his letter to Eunice Kemp. He concealed the fact that their time together had also been marred by the public pressure that arose when their affair became known. Lucia Popp was famous. The fact that she had moved out of the house she shared in Cologne with her first husband György Fischer caused a big scandal. The tabloid press was hungry for news and photos: Lucia Popp had a lover! Popp had not yet found a flat in Munich, so she and Jonas stayed at the Hotel an der Oper in Falkenturmstraße. Journalists stalked the pair near the hotel; Popp was increasingly uneasy.

Fig. 27: Peter Jonas after his illness

The way out of this unpleasant situation was offered to them by their mutual friend Eva Wagner-Pasquier, who lived in an apartment in Thierschstraße and wanted to go away with her husband Yves for Christmas and New Year. The couple accepted gratefully and were able to spend quiet days there. The story might have ended there. But in fact this offer had another lasting impact on Jonas's life: one morning Lucia and he were still in bed when they noticed someone rummaging in the wardrobe at the end of the bed – he enjoyed describing the outrage, the looks that went silently back and forth. The obviously self-confident young woman introduced herself as 'Lilo' and – as was quite common back then – wore an Eva Wagner dress; she lived next door, had the key to the flat and when they were over their surprise invited both to come for a drink when they had the chance. A little later, all three of them were now bound by a friendship that was to last a lifetime: when Lucia Popp died some sixteen years later, she was being taken care of by Lilo, who is known in Munich as Prof. Dr Dr habil. Liselotte Goedel-Meinen.

In mid-January 1978, Jonas had to return to Chicago. He moved into his new flat. Eight weeks without Lucia Popp followed: 'The most terrible separation. We both found that we could not live without the other and that every moment of absence required either a phone call or a letter. We had achieved such happiness with each other over the Christmas and New Year period … we needed all our strength, and all the strength of our love, not to go completely mad. Lucia wrote to me every single day during this period, and I wrote back to her every single day, quite an achievement for me as I have never been known for being anything other than the most irregular, sporadic and rather untalented letter writer.'[42]

For Jonas, his new job was starting under a shadow. It was difficult for him to cut his ties with Europe at the very moment when he had entered into a relationship with Lucia Popp, whose work mainly took her to European opera houses. But he went along with it and moved into a handsome flat at 1421 North State Park Way.

The first leading role

On 12 October 1977, the CSO announced Jonas's appointment in a press release. This said that he would take up the post of Artistic Administrator, which had been created for him, on 1 January 1978. 'Mr. Jonas will assist both the General Manager and the Music Director with programming, artist selection and other details of the Orchestra's subscription and non-subscription concerts in Chicago. His duties will also include organising audio and film recordings and touring programmes within and outside the United States.'[43]

He was also responsible for the Civic Orchestra of Chicago, the Chicago Symphony Chorus and the Education Department. He signed his first letter as Artistic Administrator on 17 January 1978. From 2 February onwards, his name appeared on the CSO's official letterhead under those of Solti and Edwards.[44] Peter Jonas had finally arrived in the music world.

The files preserved in the Rosenthal Archives, especially the correspondence with Solti, give an eloquent picture of his challenging, fulfilling and hectic everyday life. If Solti was travelling elsewhere, Jonas kept him well-informed through letters about the CSO in general and the quality of the guest conductors in particular. Leinsdorf's performances – 'for my taste he is always thoroughly professional, always "very good", but never "great"' – and Slatkin – 'I am not too enthusiastic about him' – did not come off well.[45] Some of his criticisms were rather amusing. This is how he wrote of another guest conductor: 'He has no sense of legato: if he is not quite an elephant in a china shop, then he is like an ox overturning a hay cart.'[46]

Again and again he reported in detail, over page after page, on the state of planning for the coming season, often day by day. Every now and then he also allowed himself a joke. He wrote to Solti that at the moment he and John Edwards were scheduled to be the first and second prisoners in Beethoven's *Fidelio*, but since neither of them expected to be able to do justice to the roles, they suggested holding auditions, so that Solti could choose the best.[47] After just a few weeks, on 24 February 1978, he confessed to Solti with striking honesty how horribly his work with the Board was wearing on him: 'By the way, I must tell you that I find these once-a-month Board meetings probably the most depressing aspect of my life in Chicago, even though I also have the impression that we have what other orchestras call a progressive board!'[48] One may assume that there would have been at least ten exclamation points at the end of this statement if he had typed the letter himself, rather than entrusting it to his assistant. But he added one more joke: 'All the very best from the Chicago branch of Local 21344 SOL TIG.'[49] In the correspondence with Solti there is also a letter dated 23 November 1979 with an amusing postscript relating how Ravel's *Boléro* had found its way into pop culture, and for a while ensured all recordings of the piece were a sell-out. It was all related to a new film by Blake Edwards called *10*. Edwards cast Bo Derek in a leading role, one that was to make her an international sex symbol. In a key scene, this girl of the hero's dreams wants to have sex to Ravel's *Boléro*. Jonas described it to Solti: 'the seduction begins, she puts the needle on the record and starts Ravel's *Boléro*. The mood is set, she waits for her hero's advances.

Unfortunately, there is something wrong with the plate. Halfway through, just as things are getting interesting, there is a scratch. The needle gets stuck in a groove and the record cannot be played any further. The woman lifts the needle, puts it back in, but it gets stuck again just before one of the great musical climaxes. As a consequence of the needle being stuck on the same beat so many times, our hero is put into a state of sexual inactivity. So the seduction is a complete failure.'[50]

Rose Records, Chicago's premier record shop on Wabash Avenue, kept Jonas in the loop: 'People are under the impression that this is the silver bullet to solve all their libido problems. Rose Records has informed us that they recommend customers (who are usually not their regular buyers) to buy their recordings from us. Something happened the other day that made us all laugh. Namely, one of the customers came back with his *Boléro* record and demanded his money back because, he said, it "did not work".'[51]

The extensively preserved minutes of the Planning Committee, the Artistic Performances and Services Committee and other committees, as well as the still-extensive memoranda to Solti, all show what proportion of the work was done by these bodies. When Jonas received an order from the administration that was ill-conceived, impractical and therefore pointless, such as the order regarding how expenses and out-of-pocket travel costs were to be reimbursed from now on, he was gripped by fear. He dictated detailed arguments, which ran to several pages, in which he meticulously demonstrated how the proposed arrangements could not work. Dated January 1979, a revision of the internal instruction is found in the files. Jonas had won this fight.

Another time, during a spell of hot weather, he threatened industrial action: as there was neither air conditioning nor windows that could be opened, Jonas and his colleagues on the sixth floor of the Symphony Center would suffer in the oppressive heat of the long summer months. He threatened the administration with a 'mass walk out', 'an industrial dispute as a result of these Victorian working conditions. Please, we implore you do something before the scandal of the 6th floor hot house and sweat shop is promulgated into the media.'[52]

Solti had decided to conduct *in situ* for twelve weeks of the season, which lasted around thirty-two weeks, and to tour for a further four to six weeks. His idea was to extend the concert season. For one thing, the subscription scheme had to be changed. Jonas proudly wrote to Solti: 'By operating some very clever mathematical gymnastics John and I have managed to fit in your subscription requirements into 10 weeks.'[53] On the other hand, the importance of the 'principal guest conductor' also increased. With Solti's arrival in Chicago, Carlo Maria Giulini had taken over this role. Claudio Abbado and Pierre Boulez followed later. Jonas worked directly with these international luminaries. The documents paint the picture of a humorous perfectionist who always wants to minimise risk. 'Just in case of disaster'[54] he wanted to be prepared for soloists falling ill. In some cases, he planned a 'survival kit'[55] months in advance, specifying who could be considered as a replacement for a part and what contact details could be used to reach the singers.

Harry Zelzer and the Allied Arts Corporation

As Artistic Administrator, Jonas also worked with the famous Chicago music manager Harry Zelzer, whom Jonas described as a 'rough, Jewish impresario', and his Allied Arts Corporation.

Harry Zelzer, born in 1897, founded his company in the 1930s under the name Zelzer Concert Management Bureau, representing only five artists. When he died in Chicago in 1978, he had shaped the city's musical life for decades. 'Harry Zelzer was one of the rare people whose musical "nose" was so extraordinary that it was enough for someone to play the first few notes of a recital for Harry to know the real potential of the artist,' Daniel Barenboim said, acknowledging his achievements. 'His tenacity and courage in presenting young artists contributed greatly to the knowledge of the public and Chicago.'[56]

At Allied Arts, Zelzer was the boss, although his wife Sarah ensured the company's success by standing by his side, albeit in his shadow, throughout their time together. In her memoirs, Sarah Zelzer, who performed in the music business under her maiden name Schectman, described her husband and boss as a businessman imbued with a love of classical music. With his clear eye for what his customers wanted, he succeeded in professionally putting on demanding concert programmes over decades. In accordance with his credo 'balance the artists to balance the books',[57] he combined big names with less well-known artists and new pieces, balancing the deficits of one concert with the gains of other concerts. 'What is a good impresario? Some people say, he is an exploiter of other people's talent. I say he is a gambler. If he finishes the season in the black, he is a good impresario,' Zelzer once said. 'One of the most important things for an impresario to know is the value of an attraction at the box office … I only really enjoy half the concerts I stage, but I'm not in the business to cater to me.'[58]

He had a hands-on style and he paid attention to every detail. He must have been a great negotiator, and he was prepared to argue with partners, managers, critics: anyone at all. 'I hadn't experienced anything like that before,' Jonas effused later. 'I remember him sitting in his office in this huge armchair talking to me. On the left side was the telephone, his most important working instrument. Every now and then the phone would ring and Harry would take the call: "Yeah, yeah." Pause. "Now listen, buddy, I am gonna tell you something."' Jonas loved re-enacting Zelzer's conversation with a musician's agent. '"I don't ask him in advance how he is gonna play the piano. You don't ask me how we gonna sell the tickets." And then he hung up without saying goodbye.' Jonas was clearly thrilled by Zelzer's hard-boiled brashness.

'Harry and I were as different as black and white, but we learned to like each other. When Harry wanted to retire, he offered me the chance to take over Allied Arts. But I wasn't interested in it.'

Zelzer's decisive skill, the key to his success, lay in salesmanship. He had always refused to set up a Board for his company and to involve trustees, but he had nevertheless managed to set up an effective distribution structure aimed at selling large bundles of tickets. For this purpose, he entered into partnerships with other companies or organisations. He also developed an innovative approach which is taken for granted today: he grouped the concerts into series and built up a subscription audience for them, which formed his regular customer base. He also sometimes offered 'special interest series', for lovers of songs, folk or guitar music, for example.[59] 'Harry made deals with agents. They shared the income. That's why the agents used to call. It wasn't about soft artistic sympathy, das war ein hartes Business [it was a tough business],' Jonas recalled.

This life took a heavy toll on everyone involved. Sarah Zelzer described how her husband left the hotel suite they lived in every day at around 7am to buy pastries for the employees on his way to the office. Between 7.30am and 9am Harry would concentrate on studying box-office intakes, promotional ideas and calls to New York managers at their homes. 'This was hard on the managers' wives. They pleaded with me to tell my husband not to call so early in the morning. Harry insisted that his best deals were made with the managers before they arrived at their offices.'[60] None of the employees, not even the Zelzers, would go into town for lunch. Instead, an errand boy was sent to collect food for the entire 'Allied Arts Family'[61] – here again that family metaphor!

After an afternoon nap, Zelzer resumed his sales work: he talked on the phone, the receiver 'glued' to his ear, as his wife put it.[62] In the evening, they visited the concerts, and sometimes several at the same time. They checked receipts until late at night. Even though the Zelzers' success was watched and imitated around town, their lives, however fulfilling, consisted solely of producing concerts. This is exemplified by one particular photograph in Sarah's memoir. It shows Harry Zelzer behind the bars of a ticket box in the Civic Theatre, in front of which is a sign reading 'This performance is sold out.' The man who is doomed to success is smiling.[63]

Over time, however, the Zelzers had to accept that the business was changing. They could hardly book Russian artists anymore, as their New York competitors were driving up the prices. Harry Zelzer was looking for a way his business could live on after he retired. Peter Jonas was only one of a series of people with whom Zelzer had dealt. Some are said to have been rejected by Zelzer himself. Paul Judy, a member of the CSO's board, recognised the value of Zelzer's company. He would have bought it himself if he had not been about to ascend to the position of President of the Board at the CSO. The position would have meant an intolerable conflict of interest. Judy convinced the Trustees to transfer Allied Arts to the Orchestral Association. Jonas finalised this merger for the Orchestral Association and, together with Zelzer, set up a new distribution system for the orchestra in 1978.

A memorandum by Peter Jonas has been preserved in the Rosenthal Archives, in which he reports to Paul Judy and John Edwards on a conversation with Harry Zelzer on 3 March 1978.[64] Originally scheduled for one hour, Jonas stayed for a total of four. This marked Peter Jonas's initiation into the world of sales, one of the most neglected elements in cultural management. The Zelzers and Jonas agreed on how they wanted to deal with artistic matters and fees. However, the procurement market, the way Allied Arts and the Orchestral Association had previously booked their artists, turned out to be fundamentally different for both companies. While the CSO marketed sophisticated products, the offerings of the Allied Arts Corporation were perceived as lowbrow and mass-produced.[65]

Zelzer assumed that the New York managers would no longer offer them the same conditions. As a non-profit company, the orchestra was regarded as a business partner of high quality, while Allied Arts was considered to be low quality.[66] Jonas explained to Judy and Edwards how important the technical aspects of ticket sales were, also in order to be able to bill correctly, and what importance innovations held in terms of negotiations with agents. All of this was handled on the basis of handwritten accounting of ticket sales. The Zelzers convinced him of how tight the monitoring of ticket sales had to be, and how much staff time had to be dedicated to this effort. In the memorandum, Jonas explained how the sales outlets in the Symphony Center could be reinforced with their own in-house staff.[67] Peter Jonas was responsible for implementing this concept. When the Supreme Audit Office of the State of Bavaria complained about deficits in central ticket distribution in the 1990s, Jonas was in an excellent position to lead the Staatsoper's sales division into the digital age.

'It all seemed pleasant and reasonable,' Sarah said of the outcome of the negotiations, 'but I was against it, as I had been from the first moment Harry broached the plan to me. I felt that our organizations were too different in too many ways for the marriage to succeed. I didn't think that the Association would appreciate his gift.'[68]

Sarah Zelzer explained in detail how she felt that her prediction had come true. The focus of her criticism was the behaviour of Peter Jonas, who in her eyes symbolised the whole misbegotten plan. During a visit to New York, she got into an argument with a manager about the fee for the concert by pianist Rudolf Serkin. Since the merger, the price for latter's performances had doubled. As Sarah had predicted, the manager justified the price increase by saying that he now saw Allied Arts as a non-profit company supported by trustees: they could afford the higher rate. Sarah Zelzer was outraged that other people's money was being thrown away in this way. She announced that John Edwards would not book the pianist on these terms.

Back in Chicago, she expressed regret to Jonas about the development. 'Well,' Jonas is supposed to have answered, 'let's book him through the CSO.' Sarah Zelzer couldn't believe her ears. 'You know, Peter,' she reportedly replied, 'the whole reason Harry gave Allied Arts to the Chicago Symphony to begin with was so that we could get together on fees and block-buying. I turned Serkin down, and so you shouldn't pay him that fee either. It's not right. That damages the purpose of combining Allied Arts with the Orchestral Association.'[69]

Vladimir Horowitz

One incident involving Vladimir Horowitz and his entourage so annoyed Sarah Zelzer that she included it in her book. Peter Jonas, incidentally, had almost exactly the same experience with Horowitz. Zelzer reports that the negotiations with his manager Peter Gelb, and the performances themselves, were always a real chore for everyone involved. As usual, he had refused to give a binding commitment until three and a half weeks before the concert. His mottos were 'keep them guessing' and 'wait until the last possible moment'.[70] Peter Jonas had to supervise a concert with Vladimir Horowitz because John Edwards did not feel like doing it himself. It was one of the concerts in the Sunday series, at 4pm. The CSO had settled with Horowitz's agents to pay out a percentage of the revenue instead of a fixed fee. That's why there were extra seats on the stage, which were sold only shortly before the concert.

John Edwards knew of Horowitz's reputation and had told Jonas to be prepared. 'Horowitz was not particularly sympathetic,' Jonas recalled. 'Just like his wife Wanda, Arturo Toscanini's daughter. Wanda Toscanini Horowitz always meticulously counted how many additional seats had been set up so that she could calculate the figures.'

Horowitz had let the CSO know that he was expecting a cheque to be delivered to his dressing room immediately after the performance, so the employees from the accounting department were called in. Everything was prepared so that the accounting, still done by hand at that time, could be finished during the concert. From around 1pm the hall was cleared so that Horowitz could warm up. As soon as the cash register closed, the cashiers sat down with their rolls to start cashing up.

'The billing was a normal working process, but the per cent rate Horowitz was to receive was tricky to calculate. Meanwhile, I was sitting in the house box. Ten minutes before the end of the concert, the financial director Bill Raye came and handed me the envelope with the cheque.' This time the amount due to Horowitz was just under fifty thousand dollars, an immensely high fee. 'I checked the calculation and put the envelope in my suit jacket. Then I waited until the encores were over. I went backstage to his dressing room, where the fans were already waiting.' But before the fans could pay him a visit, the artist needed to speak with Jonas. Wanda Toscanini Horowitz was also present. Jonas greeted them both reverently. 'Maestro, that was wonderful! What an honour to have listened to her concert!' He described her appearance and behaviour in terms that cannot be repeated here.

At first Horowitz just looked at Jonas, barely thirty years old, and eventually replied: 'My boy, do you have the cheque?' Of course he did, Jonas replied and handed Horowitz the envelope. He passed it on unopened to Wanda Toscanini Horowitz. 'Wanda opened the envelope, looked at the cheque with a disgusted expression, and then at me. Finally, she gave it back to Horowitz. After a quick glance, he threw it at my feet, whereupon Wanda exclaimed with disdain: "The great Chicago Symphony Orchestra can't even manage fifty thousand dollars!" I turned around and left.' A strong gesture from such a young man in the moment. Who finally picked up the cheque is not known. The Horowitzes had probably already spent it. Of course, Jonas discussed the incident with Edwards, who backed him up. 'I know this,' he is reported to have said, 'why do you think I wanted to go away?'

Decades later, when Peter Jonas was teaching the Master's programme in art management at the University of Zurich, he attached great importance to freeing his students from the illusion that outstanding artists are necessarily also great people. 'Why should they be?' he commented laconically.

For Jonas, the needs of the artists always came first, even though he always kept the interests of the orchestra in mind. In May 1979, for example, he wrote a harsh letter to the Düsseldorf musical director, Grisha Barfuss, to ask for a leave of absence for a singer who had been refused time off to go and perform with the CSO.

He openly acknowledged that Barfuss was within his rights to claim the singer for his own house, but he was unyielding in his demand and concise in his argument as to why good organisation at Düsseldorf could make the absence possible.[71] But for Jonas, this was about securing a central role: Manfred Jung was to sing Siegfried – and he did.

In January 1979 he assured Carlos Kleiber of 'a guaranteed number of 4 rehearsals (whoopee!!!)'.[72] In a separately signed postscript, Jonas told him about a conversation with Kleiber's aunt, who received tons of fan letters for her nephew. She had asked Jonas for advice on where to forward the letters, combined with the hope that the letters might sink into the 'morass of bureaucracy'. Jonas wrote to Kleiber that he had given her the address of the Nationaltheater in Munich. This could always be used as a scapegoat for any 'lost' mail that Kleiber simply did not want to answer.[73]

Even at this early stage, Jonas was already up to all of his tricks: a pianist once wanted to audition before Solti – Jonas generously, and more than a little confusingly, offered a whole range of options for dates for that meeting. A later letter to a colleague reveals that this was the strategy to prevent the meeting without the affront of an outright rejection. Had the pianist turned up, they would have excused themselves by pleading a scheduling error. Decades later, Jonas was reported to have advised his team, as artistic director of the Bavarian Staatsoper, that in case of doubt when it came to image rights one should simply send a fax with a request to any number at all. This way, you could always prove that you had at least made an effort.

In his Chicago years – apart from a few affairs, to which he freely admitted – Jonas had no leisure time at all. A short article from April 1978 from the small but high-quality local newspaper the *Sacramento Bee* does, however, provide an insight into a charming aside: Peter Jonas himself performed with the Sacramento Symphony Philharmonic Orchestra. He gave the narration in Arthur Honegger's *King David*. The *Sacramento Bee* reviewer singled out his performance: 'a tall young actor from England who speaks the connecting lines of Biblical text. His speech is clear, his sense of the story is absolutely compelling, his very presence helps draw us into the drama. He is magnificently a factor in the success of the performance and he doesn't even sing a note.'[74]

Total trust

Jonas allowed himself the pleasure of appearing in a speaking part a month before he wrote the letter to Eunice Kemp in which he revealed that he had met his first and most important love in Lucia Popp. Jonas wrote to Kemp: 'We again realized that both of us had found something which I thought had only existed in the deep recesses of my dream world; a total love, a total trust, a total communication and total identification with another person without sacrificing one's own sense of freedom and individuality. I have never in fact felt so free in my whole life and at the same time I have never had such inspiration, such total involvement with another person.'[75] When Lucia Popp visited him in Chicago in March 1978, she witnessed an experience that heralded the next horror in Jonas's medical history. Both were invited to a business dinner and were served soft-shell crabs from the nearby coast. The creatures, which are caught at the moment they have shed their shells and are therefore still soft, are eaten whole and can usually be chewed and swallowed without any problems. Peter Jonas, however, found he could not swallow them. The radiation treatment had severely damaged his oesophagus and stomach, and he could swallow only really soft food.

This problem was already known about, because a year earlier his doctor Bernard Levin had already tried to stretch out his narrowed oesophagus. Jonas reported to his London doctor Michael Peckham of the Royal Marsden Hospital in June 1977 that the results of this attempt were short-lived.

In April 1978, Jonas was hospitalised again, where he was diagnosed with pericarditis. On 3 May 1978 he wrote to Michael Peckham that he would like to be operated on again.

The operation that Peter Jonas wanted was a colonic interposition, in which the damaged oesophagus is removed and reconstructed with the body's own material, for example from the intestine, before then being reinserted. The anatomy of the oesophagus, its location and its poor protection make it vulnerable to injury during surgery.

Such an operation takes an enormously long time and requires high technical skills. Even reaching the oesophagus is a difficult task. Fatal complications can easily occur during the operation, and afterwards as well. In addition, patients are often not in a good condition when they undergo the treatment because they will generally have eaten poorly beforehand.

When Jonas underwent this operation, medicine had only just made the decisive advances required to make it possible in the first place.[76] It was nevertheless extremely risky. There were only a few reference cases, and the risk of death was high. Some patients had died on the operating table. Some lived only for a short time afterwards.

In Jonas's case, David Skinner, his Chicago doctor, was to perform it. The colon interposition technique was developed by Ronald Belsey of Bristol, from whom Skinner, who was about to become a leading thoracic and oesophageal surgeon, had learned the procedure.[77] The pair would later publish the leading textbook on diseases of the oesophagus. Jonas would have liked to postpone the operation until June, when the concert season would be over, 'but it became a bit too difficult. My food intake became more and more restricted.' He was in extreme pain and was losing weight dramatically. He confessed frankly to his good friend Eunice Kemp on 1 May, 'things have worsened, and as they worsened it is rather like a snowball effect, until gradually I could stand it no longer, and the last four weeks seemed to stretch out before me like a never-ending road to a distant horizon.'[78] He reported happily that Lucia had cancelled bookings for him, and would be coming to Chicago on 5 May, and they could spend four more days together before he had to go to the hospital. The orchestra did not expect him back until August. They both wanted to spend the summer in Salzburg. He remarked to Kemp that maybe something good would come from this operation. It seemed to have been the last hurdle in his race 'to really free myself from this whole thing. I will be able to defeat this miserable business with cancer and all its accompanying symptoms.'[79]

But things turned out differently. Lucia arrived in Chicago only after the operation. Not only that: Jonas would have to acknowledge afterwards that the cancer and its side effects would be with him for life, however long that might be. Although at the time he claimed to Kemp that he had 'the most complete confidence in my doctor but I have to say that I am rather frightened and especially so because I now know exactly what operations involve',[80] forty years later he could honestly say: 'I was absolutely terrified. If you have survived such an operation, you can endure anything. Even though I am beginning to doubt it again today.' While he was talking about it in retrospect, on 2 July 2019, he was sitting at the kitchen table in his wife Barbara's flat in Munich's Glockenbach district, waiting again for confirmation of yet another operation date.

Before the operation, which took place on 11 May 1978, Jonas had spoken at length with Bernard Levin and David Skinner. Besides a photo of Lucia, he also took the newly invented Sony Walkman with him to the hospital and listened to Humperdinck's *Hänsel and Gretel* twice over. Ronald Belsey travelled from England to assist David Skinner during the twelve-hour operation.

Forty years after Jonas had gone through the horror, the fear of death still haunted him. He described in the most direct language what Skinner had done to him, to his organs, how he had cut him open, placed his innermost parts next to him in a bowl, how he had thrown away what was useless, created an artificial conduit inside him and then sewn him up again. Jonas embellished his story with graphic gestures and did not spare the sound effects. His succinct conclusion: the X-ray showed that none of his organs were sitting where they should be. 'But I did wake up,' he concluded.

When he woke up the day after the operation, the first person Jonas saw was David Skinner, himself completely exhausted. The operation was an outstanding success, even if the recovery process took an incredibly long time. The following day Lucia Popp arrived. She healed him. Describing the effect that her presence had on him in 2019, Jonas chose similar language to that he had used in his letter to Eunice Kemp. Lucia, he said, was a wonderful woman who had enormous strength to give and love, 'probably because of her Slavic background, but mostly because she is very at peace with herself, her career and the world in general'. Jonas cultivated the cliché that women are generally stronger than men. He would talk about how women are not as 'mimosenhaft' [sensitive] as men, referring to his years of experience in hospitals where he had observed nurses interacting with male patients.

He and Lucia spent the summer months together in Salzburg as they had hoped. They rented a house at Sonnleitenweg 18 for the holiday season. This estate with a swimming pool was located just under twenty kilometres east of the city centre. From there they could 'enjoy a wide view over the city to the Hohensalzburg Fortress and the Untersberg',[81] wrote Ursula Tamussino in her memoir of Lucia Popp.

Funnily enough, the first letter written in German dates from 1 July 1984, preserved by Jonas in the Rosenthal Archives. In it, Jonas asks the owner of a Salzburg Autohaus to prepare Lucia's Bentley for her summer stay. Several obituaries of Jonas claimed that he learned German only in his forties. It was certainly only in those later years that he reached the high level of fluency for which he became known, but Jonas had already become acquainted with the language during his years with Lucia. Charmingly, the letter bears the reference 'Re: Inbetriebnahme [Commissioning] Bentley (SBX 34042) from my wife, KS Lucia Popp' and begins with the words: 'Der Sommer ist wieder da und wir gedenken wieder unserem (sic) Bentley ein bisschen spazieren zu Fahren [Summer is here again and we are thinking of taking our Bentley for a drive].' On the headed paper of the Orchestral Association – at that time they didn't take things very seriously – Jonas asked the mechanics to work through an enclosed checklist. At the end, he stipulates: 'ALLES WAS NOCH NOTWENDIG IST,

BESONDERS FÜR SOMMER!!!!!!!!!!! [Everything necessary, especially for summer]'[82]

After their time together, Jonas had to return to his workplace. At the hospital he had received countless greetings and good wishes from his colleagues from the orchestra. In a letter to everyone in October 1978, he asked for understanding that he could not thank everyone individually, because if he did, 'I would no doubt end up back in the operating theatre'[83] – with a habitual flourish – 'for rather extensive surgery to the manus dextra'.[84] The letter is signed only with a sweeping 'P'.

Seven fulfilling and happy years followed for Peter Jonas and Lucia Popp. Popp was Jonas's lover and companion, but she was also his mentor and introduced him to the European opera world. Whenever their busy professional schedules allowed, they spent their free time together. A caricature by Jean-Jacques Sempé shows them both listening to music on their Sony Walkman behind the panorama window of their flat at 900 Lake Shore Drive, admiring the moonlight over Lake Michigan.

900 Lake Shore Drive is one of the famous Esplanade Apartments, the first high-rise buildings designed by Ludwig Mies van der Rohe, surrounded by a continuous curtain wall separated from the building frame. Mies went on to use this approach in all his high-rise projects, including the famous Seagram Building. Jonas had chosen the most modern flat of its era for himself and Lucia Popp.

An excerpt from a 1978 letter written by Lucia to her friend Ursula Tamussino gives an impression of how she viewed her relationship with Jonas: she says that she was spending wonderful, too-short days with him. 'Peter has given me a wonderful welcome and has furnished a nice "home" for us with a lot of imagination and impeccable taste. I feel like I'm in seventh heaven and never want to leave here again. We are both very happy and feel that any further separation would be senseless. But the situation is very difficult to manage, especially as my Peter also enjoys his work, although he denies it. It makes me sick just thinking about having to do without him again. We fit so well together and I feel young, beautiful and desirable again – which is very important for me. I also see that I am having a real "body and soul" healing effect on him, just by my presence. I am also convinced that we will not be separated for long. Maybe I also have to make certain concessions, but, believe me, I would like to do that: I am still doing fantastic business. My "master classes" here have gone well – especially the second one. Peter was, as always, a great help to me, firstly concretely, secondly through his unshakeable confidence which he displays where my artistic abilities are concerned.'[85]

Walter Felsenstein and Wieland Wagner

Jonas attended Popp's performances as often as he could, got to know the most important opera houses, and he also expanded his own network. Because Popp worked in these opera houses and was involved in many standard-setting productions, Jonas gained intimate knowledge of the working conditions and style there. And being able to observe and accompany Popp in her work fulfilled that desire to soak up every novelty, everything that fascinated him, and to develop his own take on what he saw and heard.

Jonas got to know the German-language opera scene very well after spending so many years at Lucia Popp's side. Aesthetically and dramaturgically, by his own admission, he remained conservative. 'But although I longed for classical beauty on stage, I also noticed that I was more excited when something was slightly distorted, beyond the normal. But in the late 1970s and early 1980s, naturalism still dominated the stage.'

Jonas met Walter Felsenstein through Lucia Popp. As it was for so many others, the work of Walter Felsenstein at the Komische Oper became one of the decisive influences on Jonas. 'I admired him a lot,' Jonas explained. 'His image-world was entirely realised through metaphor. I was superbly impressed.'

The tradition established by Felsenstein of setting the text, music, scene and performers of an opera all on an equal footing, and of breaking with the conventions of lyric opera, helped many people to understand opera as a fully contemporary art form in the first place. His twenty-eight years at the Komische Oper Berlin fundamentally changed our understanding of opera as an art form and the aesthetics of its staging. Felsenstein is considered an authoritative voice for theatre itself, and for conservative interpretations of drama.[86]

Fig. 28: Scene from *Siegfried*, Bayreuth, 1968

In the same breath, Jonas described how deeply impressed he had been by Wieland Wagner's work as director of the 'new' Bayreuth, even during his student years. In his speech at the ceremony marking the centenary of Wieland Wagner's birth, Peter Jonas explained his view of Felsenstein and Wagner to the Bayreuth audience: 'And of course there were parallels to the work of the ultra-realist Walter Felsenstein at the Komische Oper Berlin after 1947. The ultra-conceptualist Wieland admired this ultra-realist, and of course Felsenstein influenced Wieland and Wolfgang on issues of theatrical practice – how to run a theatre, how a performance should be experienced.'

Expert opinion agrees that Wieland Wagner and Walter Felsenstein were 'astonishingly close to each other despite their aesthetic differences, when it came to a directorial concept of organising the collective'.[87] Jonas recognised the 'signs of a process of dramaturgical prophylaxis' sweeping through Bayreuth in a photograph of Siegfried Lauterwasser, showing a scene from the third act of *Siegfried*: 'It shows the surface of the so-called "Wieland disk", gently curved like the top of a huge sphere, while a softly illuminated round horizon extends over the back wall of the stage. Otherwise, the stage is completely empty. On the spherical dome, a little to the left of the centre, lies Brünnhilde, and next to her, partly on top of her, Siegfried, who is just awakening her with THE kiss. Simple, plain, epic and at the same time ravishingly erotic and deeply impressive in its emphasis on space and scale – it gives the illusion that this stage is of infinite size and thus it becomes cosmic space.' It was this image that he first saw as a boarding school student.

He said that it was 'ubiquitous' at that time, which made him want to go to Bayreuth as a student. 'For us students from the United Kingdom, who knew opera only from stage pictures and dramaturgically poor hyper-realism, the idea of such abstraction was a shock therapy that got us hooked on records of Richard Wagner's works. Wieland Wagner's visuals excited our fantasies of what was possible "out there", across the Channel on the continent's stages!'

The drama of the gifted child

Lucia Popp was more than just the companion with whom Peter

Jonas learned about the world of music. Through her, Jonas, an incapacitated man who had had to leave home as a pre-school child and who had lost his sister in an accident, found an emotional home for the first time in his life. 'Lucia was a remarkable person, incredibly normal,' Jonas explained. 'She was somebody who encouraged me when I didn't feel well. I wasn't a strong man anymore, I was a delicate man.'

In autumn 1978, the official view was that Peter Jonas was healthy. He wrote in a letter that after two and a half years and a series of operations, radiotherapy and chemotherapy, he was now completely cured of cancer. He concluded: 'There is rather less of me than before, but still…'[88] At first, Jonas enjoyed finally being able to eat again, not only for pleasure, but mainly for the energy it brought. But he also realised that he had to think, now that he was weakened: 'What's the point of working and struggling unless you are really dealing with something that gives you a reward other than a weekly salary?'[89] For the time being, he found no answer.

When, in the spring of 1979, the soprano Hildegard Behrens, another strong woman, knocked on his office door, she did not bring him an answer, but she did bring him a decisive book which would set Jonas on a path to discovering himself. 'I remember her coming into my office. She had this book in her hand and said: "This book is about you."' Hildegard Behrens was holding the recently published volume *The Drama of the Gifted Child* by the Swiss psychoanalyst Alice Miller.[90] Originally published in German by Suhrkamp, the title reached an audience of millions, offering easily accessible explanations for the suffering of many people in that generation.

'If you let yourself, you will make something of your life,' Behrens told Jonas. 'The only thanks I want is for you to do psychoanalysis.'

At first Jonas did not understand what Behrens was talking about. Jonas later described the book as key to his understanding of what childhood meant and how it shaped our psyche, our whole being. 'The moment I held it in my hand for the first time changed my life, as I'm sure it did for many other people. We are prisoners of our childhood – if we free ourselves from it, we can regain our innocence.'

Behrens, born in 1937, trained as a lawyer before she studied singing relatively late in life. Her international breakthrough came in 1977, after she had sung Salomé at the Salzburg Festival. In May 1979 she sang Leonore with the Symphony Orchestra, first at Carnegie Hall, then in recordings at Chicago's Medinah Temple. 'She was the epitome of a dramatic soprano,' says Jonas. 'She didn't have a classic legato voice, but a strong, steely voice. Hildegard was a strong, independent woman. I found her fascinating.' He was happy to follow her recommendation. He read the book but found its contents difficult to unlock. Jonas was not used to even thinking about questions of the psyche, let alone talking about them. Hildegard Behrens brought him her advice when he thought the cancer treatments were over: it was a time when he was vulnerable and unstable. After reading it for the second time, he assumed he was really ill. 'I could open the book on any page. I would always find something that applied to me. Where is my true self? What chamber is it hiding in, what are its props?'

When Alice Miller, born in 1923, published *The Drama of the Gifted Child*, she was on the verge of turning her back on the psychoanalysis she had practised for twenty years. The volume brings together three of her essays and is subtitled 'The Search for the True Self'. In it, Miller argued how the behaviours of parents in raising their children can have a permanently damaging effect and create trauma. As a result of these traumas, patients in turn fluctuated between depressive states and exaggerated feelings of their own 'grandiosity': symptoms of narcissistic disorders. Beyond the everyday meaning of the word, Miller spoke of the natural narcissism of children, their need for attention and affection. To meet this need, children would have to be able to live out their fears, anger and sadness. Ideally, children would develop a healthy sense of self, genuine vitality, and free access to their true selves and feelings.[91] 'But a mother who, as a child, was herself not taken seriously by her mother as the person she really was will crave this respect from her child as a substitute; and she will try to get it by training him to give it to her,' Miller wrote.[92] Such parents could in turn introduce unfulfilled needs for respect, echo, understanding, participation or reflection from their own childhood into the upbringing of their children. In these cases children are said to be narcissistically controlled by their parents. These parents unconsciously send out signals for which gifted, sensitive children in particular develop a high degree of sensitivity. Unknowingly, the children adopt the role assigned to them, suppress their own needs and feelings of jealousy, envy, anger, abandonment, powerlessness, fear and henceforth perceive this state as 'love'.

People who experienced this took refuge in illusions because reality was unbearable for them. Miller was not talking about illness here, but 'tragedy': 'For the majority of sensitive people, the true self remains deeply and thoroughly hidden.'[93] Affected children acquire complex defence mechanisms, such as denial, reversal of their passive behaviour into active behaviour, displacement, introjection or intellectualisation. Consequently, they construct a mask, an 'as-if personality', and become a person who plays a role and does not live as their true self. Not infrequently, such sensitive patients would be the 'pride of their parents', often praised for their talents and achievements. However, they would not possess a strong, stable self-confidence, quite the opposite: in everything they undertake they do well and often excellently; they are admired and envied; they are successful whenever they care to be – but all to no avail. Behind all this lurks depression, the feeling of emptiness and self-alienation, and a sense that their life has no meaning. 'These dark feelings will come to the fore as soon as the drug of grandiosity fails.'[94] Then these people would occasionally be plagued by fears or severe feelings of guilt and shame.

People who grew up with the image of a happy and protected childhood are completely unaware of the conflicts of their childhood. 'The internalization of the original drama has been so complete that the illusion of a good childhood can be maintained.'[95]

The truth of each unique childhood story[96] would have to be recovered during analysis. 'The paradise of preambivalent harmony, for which so many patients hope, is unattainable. But the experience of one's own truth, and the postambivalent knowledge of it, makes it possible to return to one's own world of feelings at an adult level without paradise, but with the ability to mourn.' The true self, which had withered away in a hidden 'chamber' guarded by 'prison guards', reflected the 'props of a childhood drama'. In this process, there would be no return home, but rather finding a home. Ideally, 'a new empathy with [one's] own fate, born out of mourning'[97] would emerge in the analysis.

In addition to the relevant subject matter, Jonas also felt addressed by the conceptual proximity to theatre: drama, story, role, make-up, props, an as-if personality – this language appealed to him intuitively.

The fact that Miller almost exclusively discusses an 'emotionally insecure mother'[98] who hides behind a 'totalitarian façade' struck on Jonas's memories of his own childhood, in which his father had left a strange nothingness, a void. Since Alice Miller's son Martin had made it known that his own childhood could have been a prototypical case in his mother's practice, it was known that Alice, like so many of her generation, also suffered from the consequences of war trauma.[99] This was another thing she had in common with Jonas's mother, Hilda May.

A second reading of Miller's book proved even more devastating for Jonas. He even quoted the work in his speech marking Wieland Wagner's centenary. Hildegard Behrens had since returned to Germany. He no longer had anyone to talk to, and felt that turning to a doctor was the best idea. Bernard Levin brought him together with a psychoanalyst who was then nearing retirement and taking only private patients. Levin thought that would be just right for Jonas: the psychoanalyst was not covered by his health insurance, so he would have to feel some pain after each session when he signed the cheque.

From then on, the analyst and Jonas met once a week over the course of a year. Everything went very classically. In the psychoanalyst's office there was a chaise longue on which Jonas would lie. The analyst would sit next to him on a chair. A clock hung on the wall, clearly visible to both. As soon as an hour had passed – and even during conversations where Jonas was coming very close to breaching his hidden 'chamber' – the analyst would reliably announce: 'I am afraid that's all we have time for today.' The conversation was really a monologue by Jonas. For almost a year, the psychoanalyst just listened. 'He was always writing. I have no idea what is in his notes. He taught me not to expect anything in therapy, especially not to expect that the therapist is going to pull something out of you. But somehow I felt better afterwards,' says Jonas. But, as Bernard Levin had predicted, he did feel a sharp pain every time he pulled out his little black chequebook.

With astonishing candour, Jonas told how he had gone in search of his hidden chambers and prison guards during analysis. He recalled the early separation from his parents, the loneliness at boarding school and the consequences of the violence he experienced there, against which he was not allowed to defend himself. He re-lived the loss of the nanny, the death of the sister and his later isolation within himself. Why had his parents sent him to boarding school so early? Was their decision based solely on the fact that so many parents in post-war England took this path? Or did his parents just want that excellent, academic education for which the Benedictines were famous? Was Hilda May interested in raising her son as a Catholic? What traumas did she herself carry from the war years in London? Did she suffer from the experience of emigration from Jamaica?

What was her husband's emotional world like? How had he dealt with his father's suicide and his own emigration? What was his job in the secret service, why was he away from home so often, and what did that do to him? Were his parents already estranged from one another in those early years? Hilda May and Walter had never spoken with their son about their emigration, the war period, or their early years of marriage. In retrospect, it seemed to Jonas as if they carried these invisible chains with them all their lives and completely denied their own fate. For Hilda May, her own divorce was a personal crisis that she had difficulty overcoming. The death of her daughter in 1964 placed extreme demands on her. 'Throughout her life, my mother was unable to overcome this trauma. She never fully recovered, not even by the time of her death in the year 2000 – like all parents who have lost a child in violent circumstances.'

Peter and Hilda May had little contact during his early Chicago years. His own divorce from Patricia now stood between them. She could not accept the news that another of her children was going to die: he had been given only twelve months to live. 'It was all a bit difficult, as the English say,' Jonas laughed. 'In German one would say: Es war eine Katastrophe.'

Once again, he felt that the time had come for a bit of comic relief. Jonas recounted an incident with his psychoanalyst, from whom he finally wanted to hear a sentence other than 'I think it's time now.' 'I was a young man at the time and I had violent dreams about women, almost fetishistic. I wanted to know if I was perhaps a sex murderer. Finally he reacted and answered me: "No, you are not." How did he know that? And he answered: "Otherwise you wouldn't bring up the subject without me pushing you."'

By talking about his dreams, Jonas also confirmed a central part of Alice Miller's theory: as soon as the ability to experience one's own feelings is regained, instinctual conflicts occur more frequently and are experienced with great intensity.[100]

My charming, superficial little brother

His psychoanalyst also led Jonas to reflect on the question of 'goalposts'. Whenever Jonas achieved a goal, he set himself a new, seemingly unattainable, one. Why did he behave like this? Why were his achievements never enough? Until the end, he could not – or perhaps he did not want to – give an answer. 'I do feel guilty all the same.' The Benedictines' mantra of 'ora et labora – et lege' was deeply rooted.

However, his analyst also drew his attention to the fact that he always wanted to prove himself to his deceased sister. 'I missed her a lot,' Jonas admitted. He fell silent and wept. 'She made me feel totally safe. I envied her intelligence, her eloquence. I adored her, she was my heroine! But basically I didn't know who she was. She lived a strange melange of friendships and relationships, which included older men and women. Even at St Mary's Convent she had had an unusually intense relationship with one of the nuns. I never really understood what it was. Then later, at university, she had affairs with two or three professors.' Again he repeated how important his sister was to him, still, more than fifty years on from her death – what a great influence she had had on his education. 'I really miss her.'

Throughout his life, Jonas saw himself as her 'charming, superficial little brother'. However, Kathryn had known her little brother only up until his time at Sussex. 'How shocked she would be if she could see what I have done in my life. "You?" she would ask, "then something must be wrong with the world!"'

Kathryn's way with him had had a lifelong effect; he could not break away from it even as a mature man who had known suffering. His analyst led Jonas towards a crucial observation related to the inferiority complex he felt: it was only after the death of his sister that Jonas began to develop and unfold his own talents. 'He poked me with this terrible question to which I have no answer, but which I feel has some truth in it: could it be said that I only began to grow intellectually and aesthetically with my sister's death? Maybe I have grown because my sister died. Maybe that was the trigger that released something dark and allowed me to go my own way. I don't know. An interesting coincidence.' Again he was silent. 'But you could also say that this question about my sister has nothing to do with it. The reason I started to grow was because I got sick after I started working: the illness itself left me free to develop. Or did I get sick because I hadn't processed her death?'

He looked out of the window and drummed his fingers on his mobile phone, which lay next to him on the back of his armchair.

'How I would love to see the surprise on her face when she reappears and steps through that door and thinks about what I have gone through in my life. Not what I have achieved, but what my illnesses have imposed on me. I am still here to tell that story. That in itself is an achievement.'

Over the course of their relationship, Lucia Popp, seven years his senior, also took over some of the role that Kathryn had played in his life: being his lodestar, introducing him to new worlds and offering emotional security. Only with Lucia Popp did he talk about his search, his grief and also, for the first time, about what it meant for him not to be able to have children. Even during his years in Munich he liked to claim: 'It is a crime when theatre people have children' – as if holding up the rhythm of life within the theatre, which is indeed incompatible with family life, as a justification for childlessness.

Jonas underwent analysis only one other time for a short period, when he was again under great stress in London due to his illness. The psychoanalysis he experienced in Chicago made his life more complete, he said later. He kept the book that Hildegard Behrens had given him in his Zurich flat. 'She is dead. Like so many of my friends. I can't accept that.' Jonas walked around his living room, stopping every now and then in front of a work by an Old Master. 'I dream that I am immortal. I'm standing here, I can't imagine that I won't be here tomorrow. It's so scary. I find that difficult.'

And then he is done with this topic: 'Come on, it's lunch time!'

Innovative programming

During the time that Peter Jonas was undergoing psychoanalysis, he assumed that he had beaten his cancer. There followed years in which he was able to work with Georg Solti and John Edwards on the orchestra's programming choices. Chicago audiences were used to the highest musical quality, Jonas said. 'They wanted to be carried away by Solti. They liked the fact that he was European and they wanted to follow him in his work and be driven by his baton into a frenzy of admiration and adoration. That's very naïve.' Solti knew how to exploit this situation. 'He was generous, he wanted the best conductors in the world for the CSO,' says Jonas. 'That is to his credit!'

When Jonas joined the orchestra, Carlo Maria Giulini was already the principal guest conductor, but wanted to cut back his workload for health reasons. With Daniel Barenboim and Claudio Abbado, Solti appointed two of the best conductors in the world as principal guest conductors at the CSO. Around this cocoon, as Jonas called it, he, Solti and Edwards developed a network of outstanding musicians. Solti's explicit wish was for Jonas to work on attracting the best. Carlos Kleiber, Rafael Kubelík, Erich Leinsdorf, Eugene Ormandy, André Previn, Leonard Slatkin and Michael Tilson Thomas came to Chicago regularly, sometimes for two to three weeks at a time, to work with the orchestra.

Accommodating such sought-after conductors in one season was a tremendous challenge and represented the fruit of a unique kind of planning. What was difficult about the negotiations was not so much the fee, but the arrangements as to who would take on which repertoire – and how these concerts were to be reconciled with the global performance schedules of the artists involved. It was enormously important to Solti that all his colleagues could conduct programmes that lay close to their hearts. At the same time, Solti and Jonas also had their own dramaturgical ideas about the orchestra's overall programme. 'We have always worked with the greatest artists from a good two generations. We developed a musical leadership that was the envy of the world. There was nothing like it.'

This claim was also reflected in the programme. Jonas combined symphonic and operatic works in a dramatically innovative way. Leinsdorf conducted the third act of *Die Meistersinger*, Solti *Moses und Aron* and *Simon Boccanegra*, and Abbado *Wozzeck* and *Boris Godunov*. Jonas had convinced Claudio Abbado to take on one of his most important projects, conducting Alban Berg's *Wozzeck*. Under Abbado's direction, the orchestra first performed *Wozzeck* in May 1984. The rehearsals took much longer than usual, and the costs stacked up. Jonas was under pressure and had to defend himself from the Board, which was on the verge of axing the production. His assistant at the time, Martha Gilmer, reported: 'Peter Jonas and Claudio Abbado were determined to put on something dramatic. Some of the musicians stood under a stage platform. There was no lighting designer, no props. The staff, guided by Claudio's imagination, just let it happen. It was an amazing tour de force. The budget was unclear. Peter just did what he thought was important.'[101] Edwards supported Jonas unreservedly. His success vindicated him, and the critics lavished him with praise. The Board acknowledged this joint success; Peter Jonas consolidated his standing vis-à-vis the Board, but also with the orchestra.

Later, they gave the first American performance of Modest Mussorgsky's *Boris Godunov* and toured it in New York. With Solti's approval, Jonas convinced John Cage to come to Symphony Center for a week of subscription concerts. Even the legendary work *4'33"* was performed. And they all came, the Cageists and the anti-Cageists. Leaflets of protest were thrown from the balconies. The subscribers were completely amazed. Hundreds of letters of complaint were sent to Edwards: the Board was outraged. 'It was fascinating!' Jonas crowed decades later. When he decided to play Karlheinz Stockhausen's *Gruppen for Three Orchestras*, one of the greatest challenges for any orchestra, he was accused of having 'snubbed' the Chicago audience once again. He also faced extraordinary legal challenges. *Gruppen for Three Orchestras* is considered one of the most important works in Stockhausen's oeuvre, as well as in the entire second half of the twentieth century. In it, Stockhausen divides the orchestra into three bodies, each led by its own conductor and grouped around the audience. To be able to divide the CSO into three individual orchestras the pre-existing collective agreement for the orchestra had to be rewritten. 'It was incredibly difficult, but a really worthwhile experiment! It was a time of great adventure,' Jonas said. 'He loved to start a trend. He set the tone, it didn't fit into a mould, that made it interesting for him,' Gilmer said. 'For Peter Jonas, it was fundamental to understand the score. Service to the music and to the musicians is always the most fundamental thing for him. He would not prefer something trendy to something true.' In her obituary, Gilmer wrote: 'He was a force of nature, loving the fight on behalf of the sustenance and the triumph of the arts.'[102]

At the same time, four recording studios were working with the CSO: Georg Solti worked with Decca, Claudio Abbado with Deutsche Grammophon and CBS/Sony, and James Levine with RCA. One has to bear in mind that during this time all the planning, rehearsal schedules, tour schedules, recording schedules and so on were drawn up by hand. Changes had to made using Tipp-Ex, usually several times. The pages became quite thick in these spots.

His international network was essential for Jonas's work at the CSO. 'Whoever it was, he made sure they got to Chicago,' Gilmer said. 'Peter had charisma. Artists and donors wanted to be with him. He was witty and erudite. He was tough, relentlessly tough.' Jonas also made tricky calls regarding artists' agencies. If he was dissatisfied with the outcome of negotiations, he was not afraid to withdraw from a deal. One day, a tenor booked for a difficult role decided not to perform. He just wouldn't come out of his dressing room. Peter Jonas found out about it around 10pm and needed a quick solution, because the next concert was scheduled for the following afternoon. He decided to call James Levine, then music director of the Metropolitan Opera in New York, directly. His first words in the conversation were: 'Oh, Jimmy, I'm so sorry. I didn't want to call you in the middle of the night. But I am in a dilemma. Listen, this is my problem…'

Martha Gilmer, who listened in, assumes that Jonas had deliberately called Levine at that hour so as not to get stuck in the Met bureaucracy.

British tenor David Randall stepped in for the role and rehearsed the next morning. A helicopter was booked to whisk him to O'Hare Airport so that Randall would be back in New York in time to perform.

He then returned to Chicago for the final performance. 'Peter was a genius. He was fearless. He knew how to get things done immediately. He always found a solution,' says Gilmer. 'Peter liked it when things got a little risky.'

When Martha Gilmer and Peter Jonas first met at the Symphony Center shortly after his cancer diagnosis, Jonas had greeted her with: 'There's no point in getting to know me, because I won't be around much longer.' Later, when he had just undergone treatment and was suffering from severe side effects, he could not sit, but only lie. Nevertheless, he came to the office, lay on the floor, dictated tasks and made calls. 'This shows how driven he was,' Gilmer said. When he planned programmes, he did not consult others. He was famous for throwing the programmes on the marketing team's table on his way out of the office the day before he left for Christmas. He would turn implacable and intolerant when he felt someone was out of line. 'He simply demanded top performance, no question about it. He had high expectations. The musicians always came first. We were never in doubt about what Peter thought. He had a firm point of view, we never had to guess.'

In his first years as artistic director of the orchestra, Jonas also found that everyday work in a top-class cultural enterprise could be both productive and stressful. The CSO was a 'grindstone', he wrote in a letter dated May 1981.[103] He was not well. From June 1980 to September 1981 he took a sabbatical, spent with Lucia Popp.

Ten green bottles

These years saw the development of deep lifelong friendships with Claudio Abbado, Daniel Barenboim and Carlos Kleiber. With Abbado, thirteen years his senior, who was principal guest conductor at the CSO from 1982 to 1985, he held hours-long conversations deep into the night. They shared and discussed their private passions, but also spoke of projects they wanted to realise professionally.

Daniel Barenboim had made his debut in the then Orchestra

Hall in 1958 as a fifteen-year-old pianist. As a conductor, his decades-long association with the orchestra, of which he became chief conductor in September 1991, succeeding Solti, began in 1971. For him, standing before the CSO was 'an event of shattering importance'.[104]

For Jonas, as for Barenboim, the experience with the CSO was hugely significant artistically. Their friendship developed slowly. Gradually, they came to do a lot together, discussing, going out to eat and celebrating. 'Daniel and Claudio were fantastic artists! I had a lot of fun with them. Solti, Carlo, Claudio, Rafael, Erich, Carlos: when I think about them, it doesn't feel good to me. They were all my friends. Do you know the old song about ten green bottles?' asked Jonas once. Then he began to sing the popular nursery rhyme:

> Ten green bottles hanging on the wall.
> And if one green bottle should accidentally fall,
> There'll be nine green bottles hanging on the wall.

'From those original times, the Chicago times, only Daniel, Zubin and I are left. All the others who are still alive came along later. That's hard for Daniel to bear.' Jonas interrupted the conversation because he had received a text message from his doctor in Munich. Everything had been cleared for the major operation – which would soon wind up being postponed anyway. His doctor reported that he was not expecting to find anything too concerning with his chest. That didn't really reassure Jonas. He was scared, and had to pull himself together again. 'Anyway…'

Jonas worked at the highest artistic level, and, as far as his work in Chicago permitted, he would also travel widely, especially to see Lucia Popp perform. He absorbed everything: he observed and he learned. 'I was happy in Chicago.' Headhunters called and offer letters arrived from other concert halls, but nothing would change his mind. Munich, as it happened, was not among the venues that courted him. However, in the archives there is a letter dated 21

March 1983, the first letter to Wolfgang Sawallisch.

The second would follow ten years later, on 1 September 1993. This letter is addressed to '8 Munich 20/West Germany'.[105] Jonas recommends to Sawallisch a researcher who is going to do her doctorate on Richard Strauss. Although other offers of work were not yet tempting him, he gradually became aware of a desire to work in an opera house 'where things were quite a bit of fun'.

Before Jonas was ready to talk about how Claudio Abbado aimed to win him over for the Vienna Staatsoper, he illustrated what a lasting impression Georg Solti had made. The story takes us to post-war Munich. Georg Solti told it to Jonas on one of their first tours together. It speaks to Solti's own inner struggle, and his existential insecurity as an emigrant Jew in post-war Germany. Although Solti's narrative was about his life's journey, he again drew Jonas's attention to his own family's Jewish roots, coincidentally picking up the thread that W. G. Sebald had already laid for Jonas in Manchester.

Solti told Jonas a chapter from Munich's musical history. It was a time when the Americans laid the foundations of cultural administration in the city in the post-war years: they created the very body that would later appoint Jonas as State Director of the Bavarian Staatsoper in Munich in April 1991.

Solti's story is about how a man would knock on the door of his very own office. This act became a metaphor for Jonas. In this image of knocking on one's own door, he encapsulated a nagging doubt as to whether he could meet the demands placed on him: his own demands of course, but also those of others.

MUNICH 1946–1947

Knocking on your own door

Georg Solti heard the footsteps and had to admit to himself: he had been waiting for them. Involuntarily, his back tightened and he dropped a thick pencil onto the score that lay open on his desk. His eyes lost their focus on the staves. For a moment he held his breath. He wanted to be sure. And, as so often before, he heard the knock come, but not at his door. It was the the next room over. That knock always went unanswered.

The silence that followed was disturbed only by morning sounds: the occasional vehicle, or someone entering the theatre from Prinzregentenplatz. The man waiting outside in the corridor knocked a second time. Then he entered, having received no answer. Why did he do that?

Solti heard the man hanging his heavy, dark winter coat in the wardrobe. Then he dropped his worn bag on the small, round table, over which he and Solti had quarrelled so fiercely in the past. The noises in the next room didn't stop. Solti felt an inner tension. The morning hours were precious to him: the only time to find the peace to work on new scores. He had to rehearse in the afternoons, and then rehearse a second time in the evenings, or else conduct a performance. Fortunately, the coal merchant Faltermeyer, an enthusiastic opera lover, had just brought him and his wife a sack of coal for their rooms at Maximilianstraße 6.

When Georg Solti interrupted his study of the score late that morning and stepped into the room of his colleague Ferdinand Leitner, his gaze fell on potatoes and vegetables. He was gripped by envy. His own supplies of cigarettes, brought over from Switzerland, were almost exhausted. His wife Hedi would also have to exchange theatre tickets on the black market again: alongside cigarettes, they were the hardest currency available these days.

Ferdinand Leitner noticed the hunger in Solti's eyes, but refrained from any comment and sat down. They had a lot to talk about. The Americans wanted rid of Arthur Bauckner, the Intendant of the three opera houses. That was to be expected. They wanted Leitner to take over Bauckner's roles: all three of them. Neither the Americans nor the Ministry had informed Solti. This looked like a recipe for a bitter conflict. Leitner needed to talk about it with Solti.

But Solti was already speaking. He was asking Leitner why he always knocked on his own door before entering? Leitner hesitated. How could Solti, a man of such extraordinary talent, passion and self-discipline, miss the blindingly obvious? That time was running out for the pair of them.

'I always knock. When I hear someone answer "Come in," I'll know I've been sacked.'

Georg Solti and Ferdinand Leitner

Ferdinand Leitner was keenly aware that the American military government in Bavaria, and also the Bavarian Ministry of Culture, had the power to relieve him of his duties at any time. By August 1946, the Americans had appointed Solti musical director and Leitner operatic director of the Bavarian Staatsoper under Arthur Bauckner's Intendanz. Solti had the major advantages over the other candidates of being both politically unconnected and non-Bavarian – but Solti was also a Jew. Like him, Leitner was born in 1912 and had most recently worked as Kapellmeister at the Hamburg Staatsoper. The Americans saw him as a competent administrator and conductor with sufficient professional experience in opera to rebuild the Staatsoper together with Solti, who was largely inexperienced as a conductor, although he was regarded as being extraordinarily talented.

Leitner came from a well-off family and had received music

lessons from an early age. He later studied composition and piano at the Staatliche Akademischen Hochschule für Musik in Berlin and worked as Kapellmeister at the Theater am Nollendorfplatz in Berlin in 1943–44. During the turbulent, uncertain 1930s, when he had worked as a pianist and accompanist, he had assisted Fritz Busch at the Glyndebourne Festival and as a répétiteur for Carl Muck at the Bayreuth Festival.

Now, in early 1947, Leitner was confronted with the consequences of the US military government's change of strategy in occupied Germany. Allegiances had shifted. The Soviet occupying power had become a competitor to the Americans. Now communism was the great enemy.[1]

Edward Kilényi, a music control officer in the American military government, was furiously opposed to the new directive JCS 1779, with which military governor General Lucius Clay wanted to build Germany up into an ally for the democratic powers. It wasn't that Edward Kilényi did not agree with this strategy, but the uncoordinated approach and the abrupt change in policy jeopardised the success of Kilényi's work. Clay wanted to set up state governments as quickly as possible, which would no longer be bound by the instructions of the Americans and could take over administrative tasks – such as making appointments to important posts in cultural institutions. Kilényi would not be able to fill the artistic director's post at the Staatsoper without the Bavarian ministry's say-so. At a stroke, Leitner's and Solti's trump card – not being Bavarian – had become worthless.

Leitner was loyal to Edward Kilényi, a deeply musical man. Born in Philadelphia, Kilényi had studied at the Liszt Academy in Budapest, as had Solti. Worried about his citizenship, Kilényi had joined the US army and was now entrusted with the task of rebuilding musical and operatic life in Bavaria.

Although he left Germany again in 1946 and his deputy John Evarts took over his duties and also negotiated Solti's contract, it was Kilényi who brought Solti to Munich – against initial resistance from Bauckner, whom the Americans had appointed Intendant in 1945. This decision by Kilényi sparked Solti's career.

Georg Solti, who was born György Stein in 1912, had to work as a répétiteur at the Budapest Staatsoper for eight years before he was granted his first conducting position in 1938. His parents had already recognised his excellent ear at the age of five, and at thirteen he had begun his training as a pianist and conductor at the Liszt Academy in Budapest.

In 1930, at the age of eighteen, he began his career as a répétiteur. By then had already assisted Arturo Toscanini at the Salzburg Festival. His first conducting job – Mozart's *Nozze di Figaro* in March 1938 – ended traumatically. Not because the Intendanz had refused to schedule him a single rehearsal. He knew the production well. 'But at the beginning of the third act, Mr. Lendvai, the baritone in the role of Count Almaviva ... made all sorts of mistakes, sang incoherently and seemed to have completely lost his confidence. ... Just as he had been about to go on stage, Lendvai had been handed a copy of an extra edition of an evening newspaper and had learned that German troops were crossing the border into Austria and marching towards Vienna.'[2] In the evening hours of the day when Solti was finally allowed to make his debut as a conductor, after long years of waiting, Chancellor Kurt Schuschnigg declared in his farewell speech in Vienna that he would avoid violence. The first swastikas were already hanging from government buildings.

On the night of Solti's debut, Austria's annexation by the German Reich began. During the first two acts of the opera, news of the German invasion spread. Only about five hundred kilometres away from the unfolding events, everyone at the opera in Budapest assumed that Hungary had been invaded too. 'My parents had planned a celebration after the performance. It was cancelled, of course, and my elation turned into anxiety and depression,' Solti wrote in his memoirs. 'I had the feeling that all my hopes had been dashed. That evening left a permanent scar in my heart.'[3]

As his application for a visa to the USA had been rejected, Solti emigrated to Switzerland in August 1939 to live in Zurich until the end of the war. 'I was desperately lonely and depressed,' he later confessed about his first time in Zurich, where he was spared having to witness wartime trauma despite harsh circumstances. In 1942 he was able to conduct two performances of Massenet's *Werther* in Geneva, but the turning point was his triumph at the International Piano Competition in Geneva in 1942. He received a work permit, albeit with certain restrictions, but at least he could now teach pupils, play a few concerts and survive from month to month.

Edward Kilényi

One of Solti's students was Max Lichtegg, who a few years later, in 1945, made a recommendation to Moritz Rosengarten, manager of the Decca Record Company. This would prove decisive for Solti's career. Solti first recorded the complete *Ring des Nibelungen* with the Vienna Philharmonic from 1958 to 1965 and became one of the most important artists for Decca. But for now, Solti was still a long way off such heights.

'Somehow or other',[4] Solti wrote, he had learned that his former fellow student Edward Kilényi was working as a music officer in Munich. Kilényi remembered more precisely: Gerard W. Van Loon, who was working as a theatre officer in Bavaria at the time,[5] spent his Christmas holiday in Switzerland in 1945–46, met Solti there by chance and told him about Kilényi's job in Munich. Solti then used his first wife Hedi's contacts to write a letter to Kilényi. The post did not yet work in Germany at that time. He asked Kilényi point-blank whether he could be of use as a conductor somewhere in Germany. Kilényi replied immediately: 'Be at the German border crossing at Kreuzlingen at 8 o'clock on 20 March. An American Jeep will bring you to Munich.' The open-topped Jeep arrived only at 11pm. The Americans wore thick leather jackets, but Solti had only a thin coat. 'I can't remember ever having been as frozen as I was that night,' Solti said, before going on to describe the shattering experience of seeing an utterly destroyed Munich as dawn broke over the city. For the first time he was really experiencing the extent of the devastation of war that he had been spared in sheltered Zurich. 'I would have turned back if I could have.'[6]

Solti was allowed to spend the night before his first meeting with Arthur Bauckner on a sofa in the warm American headquarters in Bavaria Studios. With the subtle irony of leaving much unsaid, Solti described his first encounter, his interview, with Bauckner: 'Kilényi introduced me to the great Dr Bauckner, who looked up from his desk and said to Kilényi: "Why are you bringing him here? We don't need him." "They told me to find someone who has no political affiliations," said Kilényi. "Oh no, we don't need him."'[7]

This was just Bauckner enjoying his new-found power vis-à-vis the American occupier. He was in fact desperate to find a conductor and would have had to offer Solti at least a guest conducting position. Kilényi was furious and sent Solti to the Stuttgart Staatsoper, where he conducted *Fidelio*. Word of this production's success reached Munich. 'That's our man,' Bauckner said, signalling a change of heart, as Kilényi's deputy and successor John Evarts recalled.

Although the Württemberg-Baden Kultusminister Theodor Heuss had made the Soltis a very attractive offer of work and a flat of their own, the future Federal President did not stand a chance against the mighty Munich Staatsoper: Solti conducted *Fidelio* again, in Munich, on 9 April 1946 and then signed his first contract, which lasted for two years. This meant that he had been given artistic responsibility over a number of performances, but not complete musical responsibility. He terminated his contract on 1 September 1946, about a month before Peter Jonas was born in London. His title changed again and again over the lives of three different contracts in the next six seasons. Sometimes he was 'chief conductor', sometimes 'musical director', but never General Music Director. In the spirit of the post-war anti-Nazi 're-education program' which was carried out in defeated Germany, Germans might have come to see how unnecessary and ridiculous such quasi-military titles as 'General Music Director' and 'General Intendant' are in a democratic society.[8] The fact that the Bavarian Staatsoper nevertheless listed Solti's job as 'Generalmusicdirektor' in a programme booklet for the 1946–47 season suggests otherwise.[9]

In the short time in which they exercised absolute control, the Americans had wanted to establish mechanisms that would prevent culture from ever again being misused for political purposes. Although the brief duration of their rule and the abrupt shift to the fight against communism make a balanced assessment of the Americans' achievements difficult, it is nevertheless clear that the US exerted a lasting influence on the basic principles of accountability and democracy in public cultural administration.[10]

The National Theatre on Max-Joseph-Platz having been destroyed in an aerial bombardment in 1943, the ensemble had been housed in the Prinzregententheater since 1944. In December 1945, of a planned repertoire of eighty-four productions, it was possible to perform only four; the sets of all the others had been destroyed in the war. In their first season together with Leitner, the programme also included *Carmen*, *Walküre* and – as so often in post-war Germany – *Fidelio*. Hardly any singers received permission from the Americans to travel to other opera houses during this period, and even had they, the paucity of transport might have made the journey impossible all the same. This enabled the Munich Staatsoper, like many other German opera houses, to work with a permanent ensemble of singers and develop individual voices.

When Solti was appointed music director, denazification was still a work in progress. His sober – and accurate – assessment was that an inexperienced conductor like him would never have been given one of the most important conducting posts in Europe if established and proven conductors had not been banned from the profession.[11]

On the basis of the first 'blacklist' published in 1945, the American military government issued numerous professional bans. Forty per cent of the members of the state orchestra lost their jobs, and in 1946 less than one per cent of musicians were officially 'available for employment'.[12]

From March 1946 onwards, the Spruchkammern [civilian anti-Nazi tribunals] took up their work under the control of the civilian Länder authorities. These reinstated many individuals, some unjustifiably. Solti's direct competitors were Eugen Jochum (1902–87), who had been General Music Director at the Hamburg Staatsoper since 1934, and Hans Knappertsbusch (1888–1965), who had been General Music Director of the Bavarian Staatsoper from 1922 to 1935 and its Intendant 1934–35. The Bavarians would have preferred Jochum over Solti, but the American military government had blocked the native Bavarian. Although Knappertsbusch was not initially blacklisted, the Americans reopened his case in October. His name had been on the 'Gottbegnadeten [God-pardoned] List', in which Goebbels and Hitler had listed the names of more than a thousand artists who were not allowed to be drafted into the Wehrmacht because the Nazi regime considered their work too important.

The fact that the Americans then considered Knappertsbusch, with whom Kilényi had also performed as a soloist, unsuitable to work as a conductor had a devastating effect on the Germans: they identified with Knappertsbusch, whom they felt the occupiers were treating unfairly.[13]

Both were allowed to return to the Munich concert halls only a short time later. The people of Munich, who, to Solti's chagrin, emphatically lauded Knappertsbusch in particular, saw the return of the two as a kind of 'vindication of German art and a condemnation of American philistinism'.[14] It was an expression of their opposition to the occupiers. The Americans' staffing decisions cost them legitimacy.

Resistance to Solti

Leitner was the first to feel this. Culture Minister Franz Fendt thought that he was not a good choice. He was not a local and, on 1 December 1946, the first elections to the Bavarian Landtag took place. The Ministry of Education had agreed to abolish the post of General Intendant on 1 April 1947. The previous General Intendant, Bauckner, had resigned. He would later call his Intendanz a 'Husarenritt [daring escapade]'.[15]

Instead of one artistic director, the Ministry planned to appoint three posts: for drama, operetta and opera. This was the second of several attempts made before 1952 to reorganise the opera house. The situation was similar to when Jonas came to Munich, when the post of General Intendant was created for August Everding.[16] Evarts wanted to impose Leitner on the Bavarians, but found no support among his superiors. The Ministry had neither informed Solti that Bauckner was unavailable for the post of Intendant, nor that Leitner was being discussed. 'Because he concentrated on his musical work, Solti was not up to date on political and administrative changes. In the last few weeks there had also been growing distance and misunderstanding between Leitner and Solti.'[17]

Solti would not accept that, as Intendant, Leitner had a right to influence his work. Leitner realised that he would not get the post of Intendant of the Staatsoper. He was wise enough not to knock on his own door a second time to find out if he was still wanted in Munich, and in early 1948 moved to the Stuttgart Staatsoper as their General Music Director, and developed Stuttgart into one of Europe's foremost operatic centres.

Of all the musicians the Americans had chosen, Solti stayed the longest. After the state elections in 1946, however, his position was increasingly up for grabs. Jochum was his greatest rival, although Rudolf Kempe asserted himself as his successor. Dieter Sattler, later ambassador and head of the cultural department at the Foreign Office, had been appointed State Secretary at the Bavarian State Ministry for Education and Culture in 1947 and led the talks with Solti.

Sattler had decided that the Jewish Solti would have to leave his post voluntarily so that no one could accuse the Ministry of anti-Semitism. His contract extension in August 1948 was thus offered to Solti under significantly worse conditions. He had to accept Jochum as his first guest conductor. In his memoirs, Solti quoted at length the report by Evarts which analysed the enthusiasm of a Munich audience after a performance by Knappertsbusch. 'An apparently well-organised claque raised its concerted voice at the end with shouts like "Wir wollen Knappertsbusch zurück an der Oper" [We want Knappertsbusch back at the opera].'[18]

Solti openly admitted how extremely difficult it was for him to work alongside Knappertsbusch and his influence in the Munich music world. He was aware of how many people did not want him in that post. 'From the beginning, I encountered a certain resistance among German musicians and music lovers who objected to the presence of cultural organisations in the American army and a non-German at the helm of the Bavarian Staatsoper.'[19]

On 31 August 1952 Solti finally resigned and took up a role as General Music Director at the Frankfurt Opera. In a Landtag debate, Hildegard Hamm-Brücher strongly denounced the Ministry's opaque behaviour. State Secretary Brenner patronisingly said, 'Solti could possibly come back as a director after a spell directing outside of Munich.'[20] What presumption.

Ferdinand Leitner's peculiar habit of knocking on his own door testified to how much Leitner had internalised a key fact: his professional existence, the possibility of working as a conductor at an opera house, was directly dependent on the American military government and the Bavarian administrative officials; on their directives, their arbitrary power, but also on their ability to enforce decisions that were correct in terms of cultural policy and art.

From then on, Solti remained extremely sensitive to the slightest signs of hostility, whether expressed by the public or by political bodies. Solti's sense of vulnerability was evident until the end of his life. Despite his outstanding success, the reactions of the former refugee prevailed over the tactical actions of the world-renowned artist.[21] Especially during his time as music director at the Royal Opera House Covent Garden, he was subjected to a campaign by the London press, which he personally accused of being motivated by hatred of him or by racism. In July 1966, after a performance in Covent Garden, he discovered that an unknown protestor had smeared the words 'Solti go home' on his car. For a Jew who had lost his relatives in the Holocaust, this attack was terrifying. Jonas would also be attacked in July 1996 with exactly these words – 'Jonas go home.'

In other respects, too, Sir Georg Solti's narratives contain many of the motifs that run through Jonas's entire life: Solti told him about people who had to emigrate because they were Jewish. He talked about being unwanted as a foreigner in Germany – at least at first – and about the battle to be permitted to work successfully as an artist within the structures of the state cultural administration.

Solti's tale of the man who knocked on his own door, discerning from the ensuing silence that he still had his job, struck a nerve with Peter Jonas. 'His story infected me, a real insecurity, and I find that this kind of insecurity was a kind of protective mechanism. One should never feel secure. Always go to work and think: today, they will find out. Today, they will realise that actually I know absolutely nothing. Always believe you are going to be fired. And all through my life – in Chicago, at ENO, and in Munich – I always knocked on the door of my office.'

LONDON 1984–1993

The agony of choice

What to choose as a next step in his career, were he to be given the option, must have preoccupied Peter Jonas for a long time. Few in the opera business would have preferred English National Opera (ENO) over the Vienna Staatsoper. But then a number-one position was on the cards in London. ENO, formerly Sadler's Wells, was the second-greatest opera house after the Royal Opera Covent Garden. When Peter Jonas, while working on this biography, recalled how he was appointed to head ENO, he was gripped once again by each twist and turn. Every single telegram exchanged between London and Chicago mattered. At the time, he followed the advice of his Chicago mentor John Edwards once more and made his choice based on what really interested him – and that was not the international standing of the particular opera house, or its finances, or its prestige. Again and again he spoke of how gruelling the never-ending battles against the policies of the Thatcher government had been. He spoke little about aesthetic questions or the style of production for which his company would become famous within a few years. Perhaps this was really how he saw himself as the newly appointed Managing Director of ENO: his aesthetic vision had not yet been defined to the degree that perhaps he had hoped for. But he was willing and able to fight a pitched battle for his chronically underfunded company, both against the government and against the Arts Council. Likewise, he was willing and able to put his personality on the line to woo audiences and sponsors alike. What Peter Jonas achieved together with his partners and friends Mark Elder and David Pountney, and with the entire ensemble of ENO, went down in opera history as the era of the 'Power House triumvirate'. Peter Jonas had more or less stumbled into his position at the CSO. He had

had no conscious wish to work for an orchestra – or indeed for a world-beating orchestra. Jonas had seen Sir Georg Solti conduct at Covent Garden during his student years, but he did not feel so taken with him that he had necessarily wanted to work for the older man. It had been a happy coincidence that had enabled him to demonstrate his knowledge and skills. Jonas recalled that: 'I *hochstapelte* my way through,' which we might translate as: 'I got in because no one noticed that I didn't know enough yet.'

In Georg Solti and John Edwards he had found two marvellous mentors who paved his way into the profession. Their importance in his professional development cannot be overestimated. In Manchester, W. G. Sebald had led Peter Jonas on a search for his Jewish and German origins. The stories the Hungarian Jew Solti told about his early days in Munich in the post-war years continued the theme. Solti had witnessed how this traditional company had redefined itself after the Second World War. Jonas had also got to know Germany and the Bavarian Staatsoper in his Chicago years through Lucia Popp. Years later, when Jonas was hoping to receive an offer from Munich, he knew the Bavarian Staatsoper in a way that even many Munich natives didn't. And from Solti he knew how unnatural it was for a foreigner to reach a position at the head of such a cultural institution.

After eleven years in Chicago, the first phase of his career, accepting a top post in London would be a conscious decision. This process, which he found agonisingly protracted, ought to be related with precision, because it reveals so much about what was important to Jonas: loyalty and commitment, the highest standards, tactical nous combined with audacity, and the will to create something great. Jonas's journey from Chicago back to London also tells a wonderfully peculiar story about the culture of his homeland.

His friendship with Claudio Abbado made Jonas hesitate for a long time, but Abbado couldn't really convince him, even with support from Lucia Popp. But the idea was too tempting for Popp as well: the prospect of Peter not only coming to Europe, but straight to her beloved Vienna! Jonas didn't really want to leave yet: something was holding him back. But both had succeeded in planting in him the seed of the idea of leaving Chicago. Ten years, however fulfilling, seemed to have been enough.

Abbado, who at this time, 1983–84, was chief conductor of Milan's La Scala and Principal Guest Conductor at the Chicago Symphony Orchestra, found himself in a deep personal crisis. Jonas and he were friends and had had many candid conversations. Jonas knew about the very first, tentative attempts from Vienna to win Abbado a post at the Staatsoper. But nothing had been firmed up yet. Abbado asked Jonas to meet with Claus Helmut Drese. Drese had cast Lucia Popp when he was Artistic Director in Cologne and when he held the same role in Zurich, so he was by no means an unknown quantity for Jonas. Drese and Abbado invited Jonas to come to Vienna with them, just in case. If the advances from Vienna were confirmed and if Drese and Abbado were indeed to become Director and General Music Director of the Vienna Staatsoper, then Jonas should come along and work as head of the operations office.

Jonas was immensely flattered, even though the offer was never made formally. 'It was a wonderful idea,' says Jonas, 'but I was hesitant.' Lucia Popp, on the other hand, was entirely enthusiastic. She had been a Kammersängerin at the Vienna Staatsoper since 1979, the year the Vienna Philharmonic had awarded her the Silver Rose. That opera house was her home. The prospect of having Jonas with her was a dream come true. 'But I was kind of nervous,' Jonas confessed. 'Today I understand the feeling better. I had an aversion, a kind of allergy to the Viennese. I didn't like this necrophilic atmosphere in Vienna.'

His mentor Solti also harboured a deep dislike for Vienna. Time and again he had told Jonas that the best street in Vienna was the one in Schwechat that led to the airport. 'I was aware of the opportunity I had here. For an Englishman! But whenever I thought about Vienna, intrigue crossed my mind. The idea of someone sticking a knife in my back.' Abbado wanted to carry on trying to persuade him, but Jonas continued his work in Chicago, outwardly unmoved. Inwardly, however, he had admitted to himself that he longed for a change.

Talking of Jonas's Chicago years, his friends praised one quality in particular: no matter where he was, no matter how he was doing, he always kept in touch with his friends. He had lost contact with one, Mark Elder, for a while because Elder worked at the Sydney Opera House from 1972 to 1974. On an early spring day in 2020, only a few weeks before Jonas died, Elder sat in the spacious, bright kitchen of his home in Highgate, north London, and reminisced about those years. It was a beautiful morning, and the magnolias were about to blossom. 'I remember how different he looked when I saw him for the first time after his cancer! But he also had this will, a very strong will! Always.'[1]

Elder had been working at ENO since 1979. The Sadler's Wells Opera Company, as it was then known, had moved to the Coliseum, and the new general manager George Harewood had arranged for the company to take a new name. 'It was Peter who organised my debut in America. Although, ironically, he hadn't seen me conduct very much. My whole career in America is directly linked to Peter.'

Elder made his US debut at the CSO in 1983. Elder and his wife Amanda travelled to Chicago for the first time the previous year, and Jonas and Elder resumed their old, familiar conversations about aesthetic questions and everything that was going on in their world.

'When Mandy and I were in Chicago in 1982, we saw him as someone who always got the job done. We didn't see him as someone who could grow into the role with a bit of luck. We thought he would do a great job running the house. I remember his way, that way! He had this confidence and this reverence for opera and singing.'

Mark Elder also saw at first-hand the outstanding cooperation between Jonas and John Edwards, which was truly amazing. As Amanda and Mark Elder sat on the plane on the way back from their first trip to the USA, it was Amanda who first uttered the idea and thus gave birth to a plan that would lead ENO into one of its most productive eras. 'Mandy said to me: "If Lord Harewood ever retires from ENO, then he is the man who should run it." It was her idea!'

In April 1984, George Harewood announced that he would retire as ENO general manager at the end of the 1984–85 season. Harewood had never heard of Peter Jonas, although Jonas had applied to him at the tail-end of his student days: the rejection letter had been sent by an assistant. 'It was up to me to bring them together,' Elder emphasised. 'It was amazing that it worked.'

Harewood met Jonas in a flat in Manhattan friends had provided. Harewood and Jonas were supposed to talk in the morning and then have lunch – but it wasn't until around midnight that they finally said goodbye. They had talked about everything from financial matters to repertoire preferences.

'Lord Harewood was a great statesman and artistic director, a proven connoisseur of opera,' Jonas enthused. 'He was a great personality. I admired him.'

Harewood, for his part, liked the idea of Jonas succeeding him. 'He was obviously a good choice. Peter made it very clear that he always wanted to work in opera houses. The experience he had had in Chicago with the orchestral repertoire was preparation for something bigger. Leading ENO was a dream for him. Wonderful!' Elder summed up.

Lord Goodman

But then Jonas received a phone call: Claus Helmut Drese asked him to meet Abbado and Robert Jungbluth, the General Secretary of the Austrian Federal Theatre Association, in Wiesbaden. Drese was awaiting the decisive offer from Vienna. Abbado was to become General Music Director, and both of them wanted Jonas to be part of the new team. Jonas agreed to the meeting. Before it took place, however, another message arrived, this time a telegram. It came from Lord Goodman, Chairman of the Board of ENO.

Jonas claimed to recall the content by heart even after all these years. He imitated the formal style in an affected singsong: 'My dear Peter Jonas, as you may or may not know the Managing Director of English National Opera, the right honourable, the Earl of Harewood, has decided he wishes to retire in the spring of 1985. We are about to conduct a search for a successor. We were wondering if you are interested in such a position. And if so, we also wonder if, without commitment, you would care to attend a meeting with myself and some Board members to discuss this matter further with views to whether you would wish to apply.'

Jonas replied by return, also with a telegram:

'Dear Lord Goodman, I would be more than happy to visit you and your Board colleagues in London, as I am on my way to an appointment in Europe in ten days' time anyway.'

The man who, with his telegram, had set in motion a carefully choreographed sequence of steps, all of which would remain non-committal until the final act, was Lord Arnold Goodman, a highly successful lawyer. He was an imposing presence, with strong, dark eyebrows and a pronounced double chin.

But his corpulence stood in contrast to his mental agility, said British music critic Norman Lebrecht.[2] Most of his clients had seen their problems solved at a stroke by a letter sent by Goodman. Whenever it seemed appropriate, he is also said to have sometimes forgotten to invoice a client. Lebrecht described him as the most influential power broker the UK had ever seen. A man for all crises, who always had a solution ready for powerful people.

In Lebrecht's view, the arts were only a means to an end for Goodman. This 'chairman of almost everything' chaired the Arts Council from 1965 to 1972, but also sat on the governing bodies of the Royal Shakespeare Company, the Royal Opera House and was Chairman of the Board of English National Opera from 1977 to 1986. It was he who destroyed the finely balanced system of British cultural funding developed by John Maynard Keynes.[3] But more on that later.

Jonas praised Goodman, although he did not detail what Goodman had achieved for ENO – other than appointing him.

'In England, tea mugs have sayings like: "Keep calm and carry on!" Goodman was the very caricature of British Phlegm. And thank God he was there! If there was an argument on the Board, Goodman would break off the discussion.' Jonas again imitated Goodman's mannerly lilt: 'This is very much the situation, but I think we are overstating the case. Let us have confidence in the General Director and let us carry on.' The minutes then only said: 'the Board took note of blablabla.' Jonas was amused. As soon as the first telegram arrived, he knew exactly who he was dealing with.

In 1984, ENO was the first British opera company to tour the United States. It put on twenty-eight performances in five cities with a thoroughly demanding programme: *War and Peace* by Sergei Prokofiev, *Rigoletto* by Verdi (the 'Mafia' production by Jonathan Miller), *The Turn of the Screw* and *Gloriana* by Benjamin Britten, and *Patience, or Bunthorne's Bride* by Gilbert and Sullivan.

Artistically, the tour was a comprehensive success, but financially a débacle, the effects of which Jonas was still dealing with in his first season in London. When he attended a performance at the Metropolitan Opera in New York during the tour, his future collaborator Maggie Sedwards saw him for the first time. 'When Lord Harewood announced his retirement, only the Board and management were involved in the discussions or in choosing his successor,' Sedwards reported. 'It was all very secret, although we were aware that conversations were being held with someone who did not live in England.'[4]

For this unknown person, one of Sedwards's colleagues used the code name 'Siegfried', alluding to Fritz Lang's film of the same name. During the performance at the Met, her colleague whispered to her that Siegfried was in the house. 'I didn't even know what this person looked like,' Sedwards said, 'but since we were all sitting together, it was pretty easy to guess who it was when this very elegant, grey-haired, dashing-looking man came in and sat down.'

The question of whether he would receive an offer to succeed Harewood excited Jonas in a way that the offer from Vienna could not have. 'That was partly related to the fact that it was a number-one position in London,' says Jonas. 'I felt more confident because of the language, but also because I thought I knew what to expect in London. Although I didn't have a clue how dangerous the London art scene was.' When Jonas summarised his career in 2006, he said he had moved to Chicago to escape London, because 'It's easy to sink under the morass of human beings and talent there, and to rise above it you have to be articulate and quick-witted.'[5]

The Coliseum

As a young man, he said, Jonas viewed the Sadler's Wells Opera Company as 'the absolute Mecca of all opera companies'. He often repeated this judgement – even though he had attended performances in Covent Garden more often with Mark Elder, as the latter countered sceptically. The history of English National Opera dates back to 1931, when philanthropist Lilian Baylis founded the Sadler's Wells Opera Company in the newly reopened Sadler's Wells Theatre. Baylis had been putting on opera concerts and plays in London since 1898, and from 1912 she was working at the Old Vic Theatre. Her passion was to provide the public with the best possible theatre and opera performances, at affordable prices. This is still ENO's mission today.

After Sadler's Wells Theatre was forced to close during the Second World War, it reopened in June 1945 with the world première of Benjamin Britten's opera *Peter Grimes*. When Jonas spoke of English National Opera as the Mecca of his youth, he meant this place, not the Coliseum where he later worked.

While Jonas was studying, the then-General Manager Stephen Arlen managed to find a new venue for the company after a tough battle: Arlen signed a first ten-year lease in 1968 and the Sadler's Wells Opera Company moved to the Coliseum in St Martin's Lane, in the heart of the West End. Jonas would also attend performances here during his later student years. A few steps from Charing Cross Station and Trafalgar Square, it is an ideal location both for Londoners as well as for visitors travelling from out of town. With its 2,359 seats, it is still the largest theatre in London's West End, and its proscenium arch is the largest among London theatres. With a width of almost seventeen metres and a depth of twenty-eight, the stage is truly gigantic.

The Coliseum was built by the leading theatre architect of his day, Frank Matcham, for the impresario Oswald Stoll. His ambition was to build the leading variety theatre, a 'people's palace of entertainment'. His production *White Horse Inn*, based on the German Singspiel *Im weißen Rößl*, was the most lavish production of its time and ran for six hundred and fifty-one performances.[6]

The revolving stage, consisting of three rings that could rotate independently or together, was itself spectacular. Stoll even used them for horse racing. Using animals on stage was not uncommon in London at the time; one theatre even had an elephant perform. But when one of the horses fell into the orchestra pit at the Coliseum, killing the jockey and injuring several musicians, the tradition came to an end.[7]

Built as a music hall, the venue was not at all ideal for an opera ensemble. The acoustics of the house were good for works with a big sound, especially Wagner, but unsuitable for operettas and works where it was important that the audience could discern all the lyrics. The house's vaudeville days were long behind it when the new general manager, Lord Harewood, had it renamed 'English National Opera' in 1974. Declaring itself the opera house of the whole English nation was no small claim. There were those who said that ENO would never have got permission for the new name were it not for Harewood's aristocratic background.

Lord Harewood

'George Henry Hubert Lascelles, the seventh Earl of Harewood, is a determined man. As first cousin to the Queen, he has a crown to throw around, and he flings it when necessary,' begins a portrait of George Harewood. 'He has a crown to throw around' – Jonas also liked to quote this phrase to characterise his predecessor. It was never clear whether this form of words was a compliment or not, says Jonas. Harewood's grandness, however, did not consist merely in the chance of having been born an aristocrat. All who worked with him at ENO and who shared his love of music and singing speak of him, his character and his conduct in the warmest terms. Despite his lineage, wrote Lesley Garrett, then first soprano at the house, George Harewood was a modest, approachable man with a disarmingly self-deprecating sense of humour, and he was not at all stuffy.[8]

To understand the circumstances in which Jonas took over ENO, one must have an idea of what kind of person opera director and later chairman George Harewood was. Peter Jonas considered himself lucky to succeed Lord Harewood. Once again, he had gained a mentor. 'Lord Harewood was royal. Er war ein großer Mann, ein wirklicher Aristokrat im besten Sinne des Wortes. [He was a great man, a true aristocrat in the best sense of the word.] He was also incredibly tolerant and generous.'

His paternal family was aristocratic and wealthy. Their Yorkshire estate is one of the most beautiful in England. The Duke of Windsor, the former King Edward VIII, said of George Harewood, with some understatement: 'It's very odd about George and the music. His parents were quite normal.'

His mother was by no means normal in the popular sense, for Mary was the only daughter of George V. 'My grandfather, the King,' was how Harewood wrote of George in his memoirs.[9] This family background necessarily brought celebrity.

He fought in the Second World War at the age of nineteen, was taken prisoner during the Italian campaign and then passed through a series of Italian hospitals and German POW camps until he was finally detained at Colditz Castle.

Harewood's memoir is a moving and finely nuanced account of his experiences. He did not allow himself any summary judgements of the 'Krauts'. In one camp, for want of any other literature, he read *Grove's Dictionary of Music and Musicians* up to the letter S. His wife Patricia later said that, whenever she wanted to cut a cake into nine parts or a melon into five, she could rely on his 'prison-handed accuracy'.[10]

Fig. 29: Lord Harewood and Peter Jonas at the Coliseum, London, 1985

The king's grandson, however, had learned more during the war than just how to cut a cake into odd-numbered pieces. George Harewood wanted to work. This in itself was unusual for a royal

– he was the only member of the royal family to have a job, and what was more, he had chosen the opera. In 1950 he founded *Opera Magazine*, one of the leading opera trade journals, still published monthly. Four years later, he completely revised and reissued a classic: Kobbé's *Complete Opera Book*. The British music writer Tom Sutcliffe judged that Harewood's life achievement was to have changed the British public's attitude to opera.[11]

Through his first wife, the publisher's daughter Marion Stein, Harewood became a close friend of Benjamin Britten. He worked at the Royal Opera House Covent Garden from 1953 to 1960. In the early years, the artistic director David Webster did not give him any particular, defined position. It was only in 1959 that he received the title of Controller of Opera Planning. After Covent Garden, he took over as artistic director of the Edinburgh Festival. His career coincided with a heyday of opera in England.

When Harewood divorced in 1967 it was one of the biggest scandals imaginable in British high society. He then married the Australian violinist Patricia Tuckwell, whom he had met waiting at Milan airport before a return flight to London. Harewood once told Jonas that he had offered to carry Tuckwell's violin to the plane. But Tuckwell had refused and asked him to carry her handbag instead; her violin simply meant more to her.

Because of his divorce, Harewood was excluded from the royal court for a long time. When the Queen, during a visit to ENO, talked to Jonas about Harewood, who was unable to attend on that occasion, she is said to have told him: 'Funny thing about George. In many ways, he is perfectly normal. He shoots, he fishes, but this opera work…'

When in 1970 the search was on for a successor to David Webster at Covent Garden, Harewood expressed interest. Arnold Goodman is said to have called the Queen's private secretary to ask Her Majesty's view. Officially, the Queen raised no objections, but she offered her blessing in the most restrained terms, meaning that the way was barred for Harewood.[12]

The tide turned when, in January 1972, the general manager of the Sadler's Wells Opera Company died unexpectedly. Harewood took over the company, got it renamed English National Opera and attacked Covent Garden whenever convenient. In his version, ENO was the people's opera house, and Covent Garden was an institution for the elite (incidentally, Solti was working at Covent Garden at the time).

Harewood brought Elder and his student friend David Pountney into the company. They developed a reputation for staging fresh and daring opera productions and distinguished themselves from Covent Garden and the 'cult of the star' there.

What Lord Harewood, Mark Elder and especially David Pountney had achieved at ENO thrilled Jonas. Pountney had already presented very successful works and was about to become production manager. 'His direction was groundbreaking. He has not only worked metaphorically, but also conceptually,' Jonas summarised his judgement at the time. 'He was clearly also influenced by Felsenstein. He transformed his entire visual world into a metaphor. I was impressed beyond measure.'

Peter who?

Finally, at the age of thirty-seven, Peter Jonas had found his own distinctive aesthetic stance, though in retrospect he was to categorise it as too conservative. Making this assessment of his own preferences, he was measuring himself against the young dramatists whom he had taught after retirement, as part of the Executive Master in Arts Administration at the University of Zurich. These students all came to him with established positions in the arts. But back when the telegram from Lord Goodman had arrived, he was still figuring out what he was really striving for aesthetically. 'I had always loved ENO. I had felt at home in this opera house,' says Jonas. 'In my view, ENO set the standard for continental European-style opera in England.' Hence his positive reply to Goodman.

In the end, Jonas flew first to Wiesbaden, then to London. He spent an afternoon with Drese, Abbado and Jungbluth: lively conversation in a pleasant atmosphere. 'But I felt uncomfortable.' Jonas felt that his role at the opera in Vienna would not really be clearly defined. Neither Abbado's appeal for Jonas to trust in him and Drese, nor Lucia Popp's vehement support for the Vienna option (she had also come to Wiesbaden to make her case), allayed Jonas's fears.

The three could simply no longer cut through. Jonas was thinking only about whether he would be offered the leadership of ENO. In Chicago, John Edwards had advised him to go for what he really wanted. And Jonas wanted to go to ENO. That Mark Elder was the house's musical director was a clear pull, as was David Pountney's position as First Director. The process of developing a new style at ENO had already begun. Because of all those intensive discussions with Mark Elder, Jonas was sure he would identify with the aesthetic approaches and goals. 'If I had been more experienced, if I had been more vain, I should have insisted on being able to start this process myself. But this way I was relieved to be able to build on it.'

But above all, he liked ENO, and this thought swept him along. 'I really believed in the company and what it stood for,' explained Jonas. 'That also makes me so angry about the current situation there, that it is having to go through such a tough time!'

In 2016, ENO had to fight for its survival anew. Once again, the Coliseum building lay at the centre of the story. The Arts Council wanted to mortgage it, which would give them the power to close the company in the long term. 'But zurück zum Stück! [let us return to the play!]' exclaimed Jonas, as he always did when he had drifted off onto a tangent.

Returning from Wiesbaden, he laid his cards on the table and told Abbado about the enquiries from London. He committed to make a decision within thirty days. If only he had known how slowly the wheels turn in London!

In London, he was met by a classic job interview set-up: Lord Goodman sat with a few members from the Board, all expecting Jonas to respond to their questions. Goodman was nice, but the others were rather strange. They asked him 'pretty stupid questions'. Even decades later, Jonas's displeasure at this meeting was plain. Above all, he took offence at the fact that the members of the Board were obsessed with one idea: they thought that the house and its programme had grown too big too quickly, and its goals were now far too ambitious. They blamed Harewood, who, they thought, was too easily manipulated. 'The Board was completely wrong,' Jonas was indignant.

But this misconception was the basis of the very first question Jonas had to face: 'How would you scale back on this ambition? How would you control the music director?' And Jonas gave a perfectly earnest, heartfelt response: 'I wouldn't. I would do the exact opposite: I would try to feed their ambition.' He knew this answer was impertinent, because what he was really telling the panel was: 'You have misunderstood the situation.' Jonas could see he was irritating his questioners. What they expected was someone who wanted to make a pronouncement that would be listened to and obeyed all the way down to the backstage groups and the workshops. 'The British think it's the Führerprinzip,' Jonas said indignantly in our meeting. In the course of the conversation, he mentioned that he had had another offer, from a surprisingly prestigious opera house. It was only for a second-rank position, but the house was clearly more important than ENO. To cut a long story short, it was a rather bumpy interview.

Over dinner with Elder and Pountney, Jonas vented his displeasure and concerns. Elder encouraged him: 'You'll get the offer! George assumes this too, even though he is not involved.' Jonas, however, didn't have long to come up with a firm answer, not only for Vienna, but also for Lucia Popp, who was still battling on to get him to come and join her there. She felt, Mark Elder recalled, that he could not cope with the enormously high demands of running ENO. 'If you take this job, it will kill you,' she warned.

Jonas flew back to Chicago. He now knew for sure that he wanted to go to London, not Vienna. But he also knew that he was in a delicate situation and that there was a danger that he would miss out on both potential positions.

Two days after his return to Chicago, he received a third invitation. Jonas rejected it out of hand. He simply had too many balls in the air. 'Isn't it funny? At certain moments you seem to emit vibrations or have a certain smell about you that signals to everyone that you want to move on.' At that moment in our interview, Jonas finally let something slip past his strict inner filter: 'I knew that my background, my qualifications were in fact perfect.'

As there was nothing he could do about the situation at that moment, he threw himself into his work and tried not to think about London. He distracted himself with long bike rides around Lake Michigan. He had to endure that for a fortnight until Harewood finally called. In his regal manner, he told Jonas that he would indeed receive an offer. Did he know anything for sure? No, no, but that will come. 'At some point I couldn't wait any longer. I had just come face to face with death! I was no longer afraid, the fear has only come back now, in my old age.'

He wrote Lord Goodman a letter, carefully wording it in Goodman's own style. He recalled it, apparently verbatim: 'Dear Lord Goodman, as you know, I mentioned to you that I have an offer to take up a very important position in Vienna. I promised them an answer, which deadline is rapidly approaching. It leads me to wonder if you have any further indication or information about your Board's decision which, as before, I am very keen to accept should such an offer be made.'

Goodman promptly responded with a telegram which, Jonas said, speaking from memory, read as follows: 'Dear Mr Jonas, as you know, we enjoyed our discussion here. At this point, I am still in consultation with my Board and I am afraid we are unable to give you any definite information. But we do ask you in good faith to hold on for a little longer, maybe as long as two weeks.'

This left Jonas in a really tricky situation. He had promised Abbado and Drese that he would make a decision within four weeks of the meeting in Wiesbaden. After receiving Goodman's reply, there were only five days left. 'So I rang up Mark: what do you think?' And Mark replied: 'You'll get the job!' Lucia urged him to trust the Viennese. Jonas waited until two days before the deadline and then decided on something really risky: he wrote to

Abbado and Drese to say that he had enjoyed their discussions immensely, that he greatly valued his friendship with Abbado, but would not be able to take up the post in Vienna. 'Claudio called me and told me that I was making a big mistake, a huge mistake. That working in London would depress me no end because the house was so miserably proletarian.' Jonas paused for a long time. 'And then I waited. And rode a bicycle. And as I got more nervous, I cycled even more.'

So Jonas was in pretty good shape when, sitting in a meeting about the coming tour with the Board of the CSO on 9 July 1984, Martha Gilmer, his assistant, knocked on the door and put a telegram on his desk. Jonas opened it immediately. It was from Lord Goodman and read something like this:

'Dear Mr Jonas, after careful considerations, my Board and I have decided that we wish to offer you the position as successor of Lord Harewood. The decision was reached *nem con*.'

'*Nem con*' stands for '*nemine contradicente*': no one was against, which means someone did not explicitly object but abstained from voting. Later Jonas found out who it had been and the reasons for their abstention: what was more, this certain someone had held out for Jonas's fiercest rival, Peter Hemmings.

It seems Jonas still felt wounded that he had not been unanimously appointed. When the Chicago meeting arrived at 'any other business' on the agenda, Jonas informed the members of the Board and his colleagues of his appointment. After the meeting, he sent a telegram to London to signal his acceptance.

Goodman had asked to meet quickly. He offered Jonas a disappointingly low salary and expected Jonas to sign immediately: 'Will you be so kind to sign this document right away?' he said, steering the conversation. The pay at ENO, for all members of the ensemble, had always been lower than that at Covent Garden. But Jonas knew he could expect an initial raise in a year's time and signed.

What annoyed him, however, was Goodman's thoughtless behaviour towards the unsuccessful candidates for the role, and one in particular. The perfectionist Jonas would never have been so casual. One rival for the post had been Nicholas Snowman, and the other Hemmings, who had excellent references and a robust network on the London scene. Snowman had been informed by telephone by Goodman that Jonas had prevailed. For some reason – 'Dinner?' Jonas speculated laconically – Goodman had omitted to extend Hemmings the same courtesy. It transpired that Hemmings, who had been seen in London circles as Harewood's presumptive heir, had to learn of his defeat from the newspapers. Hemmings became the artistic director of the Los Angeles Opera and he and Jonas worked together on co-productions.

'Peter Who?' was the reaction of an astonished public when it was announced in July 1984 that one Peter Jonas was to succeed Lord Harewood as Managing Director of ENO in June 1985. 'The choice of an administrator whose career has been American to head England's national company, which performs only in English and employs almost exclusively English artists, came as something of a surprise,'[13] noted the *New York Times*.

End of the Harewood era

When George Harewood retired in 1985, he had led ENO for thirteen years. It was the end of an outstanding career. 'He was a kind of king. I wanted to understand…' Jonas reflected, 'why he retired at the age of sixty. And why did I of all people follow him? He was very reluctant to answer me. At first he just said he wanted to take care of his estate and his family.'

'"Come on, why?" I insisted. "I have to know." Then George confessed how excruciatingly tired he was.' For decades Harewood had worked an eighty-hour week. He had grown tired of having to defend his decisions, over and over again, to the Board, the Arts Council and the Minister. Gruelling discussions about the financing of the ultimately successful US tour had eroded his exuberance, but he also felt that his authority within the house had suffered. 'George had built up an amazing circle of conductors, directors, set designers and singers. Above all, he was close to the conductors and the singers. George had wisely foreseen how English theatre aesthetics would tend to converge with the fashions of the continent. He had understood that the wave of "young Turks" wanted to work more or less on the German model, maybe with a little less discipline and a little less erudition, and in a style that he called "kind of chaotic."' Perhaps Harewood's press officer Maggie Sedwards or his chief dramaturgist Edmund Tracey could sense this direction of travel. But within the ensemble, it had not been an issue.

From September 1984 onwards, Harewood started to involve Jonas in his planning work. Harewood had succeeded in shaping ENO into what Jonas termed an 'ensemble company' with national appeal: a house in which the ensemble and its development were at the forefront; an ensemble that welcomed guest artists but always tried first to cast the great parts in-house; it was a system that went against the star cult of Covent Garden; 'the ensemble brought to maturity' was the *Sunday Times*'s verdict, at the time of Harewood's departure. With six hundred and fifty employees, the house managed around twenty-five productions, with two hundred and thirty performances, over a season lasting eleven months. Each performance had to compete with two hundred or so others on offer every single night in London.

Harewood's key decision had been to appoint the 32-year-old Mark Elder as music director of ENO in 1979. Elder had put on convincing performances conducting *Don Carlos*, *Tosca* and *Aida*.[14] Elder also convinced Harewood to bring his student friend David Pountney into the fold. Mark Elder was determined from the beginning that, as music director, he was going to improve the quality of the orchestra. In December 1979 he had taken a drastic step: he wrote to nine musicians to warn them that their contracts might not be renewed, three for disciplinary reasons, six for musical reasons. Since the post office delivered the letters only late in January, Elder was obliged to acknowledge that they were invalid. But this action showed his determination to improve the orchestra's quality.

'I was always worried that no one cared about musical quality, that they just came to see the new productions,' Elder recalled. 'My challenge was to say: "Listen, and look too!"' The process of improving the orchestra's quality took several years and finally paid off during the US tour, as Susie Gilbert points out in her chronicle of ENO.[15] Elder's commitment to a decidedly dramaturgical vision of ENO was promoted by Lord Harewood and ultimately led to the formation of his triumvirate with David Pountney and Peter Jonas, with whom he gradually transformed the orchestra through difficult and demanding negotiations with the unions. The years of the Power House triumvirate were actually 'the Elder years', judged Sutcliffe.[16] Even if Elder did not achieve a success like the *Ring* under Reginald Goodall during his fourteen years at ENO, he nevertheless developed a 'top class opera orchestra' and brought talented foreign conductors to the house.[17]

The choir also had a good reputation. Mark Elder was not only a brilliant conductor, wrote Lesley Garrett in her memoirs, but also the ultimate conductor for singers.[18] Jonas confirmed this: 'Mark was a really devoted music director, he was the indispensable opera conductor!' He thought about it for quite a while. 'The ideal general music director is always there. He is interested in what is going on in the house and also wants to know the gossip. Some directors think you can keep the GMD out of everything, but that's nonsense! A general music director must be a working member of the family. Zubin was like that too! The likes of Mark and Zubin have to be GMDs!'

Elder had already worked with Joachim Herz at ENO in 1975, when he was directing *Salomé*. In fact, Elder's boss, Charles Mackerras, should have conducted, but he was too busy and passed this task on to Elder. As a result, Elder was also offered the chance to be musical director of *Madame Butterfly* at the Komische Oper in Berlin in 1978.[19]

As a classical repertory production, *Madame Butterfly* would appear on the playbill again and again in the years that followed. This enabled Elder to travel repeatedly to East Berlin and immerse himself deeply in the aesthetic world of Walter Felsenstein. 'Going to East Berlin during those years was an incredible experience for me,' Elder recalled. 'I was touched and encouraged by the trust Joachim Herz placed in me. It was during this time that I got to know Felsenstein's legacy.'

His friend David Pountney was also influenced by Felsenstein's and Herz's tradition, but also by Ruth Berghaus. Born, like Elder, in 1947, David Pountney is one of the key figures in opera directing in England, mainly because of his position as Director of Productions at ENO, which he held for nine years until 1993. As a man with an intimate knowledge of the most important institutions, he was used to working with whatever was available in terms of singers, costumes and stage decorations. To a certain extent he was a 'slave to practice', said Sutcliffe, but also 'a highly successful pioneer of conceptual design and staging in Britain'.

Pountney had a reputation for being innovative, gifted and unapologetic. His best productions were based on an imaginative collaboration with his set designers.[20] They included Sue Blane, Maria Bjørnson, David Fielding and especially Stefanos Lazaridis. Pountney's most important works include *The Valkyrie* (1983), *Orpheus in the Underworld* (1985), *Carmen* (1986), *Rusalka* (1986), *Doctor Faust* (1986), and *Lady Macbeth of Mtsensk* (1987).[21] Sutcliffe went even further in his assessment: in his view, David Pountney was the outstanding genius of the Elder years. This is not because his productions were all wonderful. His style was eclectic and inconsistent. Like Elder, Pountney was willing to bring in highly talented artists while setting his own standards. 'Pountney was the guru of the new at ENO,' says Sutcliffe.[22] Many British directors and stage designers became known for commissions at ENO undertaken when Pountney worked there. This signature quality was reversed only towards the end of the Power House era, when it was overtaken by the distorted image of the 'Producer's Opera'. According to Sutcliffe, 'Produceritis' was seen as a contagious disease.[23]

Fig. 30: David Pountney, Peter Jonas and Mark Elder

Elder and Pountney wanted to implement strict standards for ENO productions, equivalent to those they had both seen in Berlin. The quality of the productions in England, including at their own house, no longer satisfied them. Pountney called the prevailing aesthetic 'hairdresser's opera'; Elder criticised what he called 'window dressing'.[24] 'We were far behind what Germany and Austria had achieved, behind the idea that the opera house should be a theatre of confrontation, novelty and challenge,' Elder explained.

Harewood, who was familiar with Felsenstein's work, had taken note of their project, and had started to work with them on elaborating a British version of this stage aesthetic. His great strength had lain in giving his artistic team the space they needed. But he also had firm views, defended forcefully. Elder reports that Harewood could appear incredibly Hanoverian, emphatically regal. When he wanted to push an idea through, his favourite exclamation was: 'I am going to lie down in the road over this one!'[25]

Harewood, Elder and Pountney were united in their commitment to ENO and the goal of renewing opera in England. But they disagreed on how to get there. Elder and Pountney came from a different aesthetic world from Harewood, even though the latter was quite familiar with continental European developments. Elder and Pountney wanted to change the production style of the house at all costs – and quickly. For them, opera was not a costume competition. They understood opera 'as drama and theatre'.

At the end of his tenure, Harewood was confronted with the fact 'that these young directors are not only going their own way,' as Jonas outlined the situation, 'but that they are also biting the hand that feeds them. On the one hand, George liked it. On the other hand, he had become tired of having to justify his decisions.' Pountney was held in high esteem by the ensemble; he was a dramaturgically strong director with equally strong ideas, says Jonas. 'The ensemble did not feel the slight tension between him and Harewood. The friction also had good sides, was productive. David did not get tired of these discussions at all. Sometimes he was stinging like a wasp.'

Mark Elder and David Pountney pulled together. It took Peter Jonas as the final driver to start a phase of extraordinary productivity, creativity and innovation in the ENO ensemble.

For George Harewood, it was time to go. His company bade him farewell with a production of Michael Tippett's *Midsummer Marriage*. Harewood had been fascinated by the work since its première in Covent Garden in 1955. 'This is a heavy, strange piece. Symbolism, in the sense that C. G. Jung understood it, plays a major role. It is very demanding to create a *Bildwelt* for this piece. David Pountney and Stefanos Lazaridis had created a completely individual, not at all old-fashioned visual world. A world beyond fashion. A Bildwelt of the spirit. It was a brilliant production, but economically a débacle,' Jonas laughed. 'Not at all a fitting farewell for Harewood!' *Midsummer Marriage* was a work that always meant a lot to Jonas. In Munich in 1998, he again left its musical direction in the hands of Mark Elder, and Richard Jones directed.

George Harewood appeared at the farewell gala in a purple Mao jacket. Journalists interpreted this caprice as him again 'throwing his crown around'. Harewood allowed himself another touch of irony on his last day at work when he left the Coliseum with a bag that read 'Superstar' and stood waiting for a taxi home under the sign that declared that he and Finance Director Rupert Rhymes were permitted to sell alcohol and cigarettes on the premises.

The ENO experience

This licence to sell alcohol and cigarettes was now transferred to Peter Jonas, and a new sign put up on the outside wall of the 'leaky, sometimes smelly, but very popular Coliseum'. The *Sunday Times* could hardly have described the building more aptly: it was indeed in need of renovation. During a performance of *Madame Butterfly*, a storm tore holes in the roof. Rain dripped on the second violins, but the conductor kept his cool, sent the violinists home but the performance went on uninterrupted. Jonas moved into his tiny office in this peculiar theatre and began his work.

In 1983, before Jonas moved to London, Lucia Popp and he had separated. He never talked about the whys and wherefores. She left. 'I worked from dawn until midnight. Otherwise I had no life,' Jonas confessed.

His life was as disciplined as ever. At 7.30am he did Pilates – and at that time he still had to routinely explain what it was. By 8.30am he was usually already at the Coliseum, ready to turn the world upside down, and slightly peeved that his colleagues didn't want to match him in his early starts. Sedwards laughed as she remembered his suggestion of introducing early-morning management meetings. She made it clear to him that he ought not to expect anything from her before ten o'clock. 'For some of us it was a shock. Peter was so different from Harewood. He was someone who got the adrenaline pumping, challenged us all and changed our house. He made us better at what we were doing, because he was so dynamic, energetic and focused.' Jonas also had a different relationship with the weekend: 'The Coliseum was closed on Sundays. I hated that.'[26]

In September 1985, when Jonas took over the role, the *Sunday Times* spoke of the ensemble's 'wilful determination to survive'.[27] In the first few months, when all the small and big problems of an opera business suddenly came crashing down on him, mere survival was not enough for Jonas or ENO. The deficits after the American tour were indeed a problem, although Lord Goodman was also able to use his position to make up the shortfall from additional funds. It was also a problem that the Arts Council's allocations for the 1985–86 season were too low. As one of his first official acts, Jonas had to decide together with Elder and Pountney which of the planned productions should be pulled.

Stage designer Stefanos Lazaridis called this scenario a 'theatre of poverty on a grand scale', in reference to Jerzy Grotowski. Then technical director Noel Staunton came forward, saying he felt burnt out and wanted to leave. Jonas wanted to keep him and offered him a paid sabbatical. This gesture changed everything: Staunton stayed without claiming the leave. In short: Jonas went in at full speed and yet, despite all the problems and challenges, did not want simply to maintain the status quo.

'At the same time, I suddenly realised,' Jonas admitted, looking back, 'that with all my experience at the CSO, working with the top conductors in the world and all the top musicians whose contact details were in my address book, I was not ready to lead this house. Thanks to the CSO, I was very well trained to run the organisation as such. People quickly forget how important it is to be able to deal with collectives. Anyone who is not qualified or does not have the talent fails. Theatre is always a blue-collar business. I knew how I wanted to steer the Board. But there were two areas where I was really underprepared: stage aesthetics and the thin ice of British politics.'

Through Lucia Popp, Jonas had met many directors, but had not worked with them. He had an idea of the effect he wanted to have on opera audiences, but when asked how he wanted to achieve it, he was at first unable to answer as succinctly as he would have liked. 'I was well versed in art history and design. I had taste, but I hadn't yet developed a point of view on how things should be staged. I found that despite my wonderful training, my aesthetic sensibility was still not sufficiently developed.' He was speaking in deadly earnest. After a short pause, he added: 'But that changed quickly.'

Peter Jonas, Mark Elder and David Pountney were united in their desire to create a clearly recognisable style that could at least claim to be national. They wanted to bind young artists to the house, in the tradition of German theatres. Their aim was to offer comprehensible, entertaining, exciting and provocative operas whose aesthetics were accessible to all. While they were developing this ambition, post-punk and New Romantic movements were forming in England, with bands like Duran Duran, Adam & the Ants and Spandau Ballet. They entertained fans with outlandish costumes and stylised war paint. The new generation was no longer just listening to music: they watched music – on MTV, not in opera houses. It was precisely people in this age group who Jonas, Elder and Pountney wanted to attract to ENO: 'I want the productions to be innovative, adventurous, stylish and provocative. Maybe narrowly, but the music must always come first in opera,' Jonas explained his position to ENO's circle of friends shortly after his arrival in post. 'But the look of the production is at least as important. We're a theatre, not a museum.'

The most important thing for the three was to give their ensemble's work a distinctive quality and atmosphere. 'David was absolutely brilliant in that respect,' Elder said. 'He wanted to have the best directors in the house. He was absolutely not jealous or worried about who came to the house. The same was true for me, but it was much more difficult with conductors.'

With a smile, Elder remembered how Jonas used his spies in the orchestra when he wanted to know how guest conductors were received by the musicians. 'When I came to the Coliseum for lunch after a rehearsal, often at the other end of London, Peter already knew everything. When I asked him if he had listened to the rehearsal, he said: "No, no. I have my spies!" I'm sure he did the same in Munich.'

The musicians appreciated Jonas for his extensive knowledge of their work. Maggie Sedwards knew how close Jonas was to the orchestra through her husband Raymond Ovens, the concertmaster: 'Of course the orchestra had a close relationship with the music director, but Peter also quickly found a way in with them and made them feel that the leadership of the organisation really cared about them in a way that they may not have been aware of before.'

Elder won over the best British singers of their generation. 'The artists could rely on us, they trusted us,' says Elder. 'We were a tight triumvirate that stuck together to achieve something individual and exciting.'

Chosen enemies

Popularity and accessibility were the two poles around which the triumvirate oriented their artistic work. 'At a successful German opera house, these qualities can sometimes be completely absent,' Jonas reflected in 2019. 'If I were to be asked today which attitude is the right one for an aesthetic work, I would find it difficult to answer. Now that I can look back on all that, I tend to think that the purely intellectual value of something that is interesting, something that provokes discussion and thought, takes precedence. But I wouldn't say that the other view, of wanting it to be accessible, is wrong. It's different and it fits British society better.' At the beginning of the twentieth century, according to Lebrecht, the performing arts were popular in London but were largely imported.[28] Lebrecht argued that it took the First World War to convince British theatres and concert halls to accept native artists – and it took the Second World War to convince the British public to value these artists. Lilian Baylis's work acted as a catalyst in this process.[29] In 1928, she took an extremely courageous step: she bought and renovated Sadler's Wells in run-down Islington. Her belief that she could lure the workers out of their dreary pubs helped her, despite strident accusations that she was attracting only the educated lower orders.[30] Working in adverse conditions, Baylis, who became known as 'The Lady', laid the foundations for three companies: the Royal National Theatre, English National Opera and the Royal Ballet.[31] 'My people must have the best. God tells me the best in music is grand opera. Therefore, my people must have grand opera,' was her view.[32] It went without saying that these operas had to be sung in English.

'When I started at ENO, I was very aware that people thought that if you were coming from abroad, you understand nothing. Once you've been away for eleven years, even if you're British, you're considered a foreigner.' So Jonas relied on the advice of an expert in all things London, Maggie Sedwards, who had worked in press relations for Peter Hall at the National Theatre and then moved to ENO in 1998. (Jonas would later recruit a similar expert in Munich.) Sedwards was an established press secretary, and respected in the London media scene. She knew that the key critics all had their own views on how ENO should be run and that Jonas had to be exposed to them in controlled doses. 'Maggie is a great woman, a very strong woman, a rough, tough Londoner. She helped me enormously with finding my way around the press in London.' In Chicago, Jonas had already experienced how influential critics could destroy whole careers with a stroke of the pen. 'Journalists and critics in London are like two different animals. They are cruel to their victims. The more you understand them, the more inhibited you become, because you have to anticipate an attack around every corner.'

Sedwards skilfully made the necessary introductions for Jonas. 'My first impression of Peter was that he was full of energy, like a spring. He was very elegant, extremely articulate, but at the same time he seemed quite shy, almost a little nervous. We talked about media work and I had the feeling that we would get on very well, because he is very direct when he speaks and very clear about what he would be willing to do in terms of interviews.'

When before in his life had it ever mattered that he had been born in a particular hospital? Now, however, in one of his first press interviews, he claimed to be a genuine 'Cockney', born within earshot of Bow Bells. It was a clever, assimilationist tactic: 'Look, don't be afraid, I am one of you!'

'I felt ready for politics. Not because I was familiar with the British situation, not at all. In Chicago, politics had not been so important. But I had learned not to trust people completely. I had learned to be careful.' That was surely a strong training ground. 'There was one really great misfortune in my life,' Jonas later said, with regret. 'My time at ENO coincided with the Thatcher government. Mrs Thatcher was determined to cut the cost of all the services that the left had built up after the Second World War, in health, education and many other areas.' The opposition to her government was mobilising its forces. 'We in the culture industry were just the reds under the bed for them, communists in disguise,' Jonas smiled and showed his teeth.

Thatcher's victory in 1979 put an end to the previous Labour government. Her stated aim was to liberalise markets, and she accepted any negative social consequences to that end. 'There is no such thing as society, only the individual decisions that make up the market' was her dictum, with which she held every individual responsible for his or her own lot in life. Especially in her second term from 1983, that is, the moment when Jonas was beginning his labours at ENO, the Thatcher government was systematically dismantling social structures in many sectors, cutting budgets of cultural institutions and requiring them to pay their own way to a greater extent. But what proved weightier in the long run was that the government was exerting direct influence on the management of cultural institutions, under the cover of promoting the arts, and forcing them to follow the rules of the market economy.[33] 'Don't worry, they are on our side,' Lord Harewood had told Jonas at his first meeting with Arts Council representatives. 'They are our chosen advocates.' Chosen advocates – that had been the formulation used by all people in the arts until that moment. But, as Jonas took over at ENO, the wind changed.

'Do you know what role Keynes played in promoting the arts in Britain?' Jonas asked. He continued without waiting for the answer. 'Many people know John Maynard Keynes only as the economist and do not know that he represented the British at the Versailles Conference or the Bretton Woods talks. His basic idea for the promotion of culture was extremely noble! He was the originator of the arm's length principle.'

Keynes is known worldwide as the author of the *General Theory of Employment, Interest and Money*, published in 1936. It established the economic theory named after him. That Keynes was not only a dry economist but also a passionate lover of the arts and first and foremost a fanatical supporter of ballet is less well known outside Britain. Keynes was an insider in high society, having studied at Eton and Cambridge and worked in Whitehall. But he was also 'a lion of Bohemia'. He was a civil servant and self-made millionaire, a servant of the Crown who had retained his independent spirit, according to Norman Lebrecht.[34] 'The arts', Keynes once said, 'owe no vow of obedience'.

Fig. 31: Peter Jonas and Margaret Thatcher

Without Keynes as Arts Commissioner, it is highly likely that public funding of culture would never have come into being in post-war Britain, according to Lebrecht. Until then, the British state had not supported culture. But, were the state now to implement his proposals, argued Keynes, what had happened in Germany must never happen again: that is, the direct control and abuse of culture by the state for political or propaganda purposes.

As a bulwark against this risk, Keynes created the Arts Council of Great Britain as an intermediary organisation, funded by an annual grant from the government. The Arts Council, supported by the Ministry of National Heritage at the time that Jonas was at ENO, appointed expert commissions to decide on the amount of funding for cultural enterprises and artists. This 'arm's length principle' stipulates that the state may only give the money, but not decide how it is used.

It was inconsistent, ironic, but also deeply human that it was Keynes himself who brought his own preferences into the promotion of culture: he believed that England needed a national opera and a national ballet – and so these things came to pass.

Keynes, who had hitherto lived as a homosexual, fell in love with Russian ballerina Lydia Lopokova, who was part of Diaghilev's company. Their wedding was regarded rather coolly by his friends, but celebrated in the press. As a consequence of his private *amour fou*, Keynes is said to have always preferred ballet to opera.[35]

Keynes had already encountered John Christie, the founder of the Glyndebourne Opera House, at Eton – and he is said to have hated him. And according to Lebrecht, because Keynes had disliked Christie, the Glyndebourne Festival to this day receives no public funding.[36]

In the 1960s and into the early 1970s, Arts Council funding had steadily increased. But in 1974–75, the annual grant could no longer compensate for inflation.[37] In 1981, the Arts Council passed on the cuts for the first time and removed forty-one institutions from its list of grant recipients. The Arts Council announced this decision shortly before Christmas 1980.

In the early 1980s, the Arts Council funded an average of 55 to 70 per cent of the total budget of British theatrical organisations. The Thatcher government reduced this ratio to around 30 per cent at the Royal Opera House Covent Garden and to 48 per cent from 71 per cent (the 1979 figure) at ENO.[38] The difference had to be made up by increased ticket prices, merchandising, fundraising and by income from the liquor licence. National Lottery payouts generated further income for cultural institutions.

Actors in the cultural sector were increasingly frustrated because the constraints of funding prevented them from realising their full artistic potential. Within the triumvirate, it had been Jonas's task to negotiate with the Arts Council. 'When the Arts Council was created, powerful people like Lord Goodman were at its head. Their influence made it difficult for the government to reduce funding,' Jonas explained. 'However, people with such influence also had to distribute the funds fairly. During Lord Harewood's time at ENO, this had always been the case. The Arts Council representatives were our chosen advocates.'

With William Rees-Mogg as Chairman of the Arts Council, this changed fundamentally. This former editor of *The Times* was a confidant of Thatcher and was in post from 1982 to 1988. Like Thatcher, he felt that 'cultural types were paid too much money, were lazy anyway, just reds under the bed,' Jonas commented. He met Rees-Mogg on his inaugural visit, when Lord Harewood accompanied him. 'Chosen advocates? They are our chosen enemies!' Jonas said indignantly after the meeting.

Lord Harewood was also shocked by the hostile atmosphere, which he had never experienced before. Rees-Mogg had talked only about cuts and how everything had to change. Harewood was happy to retire. The climate had definitely changed. It was now confrontational instead of cooperative.

'I liked Mrs Thatcher,' Jonas said, 'but I disapproved of her policies. With her, you knew where you stood: she was an enemy whom one could respect. The fronts were clear. I couldn't stand Rees-Mogg at all. He should have been our advocate, but instead he was an instrument of the government. Keynes's arm had been amputated!' Jonas was also outraged by the Rees-Mogg's son Jacob, who advocated a hard Brexit. Following Brexit had been especially difficult for Jonas.

Rees-Mogg senior was not the only new appointment after Thatcher's second victory in 1983. The new Secretary General of the Arts Council was Luke Rittner, who held the post until 1990. When Jonas introduced himself in the winter of 1984, Rittner launched into a long and uninterrupted monologue about why a city like London did not need two opera houses. The whole thing seemed like an anticipation of the situation in Berlin in the 1990s, when Jonas, in his capacity as chairman of the Opera Conference, advocated for the preservation of all Berlin's opera houses.

Then, too, Jonas is said to have banged his fist on the table, cementing a reputation as a potential troublemaker. 'We in the cultural scene mocked Rittner,' Jonas confessed, 'because his education wasn't all that good. He was the type who gets up at half past four in the morning, goes jogging, and then sits in the office at seven o'clock and schedules the first appointments for eight o'clock.'

The two were similar in that respect if no other. 'For us theatre professionals, who often didn't get home until around midnight after the performances, these appointments were difficult to deal with. But he wasn't being tactical about it, it was just his way.' The typical dialogue was that Rittner was said to have demanded cuts – 'cut this, cut that'. Jonas held his ground: that is not so easy, an opera house is a supertanker. If you change the course, it would be noticeable only after some time. Operas would be planned and produced several years in advance. 'He was told how the contracts with the singers worked, how the sets were produced and so on. And he, he drifted off in the middle of the conversation!' Jonas imitated how Rittner was supposed to have dozed off with his head propped up. 'And suddenly his head cocked back up, bang! He was back, finished the conversation and gave us the task of developing scenarios of what our budget would look like with a cut of five, ten or twenty per cent. And I refused! I didn't see why we had to serve them up vandalism à la carte. They would only say: "It's not all that bad after all!"'

Luke Rittner was also the author of the 'Ilkley Letter', named after a village north of Leeds, where the Arts Council had met in 1984. The letter went to around 240 recipients in the cultural sector. In it, for the first time, Rittner used a particular horticultural metaphor to illustrate the Arts Council's new strategic orientation. On 30 March 1984, the Arts Council published a paper entitled 'The Glory of the Garden'; they had taken the liberty of using Rudyard Kipling's 1911 poem as the headline for their 'Strategy paper for the coming decade'.

> Our England is a garden that is full of stately views,
> Of borders, beds and shrubberies and lawns and avenues,
> With statues on the terraces and peacocks strutting by;
> But the Glory of the Garden lies in more than meets the eye.

While Kipling alludes to Genesis, in which humans become God's gardeners, Luke Rittner used Kipling's lines to justify unscrupulous cuts and selections. The Arts Council, he insisted, had the right to decide which plants would get light and space and which would not. 'The arts, like seeds, need to grow if they are to blossom. Some of the seeds we have nurtured over the years are now bursting to grow but are held back by lack of space and nourishment. This strategy will help the Council to thin out the seed-bed and to give more room for them to develop, and for new seeds to be planted.'[39] So the glory of the garden, says Rittner, lies in weeding and selection. And the Arts Council would make this selection.

In fact, there was a need for reform: London's cultural scene – especially the four national theatres, the National Theatre, the Royal Shakespeare Company, the Royal Opera and the Royal Ballet – received significantly higher shares of funding than did regions outside the capital.[40] However, two terse sentences were sufficient for the Arts Council to explain its future policy towards the opera houses: 'The Council has always given major support to opera, which is a very important art form. That will continue.'[41] At the same time, the Ministry and the Arts Council demanded that the houses increase their productivity.

Cultural management theory knows the problem as 'Baumol's cost disease'. Unlike other sectors, services, including performances, can hardly be rationalised in terms of productivity because they consist of an irreducible, unquantifiable amount of human labour – the work of singers, the choir and the orchestra, but also the technology and the workshops. 'Everyone was supposed to get a piece of the cake, but at the same time the cake was getting smaller and smaller!' Jonas was indignant, because a fight for ever-smaller pieces of the cake was underway.

Cuts, cuts, cuts!

Together with Rupert Rhymes, who was responsible for the finances in the first years of Jonas's artistic directorship, Jonas wrote 'complicated letters' to the government. 'That was so frustrating about our work, these endless exercises in writing letters to the Arts Council!' complained Jonas, 'demonstrating this and that, justifying our position. At the end of each Board meeting, and really of each of the monthly meetings, the demand came: draft a paper about this and that! Cuts, cuts, cuts!' By the time when, just before Christmas – the Arts Council kept up this rhythm! – the statement came out indicating how much money was to be paid the following year, Rhymes would have already presented his, 'let's say, fifth draft of the budget.'

'The time when Peter started at ENO was so difficult because we had to design endless versions of the artistic programme,' Sedwards recalls. 'Again and again we had to work out budgets, and the Arts Council kept giving us new forecasts of grants. It was so insulting. Some were so low that they barely gave us enough funds to open the doors.' The increase in grants was below the rate of inflation, and so the business had to cope with de facto funding cuts. 'I found the first years particularly hard,' Jonas said. The permanent worries about funding and the ongoing experience of not being able to plan in advance according to professional standards and having to cut back or cancel productions again and again exhausted leaders across the entire cultural sector. Their energy could have been put to far better use than fighting the 'apparatchiks' of the Thatcher government. 'The Arts Council's arm's length principle is sensible, provided that the arm works,' Jonas was convinced. But now the institution that was supposed to keep the government at a safe distance had become an extension of the Treasury.

This also brought the management structures of cultural enterprises into focus. Politicians demanded that business methods from the private sector be introduced in cultural institutions. ENO was tactically well positioned for this process thanks to its leading triumvirate: Peter Jonas was able to respond to outside political demands on the management, while Mark Elder was able to concentrate on musical-artistic issues and David Pountney on staging matters.

Through his experience in Chicago, Jonas was familiar with the management methods that the government demanded. At the same time, however, his obstinacy came to the fore. He was determined to protect his house from demands he judged nonsensical or excessive. His appearance, demeanour and eloquence all did their bit to bolster his impact in the media battle. 'Peter changed the company,' Sedwards explained. 'He reorganised and refined the management systems. There was inevitably some kicking and screaming against the changes as we all had our ways of working. But he was usually right about the need for reorganisation and a different focus.'

By the time Peter Hall left the National Theatre in 1988, he was the most important lobbyist for London theatres. Time and again he had publicly drawn back the veil from the government's cultural policies and their consequences. He was outraged that one particular playwright, for example, had deliberately limited the number of parts in his new work, just so that his chances of seeing it performed would not be harmed by having too many people on the payroll. This account revealed the whole dilemma of British cultural funding.

When Rees-Mogg published an Arts Council brochure in 1985 with the pretentious title *A Great British Success Story*, Peter Hall had had enough. At a press conference, he announced that the

Cottesloe Theatre would close because its grants had once again fallen below the rate of inflation. Hall directly attacked the Culture Minister Lord Gowrie and Rees-Mogg. Hall received hundreds of letters of congratulations and encouragement for this performance.

Hall then initiated a meeting of forty-seven theatre directors who expressed their lack of confidence in the Arts Council. More than the lack of money, it was demoralisation that spurred the cultural sector into action. Many theatre folk felt that the Arts Council and the government no longer supported their work, let alone valued it. Again and again, they had to argue anew why the arts should be subsidised at all.

The Arts Council responded in its own way to this mobilisation of the theatre world. In his annual report, Luke Rittner made a direct threat: the fears of the cultural scene would indeed be realised if the Arts Council lost the confidence of the government as a result of this criticism. Lord Gowrie made Hall the scapegoat, thereby achieving greater support in the Cabinet.[42] It was every man for himself.

The triumvirate: a new style of leadership

This was the background when Peter Jonas took over ENO in 1985. He was plunged into those political battles, and that strife accompanied him throughout the entire period of his directorship. Negotiations with trade unions also demanded his attention time and again. He had little time for artistic questions, especially in the early years. But somehow that suited him, giving him time to develop his own artistic ideas. 'If there were problems, I could say to David Alden or Richard Jones, for example: "You developed this concept, choose your set designers too!" That was not very pleasant for me.' But none of his colleagues mirrored Jonas's own conception of himself as a severe leader. 'Maybe Peter felt a little insecure during that time,' his close friend Elder conceded.

'However, he never revealed this to the ensemble. His mind always worked really brilliantly.'

All intimately acquainted with Lord Harewood had spoken of him with admiration. 'Lord Harewood was such an inspiration to Peter and me. He was such a gigantic figure in the artistic world in Britain,' Lesley Garrett said, 'ahead of his time, way ahead of his time!'[43] Harewood had dedicated his life to singing and opera, Elder said. 'He was a fantastic person. Peter was the complete other side of the coin. He was able to be sneaky, clever in a way that George could not be. Before the meetings with the unions, George often took Valium because he was so nervous. In that sense he was not of this world, but he was an enthusiast with a considerable knowledge of opera. He had taste and strong views, he was a wonderful leader but not good at confrontation, whereas Peter revelled in confrontation.' Thoughtful, tactful and carefully supportive, Lord Harewood, in Sutcliffe's description, wanted to meet artists halfway. His leadership had a relaxed and open quality that differed from the hard focus of more performance-oriented managers and impresarios.[44] Peter Jonas, on the other hand, who was nervous only before Board meetings, had excellent intuition, a razor-sharp intelligence and the self-confidence to carry leadership tasks through, according to Elder. 'He really loved politics. He loved to decide what his strategy was. He loved the idea of fighting and he was brilliant at it.'

Harewood had recognised that change was needed and he had orchestrated a change. But the house Jonas took over was Harewood's house through and through. The ensemble now experienced a completely different style of leadership. 'Peter was a doer,' said Elder, 'Lord Harewood was not that at all. Peter's ability to run the house was extraordinary. It was an incredibly difficult task.'

Jonas, Elder and Pountney built on Harewood's foundations. His most influential strategic decision had been to establish the 'Norwest Holst Series', named after its sponsor.[45] With this final move, taken in 1984 as Jonas was named his successor, Harewood laid the foundation for ENO's reputation for innovative productions. In this series of performances, Harewood had brought large-scale operas by well-known extra-canonical composers to the stage. His aim was to expand the repertoire. The works had to be realised with extremely low budgets, but in return they were freed from the pressure to be 'bankers'.

Wagner's early work *Rienzi* was followed by Rossini's *Mosè in Egitto* and – the most controversial of all – *Mazeppa* by Tchaikovsky. No longer under the pressure of staging an opera that would have to be revived again and again, he radicalised his directorial style and 'unleashed a spontaneous and irreverent bravura whose impact was enormous', as Jonas, Elder and Pountney put it. Pountney would later describe the series as a 'Trojan horse'. It seems that no one was fully aware of the creative process that had been set in motion.

At the end of their time at ENO, Jonas, Elder and Pountney were of the opinion that a bluff, iconoclastic style had emerged which was markedly different from the highly aesthetic and intellectual deconstruction techniques of contemporary European theatre. During the time of the Power House triumvirate, this style changed into a 'Coliseum cliché', which would be both criticised and celebrated as 'producer's opera'.[46] As opulent sets were now out of the question, the directors and set designers – Nicholas Hytner and David Fielding for *Rienzi* and Keith Warner for *Mosè in Egitto* – opted instead for more or less ironic stylistic devices. Although Pountney's and Maria Bjørnson's *Carmen* in 1986 was not formally a part of the Norwest Holst Series, Jonas, Elder and Pountney considered the production to be a part of this trend in light of its extremely low budget.

December 1984's *Mazeppa* was a breakthrough for director David Alden, and the beginning of his decade-long collaboration with Jonas. For Sutcliffe, a chainsaw massacre was the symbol of 'ENO's brave new production world'.[47] Stage blood ran down white walls and people are said to have fainted in their seats. The titular protagonist is a Ukrainian general who wants to marry his friend's daughter, Maria, who descends into madness following her father's execution. Alden and Fielding set the plot against the backdrop of a communist regime. They created a framework which allowed them to tell this story in all its brutal realism and simplicity.[48]

For the Norwest Holst Series, the choir was not required to learn their parts by heart, and were allowed to appear on stage with the scores. Following Brecht, Alden had the chorus stand as a static mass: another allusion to Stalinist conformism.

According to Alden, any production must walk a fine line between things that address the audience directly and unambiguously, and things that speak to the unconscious, even where they may seem random and unfathomable. Alden had been inspired by Ruth Berghaus and her use of everyday objects on stage, as well as a desire to provoke contradictory reactions in the audience. It would have disappointed him had his provocations not cut through.[49]

Audiences were not yet familiar with the language of conceptual productions. Even though violence was clearly a component of the plot, spectators were shocked by what they saw on stage. 'We got a lot of angry letters,' Sedwards recalled. 'This production really created a lot of excitement. I loved it.'

Critics like Sutcliffe recognised the moral content of Alden's directing. It showed how political power is violently abused. As well as the love, the audience needed to believe the violence that they saw on stage.[50] But many critics took against the music's conscious struggle against the mise-en-scène. Elder's conducting and the singers' performances received the highest plaudits.[51] The programme attracted a younger audience, who could scarcely afford the ticket prices. Better-off theatre-goers, on the other hand, were not drawn to the Norwest Holst Series.[52]

But amid the transition from Harewood to Jonas, the most important questions remained unanswered: how could ENO's productions be made accessible and reach new audiences? And, on the other hand, how could the management raise ticket prices to generate the income the establishment needed in order to placate the Arts Council?

The leadership of Jonas, Elder and Pountney has been described as a triumvirate. The formula obscures as much as it explains. All those who have worked closely with the three report the same thing: their conversations, debates and arguments all remained behind closed doors. The three men addressed the wider ENO with one voice. 'Sometimes, within our triumvirate there were disagreements over ideas of what opera to do, or where to save money if necessary. Many of our meetings were acrimonious as we each fought our corner. At the same time, it was good, it was healthy. It was never easy-going, it was tough.'

The triumvirate did not let outsiders in. That they had arguments amongst themselves was known, but only through rumour. Nobody ever witnessed such conflicts – or at least nobody talked about having done so. They were a threesome – leading the house and acting for the house. Their congenial collaboration seems like an anticipation of the collective structures that emerged at the beginning of the twenty-first century. 'The triumvirate formed a united front for the company and was seen as such,' Sedwards said.

In this 'decade of unprecedented cynical materialism',[53] as the trio retrospectively characterised Thatcher's reign, they were able to create an atmosphere at ENO in which the ensemble was very willing to go far beyond what was asked of them, even at generally lower salaries. 'ENO was the most exciting place to work,' said Sedwards. Getting to that point had required hard work from everyone.

Creating an ondit

One thing had not been clear to Jonas at first, but he learned it very quickly:

'The success of your house is not your success, but the success of all of its employees. And that is based on the state of your *ondit*. People must be talking about whether or not the company is interesting. The company has to be on everyone's lips. If the company is on the brink financially, if one or two productions don't really come off, or if individual singers are not good enough ... if the company is exciting – if its *ondit* is right – then many things can be forgiven.'

Over the years that followed, Jonas built a strategy around this insight. His reflections on how to make the company more accessible, which directors might create exciting productions, and ways of getting new streams of income: all these questions came back to the matter of working to create a reputation. ENO is the most exciting opera company in Britain and, at its best, far beyond.

At his job interview, Jonas had stated boldly that he wanted to encourage the house and its programme to grow. 'We are in the age of the designer,' he had proclaimed. Jonas was a lover of modern designer works in general, but here he was speaking of set designers. 'Every time we broadened the boundaries of the set, every time we pushed its possibilities, we became hungrier for more resources.'

The costs for equipment increased and the stage sets became more and more difficult to construct, something which would also prove a challenge for the stage technology that Jonas was to find in Munich. In co-productions, it was becoming trickier and trickier to reconcile the requirements of shared stage spaces. 'Every time we thought about the idea of a set designer, their requirements became a huge logistical problem that left me shaken.'

Chicago had not prepared Jonas for these kinds of processes. 'You can't separate the concept for a stage set from the logistical and technical requirements it entails. I had to understand that first. My closest colleagues told me that I didn't have to deal with it, that other staff members were responsible. In the beginning, they only came to me with the final problem: how much will it cost? And to answer that question, I had to believe in their vision – or not.'

The 'director problem' was even more difficult for Jonas at first.

'In front of a room of people, I wouldn't have been able to explain what my aesthetic ideal was or why I believed in a certain aesthetic.' Jonas was serious, even if his self-perception contradicts the evidence from the end of his career. 'Unlike with stage design, I was not yet in a position to judge the direction. My visual sense has always been strong. Even experienced opera-goers confuse directing and décor when they say: "I didn't like the production. I didn't like the way it looked."' He was able to distinguish between direction and set, that was not a problem. 'But I felt unprepared to judge directorial work. How do you make it so that a scene speaks to us directly, both aesthetically and dramaturgically? It sounds very simple, but it's not.'

The directors who worked at ENO at the beginning of the 1980s all shared an outlook that interpreted operas in a non-traditional way. 'The productions were all different, but a certain sense of creative energy in the house verband sie alle [united them all],' Jonas explained. 'Nicholas Hytner never worked in the same style as David Pountney. Jonathan Miller also had his own signature. And just like Nicholas, Jonathan did not care for David's style. That didn't mean they didn't like each other as people, but as directors they were as different as chalk and cheese.'

'The work of David Alden and Keith Warner, in turn, resembled that of David Pountney.' Time and again, observers compared the production style at ENO with what they knew from theatre. Jane Livingston, who started as press officer in October 1987, was asked by Jonas in her interview what she knew about opera. 'I replied: not much, I always thought opera was rather poor theatre.'[54] Livingston laughed at this memory. On her first day at ENO, Sedwards suggested she go and see a rehearsal. Livingston did. Keith Warner and Stefanos Lazaridis were rehearsing *Werther*. 'I thought: this is Ibsen, this is theatre! I was completely hooked!' By the early 1990s, Sutcliffe judged, no one was talking any more about opera needing an injection of gifted talent from 'legitimate theatre'.[55]

Costumes and props like trench coats, suitcases or naked light bulbs soon became hallmarks of the new aesthetic at ENO. This was a triumph by Jonas, Elder and Pountney and the artists who worked with them.

'The Arts Council spoke a different language from us. We wanted to make exciting music theatre and the government wanted us to work more conservatively: "If you did a more popular programme and didn't show so many suitcases and bedsteads on stage, then people would enjoy their visit to the opera more", was their attitude. All that started when I arrived.'

The very first production in the Jonas directorship went massively over budget. Given the complex situation after the US tour, and in view of the threat of insolvency, this was no small issue, but in retrospect it did not seem too important to Jonas. 'For the first time, I understood the power a production can develop when it is well marketed. *Orpheus in the Underworld* is a popular opera. Pountney used it to make a political statement.' The set was designed by Gerald Scarfe, full-time cartoonist for the *Sunday Times*. 'Scarfe created brilliant designs for this production. Sally Burgess, as a representative of public opinion, was a caricature of Thatcher. It worked perfectly.' The visitors flocked in, and so the box office take worked out right. *Orpheus in the Underworld* became an iconic ENO production.

A huckster for musical theatre

Production had originally been planned for October 1984, but postponed for a year because of the financial deficit. The Houston Opera had already come in as a co-producer when Jonas joined. Jonas gained a second partner in the Los Angeles Opera and its artistic director Peter Hemmings, previously his strongest rival for the ENO job. A bank had also agreed to sponsor the event, and Jonas added a further £50,000 to the budget.

From the beginning, Jonas professed to be a 'huckster' for his house. Jonas knew how to combine his own artistic sensibility with the deft ruthlessness of a manager, as only ten years in commercially oriented American concert halls will train one to do, as ENO chronicler Gilbert noted. Jonas had no choice. For Thatcher's government, sponsorship was the preferred method of generating revenue within cultural enterprises.

'Mixed patronage' was the term for this form of cultural promotion. Luke Rittner was supposed to be central to this new direction for Britain's cultural organisations. Before becoming Secretary General of the Arts Council in 1983, he had led the Association for Business Sponsorship of the Arts (ABSA) since its inception. The Chairman, of course, was Arnold Goodman. The ABSA was a non-profit intermediary organisation which operated between culture and business, and is now called 'Arts & Business'. Since 1984, their 'Business Sponsorship Incentive Scheme' has subsidised sponsorship contracts.[56]

In the early 1980s, the largest share of sponsorship went to opera, ballet and concerts, probably because they were considered apolitical. Further support came from the Greater London Council (GLC), as the highest administrative authority in London. It pursued its own arts promotion strategy, in opposition to the government's social and cultural policy, and focused on the unemployed, young people, especially young women, homosexuals and ethnic groups.

The GLC was a thorn in the side of the Thatcher government, which dissolved it in 1986. But from 1981 to 1986, the words 'GLC funded' were ubiquitous in the arts.[57]

Jonas was not starting from scratch when he began fundraising for ENO. The house had been working with a basic offer for corporate sponsoring since 1978: for £2,500, the companies received tickets to premières and advertising space in publications. In 1979, ENO had set up a trust for corporate members, which had raised £30,000 by January 1981.[58] 'It was the beginning of arts sponsorship in England. The British were not used to it,' Sedwards said. 'I suspect Lord Harewood found it very difficult to ask for money. But Peter, who was influenced by the American tradition, was open to asking for support. He wasn't embarrassed at all.'

Although Jonas tackled the task successfully, he did not accept the job without protesting to the Arts Council: in January 1986 he wrote to Rittner that his house had no more 'limbs to amputate'. In global rankings, it would be sixth in terms of productivity, but eighty-seventh in terms of subsidies.[59] Jonas loved such calculations, even during his time in Munich. Except in Bavaria, the numbers were better. 'Bridging the Loch [gap] with scrounged private money, das war difficult in England,' Jonas recalled in one of his delightful linguistic mishmashes, usually the result of him switching back and forth between his jobs. 'I still think if you could get another production simply by begging for money, you should do it. In theory that didn't bother me.'

Jonas was determined to change the way audiences experienced opera. But he also wanted to change people's attitudes to culture. This inevitably led to new thinking about how culture in general, and ENO in particular, should be financed.

In 1986, the American Russell Willis Barnes, later Taylor, started at ENO. Jonas knew her from the Chicago Contemporary Art Museum, where she had been responsible for the development programme. Her task was to set up a similar long-term and cooperative programme, with its own department in-house, 'a fund-raising department, a real department that was solely concerned with using what we produced to raise sponsorship and donations from individuals,' said Jonas.

Barnes focused her attention on the so-called 'new achievers', wealthy members of the Arab community in London, but also American and Japanese businessmen.[60] Barnes was particularly successful in attracting business sponsors against strong competition from the Royal Opera House and the Glyndebourne Festival. 'She was able to do this because ENO placed itself as the cutting edge of culture,' says John Nickson, Barnes's successor.[61] It was also Barnes who suggested Jonas hold dinners and address the guests directly with a request for donations. Jonas did this not only at the end of the intervals, but also directly from the edge of the stage at the end of performances, in keeping with Barnes's attitude of being accessible. This saw the development of an art that became known as 'begging-bowl speechmaking'.

Jonas must have been very good at it. A short time later, at the start of each performance, a member of the senior management stepped in front of the curtain and explained to the audience how the Arts Council ran the subsidy system, and that income from ticket sales never covered costs, as ENO was keen to keep prices as low as possible. 'We could have been unlucky with this tactic, but it turned out to be a success,' Jonas noted. 'Contributions from the audience would fund an entire production by themselves. No company, no patron: the audience itself gave us the money.'

The members of the ensemble gradually realised that the climate had changed, especially with regard to finances, and that a clear focus on fundraising was necessary if the house were to survive. 'None of us knew how much time it would take and how much accessibility would be required from the leadership and the artists,' Sedwards admitted. 'All this had to be managed by a short-handed and overstretched management team. Peter was constantly dealing with management structures.'

Gradually, Jonas increased the number of staff. David Elliott joined as Finance Director. He brought expertise from banking with him, and introduced rigorous monthly accounting, which also involved middle management, who henceforth had to control budgets. Another new addition was Richard Elder as head of human resources, who had experience leading negotiations with trade unions in industry.

Lesley Garrett

'Back then, when I was new to ENO, there was a production of Handel's *Xerxes*, a work I adore,' Jonas recalled. ENO had included the work in its programme for Handel's tercentenary. 'A very young assistant had directed, one Nicholas Hytner. It was not at all common for assistants to get assignments, but he was brilliant.'

Hytner, born in 1956, and his set designer David Fielding created a neo-baroque entertainment world for *Xerxes*, in the style of Vauxhall Gardens, one of the most successful amusement parks in London in Handel's day. Hytner specialised in the eighteenth century and drew on a wealth of material. One critic praised his direction for so aptly exaggerating both the comic and tragic emotions Handel so magnificently brings to life.

Hytner knew that Handel operas required singers to hold a feeling and stretch it out for ten minutes. The critic Rodney Milnes was thoroughly convinced by Hytner's refined, knowledgeable, clever and enormously erudite direction.[62] For over two decades, *Xerxes* was one of ENO's great successes. Milnes regarded it as responsible for the breakthrough made by Handel's operas at this time. 'After that, no one staged *Xerxes* for a while. No one dared because they feared the comparison,' Jonas said.

However, the production was important to Jonas not only because of its outstanding quality, but also because he saw a young soprano in the role of Atalanta on one of his first visits as designated artistic director. 'Peter later told me that he fell in love with me when he saw me in this role – which is probably an exaggeration, but it was cute and a good story!' Lesley Garrett laughed uproariously. 'Peter always had a good story to tell, that's what I loved most about him!'

She was sitting in her kitchen living room in the London suburb of Highgate in the spring of 2020 when she shared her memories of Peter Jonas. It was one of those red-brick Edwardian houses with pointed gables over bay windows framed in white wood. A small, beautiful garden stretches away behind the windows of the kitchen. While Jonas had simply confessed how important Lesley Garrett had been in his life until the end, before falling silent, she laughed and shouted: 'What a responsibility!' And then she accepted the responsibility and told me about their time together.

Lesley Garrett joined the ENO ensemble in 1984, the year before she first met Jonas. Atalanta was her first role. 'We in the ensemble were all excited when we heard that this child prodigy, this exciting phenomenon from Chicago, might be coming to us,' Garrett recalled.

It was only after Jonas moved to London that they got to know each other personally. Jonas invited her to lunch. Garrett assumed that he wanted to meet all the ensemble members. 'I thought this was just a routine thing, but during lunch I realised quite clearly that he and I got on very well. I knew that he and I would be involved in some way. I think we both knew.'

In late 1985, when Jonas asked her out for the first time, she saw that the moment had come. Lesley Garrett described Peter Jonas in her memoirs as follows: 'He was one of the most attractive men I have ever met, with a combination of good looks, power and enormous vulnerability that I found irresistible. PJ, as he was known, is ridiculously tall and in his youth was built like a rugby prop forward ... [B]y the time we met he was spare and rangy, which highlighted his striking bone structure and breathtaking blue eyes. The attraction between us was palpable and undeniable, though we spent some time trying to deny it to each other and ourselves.'[63]

In early 1986, Garrett moved into Jonas's flat in Islington. The famous architect Piers Gough had designed it. Jonas filled it with modern art. Friends called his flat 'the Pristine Chapel'.

For Jonas and Garrett, everything revolved around ENO. It was their world. Garrett had studied at the Royal Academy of Music. Her path into the world of opera had been hard. This engagement was her big chance. Like Jonas, she also sank into her work. 'We had a passionate relationship.' Lesley Garrett, a few weeks before Jonas's death, smiled as she looked back on that time. 'But we were also passionate about our jobs and the Coliseum, English National Opera. Everywhere you look, there was passion! Peter was very enthusiastic about the team he was creating, the family at ENO. He was a very strong man.'

She was happy then. But the seeds of their future separation were already evident. 'Although we were passionate about each other – and that never stopped – from a practical point of view it was almost impossible to maintain the relationship because we were very different people. Our backgrounds were very different.'

For Lesley Garrett, life at his side opened up a previously unknown perspective. 'There was a whole world that I had only ever glimpsed through a gap in the curtains. Now I was going in through the front door! I no longer had to scrounge tickets for the dress rehearsals at Covent Garden. We went to all the premières.'[64] Garrett had visited Paris before, but had travelled by coach and stayed in a tiny hotel. Now she and Peter flew first class and were the guests of Daniel Barenboim or Eva Wagner-Pasquier.

As much as Garrett was attracted to Jonas, she also felt that living by his side would keep her from certain things she wanted for herself. 'He needed someone to support him in his work, to subordinate herself to it, so that he would be satisfied. I was too interested in my own career and my own life. I had fought hard to get where I was.' Garrett came from humble beginnings and was not prepared to put her own career second.

She was silent for a moment and looked out into her enchanted garden. 'Peter needed a full-time "theatre wife". That was a role I did not want to play. As much as I was dazzled by his lifestyle and we by one another, I knew I had to make my own way in the world. I could not live in his shadow.'[65] Garrett thought of Peter as being more open-minded and adventurous than she was. Therein lay a lot of the attraction. But Garrett was also proud of herself and her background. 'I didn't want to be moulded by anyone. I didn't want to be Eliza Doolittle to his Professor Higgins. So I decided to leave. He also realised that he couldn't do that to me.' She wrote him a farewell letter and moved out at the end of 1987. 'It was right, even though it was hard, because we still loved each other.'

Lesley Garrett fell silent. She did the only thing she could, and took some time for herself. 'PJ knew I was wounded. He knew it was painful for me when he married Lucy so quickly.'

Their story would find a new beginning later, at the end of his directorship: on New Year's Day 1993, after Lesley Garrett had given birth to her first child, Peter Jonas was the first person after her husband to visit. 'From that moment on, everything was complete,' Garrett recalled. 'Now we could move on. Since then we have been the closest of friends.'

A new stage aesthetic

In his first year in London Jonas kept a low profile. After a meeting with Rittner in November 1985, however, he started to speak openly of the Arts Council's bias against the opera houses. After two gruelling years, Peter Jonas was beginning to rebel, noted *The Times* in December 1986. Jonas's attitude was combative: 'Opera houses must not be run by weaklings: we are hucksters.' It was quite a slogan.

Perhaps such a strident battle cry concealed some lingering trace of self-doubt. In the end, however, Jonas was completely without fear, even regarding his personal circumstances. He did not fear any consequences, even if on a personal level – knocking on his own door – his illness might strike at any moment. 'Through the incredibly painful and brutal experience of his cancer,' Mark Elder said, 'Peter was completely fearless.'

Jonas risked attacks. They did not come out of the blue. It was only at the moment of his departure that he revealed how he had been openly threatened by the government. 'In those dark years of the eighties one used to receive threatening telephone calls in the morning at home from somebody saying, "I think you should be a little more discreet, Peter, if you really have the advancement of your organization at heart." Or it would be, "We're getting a bit fed up in Whitehall that you're talking too loud," things like that. Another day somebody would ring and say quietly that I was complaining about Rees-Mogg too much.'[66]

Jonas did not name names, but it became clear that he was talking about certain civil servants. 'Such people can be surprisingly devastating.' Jonas was not popular in these circles. Some described him as a megalomaniac. He would have replied that that was a question of perspective and circumstances.

After Peter Hall left the National Theatre, Jonas became the unofficial spokesman and lobbyist for the Big Four companies in London. 'I told my press officer at ENO again and again: "Always go into work and think: Today, they will find out."' Jonas rapped his knuckles on the arm of his chair. '"Today, they will realise that actually I know absolutely nothing." Always believe you are going to be fired.'

Again Jonas recounted how Solti had spoken of the old days in Munich. 'I completely understand what Peter means when he says he expects that "they will find him out"' said Maggie Sedwards. 'It's the insecurity that what you do will never be good enough. For him it was really deeply rooted. Peter never felt that what he had achieved was good enough.' Coming into a mature organisation as Director General is never easy. You have to do more than just integrate: you have to understand how the organisation works right away. From day one Jonas struggled, especially with the Arts Council, and then around the short- and long-term planning of the artistic programme, which was forever changing, as the Arts Council could not decide on the grant amount. 'He had to attend endless meetings inside and outside ENO,' says Sedwards. 'I really don't know how he did it with only twenty-four hours in a day.'

ENO also took high risks in its programme. On 25 April 1986 came the British première of Busoni's *Doctor Faust* and, just under a month later the première of Harrison Birtwistle's *The Mask of Orpheus*. 'The *succès d'estime* of that time for me was Busoni's *Faust*, a production that influenced my whole life.'

After retirement, Jonas would move into the house in Zurich where Busoni had composed parts of *Doctor Faust*. '*Doctor Faust* is an incredible, evocative sound picture of the German struggle with its soul, their hunt for answers. I have always felt this. When we staged this work in London, we managed the opening scene so effectively. Busoni is not immediately accessible, but almost.'

Looking back, he considered Pountney's and Lazaridis's work to be a 'worthwhile, important, courageous production'. From an economic point of view, he was taking a big risk. 'Just imagine both productions, *The Mask of Orpheus* and *Doctor Faust*, being on the programme in London at the same time, today. It is unthinkable that they could both sell out!'

Just as Jonas reorganised the financial systems within ENO, he changed the process for new productions: directors and set designers still had a free hand, but had to present their models for the set and discuss their concept by a set deadline. 'Later, in Munich, I did things differently,' says Jonas. 'There, the team presented the model and concept in front of the whole ensemble.' In London, he didn't think that would have been practicable. 'At that time, I was developing an aversion to directors who come to a piece with a certain idea, but then it becomes clear that they have no idea how to present it.' When such directors explained that they wanted to leave the development of this or that scene to the singers in the rehearsal process, Jonas flew into a rage. 'I suppose the way I showed my disapproval was very intolerant. First and foremost, I was lucky to be able to work with such talented, vibrant directors and set designers with so little opera experience.'

But Jonas also saw what little chance a director would have had coming into ENO, which had been shaped by Harewood, Elder and Pountney, and trying to implement his own clearly defined ideas. 'There was a collegial atmosphere at ENO. The different working styles had to be brought together and they had to be valued as a house style.'

Jonathan Miller left a distinct footprint on ENO. In 1978, Harewood had commissioned him for his first production there, *The Marriage of Figaro*. *The Turn of the Screw* followed in 1979, and in 1982 there came the now-famous *Rigoletto*, the production that went on tour to America. It was set among the mafiosi of Little Italy. Miller had faithfully reconstructed the New York of the early 1950s. Although Sutcliffe noted critically that the world of the mafiosi was mere decoration and that Miller had not penetrated the essence of violence as Alden had in *Mazeppa*, he praised the production as a dramaturgically well-grounded and intellectually profound examination of the themes of the work, 'not just window-dressing, decoration, culinary opera'.[67] The production became one of the greatest successes of Harewood's era.

Sir Jonathan Miller (1934–2019) was one of England's great intellectuals. He first trained as a neurologist, then in the early 1960s, together with Peter Cook, Dudley Moore and Alan Bennett, he founded *Beyond the Fringe*. Their groundbreaking success ushered in the satire boom of the 1960s. Miller left the troupe when the show transferred to Broadway.

'Miller was a tremendously talented babbler. He could philosophise on all subjects,' Jonas enthused, 'from syphilis to pride, from quantum mechanics to medicine. He was incredibly well educated and extremely entertaining. People called him a polymath. The way they launched *Beyond the Fringe* was extraordinary! They had come straight from university.' Jonas searched for a recording from the internet. 'Look! Dudley Moore sits down at the piano and improvises in the style of Beethoven… Do you understand the words [from the source tune]? "Hitler has only got one ball…" They also liked to mock tenors, especially Peter Pears. That was great!'

When Jonas met Jonathan Miller and worked with him on the idea for the later long-running success *Mikado*, colleagues told him, 'Jonathan is not a director, he doesn't direct people. He develops one or two ideas in his performances.' Jonas replied that this ethos was that of continental European directors who set a strong dramaturgical idea and allowed the actors to work out that idea within a strong set. 'Then you have a production like *Mikado*!'

Sutcliffe judged that 'the best of Jonathan Miller and David Freeman were harbingers of the English National Opera's so-called Power House regime.'[68] 'Miller was part of the furniture, so to speak,' says Jonas. 'In a way, Pountney was right, Miller was not a director. He was a university scholar who could direct. They didn't like each other.'

Jonas's only serious argument with Pountney came over the question of whether or not Miller should get the commission for *Rosenkavalier*. In the event, the production did not happen until 1994, by which time Pountney had left.[69] 'The success of *Mikado* sealed David's departure forever. He rejected that style and was jealous of Miller's success,' says Jonas.

For Miller, 1988 was 'finito at ENO', as it says in his biography,[70] with the caveat 'for now'. After 1994, after the Power House triumvirate had come to an end, he would find himself producing at ENO once again.

Once, returning from one of those incredibly depressing meetings with the Arts Council, Jonas met Miller in a trendy brasserie in north London. 'I really didn't know what to do anymore and cried a little on his shoulder,' Jonas recalled. 'And then we hatched a plan to make *Mikado* in the style of a revue, a cabaret.' Miller wanted to realise the show with a very small budget, but with one of the most demanding stage designers at his side: Stefanos Lazaridis, who usually worked with Pountney or Alden. The idea was that everything should be done on a single set. There would be no scene changes.

Lazaridis created a 1920s scene, a hotel lobby in a British seaside spa town, all in shades of white. The lush palm trees had blanched and provided a magnificent backdrop for the revue-style choreographies. The costumes were by Sue Blane, who was particularly known for her designs for singers and dancers. What emerged became one of the most successful ENO productions of all time.

Gilbert and Sullivan's *Mikado* is synonymous with comic opera in nineteenth-century England. With a great dose of black humour, composer Arthur Sullivan and his librettist William Gilbert create a satire on Victorian England in an exotic setting: the Japanese emperor Mikado bans flirting, under threat of death. A game of confusion develops around the question of who is still allowed – or obliged – to behead people. We meet the kimono-maker Ko-Ko, in love with the beautiful Yum-Yum. Everything threatens to fall apart, and the entire court is exposed to ridicule. For Jonas, this was the perfect political satire on Whitehall and its apparatchiks. But the operetta was also cheerful enough to appeal to the widest possible audience. If this all suggests shades of Monty Python, that is no accident: Eric Idle was the first to play the part of Ko-Ko.

'The combination of Jonathan Miller and Eric Idle was heavenly!' exclaimed Lesley Garrett. 'We were working on something absolutely unique. We laughed all the time and thought: if the audience laughs half as much as we do, then it will be a success.' She recalled how during rehearsals – she and Jonas were still living together at that time – Jonathan Miller would ring Jonas in the evenings and need 'coddling'. 'I'd been rehearsing with him all day and when I got home Peter was negotiating all these things over the phone,' Lesley Garrett laughed. 'There was no escape!'

As Ko-Ko, Eric Idle (not a singer himself) had the opportunity at one point in the performance to recite to the audience a list of people 'who would not be missed'. He improvised a kind of political speech at this point, different every night. 'Anyone could find themselves on this list: muggers, joggers, buggers, floggers or girls that tell stories of the Tories they have kissed. The scene has never offended anyone, and yet it was provocative in its own way,' says Jonas. 'Those were moments of classic beauty! You have to watch the rehearsal film of *Mikado* to get an idea of Miller's tempo and energy,' he insisted, tapping away on his iPad. He was looking for a particular recording with Lesley Garrett and ranted: 'I am so bad at this!'

The recording he was looking for shows a rehearsal with Garrett as Yum-Yum and Eric Idle as Ko-Ko. Miller himself can also be seen. The rehearsal process had just begun, and Miller explained his concept. You see tense, beaming faces. Miller speaks at length, not always in simple terms, but always intensely. With Lesley Garrett, he honed her line 'I am a child of nature,' working out every vowel, every timbre. Jonas also appears in the rehearsal film for a moment, gesticulating with his right hand as he often does.[71] 'You have to watch the recordings, absolutely! You absolutely have to make sure you see the original cast,' Jonas insisted. He specifically searched for the Yum-Yum aria, which Lesley Garrett performed. 'The sun, whose rays/Are all ablaze' is – as Lesley Garrett herself had said to Miller in rehearsal – 'a little moment taken out'. And then Jonas took a little moment to listen to her singing. She had perfect pitch, flawless breath control, a pure sound.

If you ask Jonas's closest circle what their favourite productions were during his directorship, there is a surprising degree of agreement: *Lady Macbeth of Mtsensk* is often mentioned, as is *Rigoletto*, interestingly, although it dates back to Harewood's era, and then again and again: *Mikado*.

'Why *Mikado*? Because of the effect it had. No one had staged *Mikado* in this way before. It completely destroyed the historical concept of Gilbert and Sullivan's operas,' Sedwards explained. 'It was the funniest thing in the world!' ENO leadership bet heavily on it, with almost twenty performances from September 1986. 'The production was a success, just a success,' Jonas beamed. 'The singers were great, Lesley on her way up. The audience was delighted. They played to a sold-out audience. In the house, it was fun for everyone. They loved performing with Eric Idle,' Jonas could not stop raving.

He had never spoken about any other production in such detail. 'Since then, all ENO managers have put this production on the programme again and again. And it sells immediately! It has survived several residences, travelled around the world, been filmed several times and is available on DVD. It's been the most successful commercial opera production ever known!' Jonas laughed, clearly pleased. Politically, the *Mikado*'s success was highly significant. 'That was our lifeline!' said Jonas. 'Thatcher forced cuts on us and then suddenly this very cheap show, in money terms, came along and raised enormous amounts of money! Not so much that it could have saved us or replaced the grants. But it meant that we could finally shut up all those apparatchiks who were always criticising ENO for not being popular enough. ENO was suddenly present in the media. It was our first time on domestic television, all the people were watching us from home!'

Jonas had achieved his goal of having an '*ondit*' among the public, but also among international colleagues: ENO could do more than just the classics. Jonas was convinced that he had built his international reputation around the *Mikado*. 'Many houses wanted the production as a guest performance. Everyone came to see the show, especially artistic directors from Europe! That was the peak, when everyone thought: this is the place to be! Everyone thought so: public figures, wives of opinion-makers, even people who weren't interested in opera.' Jonas hesitated before adding: 'You could say this success was well-deserved.'

As for many of his colleagues, the UK première of Shostakovich's *Lady Macbeth of Mtsensk* in David Pountney's 1987 staging was another key production of the Power House era. 'It was incredibly exciting. It represented what we were,' Elder enthused. 'That production was our flagship. Stefanos Lazaridis had created an exceptionally powerful and physical concept.'

In retrospect, however, Jonas spoke more about *Hänsel and Gretel*, a work with which he personally associated a great deal. 'I remember the meeting when I said to David: "I would like you to stage one of my favourite works, *Hänsel and Gretel*." He flatly refused, said I was crazy.' Jonas asked Pountney, who saw himself as a champion of dramaturgical rigour, to study the opera once more. 'I was sure that he would realise that it was not a piece for children. It tells so much of the damage we all suffer at the hands of our parents. The music is so intrinsically Wagnerian, Humperdinck was Wagner's assistant. I was sure David would agree.'

When the production premièred in December 1987, it showed an ENO at the height of its powers. The audience reacted enthusiastically.[72] Pountney and his set designer Lazaridis set the play in post-war Britain. In a typical city park, against a starry sky, one saw the kitchen of a family that had fallen through the cracks of society. The critics acknowledged the serious message.[73] 'David delivered it brilliantly. The production was a huge success,' was how Jonas summed it up.

Pountney's translation of the libretto also contributed to the production. He had some experience here, for example in 1982's *Flying Dutchman*. The policy at ENO of performing all works in English necessarily demanded a libretto translated with craft and artistry. Although the decision to sing in English had long been seen less as a 'liberating commitment' and more as 'a compromise for the mass market, which would guarantee second-best standards',[74] Jonas, Elder and Pountney mounted a skilful defence of their stance.

A translation is necessarily a compromise. But the meaning of a text can sometimes be conveyed more directly in translation than it can in the original. Not only English-speaking opera-goers would have noticed that Andrew Porter's translation of the *Ring* was easier to understand than the German original. Naturally, the three recognised how the prosody of the English language, and the interplay of its vowels, consonants and sound changes affect the beauty of the tone and the length of the line in song. It follows that no Italian opera could be performed authentically if it were sung in English.

But if one takes this understanding of 'authenticity' to its logical conclusion, then an Italian opera could be performed authentically *only* if cast exclusively with Italian singers. The triumvirate concluded that it would be more honest to present opera in England in such a way that its message could be directly understood by the audience. In this way, opera could fulfil a social and civic function.[75]

Performing in English also offered the strongest argument for the government to maintain two independent opera houses in London: at Covent Garden, operas were performed in their original languages. It went without saying that the triumvirate rejected the use of surtitles above the stage – 'theatrical condoms'[76] – outright, on the same basis.

When ENO had to introduce surtitles in 2005, in response to public demand, Jonas countered that they would also have to hold public executions there if the public so desired.[77]

David Alden

Peter Jonas and David Alden met in 1985 when Jonas was preparing to take up his role in London. During one visit, Jonas was keen to see the production that had caused such an uproar there. He did not yet know *Mazeppa* well and – as always – prepared himself intensively before attending: 'There I sat in the auditorium and I saw the audience around me growing angry. The chainsaw massacre infuriated everyone. During the break, people were arguing with each other. The production was absolutely groundbreaking! It had a strong concept. David Alden had cast experienced singers and directed with the sort of eye for detail normally only seen at the National Theatre. I knew then that I really wanted to continue working with him.' Alden, an American among the British, had been working on a *Don Giovanni* in Houston in 1976 when Pountney had met him and offered him a job at the Coliseum. Alden, born in 1949, was considered one of the most important and distinctive reformers of the English-speaking opera world.[78] It was clear to Jonas from an early stage that 'David is a brilliant person.'

Like Pountney, Alden was able to work brilliantly with Mark Elder. Pountney's and Elder's decision to bring Alden on board at ENO was a matter both of conviction and of artistic commitment, as Sutcliffe accurately put it. Alden's political motivation and craftsmanship set new, higher standards. For him, operas were 'psycho-historical mysteries whose resonances and implications (submerged in music) invited daringly imaginative amplification and experimental synthesis – so that they merged with the imagery and philosophy of life and art today.'[79]

Alden's directorial style was no doubt rooted in the German tradition.[80] He also directed the characters in the chorus precisely and in detail. For many in his audience, his productions were a way of telling the truth, simply and convincingly, about both the people in the dramas and about the politics that touched their lives.[81] For ENO, Alden was 'a constant winner'[82] and it was predictable who would not like his work. According to Sutcliffe, his work required the full and unwavering support of Jonas, Elder and Pountney.

For Jonas, this was to become a lifelong artistic friendship. Alden's most important works are associated with Jonas's directorships.

At ENO, Alden worked primarily with David Fielding, whose stage worlds, Jonas said, were ahead of their time. This was also the case in April 1987 with *Simon Boccanegra*, a production of which Jonas was especially proud. '*Simon Boccanegra* was great! Together with *A Masked Ball*, these were the most important flagships of our work.' Mark Elder, the musical director on the production, and the one who received the highest praise, was of a similar opinion: '*Simon Boccanegra* by Alden was unforgettably beautiful! It belonged to a different kind of theatre. For me it was exactly what I wanted, a dream come true! This modern production with this great, human eternal music. It made the music seem like the best of all music. What Alden had the singers do, what they achieved, went far beyond anything else! David Alden set the singers free, in the most extraordinary way.'

But Elder also reported that Alden conducted the rehearsals in a way that he found exasperating. He was always changing his mind, nothing was fixed, he was always rethinking everything. 'But he made the singers feel empowered!'

'Peter Jonas never attended many rehearsals,' David Alden recalled. 'I can remember only one single piano rehearsal in London. When the stage rehearsals began, he came regularly and early enough to still comment and suggest changes. When he had hired someone, he trusted them. You have to take that risk, even if it turns out badly. That was the basis of how he did his job. He did not want to disturb people or their creativity. Now and then he had to mediate between directors, singers and conductors. But at the same time, he always kept his distance.'[83]

Unlike audiences, Sutcliffe said, '[m]any critics (but not his ENO audience) seemed incapable of looking behind the conscious indecorousness of the productions, the rejection of specific period, the desire to free the stage picture from the weight of extended naturalistic and dramatically irrelevant filling-in.'[84] Tom Sutcliffe sided entirely with Alden here. Jonas defended the production before the Board: *Simon Boccanegra* merely marked the beginning of a new production style at ENO. The Company would now dispose of much of the décor left over from earlier productions.

Max Loppert of the *Financial Times* was overwhelmed by the visual stimuli in *Simon Boccanegra*. The things that bothered him – the bare light bulbs, a single wooden chair or various styles of clothing – his critic colleague Milnes later referred to as 'design tics'. For more than a decade, the feature pages of the British press attacked Alden's work incessantly.[85] The bold and provocative approach that David Alden and David Fielding had developed at ENO seemed in later years to have become something of an end in itself and, as such, eventually lost audience support.

Peter Palumbo

The cultural scene in London was – and still is – a tough place. A good part of the pressure came from the media. Jonas prepared very carefully for press events, and Maggie Sedwards, head of the PR department, carefully managed his media presence, always careful not to expose him to too much journalistic attention.

Due to the numerous disputes about the financing of ENO, his presence inevitably attracted a certain amount of commentary: 'His decisions were not always praised. He could be quite fiery in his answers, although he learned to tone it down,' Sedwards recalled.

Soon the press realised that Jonas was someone to be reckoned with. That he had a deep knowledge of opera and had known the company since his youth. He ticked a lot of boxes for journalists. 'Peter was also extremely personable and articulate. He had this ability to say something that was probably already public knowledge in such a way that his interviewer felt he was being told something private.'

In their obituaries, journalists picked up on his quirks, his little eccentricities, which had been passed on from article to article over the decades. It was mentioned that at times he appeared at premières wearing a pink tie, which, for this style-conscious person, was most likely not a lapse of taste but rather an ironic comment on his state of health: he was 'in the pink'. Or that, instead of a company car, he had requested his own parking space and a company car with a licence plate reading 'ENO 1'.

That much was true, Lesley Garrett confirmed. At first he had ENO 666. 'That's the devil's number,' she had warned him. 'He changed it to ENO 159, which was the number of a key bus route to rehearsals.'

On the London scene, a story would have a hard time cutting through if it weren't about a personality or a production. As early as 1985–86, ENO was the first company to try out a participatory approach to communications and outreach programmes.[86] The media were not interested in these questions at all, Jane Livingston recalled. All foreign media representatives went to her first, because she administered the press tickets. 'Every foreign journalist who came to London wanted to visit ENO first. ENO was really the place to be. They all wanted to come to ENO.'

Jonas had also already built up a strong back-end operation. 'Peter was such an enabler,' said Sedwards. 'It was his overview, his intellectual and dramaturgical rigour that carried the entire artistic programme. His artistic contribution was outstanding. None of what the artistic team wanted could have been realised if he hadn't created the framework that made it all possible.'

John Nickson, responsible for fundraising from 1989, emphasised Jonas's natural authority, which was immediately clear to him. 'He had the ability to inspire and make you feel that you would do anything for him. Everyone felt that, inside but also outside the house.'

Jane Livingston worked with Jonas from 1987 until he moved to Munich. 'When I joined the ENO ensemble, he was already a very strong leader,' she said, 'a marvellous spokesman for the arts and the ensemble, brilliant in interviews. I was part of an ensemble, a company. This word somehow seemed to disappear later. Peter only ever said Company with a capital C! The whole feeling was that of an ensemble, the difference and the impact Peter made: the empowerment, the ensemble feeling, the family feeling!'

Lesley Garrett also spoke as first soprano when she said: 'Peter was highly respected in the house. Everyone was proud of ENO. We had the feeling that we really were a powerhouse.' He himself reported that during this time his colleagues often accused him of being 'too German' and 'too centrist' in his leadership style.[87]

Jonas, like so many people in leading positions, was prepared to gear his entire lifestyle around the demands of work. 'During my time at ENO, I worked from morning until late at night,' he said. 'Almost every evening I attended a performance.' Sedwards also noted that, with almost twenty productions per season, and the media attending the first two performances, there were endless press days. As fundraising became more and more important, supporters' evenings were instituted. 'Peter, along with most of the management team, was generally at the theatre most evenings.'

In June 1987, Margaret Thatcher was elected Prime Minister for the third time in a row. She drove ahead with market liberalisation. Grants were still below the rate of inflation, and fundraising became more important than ever. On 19 October 1987, the Dow Jones index plummeted by almost twenty-three percentage points. This day went down in history as Black Monday. Although some dissenting voices felt George Harewood was not qualified because he was accused of being too lenient toward his successor, he was elected chairman of ENO's Board in October 1986.

In early 1988, cultural institutions had to face a new funding principle, known as 'Incentive Funding': Arts Council grants now depended on whether the arts organisation had acquired a certain amount of money from other sources. The 'arm's length principle' and forty years of consensus in British society were upended: the free market now had a direct influence on public funding. Previous fundraising successes would be taken into consideration only in the sense that sums raised prior to the assessment would be taken as a baseline.[88]

Decades later, the memory of these noisome innovations still infuriated Jonas: 'The government betrayed us! This was not a formal betrayal. There is a social contract. You want us to be more productive? All right, then we'll grab the money from somewhere else. You want to take away our money? Good, that means you are my enemies forever. I was young, I had eleven years in Chicago behind me. I had a simple us-and-them view. There was nothing in between, and that is more or less in keeping with my character. Either we share everything and kiss and hug each other or nothing at all.' Jonas was driven by something very basic. 'For a director, there is always the danger that the government will cheat you. After that, you are seen as someone who has been cheated. And I must say that I have no sympathy for colleagues who decide to cut their programme in such situations. Of course, sometimes you have to cut something. Basically, however, one should fight in an almost bloody way to keep the programme. And, if possible, expand it.' And Jonas found more drastic words to express his displeasure. 'Today I understand that there are other ways. But that's how I do it. Honestly, I cannot go and lick the asshole of a government if they behave badly. And I really don't care if the finance minister is a powerful person. If he behaves badly or dishonourably, I will say so.'

And Jonas did.

While grants to the Arts Council from the government had increased by 8 per cent, the Arts Council increased the grants to ENO by only 2.5 per cent. The basic funding of cultural institutions was still insufficient. In early 1988, Jonas spoke out publicly: he said that ENO felt betrayed by the Arts Council in its efforts to reach a wider audience and generate higher revenues through ticket sales and sponsorship. For years, cultural institutions had been told that the Arts Council had no money itself. Now that there was money, the national theatres were not the first priority.

The Arts Council responded in its own way, and pressed ENO finance director David Elliott to ask Jonas to adopt a less confrontational style.[89] Peter Jonas, however, had fully assumed Peter Hall's role as lobbyist.

'Peter was a charismatic person. No one who encountered him could escape his power. He was tall, handsome, powerful and artistically motivated. People respected that,' says Lesley Garrett. 'He also had many battles with the unions in which he had to prevail. He was fierce, no pushover, and people saw that,' she recalled. 'He fought for the house, always driven to work for the greater good and by his vision that art is for all people. Everyone in the Coliseum shared this passion. That's why it was a powerhouse, because that was what we all wanted: to reach that goal, to be guided by it. He was a fantastic leader!'

In 1988 Thatcher made a staffing change that would work out wonderfully for Jonas. She appointed as Chairman of the Arts Council a man of whom the *Independent* would later write, when his term in office came to an end: 'Peter Palumbo is a rich man with dreams too big for Little Britain.' Palumbo thinks bigger 'than the Arts Council, the Tory governments he supports and the British economy'.

The fact that William Rees-Mogg had been replaced was itself a ray of sunshine for Jonas. But the fact that he was succeeded by a man who, at last, was no mere acolyte of Thatcher and who was as passionate about architecture and design as he was – that was a godsend. Jonas, forever forging friendships with people from his professional life, later invited Palumbo to his wedding, to which the latter brought a keenly anticipated gift.

Palumbo met Harewood and Jonas within days of taking office. He was pleased not to be greeted like the big bad wolf, Jonas commented afterwards, alluding to their shared Christian name.[90] Despite his stubbornness, Palumbo seemed to have a good relationship with Thatcher. You could go to her office, he said, her door was always open. Although the arts were not at the epicentre of her interests, she made you think they were important to her. Thatcher is said to have read all her briefings. She understood them and the way she questioned her counterparts was forceful and dazzling. Tell me what the arts cost, what they produce, Thatcher is said to have asked. 'Give me examples. What is your evidence for this statement? Don't talk to me about government money, there is none. It's taxpayers' money.'[91]

On an artistic level, the triumvirate's successes were far from uninterrupted. Although success seemed assured for the UK première of Philip Glass's *The Making of the Representative for Planet 8* on 9 November 1988, with Doris Lessing as librettist, the production flopped.[92] But Jonas had used his earlier successes to put pressure on Covent Garden. His argument was that ENO produced more successful British singers than its competitors. He underlined the differences between the two houses. 'ENO is not a place for star canary fanciers.' In Covent Garden the best seat cost £70. At the Coliseum it was only £21.50. In 1988 ENO was subsidised at a rate of just £16 per seat; other houses received £20. But inflation and the attitude of the Arts Council created pressure to change the pricing policy at ENO. Taking advantage of its popularity and the high number of visitors, ENO had tried to exploit income from ticket sales by means of a differentiated pricing system. During the Thatcher era, the highest prices increased eightfold, from £6.20 in the 1978–79 season to £49.50 in the 1988–89 season. The lowest prices rose from ninety pence in the 1978–79 season to £2.50 in the 1988–89 season.[93]

As with all other West End theatre operations, the Coliseum sold tickets through seating charts. Printed tickets were crossed out on the chart when sold. Electronic sales systems were still a long way off. It was possible in those days to book with a credit card, but many customers paid cash on the spot. Those who ordered their tickets by post had to enclose stamped envelopes. The money had to be taken to the bank every day for around two hundred and thirty performances a year, with 2,359 seats per performance. 'All of this was incredibly labour-intensive compared to today's computer systems,' says Sedwards, who was responsible for ticketing. 'I've had some struggles over seat prices, mainly because the Board has always felt that one of the answers to our ongoing financial problems was to raise prices. But we ran the risk of losing our regular audience if we set the prices too high. It was an ongoing argument.'

The usefulness of market research was known at the time, but the results of market studies were implemented in only a rudimentary fashion. Sedwards knew the pitfalls of pricing: 'There will always be a section of the audience willing to pay a high price to sit in the best seats. The trick is to balance the pricing in the middle segment so that you don't shoot yourself in the foot by charging too much, especially for the second tier – for example, the seats on the side. And the top part of the Coliseum, the balcony, must always be sold at the lowest prices to be accessible.'

ENO was able to conduct a few surveys with the support of universities. The studies concluded that subscribers were interested only in new productions. If there were too many revivals, they didn't want to book. The financial bedrock of each season was generally a revival of a previously successful production. This was especially the case where there were fewer new productions planned for a given season, not least as advance ticket sales for new productions are never as reliable as they are for revivals. This meant that when it came to revivals, ticket sales were crucial. 'We have always struggled with the question of how to set the ticket prices correctly,' says Sedwards.

Pan Am flight 103

Peter Jonas had planned to fly to New York on 21 December 1988. He wanted to meet James Wolfensohn, the president of the World Bank, and then his aunt Elizabeth Melamid, in order to be back in London on Christmas Eve. He was already acquainted with Wolfensohn through Daniel Barenboim, who had known him since their childhood. Jonas was coming to Wolfensohn with an important mission. He was seeking advice on how ENO could acquire the land on which its building stood. This issue had been in Jonas's in-tray since his early days in post. In 1987 property consultants had been commissioned to look into the issue, and now Jonas was preparing to become more hands-on. Wolfensohn knew the landowner from school and might have been in a position to make a decisive intervention.

The travel agency had made Jonas a special offer. A cheap Pan Am flight was due to leave Heathrow at six o'clock. Jonas had never liked Pan Am and had always preferred Lufthansa ever since his Chicago days, but there was no way around it: he had to book the cheapest flight. A short time later, his office noticed that the monthly meeting of the Board was to be held on that very Wednesday, starting at two. Jonas conferred with Harewood. No one expected the meeting to last more than two hours. The meeting sailed smoothly through the agenda at first, until the chair called for 'any other business'. 'Some busybody was griping about a production,' Jonas waved his hand through the air. 'I don't remember which one. It wasn't important, but it triggered a discussion that was pointless and tedious. Even the chair, George, was bored, but he was not strong enough to bring the discussion to a halt. They talked and talked. It was now 4:30pm, 4:40pm. I was starting to panic.'

He had wanted to take the Tube, but now he asked his secretary to book him a taxi. It got stuck in traffic at Knightsbridge. Jonas arrived at Heathrow only forty minutes before departure. 'Because of my luggage, which was too big to take into the cabin, these bastards decided that I was too late. I should have been there at least an hour earlier. I was so pissed off!' Jonas was visibly still angered by the memory. 'Thank God we had booked through the travel agency. I called there and the agent just said: "Lucky you, now you can fly British Airways! It's a bit more expensive and it leaves an hour and a half later, but you'll still get the flight." He arranged everything for me and it was a wonderful flight! I read a novel by Iris Murdoch, everything was wonderfully relaxed.' Jonas made one phone call before departure. He called Lesley Garrett. 'Peter was very upset. "The Board meeting overran! I missed my fucking plane!" he was shouting down the phone. It was the only flight Peter missed in his whole life!' Garrett said. 'We had no idea that Peter had cheated death once again. He has cheated death all his life, this is just the most dramatic example!'

When they landed in New York, they were confronted by ten or fifteen British Airways employees in the baggage claim area who had to tell the passengers the terrible news: Pan Am Flight 103, on which Jonas was originally due to arrive, had exploded over the small Scottish town of Lockerbie. British Airways staff wanted to warn passengers of the situation that would await them after clearing customs: hundreds of journalists and photographers were waiting for the six people known to have been rebooked from Pan Am 103 onto the British Airways flight. Such rebookings were a familiar phenomenon on evening flights from Heathrow to the USA; the traffic during London rush hour was difficult to calculate, and passengers routinely arrived late. 'The news was a bit of a shock for me. I took a taxi to the hotel and went to inform my office that I had missed the flight. But it was late at night in London. There was no one left in the office.' Jonas reached his relieved assistant at home and then called Harewood. The latter kept his composure and, as was his way, remained focused on the essentials. 'Peter, thank God! We thought you were dead. There would have been no alcohol at tomorrow night's performance. I was on the verge of appointing a provisional management for ENO.' Harewood alluded to the old law that demanded a named person be individually liable for alcohol sales.

'I had just narrowly escaped death. The ENO Board saved my life,' Jonas wandered through his living room once again, stirred by his memories. 'I just wanted to tell you this funny story. Zurück zum Stück!' It clearly wasn't a tale that he had often told: hardly anyone in his inner circle was aware of it.

Innovative musical theatre marketing

From his apprenticeship with Edwards and Solti, Jonas knew all about the discussions over what subscribers expected and how to develop the programme to match these expectations. In America, however, Jonas had also developed an understanding of cultural marketing that was ahead of its time. He knew what strategic marketing could mean for a business. For him, having an individual visual identity, a recognisable brand, was an absolute must, although it took a long time for the cultural sector to accept and implement this notion.

'When I first came to London,' Jonas recalled, 'the city was still a pretty uptight place. I didn't really like what I observed. I really wanted our work to be noticed by the media.' Jonas was not merely concerned with ticket sales and distribution alone. What he wanted was for his house to be the most talked-about in London.

'People should have the impression that tickets might well run out, but that maybe they might actually be able to get some after all. That was how we had to do it.' Jonas was in his element and counted off with his fingers. 'We had to build an *ondit* that said that a) we had something special to offer, b) it was hard to get tickets, and c) it made sense to buy subscriptions if you were a regular customer, because otherwise you didn't have any guarantee of being able to see what you were interested in.'

In his vision of what he wanted to achieve as artistic director, he was inspired by Walter Felsenstein. 'One thing I learned from studying Felsenstein was: the job of the artistic director was not only an artistic, managerial, coordinating or a political task, but also very much linked to the whole process of buying tickets. But the 1980s were a different time in that respect! For Felsenstein, the performance began from the moment someone on the street happened to see a poster for a performance: somehow it grabs their attention, their imagination: that's the beginning of the performance! And further: the prospective customer comes upon the idea of buying a ticket. How are they treated? How easy or difficult is it to get a ticket? The little mini catharsis of actually getting a ticket! The anticipation of arriving at the opera house. The quality of the nibbles. How the programme booklet feels in the hand!'

Here Jonas set off on a tangent and revisited the seemingly endless discussions in Munich with his dramaturges about how thick the programme book ought to be. The dramaturge, of course, also had the budget in mind, and cited the costs. Jonas replied to him: 'this here is not thick enough. It has to be thicker!' In London, Nicholas John, who had been hired by Harewood in 1976, had reworked the structure and content of the programme booklets. He included in-depth essays, evocative quotes and images: these programme booklets were exemplary among their kind. This was probably the basis of Jonas's obsession; for him, the programmes could never be lavish enough. 'Finally, the guest sits in the auditorium in the midst of the other guests, the lights go out and at last the performance itself begins, with the approval or disapproval at the end, one's own and that of one's neighbours. The discussions afterwards. Or you read the programme later on your own. The performance experience lasts longer than these two and a half hours! And the artistic director has to shape each of these moments, each on its own and all of them together as a whole. All this became strangely clear to me through this other world in America.'

Jonas cut off this discussion because he had again grown terribly cold.

When he started again, he declared: 'Marketing, public relations and fundraising – it all has to come from one source to make a visit to a performance exciting! I wanted everything to be of one piece: our image, our logo, the posters and everything beyond the performance. We didn't do everything right at ENO back then. I continued working on it later in Munich. Everything has to follow a technique. But public relations and fundraising in London were well on track.'

Jonas had been initially dissatisfied about various elements of the PR effort at ENO. Apart from routine announcements of the programme in big-circulation daily press and music magazines, ENO did not advertise its ambitious programme. Jonas felt that their outdoor advertising simply did not convey what he felt the 'Power House' stood for. Jonas wanted to do a publicity stunt to increase ENO's profile, cause a stir in London, and make it the talk of the town.

Maggie Sedwards again: 'Peter and I had some pretty heated discussions, mainly about ENO graphics, on the front of the house, on posters and leaflets,' Sedwards recalled. 'We are both quite explosive… He said: "I want this to be done in this way." And I replied: "But that's wrong, you can't do that." Never tell Peter that you can't do something, because then he will immediately want it even more! Actually, they were stimulating times, and underneath all the disagreements, we got along incredibly well.'

ENO had been pouring serious efforts into their marketing since 1981. Harewood had realised that he had to take trends seriously in order to understand what his viewers found exciting. He had sought advice from external companies; the first audience surveys emerged.[94] 'I understood that he wanted changes. But there was such a limited advertising budget at the time that I couldn't see how we could change everything radically and still have money available to produce the materials that actually told people what operas were on and when they started,' Sedwards said.

She decided to leave ENO. This gave Jonas the opportunity to completely reorganise the marketing. Keith Cooper, who had already proven his talent for these tasks at Opera North, became her successor. 'Keith Cooper was completely in tune with Peter's ideas and delivered exactly what Peter wanted.' Sedwards outlined the new constellation: 'Keith, in turn, ensured that he was allocated the budget increases that this demanded. Like Peter, he was very demanding and energetic, just the right person for Peter to work with.'

The way in which ENO combined marketing, public relations and fundraising in the following years had never been seen before in Britain. No one had really done PR and marketing for the arts. Those who, like ENO chronicler Susie Gilbert, see these developments in marketing and fundraising as a mere consequence of Thatcher's policies have misunderstood Jonas's thinking. In the years of Thatcher's government, ENO fought 'with a doggedness and fury worthy of its time', writes Gilbert. Thatcher's policies had driven marketing and the 'hunt for sponsors' inexorably forward until it 'eventually ceased to be a mere adjunct to the artistic work of the company and became a central part of its thinking'.[95] How Jonas wanted his house to be perceived, the people for whom ENO played each night, and what the guests experienced at the Coliseum had always been central to his thinking.

He didn't need the Thatcher government to come to this way of thinking: 'One should be business-minded and use branding to the best of one's ability.' But everything: business, politics, and the demands of the Arts Council, 'must be a slave to artistic ideals and visions. Ideals can move mountains.' He had also seen modern marketing techniques used in the cultural sector in the US. Inspired by their success there, he wanted to apply these ideas to ENO.

The 1989–90 season was ENO's first public outing with Jonas's new marketing vision.

Like many important buildings in London – 'all of them, really, except Buckingham Palace and the Palace of Westminster', Jonas noted – the Coliseum is hidden away in a dense row of buildings, its façade integrated with its neighbours on St Martin's Lane. If you are coming from the National Portrait Gallery or looking for the Coliseum from the north, from the intersection of Cranbourn and Garrick Streets, you have to look up to the sky to see the famous tower with the rotating globe, the ENO emblem. Especially after dark, the building and its surroundings look magnificent. But it is easy enough to miss it among the crowd of competing theatres in the West End. 'We needed a different way of making it clear that we were there as a company – and of making it clear who we were.'

Keith Cooper first developed a classic image campaign. It focused on ENO as an opera house with its ensemble. Nine black and white studio shots in a poster series show ENO employees, all in different roles. Cooper commissioned two of the most famous photographers in the country, John Stoddart and Anthony Crickmay, well-known from the world of showbusiness and magazines. Normally, ENO would not have been able to afford them. But because of the prestige associated with the assignment, they were willing to work at a much reduced rate.

Cooper worked exclusively with ENO staff on the campaign: no agency or studio was commissioned. All rights, except for those of the photographer, remained with the ensemble. Cooper later reported the cost as having been £8,000.

In retrospect, Jonas, Elder and Pountney looked upon this episode – with a hint of irony and self-awareness – as 'the adman's discovery of opera's blend of corny emotion with glamour and spectacle'.[96] And the campaign was based on precisely this mixture, advertised liberally around the city centre, on buses, the Tube and on billboards. ENO thus targeted a fashionable younger audience by emphasising how young the ensemble was, and the commitment brought to its work. Market studies had shown that the younger audience did not respond to conventional posters with information about plays or dates because this information had no meaning for them. 'We want to break the usual ways in which people perceive opera,' says Cooper. 'It was designed to appeal directly to those who were thirsty for something new, different and exciting,' explained John Nickson. 'There were signs that ENO was reaching a new audience that identified with the artistic goals of the house.'

The series was titled 'Noted for the Company we Keep'. The slogan was aimed at the elusive upscale segment of affluent 18- to 35-year-olds, reported the weekly newspaper the *Stage*, quoting Cooper as saying: 'Everyone, but really everyone wants to sell to them.'

Fig. 32: ENO advertising poster

Jonas wanted an '*ondit*' – and here he succeeded once again. The burning question in London's cultural scene at the start of the 1989–90 season was not who would be the new director of the Royal Shakespeare Company or other such matters, wrote Jeremy Myerson in the *Stage*.[97] Everyone was interested only in whether the 'handsome Karl Phillips' would really, truly work as a stage

319

technician at the Coliseum. And he did. Keith Cooper's August 1989 campaign was a smash hit. The poster showed 'gorgeous Karl', or 'beautiful, ravishing Karl', as Karl Phillips was known in the ensemble. John Stoddart had spotted the young stage technician with distinctive features, dark eyes and shoulder-length dreadlocks standing in front of a sloping antique column and taken his photograph.

Phillips puts his hands on his hips at belt level, his muscular upper body naked. You can see the edges of a tattoo on the right upper arm. 'Scene stealer or scene shifter?' the slogan asked knowingly, in a modern typeface.

This first design became the subject of countless conversations on the London Underground. Phillips was interviewed on the *Six O'Clock News*, followed by articles in the *Evening Standard*, the *Observer* and the weekly the *Stage*. The ad immediately became an iconic pin-up piece. Mountains of fan mail arrived for Phillips at the Coliseum, many people asking for a copy of the poster. In addition, he received numerous offers to pose for painters.

A poster showing Lesley Garrett was also published at the beginning of the 1989–90 season and immediately became the object of fierce controversy. In Stoddart's shot, Garrett wore a black crepe dress, a sheer chiffon coat, also black, draped around her legs and bare feet. She lay rather than sat, her head thrown back lasciviously, her dramatically darkly made-up eyes closed, both arms folded in front of her chest. Her luxuriant hair flowed down her back, a single curl on her collarbone. Her face bore 'an expression of indefinable ecstasy',[98] to use her own words. The slogan on their poster was an ENO battle cry: 'She makes music theatre'. No dusty opera divas sing at ENO: here you can meet attractive, sexy young women. In general, it is not opera that is on offer here, but musical theatre itself.

At the foot of the poster was a very small reference to the production: *A Masked Ball*, on from 4 September 1989, and its sponsor British Steel. *A Masked Ball* would bring Garrett even more turmoil – and Jonas a critique from British Steel, which he coolly dismissed.

The third motif to open the season featured David Freeman, founder of the Opera Factory London, a venue associated with ENO and known for its experimental productions. Stoddart had photographed the opera director in a classic portrait pose. Freeman, who was wearing a dark jacket with a light-coloured shirt and an open collar, looked head-on into the camera. He rested one arm on a stage prop. 'His direction could change yours,' the slogan claimed.

In early 1990, Anthony Crickmay's designs followed. Micky Titchmarsh, a muscular young man, was the 'Flyman'. He wears classic work clothes, dungarees made of denim, but without a shirt. In his hands are the thick ropes of the flying scenery. He has a dark moustache, his eyes upturned. A 'flyman' is a stage technician who looks after the the scenery stored on ropes in the upstage space and moved about by hand. 'High flyer low profile' was the slogan.

Another poster showed Eileen White. She wears a dark evening dress and beams. The tightly combed-back hair accentuates her smile. She is heavily made up, wears earrings and holds up a wine glass as if to offer a toast, right arm on her hip. 'Not all our rounds are applause!' read her slogan.

In another of Crickmay's shots, drummer John Harrod is described as 'Never Hum Drum'. He sits on his instrument as if on a barrel, drumstick slung over the shoulder. Harrod is fully dressed, in dark trousers and a loose shirt with the sleeves rolled up, revealing muscular forearms. Like all others in the series, he was very attractive.

First-class photography married with jaunty slogans. Traditional music critics rejected this campaign. That was the whole point. In *The Times*, Robert Morrison asked, 'Is this hard sell or soft porn?' and in the October issue of *Opera* magazine, the renowned editor Rodney Milnes raged at the 'Extremely Naff Opera'. Whereas Covent Garden inspired unrestrained yawning in the merciless Milnes, he was outraged by ENO's titillating pin-ups, which in its 'archaic triviality'[99] was miles away from the sophisticated principles of a Lilian Baylis. He complained that their best advertising spot, at the exit of Leicester Square Station, which leads directly to the Coliseum, there was now a parade of meaningless, haughty portraits of ensemble members. Alluding to Marilyn Monroe's role of Lorelei Lee in *Gentlemen Prefer Blondes* and the famous line from *Fidelio*, he described Garrett's outfit as something 'that Lorelei Lee would have called a "gauzy negligee"', which 'hinted at nameless pleasures'. David Freeman, on the other hand, looked wonderfully moody, and Phillips he described as a classic muscleman, his thumb hooked in his belt, his eyes smouldering. What would come next, Milnes asked. 'David Pountney in the shower?'[100]

In his view, the whole thing was neither provincial, because this accusation would be 'unfair to the provinces', nor vulgar, as it lacked 'the healthy vulgarity of the tabloid press'. Instead, he said, the flavour of the campaign was 'swinging', libertine, in short: Extremely Naff. Such criticism fuelled the campaign. Pountney wrote back in a letter to the editor, accusing Milnes of using his editorial to reinforce the very prejudices against opera that ENO was trying to dismantle. For him, Milnes was partly responsible for the fact that younger audiences were not interested in opera.[101]

Jonas uncompromisingly defended the new line against all critics. Studies from market research had shown that despite all the progress made in reaching further audiences, large groups of the population were still deterred from visiting ENO by opera's fuddy-duddy image. 'The importance of the success of the marketing campaign within Thatcher's cultural policy cannot be underestimated,' Jonas stressed.

'It was the safeguard for our production style.' The house needed the audience's approval to justify the new style of directing. For Jonas, the marketing strategy was exactly in line with Lilian Baylis's goals; clearly, the campaign raised the profile of the house among non-customers. ENO did not want to be a 'temple of art that people admired from afar', as Nickson put it. 'Jonas, Elder and Pountney wanted to give the audience an experience that not only moved them emotionally, but also made them feel part of ENO.'

All nine poster designs had the full support of the Board – at least according to the minutes.[102] Not that the members of the Board were typical users of the Tube. The mere fact that Lesley Garrett could be seen there – and in such a pose – outraged many. This image was not only unusual for Garrett herself: it was a shock. In Garrett's view, this image of her departed from how one would imagine a typical opera singer, 'Montscrrat Caballé, for example'. As a result, she received her first record and television contract. 'My career diversified enormously after Keith Cooper's campaign started,' Garrett acknowledged. But as with Karl Phillips, the consequences were not all pleasant. In her memoirs, she confessed that she received bad offers as well as good ones – and 'some very strange ones'.

The poster with Karl Phillips may not have been as consequential for him as Lesley Garrett's was for her, but within the campaign it was by far the most successful. Today, the display is considered a collector's item and is the subject of scholarly discussion. Peter Jackson, a British social geographer, interpreted the motif as early as 1991 as a particularly impressive example of a homoerotic depiction that does without bow and arrow, but nevertheless plays with the column as an art-historical quotation. Perhaps, Jackson asked, 'we are dealing with a politics of ambiguity, in which homoeroticism plays a complex and largely unacknowledged role among those who would claim an exclusive heterosexuality? For it is surely this ambiguity within hegemonic masculinity, between sexual practice and sexual fantasy, between overt representation and covert desire, that this advert seeks to exploit.'[103]

In a later publication, he read the photograph as an example of one of the images of masculinity that originate in a particular realm, can shift over time, enter new realms and take on new meanings when perceived by different audiences. 'His dreadlocks may be novel, but his look and pose are familiar from other contexts, particularly the twilight world of homoerotica and physical fitness magazines.'[104] Jackson pointed out that apart from a few newspaper articles and letters to the editor, little was known about how the advertisement had worked. 'Did it appeal equally to men and women, homosexuals and heterosexuals? To what extent does the effectiveness of the image depend on the creation of hidden homosexual desires and sexual fantasies in those who claim to be exclusively heterosexual? Why was an image that seems more at home in the world of popular culture used to promote a more "elevated" art form like opera?'

Writing with Nigel Thrift, Jackson interpreted the 1989 ad from the perspective of its makers. Rather than targeting specific market segments by clearly associating their product with a single, specific lifestyle, marketing strategists increasingly sought to exploit the contradictory and shifting boundaries within which people conceive of their identity. Different groups in the audience understood the ad in their own way. The success of the ad was based on deliberately addressing the different groups ambiguously, Jackson and Thrift judged.[105]

This analysis certainly applies to designs based on John Stoddart's photographs. Not only his iconic shots of famous personalities such as Pierce Brosnan, Anthony Hopkins or Catherine Zeta-Jones, but also his *Risqué* series make it clear how skilled he was at staging erotically charged shoots.[106]

ENO's new visual language was so pervasive that the public came to associate images with the campaign that had never even been used on a poster. A well-known photograph shows singer Thomas Randle and a snake. Nicholas Hytner had originally intended to use a real snake in his famous 1988 production of the *Magic Flute*. The snake dealer had warned Randle, who played Tamino, that the snake would react to birds, and so Randle had better keep the snake well away from the bird dealer's cage.

Fig. 33: Peter Jonas as general director of ENO

Randle once forgot this warning during a rehearsal and found the snake started slowly tightening its coils around his neck. This, however, was not the decisive reason for the live animal being dropped and replaced by a model: one of the other singers admitted to a pronounced phobia of snakes.[107]

The photograph showed Randle, dressed all in white and embraced by a fat snake. It could be interpreted as the presentation of a black man – a muscular, sweaty man – who, between sexual exploitation and homoerotic desire, is exposed to one's gaze. Contradictory indeed.

Cooper had also commissioned a shot of Jonas, the familiar half-profile of him wearing a striped jacket and roll-neck. Jonas decided against using it in the campaign. The director himself had no business being there. It would have been interpreted as an expression of his vanity.

'Many thought we had gone too far. But sometimes you have

to do something like that. In the 1980s, opera in London was still seen as an art for the older elites. No one had any idea about the people who worked in the opera,' Jonas said, in his summing up of the reaction to the campaign. 'The Arts Council forcefully criticised the campaign. They didn't like the fact that the posters were on the buses and the Tube. We wanted to address ordinary people and show them who the people in the opera are. Every now and then I had to slow Keith Cooper down, but not very often.' Jonas reflected. 'I didn't slow him down often enough.'

Keith Cooper often focused on the radical accessibility of a production in his press campaigns. He picked up on the fact that Verdi also had to suffer under censorship, gave out only little information and few pictures, and built-up tension around what would actually happen at the première. 'You can call it hyping it in advance. But as always, when you do something for the first time, there is resistance.'

The campaign was very well received by the ensemble, which was itself the focus of attention. Moreover, colleagues who contributed backstage were finally brought into the public eye. In the *Stage*, the poster with Karl – 'you know, the guy who earns so little he can't afford a shirt' – took on quite a different meaning: it broke with the cliché of the stagehand and his slovenly image, with an appearance of 'robust ill-health'.[108]

ENO kept up its reputation for running sexualised advertisements. In 2010, a new production of *Don Giovanni* was advertised with a torn-open condom wrapper and the double entendre 'Don Giovanni. Coming soon.' This reminded the press of Cooper's 1989 campaign.

This was far from Keith Cooper's only success at ENO, before he was poached by the Royal Opera House's artistic director Jeremy Isaacs, much to Jonas's chagrin. ENO still uses the logo that Keith Cooper designed in 1991–92 with Mike Dempsey of Carroll, Dempsey & Thirkell. This firm had already made a name for itself on the scene through its work with the renowned London Chamber Orchestra, and Cooper invited Mike Dempsey to the Coliseum to introduce him to Jonas. In discussion, Jonas was open to Dempsey's ideas, but above all to the criticisms that Dempsey made. The work of the marketing department seemed 'relatively aimless and uncoordinated' to Dempsey. Dempsey criticised the elaborate approval procedures in which the respective production manager was allowed to veto poster designs. This process meant that often a poster's fate would depend more on its reception by the institution itself than its impact on the target audience.

It is not surprising that Jonas was amenable to this criticism, as he was constantly reviewing the structures and processes in the company. Streamlining the approval process meant that he would become the one to issue approvals. He promised Dempsey that all his criticisms would be resolved if Dempsey offered him a logo as iconic as VW's.[109]

Fig. 34: 1991–92 ENO logo

Dempsey's classically simple, timelessly beautiful design features the letters E and N, the N boldly set above a circular, singing O, sometimes rendered in bright red. The E and N create the impression of narrowed eyes over a mouth singing a high note, as if in a crescendo. 'When I saw the logo for the first time, I didn't like it,' confessed Mark Elder. 'But I was so happy that we would get a new logo, that money was being spent on making our image fresh and challenging. The message of the campaign was: "We have confidence. We want you to come!" I was so relieved, I had longed for all this when I worked at the house in the 1970s. Peter wanted the campaign to reflect the company's courage and confidence. I thought that was wonderful. The right choice at the time!'

None of his successors had anything like the same understanding of the nature of design, according to Dempsey, who remained with ENO throughout Jonas's directorship and also oversaw the 'Everybody Needs Opera' campaign.

When Rose Design was commissioned to come up with a redesign in 2014, it fell back on this logo. It is the utter simplicity that has made it so long-lasting.

Jeremy Isaacs had once revealed how envious he was of ENO's marketing success to Jonas at a dinner. Keith Cooper worked for Isaacs from 1992, and while there he initiated the BBC series *The House*. In the style of a docu-drama, a BBC team followed the Royal Opera House at work for several weeks in 1995. The camera was allowed everywhere: backstage, in the director's office, the box office and in the workshops. The result was some beautiful shots and some intimate insights: how hard Denyce Graves fought for her voice before her debut in the role of Carmen, but also how stage technicians risked life and limb for an art form that paid them a pittance. Royal Opera sales skyrocketed after the broadcast. But four million viewers also saw in prime time how incompetent and unprofessional the largest opera house in England was, especially in financial matters, and how Cooper dismissed a member of staff and threw his phone against the wall. Ultimately, this scene cost Cooper his job and his reputation in the industry. 'Keith Cooper was a great talent. Unfortunately, the documentary shows him at the wrong moment. His career never recovered from that,' Jonas summed up. 'In marketing, he was a great visionary.'

The year 1989 and the tour to Russia

The year 1989 had begun unremarkably. In March, Jonas had refused to make up a further deficit of three hundred thousand pounds. For the third year in a row, Arts Council subsidies remained below the level of inflation. The recession was making itself felt, although Russell Willis Barnes was seeing the first fruits of the house's fundraising programme. Because the required wage rises could not be implemented with the current Arts Council grants, the musicians' union threatened strikes.

Jonas was on top form, copying a strategy he had learned from Edwards in Chicago: he invited all the participants up to his tiny office, closed all the windows beforehand and turned up the heating. When the first people commented that it was so terribly warm in his office, he asked for their understanding: he, a cancer patient, was not feeling so well; this morning he had been so terribly cold, surely everyone could agree on such-and-such? He just let everyone cook and sat out the negotiations until he had achieved what he wanted or could accept. The financial situation was as tense as ever. One might have understood if he had simply accepted the job offer from the Salzburg Festival, which was now courting him for the first time. But the festival business never appealed to Jonas.

What's more, he had recently met and fallen in love with 34-year-old Lucy Hull, a music agent. On 22 November 1989, the feast day of St Cecilia, patron saint of music, they held an elaborately staged wedding. Instead of having a wedding list at the usual department stores, the bride and groom left a list with a wine merchant in London. Jonas found this a democratic idea, as it allowed guests to choose wine according to their own budget.

For the wedding, the couple commissioned a world première performance by Mark-Anthony Turnage of the poem *All Will Be Well* by W. H. Auden (taken from Auden's translation of Schikaneder's libretto of Mozart's *Magic Flute*, the duet between Papageno and

Pamina, '*Bei Männern, welche Liebe fühlen*'). Among the guests were Valerie and Georg Solti, Michael Tilson Thomas, Lucia Popp, Josephine Barstow, Nicholas Hytner, Jonathan Miller, Alfred Brendel and Jeremy Isaacs. There was also Peter Palumbo, who had delivered his gift the day before: on 21 November 1989, the Arts Council had announced that the grants for the year 1990 would increase by 11 per cent. Palumbo had promised Jonas to announce the decision in time for the wedding. The day after the wedding, the Royal College of Music named Jonas a Fellow.[110] Some of his friends thought the wedding was a mistake even then. Others, outsiders, chalked it up to vanity.

1989 was also the year in which Jonas took advantage of a tiny, never-acknowledged mistake by Thatcher to make ENO the first foreign opera company of distinction to tour the Soviet Union. Jonas didn't need to do much about it, he just made a phone call and had a meeting with Thatcher. But the enterprise wouldn't have worked without his chutzpah.

During a meeting with Gorbachev in 1989, Thatcher had strayed from her notes and improvised on the new bond between the two countries and the 'British Week' to be held in Kiev and Moscow the following year. England would send the best of everything, the National Ballet and 'our English National Opera', Thatcher is reported to have said.

The transcript of the speech was never published, but the newspapers reported on it – and Jonas received calls from journalists who wanted him to confirm the news of the ENO tour. 'Thatcher didn't know her way around the cultural scene,' says Jonas. 'I suspect to this day that she mixed us up with the Royal Opera House.'

He knew what to do: he thanked Thatcher for her confidence and accepted the task. Thatcher's office allowed him twenty minutes with the Prime Minister and he was briefed: he had to be quick and present a paper. This was a pushover for Jonas. 'Clever as she was, Thatcher admitted nothing and promised to find the money for the tour. And at a time when she was cutting back wherever she could!' Thatcher kept her promise, even though a new employee was to play a not insignificant part in financing the tour.

From 1986 to 1988, Russell Willis Barnes succeeded in tripling the volume of sponsorship received by ENO. In April 1987, the Arts Council had recognised that ENO had a better return on investment than any other UK theatre company in terms of the grants it received per seat. At ENO, the rate was less than £20, for the others it lay between £30 and £40. At the same time, ENO's artistic achievements were appreciated by audiences, critics and in international theatrical circles.

When Barnes left ENO in 1989 for personal reasons, John Nickson succeeded her. He had not known that Jonas was looking for someone for fundraising, but had contacted him to arrange a contract with Rank Xerox. Through his work for the British Council, Nickson had learned of the company's plans to expand into the Soviet Union and open an office in Kiev. Nickson had reported to the company's chairman that Thatcher and Gorbachev would attend the opening performance of ENO in Kiev together, during the British Week. This resulted in a contract worth £250,000. Nickson had approached Jonas with this idea and received not only his approval for the contract, but also a job offer.

On his first day at the Coliseum, Jonas was still grateful for the Rank Xerox plan, but informed Nickson matter-of-factly that there was still a £50,000 shortfall, and if the money did not appear within the next four weeks, the tour would be cancelled. 'If it proves impossible to raise the money in the end, no one will blame you. I will of course give you all the help I can,' Jonas said by way of encouragement. For Nickson, it was just the right mix of risk-taking and trust. 'Peter had an extraordinary natural authority that was palpable,' Nickson rhapsodised in retrospect. 'He had the ability to inspire. You could feel that in the ensemble, but also outside.' Their collaboration saw the first truly professional fundraising effort for the arts take place in England.

Just under six months before her resignation on 22 November

1990, Thatcher appeared together with Mikhail Gorbachev on 7 June for the opening night of British Week in Kiev. 'This was a major political coup,' says Jonas. 'She was not interested in opera, but if opera was of use to her in diplomatic matters… Whether you like her politics or not, she was extremely clever, quick, with an extraordinary capacity for improvisation. You can't imagine what she would have made of this Brexit mess!'

Around four hundred people had been booked for the tour, which lasted until 24 June and went from Kiev via Moscow to Leningrad. The Russian stagehands were said to have been utterly astonished when they saw the hairstyles and earrings of their British colleagues. The British stage technicians had a woman boss, Louise Jeffreys. To the Russians, this was inconceivable.

'When Thatcher entered the ceremonial box, it was as if the Tsarina had returned,' Nickson recalled. 'The applause was so powerful that I thought the roof would blow off. That was the first signal to us that something really significant was happening in the Soviet Union, which collapsed fifteen months later.' Lord Harewood had a similar effect on the crowds. He had travelled along as Chairman of the Board and wore a full beard at the time, which gave him the typical 'Hanoverian, Romanov look', according to Jonas. When he entered, the shock was palpable: Harewood looked too much like the last Tsar.

The audience, but also Soviet functionaries, who were quite used to traditional set pieces, were thrilled by the performance. For many, *Xerxes*, performed on the opening night, was the first Handel opera of their lives. Moreover, the overall lightheartedness of the staging made an impression: Russians were not used to laughing at the opera. Thatcher did not let the KGB keep her from an unplanned backstage visit after the performance. A staff member whispered to Jonas in passing that he should be prepared to say a few brief words to her. This was a moment for Jonas to shine. He probably used the opportunity to explain to her why ENO needed a higher basic subsidy.

Apart from *Xerxes*, the programme included Miller's *The Turn of the Screw* and a *Macbeth* by Pountney and Lazaridis. After the

Macbeth première in April 1990, ENO's opera committee had wondered whether the productions had fallen into a 'stylistic straitjacket': *Macbeth* came across to the committee as a bad parody of the house style.

In Russia, it had a completely different effect: the play was recognisably set in an Eastern European dictatorship and spoke directly to the Russian audience. The tour closed with a small deficit: too much overtime had been paid out because of the endless rounds of applause.[111]

The 20+ season

In addition to the marketing campaign and the preparations for the tour, the ENO management team also planned an innovation in programming policy. With the programme for the 1990–91 season, they wanted to break out of the established canon of operatic literature.

They presented their plans under the heading '20+'. As a tribute to the bicentenary of Mozart's death, three of his works were on the programme, but otherwise only twentieth-century works featured. Most were pieces audiences had never heard before. The programme included *Wozzeck* with Pountney, Lazaridis and Elder on the production team, *Bluebeard* and *Oedipus Rex* as imagined by Alden, Lowery and again Elder, and the world première of *Timon of Athens* by Stephen Oliver, in a production by Graham Vick, musically directed by Graeme Jenkins. At last, a woman was directing at ENO: Julia Hollander had received the commission for Frederick Delius's *Fennimore and Gerda*.

'We hope that the season will, in its selection and presentation, reflect the turbulence of the century we live in and the changes in society and its boundaries that have taken and are still taking place,' Jonas said at the press conference.[112] He did not convince *The Times* editor Griffiths.

The ENO interpretation of Verdi had shown that works from

the nineteenth century could also bear witness to major upheavals in social or intellectual life. Most of the works on the programme in the 1990–91 season would be from the period 1900 to 1925. But Griffiths also acknowledged the enormous risk that ENO was taking with this programme, especially given Covent Garden's thoroughly traditional schedule. In addition, the house would have to pay royalties of £145,000 for these works.

Jonas clearly enjoyed pointing out that this sum was roughly equivalent to what ENO had to pay in taxes to the state. The real risk was that ENO was departing from its strong existing reputation for reinterpreting the classical canon. 'Risk is what this company is about,' Jonas announced confidently.

He used the podium of this press conference again to rail against William Rees-Mogg and the Arts Council: artists, he said, should have voiced their criticism much earlier and more loudly. Rees-Mogg had harmed the arts. Jonas expressed his hopes for a better future with Peter Palumbo at the helm of the Arts Council.

No wonder the *Guardian* described Jonas as a notorious fighter, 'deliberately modernist and wonderfully uncompromising'. Political caricature has been popular since the eigthteenth century; it was still going strong in the twentieth. Jonas was a prime candidate: his elongated limbs, the head slightly tilted, the eyes looking down from on high, the smoothly drawn crown, a slightly protruding ear – and the obligatory, extended index finger. 'Radical Reign of a King in the Coliseum', was the title of the *Guardian*'s overview of the 1990–91 season, which was to be a 'great success' and promised an 'operatic revolution'. Here Jonas was also referred to as a 'self-styled huckster',[113] a term which would resurface in his obituaries.

In order to get the financial plans for the 1990–91 season past the Board, Jonas later admitted to resorting to trickery: 'he had pulled the wool over the eyes of the Board'.[114] Indeed, ENO had to raise ticket prices once again, this time by 18 per cent. The most expensive ticket now cost £37.50. Of course, even this was not enough to balance the budget.

In order to persuade the Arts Council that the twentieth-century season was financially viable, Nickson agreed to Jonas's wish that every opera would be sponsored. That goal was achieved. Nickson suggested to Jonas a novel form of audience sponsorship to fund the revival of Pountney's production of Shostakovich's *Lady Macbeth of Mtsensk* (the production had premiered in 1987 to great acclaim). For several weeks in the lead-up to the revival, either Jonas or Nickson stepped in front of the curtain before performances and asked members of the audience to become production sponsors.

Their efforts were a great success and raised more than £100,000. The average individual donation of around £40 also exceeded expectations. 'We were successful with the campaign,' says Nickson, 'because our audience understood our situation and were motivated to give. Without Peter's inspiring guidance, none of this would have been possible. He made us all, the ensemble and the audience, believe in the cause. In the arts, this was the first example of crowdfunding in England.'

Fig. 35: Scene photo from *A Masked Ball*, London, 1989

'There were other productions I was secretly proud of,' Jonas confessed. '*A Masked Ball* and *Die Fledermaus*.' Nicholas Hytner was actually intended to direct *A Masked Ball*, which premièred in September 1989.[115] There had reportedly been an hour-long

336

wrangle at the Board meeting: Lord Harewood needed some convincing before David Alden and David Fielding got the job. This production became the work of which the triumvirate was proudest.

The *Guardian* would illustrate its obituary of Jonas with an iconic image from that production: the rider of the apocalypse looming over the ball. Sutcliffe thought that *A Masked Ball* by Alden and Fielding was as bold and individual as their *Simon Boccanegra*.[116] Fielding's stage design was marked by striking, bold symbols, which to Sutcliffe were captivating, clear and touched by sublimity.[117] A neoclassical gold frame, as large as the proscenium arch, hemmed in the scenery. In the very first scene, Gustavo leans on a gigantic hourglass, in which the sands of time ran. The final scene in the ballroom was dominated by the horseman of the apocalypse on a clock face with racing hands.

There were the usual waves of boos and bravos in the hall itself, but also 'fisticuffs' among the audience in the foyer. 'Turmoil at the opera' the *Evening Standard* wrote on its front page the day after the opening night. Until Jonas moved to Munich, he had this cover hanging on the wall outside his office. That was what he wanted to achieve: for a brief moment, his opera house was the place where society came to terms with itself.

At the beginning of the 1990–91 season, the triumvirate faced difficult challenges. Gilbert even spoke of a crisis. The triumvirate had made decisions that had not been passed on to the planning team. They had also made decisions that had not been thought through in terms of their branding implications. The business was no longer running smoothly, and staff had plenty to criticise.

No one doubted the artistic value of the 20+ season. But marketing director Cooper estimated their target audience as numbering only 20,000 people. At the same time, however, ticket prices had increased and the number of performances decreased in comparison to the previous seasons. The recession was taking hold. The season generated a deficit of one million pounds. Debts now amounted to £2.3 million. Hytner argued in retrospect that the triumvirate had adopted demands and values from continental Europe that did not work in British theatres. Even Pountney pointed to a 'Coliseum Cliché', as costumes and props were being used again and again.[118] For Jonas, an opera house was not democratic by nature. He saw himself as the driving force, 'ruthlessly pressing for *Lebensraum*', as he said, to realise his artistic goals. 'You will never achieve satisfying everyone – nor should you try to. Avoid the tyranny of the reader,' he said by way of defending himself.[119] ENO chronicler Gilbert saw here the first signs that the triumvirate was disintegrating.[120]

The Wall fell, and Thatcher's resignation on 22 November 1990 was celebrated as 'Enlightenment Thursday' in the British art world. Jonas received numerous letters from customers during this time. In times of recession, visitors felt the need for more traditional productions. The triumvirate did not grant them this wish. It was said to have grown deaf to criticism. Edmund Tracey, who had already served as chief dramaturge under Harewood, warned in an internal paper: 'We have become very blunt … the Coliseum and ENO have a reputation for being pretentious and not fun.'[121] The documents bear witness to tensions between the management and the Board, which did not seem to have a clear role. 'The seasons 1991 to 1993, Jonas's last at ENO, were difficult,'[122] Sutcliffe summarised. 'The mood turned against his leadership. During the recession, viewer numbers declined.'[123] The triumvirate made bad decisions; their way of working was breaking down. Pountney's *Don Carlos* and Hytner's *La Forza del Destino* were failures. Prices had been driven as high as the market would allow – a decision that cut against the principles of the founder Baylis. The result: audiences voted with their feet and stayed away.

When Johann Strauss's *Fledermaus*, 'the most un-ENO-piece', a relic of the Viennese era of opera par excellence, premièred in December 1991, directed by Richard Jones, ENO's programming policy reached its aesthetic peak. For Sutcliffe, it was 'one of ENO's most ambitious productions in the decade of producer's opera'.[124] With this daring and meticulously detailed production, ENO set a 'new standard of excess', according to Sutcliffe.[125] Jones was, for him, 'the most original and perceptive of the native British directors',[126] a formulation not entirely without irony, since Alden, the American, was no 'native British director'.

In the *Spectator*, on the other hand, Rupert Christiansen offered a scathing verdict. Jonas fundamentally didn't like opera, he said. The music, which Jonas doesn't waste a second on, bored him. Above all, however, Christiansen rejected the jokes because of their 'complete irrelevance', even those during the overture.[127] Opinions have always differed about humour. For Sutcliffe, the manic intensity with which Jonas would often and unashamedly direct jokes on stage was already evident in the overture.[128] Elegant, gloved hands and champagne flutes danced on the curtain along with powder puffs, the hands plucking chocolates from heart-shaped boxes. 'Think about how it's done normally – and then do it differently,' Nigel Lowery had said of his set design.[129]

But Lesley Garrett as Adele stole the show. She wore a stunning Gaultier-style turquoise bodice with pearls, long pearl-studded gloves in the same colour, black stilettos – and nothing else. In Adele's aria in the last act, she took off her clothes and threw her costume in the air. She was visible only from the back, and just for a moment, but her photo was in every newspaper. 'That was unusual on the opera stage,' Jonas commented.

'It's very difficult to talk about this *Fledermaus* business,' Lesley Garrett told the *Independent*, 'because people are determined to think it was a calculated thing, that it was all publicity for me and ENO. But it wasn't like that at all. Actually what I did was born out of the music – you don't have to believe me, but look at the words and they're all about stripping. Besides, I didn't do a strip-tease. What I did was a very fleeting moment of artistic nudity which was just part of a show that was full of extraordinary visual moments. You have to take it in context. It was a crazy, wonderful, visually extravagant evening of which my bottom was the sensation. I completely upstaged the whole thing.'[130]

Surely the London newspapers would have put the photograph on the front pages even without Keith Cooper's insistence. He could have intervened only by *not* releasing the photograph for press purposes. But why should he? The attitude of his boss was crystal clear: 'Competition was fierce in London's West End. Getting a full-page photograph in the major British dailies helps the house. All seventeen performances were immediately sold out. I have been criticised for being opportunistic. Honestly, I didn't mind this criticism, even from the Board. If you can get such advertising for free, you should take it. The tickets were sold out, end of story.'

Jonas was unrepentant towards his sponsor British Steel, which rejected the production outright. He is said to have replied – in writing – to Goodison, British Steel's representative, that in government circles his company had the scent of roses only because ENO was so venturesome and innovative.[131] 'End of story.'

Once again: Peter who?

'I was very happy at ENO. As is often the case in my life, the first six months were very difficult, the next two and a half years or so were rapid, happy and successful – although I don't know what success really is. I was always being courted. And not only by women. But whenever I was sattelfest [saddle-fast], offers came. It's like the stock market in this industry. As soon as there is a good *ondit* about some aspect or other, offers always come along. Whether you are qualified or not. I think I was always unqualified.'

When Jonas began to talk about the offers that reached him during this time, he once again found it difficult to speak. His voice was raspy, yet amazingly strong. 'After my third year at ENO, I was approached by the chairman of the Aufsichtsrat [supervisory board] of the Zurich Opera. He wanted to have lunch with me. I invited him to my London club. It was a good lunch, a polite conversation. But I couldn't do that. I'd only been in London for such a short time.'

A year after the visit from Zurich, the 'président du conseil' of the Opéra de Paris contacted him. The new building at the Bastille was nearing completion. 'For me, Paris has always remained traumatically linked to those six months as a student. Besides, I am more inclined towards German than towards French. He insisted that I should come look at the new building.'

'I was young, inexperienced, unqualified by my standards. It was really a Verführungsaktion [seduction].' When Daniel Barenboim was offered the position of general music director of the Staatsoper Unter den Linden in Berlin, he wanted Jonas to come along with him. 'That was the only phase in which our friendship cooled down. Daniel accused me of having no ambition.'[132] Jonas, however, did not feel equipped. 'I know the limits of my intelligence. For a few months Daniel didn't speak to me.'

After that, De Nederlandse Opera also contacted him. 'There, too, I declined. I had no idea that I would later spend over a decade on their Board. But my time on that committee brought me a lot of happiness. Then when the Salzburg Festival came along, I was really quite amazed.' He didn't consider himself nearly experienced enough, despite the knowledge he had gained during his time with Lucia Popp. 'The committee expected me to appear in Salzburg in person. I had to fly there and talk to the committee. I told them I couldn't take it on!' Jonas stayed overnight in Salzburg. When he sat on the plane on the return flight and opened the newspaper, he saw his photo: The *Wiener Kurier* saw him as a possible successor to Karajan. Jonas was greatly vexed.

Three weeks later, he got a phone call. The Austrian Prime Minister and his Minister of Culture could not believe what they were being told. They assumed that the Commission had not pushed hard enough – after all, *who could refuse the Salzburg Festival?* – and they requested – no, demanded – of Jonas that he please explain his refusal in writing. You must justify yourself, Jonas was told. Jonas obliged.

Then August Everding called him. 'Once I went to Amsterdam to see a performance,' Jonas leaned back in his chair and ate a biscuit. 'I can't remember which one it was. I had just checked into the hotel when the phone in my room rang.' Everding chatted with him and invited him to come to a meeting of the Association Internationale des Directeurs d'Opéra, a forerunner of the industry association Opera Europa. When they met two weeks later, Everding took Jonas aside. Could he see himself in Munich? After the Bavarian state elections in October 1990, the search for Sawallisch's successor was set to begin. 'We talked about it,' says Jonas. 'I didn't get my hopes up and didn't give it a second thought. I thought it was pretty silly. Months went by.' Are we to believe that Peter Jonas did not really think about the possibility of being appointed to the Bavarian Staatsoper during these months – hardly credible.

During his next visit to Amsterdam, again at the same hotel, Everding called him once more. The CSU had again won the state elections, and the race for Sawallisch's successor had begun. Everding wanted to know if he could throw Jonas's name into the ring. The now-customary exchange followed: it made no sense, he should not be considered for it; but Jonas could not ignore the request – 'Do me a favour!' Everding even travelled to London and met Jonas at his club for lunch. The minister had officially asked him to make contact. 'I didn't think it was for me.' Everding persisted and accused him of having no manners, and of insulting the Bavarian Minister of Culture with his behaviour.

A month later, Jonas agreed to visit Munich. Curiously, he later recalled that he had to get up at six o'clock to catch the first flight to Munich from Cannes, where he had given a speech at the film festival. 'Okay, if I have to,' was his attitude.

In the Bavarian State Ministry for Education, Culture, Science and the Arts, in Salvatorstraße 2, Jonas met Minister of State Hans Zehetmair for the first time. He was extraordinarily charming, Jonas recalled, and he also noticed that Zehetmair had a folder with the official state coat of arms on his desk, 'surely from the Bavarian secret police,' the Briton in him whispered. When Zehetmair opened the file, Jonas recognised an article that had recently appeared in the *Financial Times* – full-page and with one of those caricatures showing him with elongated and sticking-out ears, as he noted with obvious amusement. Jonas knew the final sentence of the article by heart: 'Some people would say that Peter Jonas is not a creative person, but just an actor playing a role – which only goes to show that there are no great roles, only great actors.'

Peter Jonas found this characterisation clever, as it struck at the heart of his insecurities at the time. Nevertheless, it was not unkind, it held a grain of truth, and was at the same time polite – again, something important for Jonas's inner Brit.

'Hans Zehetmair then proceeded to give me the whole Spiel,' Jonas reported. He asked whether Jonas had noticed that all of Europe was after this job. Jonas baulked – 'I was offered a job like this on a plate! No commission, nothing!' – and threw in names of people he thought were better suited for the job. Zehetmair replied that he was not asking him for recommendations, but whether Jonas wanted to take up the position. Jonas asked for thirty days to think it over – 'and off I went'.

Two weeks later he accepted an invitation from the German Embassy in London to a reception, 'the usual thing, canapés and champagne'. Hans Zehetmair was there, with his colleague Toni Schmid. 'What a coincidence!' Of course, they had a private conversation: 'The whole Spiel again!' Toni Schmid did a superb job of describing the opportunities the position offered. 'He spoke excellent English, with a Welsh accent. We had some more champagne and then went home.'

Jonas's charms evidently worked on the Germans. 'I had the impression,' Hans Zehetmair recalled, 'that Sir Peter was rather acting a part. But I was a person who trusted his employees and said: "You do it." The question of who should be the director of the Staatsoper was the chief issue for me.'[133]

As an avowed Latinist, Zehetmair described his role in the negotiations humorously as *'pontifex'*, bridge builder. 'The Munich Staatsoper, this urbane Bavarian house, which is one of the best-attended and one of the most profitable, needed, in quotation marks, a breath of fresh air,' Zehetmair said. 'So the point was that, with all due respect to my predecessors, I wanted to set a new tone. I was very impressed by Sir Peter Jonas's CV. At the time he was just Peter Jonas, not yet a Sir. He was interesting to me from the very first moment.' At that time, Bavaria's cultural administration had a reputation for signing up well-known names and paying them high salaries but not taking any artistic risks. His appointment was a testament to the new international standing that British opera had achieved through the Power House triumvirate.[134]

'Slowly I started to really think about Munich,' Jonas explained. 'Just that week I had had a terrible spat with the Arts Council. I said to Lucy: "I'm taking this job." Then I waited until the twenty-eighth day and called Toni Schmid to arrange another meeting in Munich. Two days before, I had another run-in with the Council.' The deep-seated, well-fed anger with the Arts Council was the ideal seedbed in which the thought of Munich could germinate.

Another factor in Jonas's favour was that Zehetmair is said to have been very annoyed with a seasoned German director who thought himself the heir apparent, due to his existing position, and had demanded an appointment with Zehetmair. That says a lot about how Jonas approached the game. Jonas was not only a strategist, he was also a tactician. 'For some reason, I don't know why: I will do it.' He did not want to elaborate on why he suddenly made the decision to say yes, and take the job as Staatsintendant (State Director) of the Bavarian Staatsoper in Munich.

Herbert Meier, theatre advisor at the Staatsministerium (Ministry), took over negotiations, in which Jonas was represented by Thomas Bär from Zurich. After a protracted lunch in Bär's office, a deal was reached.

Jonas thought he had been able to keep the news confidential. However, on the morning of Good Friday 1991 he was woken by an angry caller from the Arts Council who had read of his new appointment on the front page of *The Times*. 'The head of ENO says goodbye and goes to Munich,' wrote Richard Morrison. 'His departure marks the end of the most exciting era in the history of English National Opera and an immensely fruitful partnership with Elder and Pountney.'

Not only was the Arts Council raging: Jonas was furious too. He had wanted to inform the ENO ensemble personally. Someone had leaked the news of the appointment to the German press. 'It was clear who it was,' says Jonas, 'a well-known personality in the German theatre scene.' Schmid, who was responsible for the press work of the Staatsministerium at the time, apologised to him by telephone, but at the same time asked him to plan the press conference in which Jonas was to be introduced to the public in Munich. Like the consummate professional that he was, he agreed to the following Thursday, 5 April 1991, without batting an eye, but a little later, in the privacy of his office, he had to admit that the prospect of facing the German press – and then having to speak German! – daunted him. The fact that he was not at all known to the general public in Germany did not exactly reassure him.

While media representatives may not have been counting on anything earth-shattering from the press conference, because they did not expect detailed information about his Intendanz at this early stage, this event was always associated with one very physical memory for Jonas. He was supposed to enter Munich's Nationaltheater through the main entrance and climb the big staircase all by himself. 'Although I had always had the ability to look confident and my height helped me, I felt so small. The truth is, I was always terrified in these situations. Even though I was used to dealing with the press and photographers, this time I had to speak in a foreign language. No matter how well you speak it, the nuances, how you control the conversation, it makes so much difference. If required, you have to be quick on your feet. Sometimes you need to be quick on the uptake! I wanted to avoid embarrassment at all costs, that was my biggest concern.' His concern was understandable, but in the event it was unfounded: as soon as he arrived in Munich, he was able to convey his most important points in perfect German.

For his first press conference in Munich, Jonas employed a tried and tested tactic, though one that he no longer needed in

London: he made a plan of what he wanted to convey and jotted down key phrases on cue cards. His German colleagues did not notice any problems with his command of German: when Peter Jonas said that he can barely speak German, Zehetmair judged that this was merely the Englishman 'fishing for compliments'. In fact, any exotic quirks in his German gave him a special charm. 'Often I wasn't quite sure if he was just playing it up. Given his intellectualism, I think a lot of it was put on deliberately.' On the eve of the press conference, he put his artistic programme down on paper in broad outline. 'The night before, I was pretty scared,' Jonas repeated several times in retrospect.

That basic plan split the new season into five, maybe six slots. One slot had to be reserved for the Munich house gods: Mozart, Richard Strauss or Wagner, the second slot for something from the Italian repertoire. The third slot, however, was to be filled with a work from the Baroque period, Handel, Monteverdi or Cavalli. 'The last time *Giulio Cesare in Egitto* was performed was in 1955,' said Jonas. For the other slots, he wanted to choose works of classical modernism, if possible a commissioned work, and lastly, 'being cheeky', he named the final slot simply: Love. 'Here I wanted a work that I absolutely love. *Die Königskinder* by Humperdinck or *The Cunning Little Vixen* by Janáček. My contract was only for five years at that time, but the pattern remained the same for the whole thirteen years.'

When Zehetmair opened up the press conference for Q&As, Jonas fielded the questions he had been expecting: ENO is famous for its modern, radical productions, so would Munich audiences be frightened by his directorship? He did not know what was radical or modern, Jonas countered: he only knew good and bad. But then someone asked a question Jonas remembered vividly. On the podium with him were Peter Schneider, who would be chief conductor of the Bavarian Staatsoper until 1998, and Gerd Uecker, who was opera director in Munich until he began his Intendanz at the Semper Opera. Would they make all the decisions as a troika, asked a woman (who knew her way around ENO because she had worked there as an assistant director, but who also knew the Munich opera). Many members of the Staastoper ensemble were in the room with them. In an opera house there is always teamwork, the expertise of the departments is always needed, Jonas replied.

'But who has the last word?' she added. 'Everyone fell absolutely silent, you could hear a pin drop,' Jonas described the moment. 'The background to her question was an infamous civil war between Sawallisch and Everding and their wives. Sawallisch and Everding were like oranges and milk. I had already been inoculated by the ministry about the damage done to the Opera. In every corner of the Staatsoper there was a principality, a county or a duchy. No one had been able to solve it. And these princes were all sitting in the room.' This included Peter Schneider, who made it clear that he had concluded a contract with the Staatsministerium, not with the Intendant.[135] Jonas, quick-witted, shot back: 'That's quite clear. There is only one boss, that's me.' This statement did not make him popular, among the staff least of all. But Jonas thought he had won Zehetmair's heart. With that, there was nothing left to be said. 'That was the beginning in Munich,' Jonas smiled.

The London legacy

While his negotiations with the Bavarian Staatsoper were still in progress, Jonas had to solve a problem that ENO had been facing since 1986 – and the reason for that fateful booking on the December 1988 Pan Am flight to New York. The land on which the Coliseum stood was owned by the Stoll Moss Theatre Group, which in turn was owned by the Australian businessman Robert Holmes à Court. ENO's lease on the Coliseum would expire on 31 March 1996. The Board expected Jonas to solve this problem, because there was a risk that the company, although a national theatre, could theoretically go bankrupt.

As a limited liability company subsidised by the state, ENO had Coutts as their principal banker. The director of the bank – the aptly-named David Money-Coutts – and his employees, who wore Stresemann suits to work, were aware that the state regularly did not pay out the announced subsidies until after the end of the financial year in April. Nevertheless, Money-Coutts had to insist on an overdraft. The bank made its money from interest: ultimately from taxpayers' money, because ENO had to show the interest on its balance sheets. 'This one particular bank was cross-subsidised by the state,' Jonas complained. 'That's how Britain works!'

In addition to the burden of avoidable interest payments, the gradual expiry of the lease agreement was a particular burden on the balance sheet. Jonas compared their situation to a ship heading for an iceberg: it was not clear whether ENO would have been allowed to continue trading after the end of the contract.[136]

At the end of each financial year, Jonas and his financial director asked Money-Coutts for an overdraft. Again and again, the same discussion developed around the question of what assets ENO had to offer. The fact that it was a national theatre, that the government had announced the subsidies, was irrelevant to the bank. The income from ticket sales, on the other hand, could not be planned with certainty.

Moreover, this income appeared on the balance sheet as debts, because the performances for which people had bought tickets had not yet taken place. So for the bank, this income was not safe. 'We then had to work out a complicated cash-flow calculation to prove that we could do it,' Jonas explained.

'Although this bank specialised in cultural enterprises, it was still a bank. It had to judge things according to finance law, not government affairs. Dealing with such things took an enormous amount of time. Can you imagine how great it was to come to Munich? This freedom!'

A 1988 feasibility study had shown that the purchase of the land was the best option for ENO. In order to receive some advice from the head of the World Bank, James Wolfensohn, on how ENO might best approach Robert Holmes à Court, Jonas had flown to New York shortly before Christmas 1988.

Wolfensohn had tipped off Jonas that the Holmes à Court

empire was not as solvent as was widely believed. Possibly he would be willing to sell. The Arts Council had authorised Jonas and Harewood, as Chair of the Board, to begin negotiations. Even after three meetings, in which Holmes à Court, who was considered eccentric, had appeared 'stuffy and inscrutable', no solution had been reached. Then Holmes à Court died unexpectedly in September 1990. It took his widow, Janet, only a few days to give Harewood and Jonas a price they could agree to, at least in principle: the property was expected to cost £2.5 million. Now they just had to find the money.

Naturally, the Arts Council refused. For the last time, Jonas's dauntless courage proved its worth as he went straight to David Mellor, who secured £2.8 million in funding from the Office of Arts and Libraries. The Arts Council covered £0.8 million of this; the rest came through Heritage Funds.

Jonas was rightly proud of this achievement: the Conservative government had paid for land for ENO. For Tom Sutcliffe, this is Jonas's legacy: the fact that the ensemble now had its own premises made it more difficult for politicians to abolish ENO or to merge the two opera houses. Justifying public funding for this purchase would never have been possible if ENO had not previously become 'a popular artistic pace-setter' in the 1970s and 1980s.[137] 'But the Arts Council was furious!' Jonas recalled. And the Arts Council responded in its own way, demanding that the purchase come with a condition: the building and land belong to ENO, but only as long as it maintains a full-time opera and ballet company. Otherwise, the building reverts to the Arts Council, which can sell it or use it for other purposes. Stoll Moss's cash crunch, low property prices during the recession and the upcoming election campaign: all three factors had worked to Jonas's advantage.

Rodney Milnes wrote quite correctly in *Opera* magazine that ENO would now be trapped, 'a sweet trap, but a trap nonetheless'.[138] Because now ENO would also have to finance the renovation of the building, to the tune of tens of millions. Jonas was involved in this only by chance. When he publicly thanked ENO in March 1992 and compared the significance that the acquisition of the land had for ENO with the fall of the Berlin Wall, it was already known that he was set to move to Munich.

During a flight back from Australia, the businessman Garfield Howard Weston had closely followed the *Daily Telegraph* reports on the purchase of the property. Through his secretary, he invited Jonas to have breakfast. 'Peter, I was so pleased to read this,' Weston is reported to have said. 'You got £2.5 million from a Conservative government, that's unheard of! This morning I spoke to my family. We decided that we wanted to give you a gift.' Then he pulled a cheque for one million pounds out of his pocket and handed it to Jonas. 'Do with it what you want for the Company!'

Jonas had to report this donation to the Board. His concern was that the Arts Council would take the money away from the house if they ended the financial year with a surplus on the balance sheet. A justified concern, because it would be that time again in April. To prevent this, Jonas risked another deficit and put the donation in a blocked bank account so that it could be spent only on the restoration of the building. 'If there's anything I'm glad about, it's that. My successor spent the money on a study to see whether the Coliseum was too big for the company and whether ENO would be better off moving to a smaller building.'

The size of the Coliseum is still a huge challenge for ENO today. When in 2016 the Arts Council once again failed to champion the arts and cut ENO's subsidies by a third in one fell swoop, Jonas also raised his voice in an international chorus of solidarity. He immediately saw that the drastic job cuts in the choir and orchestra resulting from the budget cuts were not the real problem.

Rather, the reduction of the season to nine months could give the Arts Council a basis to argue that the company and operations that were tied to the purchase of the property in 1992 no longer existed. In 2016, the house did not publish any figures on occupancy. They were probably shamefully low, even though perennial favourites such as *Mikado* were still playing to sell-out crowds. The sheer size of the venue overwhelmed the management, which in those months was briefly led by a former McKinsey manager with no previous opera management experience.

Farewell in a wheelchair

Regular operations at the house required full commitment as before, regardless of who was at the head of ENO. The recession caused problems for all cultural enterprises, and ENO also had to take certain countermeasures. In August 1992, Jonas and other executives advertised a new offer of two tickets for just £15 for the revival of Miller's *Rigoletto* outside the Coliseum in St Martin's Lane, and at the Albert Hall and Kenwood, with staff in sandwich boards. At the same time, the 'Everyone Needs Opera' campaign ran with posters designed by Mike Dempsey. The battle for audiences, the battle for public and political perception and, above all, the battle for Arts Council support continued at all levels.

But this was the swansong of an era that had been harshly criticised by the press as 'self-important navel-gazing' (*Independent*). 'Compared to the need for jobs and housing, the need for opera is a somewhat ephemeral,' *The Times* commented.[139] 'We knew we were priced a little too high for our market and that the recession would affect our work,' Jonas said. Perhaps it would have been more appropriate to say 'Everyone needs the Arts', Jonas conceded, pointing out, in another swipe at Thatcher, that without the arts there would be no society.[140]

'My time at ENO was really a remarkable time,' Jonas concluded. 'Suddenly there was something like hope that opera in London could be intellectually and artistically important. That moment is over. In the 1980s there had been this one moment to build a vibrant art world as a counterpoint to Thatcher, and as a polemic against her. People like David Pountney, who passionately believed that the principles of European opera were important on stage, and Mark Elder as the driving musical force in the ensemble were so important for this. It was also important that people like David Alden, Nicholas Hytner, Richard Jones and Jonathan Miller were all at the house at the same time, even though they were all very different and sometimes very much opposed to one another. They all had the ability to do exceptionally interesting work; they were all loyal to ENO and collegial with each other. What satisfies me about this is that their styles couldn't be further apart from each other.'

Then he fell silent for quite a while. 'When I look back at my significance for the company, however much the era was celebrated and considered successful, I wonder if I had any significance at all.' And then he made a strikingly candid confession: 'For me personally in the sense that my share price went up. I seemed to be in demand.'

The ensemble was saddened by the news of Jonas's departure, but permanent change was such an ingrained part of theatrical life that everyone would have expected this moment to come sooner or later.

Close companions like Maggie Sedwards understood his decision. 'The Bavarian Staatsoper is one of the greatest opera houses in the world. It was right for him to return to the international scene at the highest level. After years of trying to balance ENO's finances, he would work within generous German funding structures, with a huge, international ensemble. The sheer size of the operation must have had an immense appeal for Peter,' says Sedwards, who, like many others in the ensemble, drew a positive balance sheet of his directorship. 'One of Peter's great achievements is that when he, Mark and David left, ENO was recognised as a necessary and important member of the arts in this country. The years that Peter, Mark and David led ENO were without question the most exciting in opera and the creative arts in London. The work was amazingly progressive.'

Jonas, Elder and Pountney drew a balance sheet of their own, published in 1992. That volume, the slim and richly illustrated paperback *Power House: The English National Opera Experience*, functions as a testament to the triumvirate and is considered the 'best available record of a truly remarkable period in post-war British cultural history'.[141] A photograph by Bill Rafferty takes the viewer directly into the opera house's machine room. It is an image from *Lady Macbeth of Mtsensk* as directed by Pountney, one of the company's most important productions. Most of the lyrics are said to have been written by Pountney and Nicholas John. From 1985 and until his death in 1996, John was the ENO dramaturge. It was he who is said to have coined the term 'Power House' for the triumvirate's tenure, even though Harewood had already spoken of the 'Musical Powerhouse' in an address to the company in 1979.[142] In his function as chairman, Harewood had contributed a foreword to the volume; it represents his own ethos *in nuce*: 'If you ask what is the aim of an opera company, the straight answer must be "to perform opera to as high a standard as lies within the company's possibilities – and then to raise the standards a bit higher". All other considerations – of place, specialisation, casting, tradition and so on – are secondary.'[143] The triumvirate had achieved this admirably. The whole had become greater than the sum of its parts. Harewood goes on, now addressing Jonas: 'A manager is responsible for the work of a company as a whole, and, while it might theoretically be possible for individual productions to flourish in spite of him, a company style could hardly develop without his enthusiasm.' Harewood added: 'I hope that the groundwork was laid before Peter Jonas arrived,'[144] indicating that in the latter he sees a worthy successor to the great Lilian Baylis.

After Harewood's preface, Jonas, Elder and Pountney launched into their polemic: without mentioning her name, they embarked upon a criticism of Thatcher. Their position was one of a clear commitment to opera, first and foremost; and, in particular, opera sung in English. They defended this position against left- and right-wing ideologies that oppose the concept of publicly funded opera houses from their respective standpoints. 'Opera is an easy target for the ideologues of the left who refuse to distinguish between Rembrandt and rap, Keats and *Kilroy* or Bach and a busker. From the right comes the less verbose but no less deadly cavalry who want to scythe down the whole notion of subsidised culture.' And then they name Thatcher after all, quoting her 'disgraceful remark'[145] – 'There is no such thing as society.' Art, they say, has the task of entertaining people, but also of disturbing people and questioning the present state of things.

Precisely because ENO was publicly funded, the house had to take on this second task, with all of its risks. And when the triumvirate then reflected on the 'ideal conductor' of operas they did take care to refer to this future leader as either 'him or her', although the stage of their day was very much a man's world. And indeed, Elder's successor was to be a woman.

In their book, the triumvirate acknowledged the consequences of their management decisions: on seat prices, advertising or the colour of the carpet in the hall. But Jonas also took responsibility for his company's aggressive marketing strategy, a strategy that he felt was ahead of its time, but above all due to the fierce competitive pressure in London. 'I don't apologise for that, London is not Munich,' Jonas shrugged. 'We had to sell tickets! Only when a production generated interest was there a run on individual ticket sales. Every single night we competed with all the other attractions in the West End.' Once again he took out his copy of *Power House*, leafed through it and looked at some of the pictures. 'It's been a long time since I last looked at these images, but what strikes me is how current, how contemporary many of these sets seem. They don't look dated at all. You could expect them on a stage in Gelsenkirchen or Duisburg today.' And then he added to this sharp little remark in a typical way: 'That I find a little bit interesting, remarkable.'

But the retrospective in the book also reveals what many testimonies from life on stage and in the orchestra pit had long made clear: it really was a man's world. Jonas knew the question, but he didn't want to answer it, not with regard to his time at ENO. 'It was a different age. ENO was not dominated by men, even though we were only men in the leadership team. We had female directors! Although I do wonder why Julia Hollander didn't have a breakthrough.'

The fact that the technical manager Louise Jeffreys had astonished the Russian workers during the company's tour seemed to Jonas unremarkable. There were also many stereotypes on stage. As radical as the approaches of the productions were, the question of how women were represented was not much-discussed then. For

Jonas, how his directors portrayed female characters was an issue of artistic freedom. He would never have touched or discussed the matter.

Mark Elder also found that ENO had succeeded in doing something in the triumvirate period that no one else achieved: 'We made our theatre a theatre of excitement, novelty and iconoclasm, to such an extent that, by the end of the 1980s, theatre was coming to us for inspiration for what they should be doing.' Elder had been dreaming about this even before Jonas and Pountney came to the house.

Recently, however, numerous voices have argued that ENO got lost amid its own clichés. The 'concept opera' – 'the producer's interpretation of the composer's intention'[146] – was losing its power. Audience numbers declined, while Covent Garden's popularity rebounded. In its own way, the company's approach had become exclusive. The cohesion of the ensemble was slowly dissolving, and more and more singers were taken on only for individual engagements. British singers were more frequently performing abroad, ENO having contributed to their good training.

Despite these signs of erosion at the end of the Power House era, critics acknowledged the significance of the directorships of Peter Jonas, Mark Elder and David Pountney both for ENO itself and for English opera history, and in terms of how their company's aesthetics and musical quality had set international standards. Jonas's appointment in Munich was a direct consequence of this development. 'Lord Harewood, Peter Jonas, Mark Elder and David Pountney helped opera to play a full part in British theatrical life,' judged Sutcliffe.[147] Gilbert wrote that 'a period of astonishing zest, drive and creativity, with 1985–87 marking its high point, with a succession of extraordinary and exciting productions that challenged traditional and complacent attitudes to opera as an art form, as well as making the Coliseum one of the most dynamic theatres in Europe' had come to an end.[148] The directorship of Jonas, Elder and Pountney catapulted ENO into the international limelight, 'far outstripping the troubled Royal Opera at Covent Garden through a combination of big and bold theatrical ideas, an unswerving commitment to high musical standards, and long-term artistic goals which have broadly survived the financial constraints imposed by dwindling subsidy' judged Hugh Canning in the *Sunday Times*. 'Everything has a sell-by date. It's time to go,' Jonas had told Pauline Peters of the *Evening Standard*.[149] 'He is convinced that he has become a different person since he joined ENO: more mature and possibly tougher. He claims that nothing scares him except premières,' Peters wrote.

Fig. 36: The Queen and Peter Jonas

For his services to opera in England, in 1991 Peter Jonas was awarded the honour of 'Commander of the British Empire' by the Queen. The sculptor Nigel Boonham made a bronze bust of him, now in the National Portrait Gallery.

Mark Elder, who had been working at ENO since the end of 1979, had wanted to leave the house earlier, but Jonas had changed his mind, whereupon Pountney also decided to leave the house along with his friends. Perhaps this decision was misguided, Elder said. 'Peter should have let me go and organised the next music director.'

Certainly, this decision contrasted with the forward-looking and carefully orchestrated way that Lord Harewood had prepared his departure. ENO's Power House had run out of steam and Peter Jonas was on his way to run the Bavarian Staatsoper in Munich, leaving a large deficit and leaking roofs to his successor. In autumn 1991, Dennis Marks became the new managing director of ENO. Sian Edwards was appointed as new music director. Both were largely inexperienced in opera matters. Marks had been a BBC producer and had no previous experience of running a theatre. Sian Edwards was equally innocent. ENO 'in disarray' was how Norman Lebrecht summarised the situation.[150]

That neither Marks nor Edwards were suitable successors quickly became clear, if it had not already been plain at the time of the appointments – a state of affairs that could have been avoided. The large deficit that Jonas left to Marks, which came to £2.3 million,[151] was considerable, but this was a situation that Jonas had also encountered when he took over from Harewood. ENO had never been adequately funded. 'Unfortunately, my successor was not successful. He didn't have a lucky hand with the workers in the ensemble,' Jonas commented. 'You can be as brilliant as you like, but if you don't really get on with the people who work there, it won't work.'

Marks also openly spoke out against the production style of the house. The directors in the German tradition had lost themselves in revivals and clichés. He reorganised the departments and split Pountney's old department.[152] Edmund Tracey and the casting director Jeremy Caulton both left. Nickson stayed until 1996, Livingston until her retirement. The 1995 Stevenson Report discussed the option of a 'reduced role for ENO' and the fundamental question of how much opera and how much dance a world city like London 'needed'. By that time, both the Royal Opera Covent Garden and ENO had the lowest subsidies in Europe.[153]

Jonas almost didn't see his farewell performance of Verdi's *Macbeth*, which Pountney produced, in June 1993. The day before he had played a cricket match on a glorious summer day.

The Royal Opera House team was pitted against ENO. That Jonas should play for ENO was a matter of honour.

The match had lasted longer than expected. Drenched in sweat, he sat in his car, air conditioning cranked up, and sped home to change for one of his various farewell dinners. Donatella Flick, the then wife of Gert Rudolph Flick, who sat on the Board of ENO, had invited him. At first Jonas was still quite well, coughing only a little. Then, within hours, a simple cold turned into bacterial pneumococcal sepsis. At breakfast he collapsed. His wife Lucy called the doctor, who arrived by bicycle and admitted Jonas to hospital with a high fever. Jonas had had his spleen removed during his first round of cancer treatment, at a time when its importance as the ultimate barrier against bacterial infections had not yet been recognised. Jonas could have really done with his spleen now. He was treated with strong antibiotics in hospital for over three weeks. This did not agree with him at all.

A National Health Service car and a nurse accompanied him in a wheelchair to the farewell performance at the Coliseum. 'That was sad,' Jonas commented succinctly. 'The Curse of Macbeth.' After all, this was the first time he had worn the kilt he had bought specially for the farewell party, which bore the legend 'Scotland'.

As Peter was being driven back to the hospital, the ENO ensemble partied to mark the end of the Power House era.

MUNICH 1993–2006

The dinosaur

It all came together in the image of a collapsing dinosaur, a key concept in the production of *Giulio Cesare in Egitto* at the Bavarian Staatsoper in Munich (BSO), which premiered on 21 March 1994. The dinosaur symbolized the beginning of something new – something unheard of. An aesthetic entirely new to the world of Munich opera, and one that would be hotly debated by the city's cultural establishment.

For Peter Jonas, the production was the fulfilment of everything he had longed for in his work. His love of Handel, and his attitude to directing as interpretation rather than representation, united with a strong directorial concept and a dash of humour. 'If you were to ask me today, what if I had been fired after *Giulio Cesare*? It would have been worth it! Everything in my life had led to this moment,' Jonas said emphatically. In the production by Richard Jones and Nigel Lowery, the falling dinosaur stood for the fall of the Roman Empire and its obsolete order. In a figurative sense, however, the metaphor could be read as the overthrow of the old order at the Bavarian Staatsoper in Munich. This production became the turning point of Peter Jonas's tenure, making dinosaurs the symbol of his Intendanz – and of the Handel renaissance in Germany.

Nothing in the previous months and weeks – or even the last days – before the opening night indicated the effect the production would trigger. Jonas was under pressure. He had thought that he had planned the beginning of his first season, 1993–94, pretty cleverly. Over the first weeks, only standard repertoire and revivals were on the programme. The first new production was *La Damnation de Faust*, which they were able to prepare in peace.

The national feature pages reviewed the production positively.

The *Frankfurter Allgemeine Zeitung* wrote that the opening night, directed by Thomas Langhoff, was promising in every respect. For Anne Midgette of the American magazine *Opera News*, it was an unqualified success.[1] Jonas and the BSO seemed to be well on the way to working out a new, contemporary stage aesthetic.

Behind the scenes things looked different. At first, the stage technicians had judged the technical set-up was impossible. They were not experienced enough for what was now being asked of them. Jonas held seemingly endless crisis meetings until late at night. In the end, the implementation succeeded, 'but with great blood, sweat, tears and rows. How we did it, I don't know to this day,' Jonas sighed decades later. 'I found the work unforgettable, not least because of the set design by Jürgen Rose. I was also impressed by his influence in the house.'

Fig. 37: The dinosaur

Immediately after the première, rehearsals began for *Un Ballo in Maschera*. 'The production was an embarrassment. I made several weak decisions here,' Jonas confessed. For one thing, he should not have commissioned Tom Cairns to direct. Jonas had been delighted by the latter's production of *The Knot Garden* by Michael Tippett at Covent Garden. He had expected a much more abstract interpretation of the court scenery in Verdi's opera.

In retrospect Jonas also thought it a mistake to have entrusted Peter Schneider with the baton. Jonas had bucked against 'German Fachdenken [pigeonhole-thinking]'. What was the point of these discussions about innate *Italianità*? Why shouldn't an Austrian conductor be able to conduct Verdi? Jonas thought it was all 'rubbish': 'this proved to be not a good decision.'

In addition, the concept for the set again placed enormous demands on the technology at the BSO. In order for the production to be included in the programme, it had to be possible to store the scenery. This was simply not feasible with some of the items. Compromises had to be found. On the day of the première a singer called in sick. 'The whole thing was expensive and half-baked,' Jonas commented.

The audience booed Schneider, his conducting attracting bad reviews; the *Financial Times* called it 'as un-italianate as you can get'.[2] But boos were also mixed in with applause for the singers. The *Frankfurter Allgemeine Zeitung* saw in the production 'not a state-threatening catastrophe, but rather a disappointment, which of course weighs heavily enough, precisely because it was supposed to mark a new beginning'.[3]

After the première, Jonas's postbag of complaint letters and hate mail (some anonymous), previously negligible, increased. 'The production uncovered a hornet's nest of hatred towards me. Xenophobia ... insults that a half-Jewish emigrant should have no place at the Staatsoper ... But at least it woke me up and put me en garde. After *Un Ballo in Maschera*, I didn't expect us to make it.'

This was also because preparations for *Giulio Cesare in Egitto* involved difficulties of a special kind. Jonas had placed the musical direction of the production in the hands of Sir Charles Mackerras, one of the leading specialists in the field of Baroque music. However, after Mackerras heard about the initial thoughts of the directing team, he 'bombarded' Jonas 'with phone calls expressing his concerns about the concept'.[4]

He was not the only one who called. Richard Jones was also worried about whether Mackerras could identify with the concept. Jonas knew what to expect from Jones and Lowery. They had been responsible for the famous ENO production of *Fledermaus* with Lesley Garrett as Adele. Gerd Uecker, BSO's operations director, had attended a performance, and Jonas knew that Uecker enjoyed it greatly. Jonas then decided to commission Richard Jones and Nigel Lowery for the Munich production of *Cesare*. 'Their concept was truly revolutionary for German theatre. I felt that this would enable me to achieve one of my most important goals. Ever since I was a child, I have admired Handel. I didn't understand why his works played such a minor role in the German theatre scene. For me, everything that the word opera encompasses was there in Handel: drama, melodrama, tragedy, but also comedy, farce, pantomime, the ridiculous, madness, metaphor, the great myths of antiquity under the microscope of incredible music. It took the historian Edward Gibbons a full six volumes in his work *The History of the Decline and Fall of the Roman Empire* to trace the fall of the Roman Empire, Handel only four hours, but in an entertaining, funny and moving way that makes the audience laugh as well as cry.'

But now clouds were gathering. Mackerras and Jones were not seeing eye to eye. Jonas decided to 'take the bull by the horns'[5] and, the day after the première of *Un Ballo in Maschera*, on 1 February 1994, held a summit meeting at Mackerras's house in London.

Richard Jones and Nigel Lowery had made impressively meticulous preparations for the meeting: they had brought a sketchbook that contained precise details for every scene and every aria of the opera. They supported their interpretations of individual moments by playing extracts on a tape recorder. 'It was quite a performance by the others!' Jonas recalled. 'At the end of the day, Charles Mackerras smiled and said in his Australian accent: "Listen, boys. This is absolutely brilliant. I have never seen anything like this in my whole life. But there is no way that I can conduct that opera. I simply cannot conduct the first scene with a dinosaur on stage.

Peter, forgive me, we have known each other for twenty years. Don't change it, get a younger conductor."'

Jonas now had to follow this advice, forty-eight days before the opening night.

In the end help came in the form of the agent Jonathan Grove. Grove suggested the young and largely unknown Ivor Bolton. Jonas knew very little about him. 'Reports about his musical genius abounded,' Jonas related. Bolton was considered a talented Baroque conductor and brilliant harpsichordist: 'he was possessed of an inquisitive mind, high intelligence, dramaturgical acumen and an energy as stimulating as it was inspiring.' Although many warned him that hiring Bolton was playing with fire, Jonas flew to London again to meet with him. 'This young man was music incarnate, for whom nothing seemed impossible. After his first meeting with him, Richard Jones was breathless with excitement.'[6] Jonas smiled as he described the shock he caused in the directors' meeting with the news that the inexperienced Bolton would replace the seasoned Mackerras. 'Then I intuitively did the only thing I could do: I showed the sketchbook to my colleagues. After the experiences with our first two productions, it reawakened their enthusiasm for preparing the production.'

When Bolton took over rehearsals in February 1994, he transferred that enthusiasm to the Staatsorchester as well. The players had little experience with the Baroque repertoire at the time – *Giulio Cesare in Egitto* had last been produced in 1955 – but, in Jonas's words, they were 'great musicians with a positive attitude'.[7]

Barbara Burgdorf, the orchestra's concertmaster, had decided to take over the first desk for the Handel production. 'The renaissance of Handel and Baroque operas was not everyone's cup of tea,' Burgdorf recalled. 'I was fascinated by learning this new language. With Ivor Bolton, an atmosphere was created at the Staatsoper that is familiar from youth orchestras. He was a young enthusiast who did not see himself as an old-school conductor. He made us feel like we were working together as a big family.'[8]

After the first rehearsal, some musicians approached Jonas, he wrote, 'amazed at the musicality of this young man, worried about his lack of German language skills, but overwhelmed by his talent'. Anne Midgette of *Opera News* said after the première that Bolton had achieved a heartfelt, if not very Baroque, performance with the State Orchestra.[9] He released energies among the musicians which no one had hitherto imagined. 'When Ivor Bolton conducts, he celebrates the moment,' said Burgdorf. 'He has fantastic timing, never just beating the beat. That would go against his inner musicality. With his exuberant Baroque charisma, he sweeps everyone along with him as he conducts.'

The musicians felt 'that they would be able to grow with him in this area of the repertoire, and he with them; and that's exactly what happened',[10] as Jonas said. Years later, from among this circle the Monteverdi Continuo Ensemble was formed, specialising in the works of the early Baroque. 'This splendid ensemble within an opera orchestra of symphonic proportions was a unique, quite extraordinary undertaking,'[11] wrote Zubin Mehta, later its general music director, in his memoirs.

Ivor Bolton is regarded today as one of the best interpreters of Baroque music and as a proven expert on historical performance practice.

People's Republic of Technology

Now that Jonas had completed the team with the addition of Ivor Bolton, barely seven weeks before the première of *Giulio Cesare in Egitto*, he had to turn to the familiar, recurring and far more serious problem: the stage machinery and its state of disrepair. The problem had been bothering the Staatsoper for some time, and costly maintenance work had not yielded the desired result. The question of liability for the equipment had been disputed for years.

The Intendanz of Wolfgang Sawallisch, Jonas's predecessor, had also been overshadowed by this issue. Sawallisch's last season had been cut short due to the need for repairs to the hydraulics. It had been among the reasons why Sawallisch decided to end his Intendanz prematurely. He had originally wanted to stay until the end of the Festival in July 1993, but instead left the Staatsoper in the spring.

Jonas, in turn, did not arrive in Munich until mid-July 1993, severely weakened by sepsis. The past two years of preparatory work for Munich had demanded an iron discipline. He had flown to Munich for three days a month, dealt with a heavy workload of talks and discussions and then attended a performance. It seemed to him that, whenever he was in Munich, problems then arose at ENO that demanded his urgent intervention.

After Sawallisch's premature departure, Gerd Uecker and his team had run the operation. Moreover, a tour – artistically successful – that had taken the State Ballet to New York in February and March 1993 had produced a 'subsidy requirement of 2.27 million Marks', as the Oberste Rechnungshof [Supreme Audit Office] complained. Estimated sponsorship income had proved 'completely uncollectible',[12] according to the Audit Office.

The handling of the Staatsoper's financial resources also became the focus of the international press. As Midgette wrote for *Opera News* in June 1993, 'The Bavarian State Opera is a fine example of a wealthy West German house realizing it's time to do something about its image. It's also a fine example of how much money a theater can swallow. Internationally, the house has attracted much attention recently by having had to close for two full seasons in the last five years for renovations to its hydraulic stage machinery, each time at a cost of about $2.4 million over and above the annual operating budget. The failure of the hydraulic system could be a metaphor for many productions in wealthy West German theaters: lots of money poured in, little quality control.'[13] The *New York Times* noted: 'Last summer a bacterial infection of the theater's elaborate hydraulic system, which controls all the stage machinery and which was constantly clogged with yellow slime, forced the theater's closing for repairs. All last season the company had to perform in ad hoc spaces, mostly in concert versions, and to tour. The repairs cost Bavarian taxpayers $22.5 million, along with

$5.75 million for improvements undertaken while the building was closed anyway.'[14]

The stage technology of the Staatsoper was said to be the best in Europe. But it still didn't run anywhere near perfectly, despite the expensive renovations. Together with the new technical director of the Staatsoper, Gerhard Zahn, Jonas searched for the reason why. 'I simply didn't understand the problems with the technology. What I needed were simple, understandable explanations of how we could solve the problems,' Jonas recalled. The production plan came out shortly after he took office. Several productions were scheduled with high budgets for the stage design. The crisis meetings went on deep into the night.

At that time, the BSO had about two hundred employees in the technical areas on and backstage, but also in the workshops. Conflicts between plant managers and the house management further aggravated the situation. 'The technical team is comparable to an army: firmly controlled, but with humanity. Some of them seemed to me to be psychologically paralysed. The change to computerised systems was not easy for some. Despite all the repairs, there was little confidence in the technology.' Jonas banged his fist on the table. 'But I wanted to understand how this Volksrepublik Technik [People's Republic of Technology] worked.' He chose here a term which cannot have made him many friends in the technical department. Generally, the professional pride of stage technicians dictates that they try to meet all the demands placed on them by the director and the set designer. In theatre, that is a question of honour.

For outsiders, however, it is hardly possible to understand what happens during scene changes, both backstage and among the flying machinery. When the stage machinery did not function smoothly, as in Munich in the early 1990s, and when modernisation required older stage technicians to adapt to new processes, then friction between the artistic and technical teams was guaranteed. But Jonas was determined to understand the technical side of the operation, with all its challenges and problems. This meant that the stage technology was much more closely supervised by the new Intendant than it ever had been under his predecessors.

To facilitate cooperation between the directorial teams and the house staff, Jonas wanted to try something with the BSO that had worked before at ENO. He hired Louise Jeffreys as production manager, who was to sound out the directorial teams' wishes and communicate them to the house management. In principle, this could have worked, but there was a language barrier. 'Suddenly there was a rumour that the German technicians were to be made to take English lessons,' reported costume and set designer Jürgen Rose, who had experienced the teething problems in the workshops and the technical department. However, Jonas quickly withdrew this idea. 'Jonas was a highly intelligent man and with his own antennae he could sense that this was the wrong way to go.'[15]

Richard Jones and Nigel Lowery came into this mix with their imaginative, meticulously choreographed and extraordinarily complex stage design, which was also based on translating Baroque stage design with its borders, transformations and effects into a modern aesthetic.

'We were aware that we wanted to do Baroque theatre in an incredibly ambitious way, which had easily never been presented on this scale before,' Jonas recalled. 'The dinosaur reached up to the top of the stage. When the moment came for it to collapse, its joints had to function smoothly. Its tail was incredibly long and thick. It had to completely fall over and then disappear into oblivion, like a shark.'

For the choreography of the ballet dancers who portrayed soldiers and slaves, Jones and Lowery had hired the young and then-unknown Iranian Amir Hosseinpour. 'For four and a half hours the singers and dancers were not just directed, but choreographed. Every single movement was choreographed to the music,' Jonas recalled with glee.

Then the final rehearsal week began. The main piano rehearsal experienced some interruptions, which was to be expected. It is said to have lasted almost ten hours – until at midnight Jones and Lowery offered to lower the technical requirements. 'I didn't want that. I wanted everyone to keep trying.' The vehemence with which Jonas recounted the conflict gave an idea of how much pressure everyone was under. 'We had to accept that things could go wrong. We were so close to disaster, but it was also kind of thrilling, incredible, almost like a drug rush, to live with so much risk.'

The main orchestra rehearsal is said to have lasted only about seven hours. But that too was interrupted. In those days, those close to him saw the usually-cool Jonas show signs of insecurity. Many staff members, on the other hand, were completely enthralled by what they saw on stage. The Staatsoper photographer, Wilfried Hösl, had taken his photographs to the editorial office of the *Süddeutsche Zeitung* after the main rehearsal, as was still customary at the time, and saw important critics standing around discussing the photos. 'That's when I realised: Something is happening! It was clear to me that it would be a super success.'[16] The first guests were admitted to the dress rehearsal, and word of mouth did the rest.

21 March 1993

When the première began at the Nationaltheater in Munich, exactly two hundred and sixty-four years after the extended version debuted in London, Jonas recalled that the atmosphere was, 'How shall I put it? Feverish!' Outwardly, he tried to keep his composure. He looked different somehow. He was aware of what the failure of this production could mean for his house and for him personally.

The stage curtain had been changed. It now showed a cosmic backdrop against which a man and a woman were gliding towards each other, captured at the moment just before their fingers touched. The new curtain sent a signal: that evening, something unheard of was about to begin. During the overture, the audience saw a huge folding map of Egypt, transposed to the Munich district of Haidhausen. Then, when the second curtain lifted, it revealed the dinosaur. Ten minutes later, just before Achilla presented the severed head of Pompey in a Karstadt bag, Richard Jones had staged two minutes in which the music paused. In this silence, the dinosaur toppled over in slow motion, sank into the stage floor and was hidden from the audience's gaze.

'At that moment, the rancour in the auditorium, which until then had been brooding quietly, suddenly broke loose,' Jonas recounted. From a gallery someone shouted: 'Stop it, kids!' Whistles, boos and bravos clashed. 'I had never experienced anything like this before. Ivor just waited. The first interval was so exciting! There were so many debates among the audience! Everding came to me: "Peter, that was some debut!" I said: "No, August, that was *Faust*!" Everding countered: "No, *this* is your debut!"'

In the second interval, the tension was palpable: people were excitedly discussing the production in the bars. Bolton had responded to Jonas's suggestion to play the first movement of Handel's *Concerto Grosso op. 3* as an entr'acte at the end of the second interval. This catchy, accessible movement, lasting just under nine minutes, gently brought the audience back into the auditorium. When the final curtain came down hours after the dinosaur had collapsed, a battle of boos and cheers broke out. It lasted a full twenty minutes. Something remarkable happened backstage after the end of that performance, as the producer Aron Stiehl recalled: 'Richard Jones apologised to Jonas after the première. He was completely devastated.'[17] Richard Jones must have assumed that his direction had proved Jonas's undoing.

The following morning, the managers met. Some had not gone home after the première party, said to have lasted until five in the morning. No reviews were yet out. Only the Munich *Abendzeitung* had run with a negative story about the scandal at the opera, calling the première 'an insult to Handel', 'superficial, weakly staged and musically boring', as Jonas put it in the sleeve notes for the CD. The article, however, appeared 'with a lurid headline and a picture that whetted rather than curbed the public's appetite'.[18] The sales figures for the following performances, however, were already on the table at the directors' meeting: they were cruelly low. Handel did not seem to be doing well in Munich. A letter arrived by messenger, sent by the Staatsministerium for Science, Research and the Arts, which was to cause a great stir and eventually cost Minister Zehetmair two bottles of French wine. More on that later.

For lunch, Jonas met up with a friend, the graphic designer Pierre Mendell. 'He cheered me up a lot,' sighed Jonas. On the first day after the première, however, the first reports arrived from the Oscars ceremony, also held the night before. Steven Spielberg had scooped ten Oscars, including for best director, for *Schindler's List*. But he had also won three Oscars for *Jurassic Park*. The newspapers were full of pictures of dinosaurs. It was pure coincidence, but the Staatsoper had Hollywood on its side. They didn't need any more advertisements for *Giulio Cesare in Egitto* after that, said Jonas.[19]

On day two after the première, Jonas was sitting in his office in the evening when the head of the PR department, Ulrike Hessler, came in smiling. She brought the first issues of the Munich newspapers. The *Abendzeitung* had run a scathing critique. *Tz*, however, the second Munich tabloid, had 'absolutely rhapsodised' about the production, in Jonas's phrase. The *Süddeutsche Zeitung*, in turn, had given the production an extremely positive review, dedicating a whole page and illustrating it with lavish photos. The chief dramaturge Hanspeter Krellmann came to Jonas's office on the third day after the première with copies of *Die Welt* and the *Frankfurter Allgemeine Zeitung*. They had both run overwhelmingly positive reviews. When the following day began with another positive review in *Die Zeit*, Jonas knew he was on safe ground as far as the critics were concerned. 'You'll see, now they'll storm the box office,' Hessler promised him, 'no matter whether the guests want to see a scandal or the opposite'. She was proved right.

Demand for the second performance remained low, but the third and fourth performances sold out in a few days. All other performances enjoyed high sales figures. The pattern of sales was new at the Staatsoper: the cheapest tickets and the standing places with poor visibility went first. The most expensive seats sold last.

A young audience was responsible for the new pattern. They were claiming the Staatsoper for themselves. The 'scandal'[20] had become a cult: tickets for this show remained highly sought-after, throughout 103 performances over ten years.

Until that turning point, Jonas had had to tread very carefully with his Baroque programme: only *Xerxes* was planned for the following season, and even then just as an option. Now that it did indeed look feasible to stage these Baroque operas in an exciting way, Jonas would also be able to add works by Monteverdi and Cavalli to his programme. Had the sales figures for the *Cesare* production remained disappointing over the long term, *Xerxes* would have been axed, and the later series stillborn.[21]

Jonas's third première, only seven months after the start of his Intendanz, was 'the first to wake up the audience,' Egbert Tholl wrote in the *Süddeutsche Zeitung*. 'At that time, in the 1990s, [Richard Jones] was at the top of his game, extremely imaginative, made irreverent by his devotion to the music.' In the meantime, the visual worlds of Jones and Lowery are among the 'icons of director's theatre',[22] Tholl noted. What later became known as '*Bildertheater* [theatre of images]' in opera had found its way to the Munich Staatsoper.

The image of the collapsing dinosaur is now emblematic of the beginning of a new chapter in the history of opera. The photograph by Wilfried Hösl was rightly included in Carolyn Abbate's and Roger Parker's *History of Opera*, now published in English, German and Italian. It states: 'After two centuries of almost complete neglect, Handel's operas have been rediscovered and re-staged over the last thirty years, often in the form of surprising, post-modern productions. This photo is from the opera *Giulio Cesare in Egitto*, which marked the Handel Renaissance at the Bavarian State Theatre. This production, with well over a hundred performances, always ensured a sold-out house from 1994 to 2006.'[23]

A recording captures the audience's imagination and changed atmosphere in Munich. *Giulio Cesare in Egitto* was a production with an unheard-of new aesthetic; for some it was a relief, an adventure; for others an insult. 'We demanded incredible tolerance from the public,' Jonas emphasised. 'When the severed head of Pompey was brought out in a Karstadt bag, it was surprising for some, but really shocking for others. The excitement and thrill of theatre often comes from pushing the emotional envelope, juxtaposing the unexpected.'

The letters of complaint

A letter was delivered to Jonas by messenger from the Staatsministerium for Science, Research and the Arts the day after the première, and sparked Jonas's first Munich feud. Jonas wrote about this in the sleeve notes of the CD:

> 'A letter of outrage arrived on ministerial letterhead from the minister's personal assistant admonishing me for being so irreverent to Händel and to Munich's traditions and expectancy. Spitting inflammatory prejudice it started a series of skirmishes between this civil servant, who had led the boo claque from his complimentary seat at the première, that never let up even when he subsequently became head of the theatre department at the ministry before being transferred after trying to interfere just once too often.'

An intensive exchange of letters began, in which the two correspondents did not hesitate to include colleagues in the distribution list. In one of his letters Jonas wrote:

> '[…] finally, you are also a civil servant of the Free State of Bavaria and personal advisor to the Minister of Education and Cultural Affairs, i.e. our legal entity. I have always been very impressed by the noble tradition of civil servants in Bavaria, which is comparable to that in France and Great Britain and which follows

the line of tolerance, independence and integrity in a democratic society, striving for objectivity and not allowing itself to be influenced by political influences or cultural–political intrigues. No one forbids a première visitor to express his opinion openly and clearly, but the objectivity of a public servant is based on a noble and healthy principle. That you shattered this principle was a shock and a disappointment for all of us. For me personally, it was also an unforgettable expression of licence and intolerance that I would never have expected from someone who is supposed to support all of us here, regardless of personal taste.'

Jonas could not forgive someone who represented the opera's owner and operator booing at a production of his own opera. Minister Zehetmair had to personally repair the damage from this first collision, using the aforementioned bottles of French wine. However, the working relationship between the adversaries remained fractured until the end.

Jonas had a drawer he called the 'stink box' for all the hate mail. He studied the letters carefully: he wanted to learn from them how to better understand, if that were possible, as some of the letters testified to an inconceivable narrow-mindedness, bigotry and presumption. As long as they were not anonymous, all received an answer, not always from Jonas himself. Sometimes, especially if they really angered Jonas, he also asked Hanspeter Krellmann or Ulrike Hessler to draft the reply.

Jonas particularly remembered his correspondence with one particular gentleman from Munich. In his first letter, the author had come to the conclusion, after intensive examination of the current productions, that it was impermissible to bring such an aesthetic to the stage. That is why he no longer wanted to visit the Staatsoper. Jonas replied, asked him to come back and try to understand the production. In his reply, he enclosed a cheap ticket that he had paid for himself. The gentleman not only came back to see the performance again, he wrote later. He was starting to get into the swing of things and would attend one more production.

Then a third letter arrived, in which the gentleman thanked Jonas for helping him to understand the aesthetics of the production. A rare moment of happiness.

Another letter, written by a gentleman with a doctorate, took issue with Konwitschny's production of *Parsifal*. Although the author presented himself as a 'long-time opera-goer', he was a little confused with the spelling of 'Parsival' or 'Parzival'. Nevertheless, his argument revolved around the principle of faithfulness to the work and the wish for salvation. He received a detailed answer from the head dramaturge.

Another letter expressed the presumption of the city's Kulturbürgertum [cultural bourgeoisie] in a single sentence. 'I am appalled at what you did to my *Magic Flute* yesterday on the stage of your opera house.'

Another gentleman, a doctor who said that he had felt 'at home' at the Staatsoper since 1953, wrote: 'How did you come to have Mr Schneider as chief conductor?' He felt musical standards were now at their most unsatisfactory level since the beginning of Jonas's Intendanz. He accused Jonas of 'mishandling' the selection of directors, giving only *Xerxes* any credit, and spoke of 'cretinism' and 'tedium' among the directors. In particular, he found the staging of *Idomeneo* 'bland': 'Here, too, the Jonas trademark: tedium.'

Though this letter was actually rather pitiful and lacking in substance, it made Jonas really angry. It hurt him more than the others. He asked his chief dramaturge Hanspeter Krellmann to draft an answer. Four years later, the doctor was still working on Jonas. This time he decided to make a denunciation, and wrote directly to the Minister of State. He criticised Jonas and Zehetmair for selecting directors who thought only of using works to express their own brilliance and for whose productions one needed an instruction manual – 'scenic rubbish'. 'There were forces that wanted to get rid of Sir Peter,' Aron Stiehl said, outlining the mood.

At the end of his first season, Jonas was given a particularly disgusting package. An anonymous, typed letter, wrapped around some faeces, read:

'STAATSINTENDANT PETER JONAS (personal correspondence)

Re: the '*TANNHÄUSER*' première and the 1993–94 season: Fuck all the shit and yourself!!!!!!! M.' Followed by an illegible signature.

On the very weekend that Chris Dercon announced his resignation as the Intendant of the Volksbühne Berlin, Jonas told me during a walk through Zurich that Dercon had also received such packages, that this was 'a typically German way of reacting'. These letters hit home for Jonas, even if he did not mention them to friends like Daniel Barenboim: 'Peter was too proud to talk to me about the hostility he had experienced during his first time in Munich.'[24]

Jonas saw something positive from the letters. For him, his difficult first years in Munich showed that the performing arts still belonged to the core of society, 'that is, they mean something'.[25] He would rather live with his 'stink box' than with the idea that there was nothing to discuss about his opera apart from sales figures. 'Since Jonas appreciated opposition and resistance, he was able to get something out of the letters of complaint,' said Christine Lemke-Matwey, writing for the *Süddeutsche Zeitung* at the time. 'This German, Bavarian fervour with which some of the letters were written shocked him at first, but he also felt that they were issuing him a challenge: let's see which one of us will last longer! Maybe not in the next season, but in two years we shall see!'[26] He tried to counter the letters of complaint and hate mail with his own weapons. In the words of Jane Kramer, these were his 'presence, intellect, and a kind of infectious and highly articulate imperviousness to the claims of stupid or offensive people, which gave him a moral high ground often described by his admirers as "the British confidence", and by Jonas himself as "ten years' training" with the monks.'[27]

There were letters that upset Jonas, but also those that cut him to the core, letters like the one from a woman who asked him, as a 'half-Jew', to leave Germany, and who wished to see him deported.

Here his weapons were blunt. Jonas knew of such attacks from Solti, whose car had been smeared with 'Solti go home.' Now he experienced first-hand what such words can trigger.

Another gentleman took up the cudgels, arguing in terms of the 'health of the Volk'. For Tom Sutcliffe, such attacks were echoes from the Weimar Republic and the Third Reich.[28] Parts of Jonas's family had reacted with horror to the news that he had moved to the former 'capital of the movement'. While his father had tried to keep quiet about his family's Jewish origins, Jonas was made keenly aware of this heritage by his aunt Elizabeth Melamid during his childhood and youth. When Jonas arrived in Munich, he had not yet really reckoned with the Jewish heritage in his family. That was another reason why hate mail came as such a brutal shock. He tried to play on his status: he liked to call himself a 'guest worker in Germany'. 'The English hate the word culture. The British believe in heritage, land, houses, dogs, even art – but not culture. Germans have culture. Germany has always been the most cultured country. German culture acts like a magnet.'[29]

Many years later, in 2005, he was able to spark a provocation that might have ended a German director's career. He said: 'I am proud of German culture.'[30] He had 'exorcised' the ghosts that had visited him in Munich. That involved never forgetting the past. 'As for his grandfather, Peter Jonas has come home,' Jane Kramer wrote in the *New Yorker* about the irony 'that the city that had nurtured Hitler in the country that his father had fled because of Hitler was now nurturing him.'[31] It was an irony Jonas came to enjoy.

PJ and the Free State of Bavaria

The *New York Times* was also aware that disputes between August Everding, the former general director of the Bavarian State Theatres, and Wolfgang Sawallisch, the former General Music Director and Staatsoper Director, had plagued the house for years.

'One source of friction was that Mr. Everding, while no firebrand, resented Mr. Sawallisch's conservatism in matters of repertory and especially staging,'[32] noted the music critic John Rockwell. But the conflict between Everding's wife Gustava and Sawallisch's wife Mechthild, who was cruelly called 'Machthild' by some columnists [Macht meaning 'power'], also had a paralysing effect on the house.[33] There was a real 'civil war' going on there, Jonas said. All communication went through the minister's desk, which created a truly stressful and complicated situation. Hans Zehetmair found an idiosyncratic way of managing it all. He described it as a 'supposedly Solomonic' solution: he appointed Everding as General Director of the Bavarian State Theatres and Sawallisch as General Music Director and Intendant of the BSO. Zehetmair described his solution as follows: 'General Director August Everding was thus formally enthroned above the three state theatres and the state directors, but it was clear from the outset that they would not allow themselves to be talked into falling under his authority. The result was a strange situation in which August Everding, the personification of German theatre both nationally and internationally, was a kind of unlanded King in his own country.'[34]

Jonas had answered the question of who would have the last word during the press conference when introduced as the new state director: 'Der Chef bin ich [I am the boss].' For Zehetmair, this answer must have been a source of enormous relief. For the 'princes' from the various departments of the Staatsoper, however, it was a highly unpopular announcement.

In Sawallisch, 'a gifted man had been promoted to precisely the high position appropriate for his talent, which rendered all limits and excessive demands clearly visible,'[35] Wolf-Dieter Peter judged in the *Deutsche Bühne*. Sawallisch saw dedicating an entire season to the work of Richard Strauss as an innovative programming policy – 'a radical enough idea, in a sense, though hardly calculated to sell a lot of tickets,'[36] Midgette noted in the *New York Times*. With Herbert Wernicke's *Judas Maccabaeus* of 1980, his *Flying Dutchman* of 1981 and Nikolaus Lehnhoff's 1987 *Ring des Nibelungen* with stage design by Erich Wonder, Sawallisch had sought to connect with emerging trends in music theatre, Wolfgang Schreiber emphasised. 'But then the scenic and musical traditionalism increasingly paralysed the house and its defective stage technology,'[37] Schreiber summarised.

'Munich likes to think of itself as the "secret capital", the "artistic capital" of Germany,' Jonas told John Rockwell of the *New York Times* in July 1993. Jonas thought this competition between Berlin and Munich was healthy. That the man who was responsible for ENO's 'provocative, scrappy, even defiant stagings' had been appointed to the Munich Staatsoper, which stood for the 'moneyed, placid conservatism of the Bavarians', astonished Rockwell. He mused that 'maybe this blend of guardedly revolutionary rhetoric and judicious conservatism is the only way Mr. Jonas can eventually introduce real reform into this wealthy operatic museum. He can praise his predecessors and still talk of radical changes by using the theater's yearlong closing as an excuse. And by stressing Munich's progressive artistic past (which in truth was only periodic and was rarely reflected in its opera), he can postulate an ideal audience that may not yet exist. Mr. Jonas is no naif; he recognizes that despite his all-embracing manifestos, he may have trouble pleasing both the conservatives and the progressives.'[38] This analysis goes to the heart of the dual strategy Jonas pursued: he had been appointed to transform the Staatsoper. Anne Midgette found it indicative of the Germans' attitude that many people feared that Jonas's arrival meant a break with the house's traditions, while it was obvious to an outside observer that such change was exactly what the house desperately needed in order to truly rise to an international standard.[39]

With his programme Jonas wanted to 'provoke, disturb and challenge': he repeated this intention again and again. But in doing so, he did not want to repel regular audiences, especially since he did not yet understand what motivated those faithful attendees. To begin with, he wanted to understand the social structures in Munich and Bavaria, and especially how the Staatsoper functioned, what the working conditions were like at the house and what the subscription system demanded.[40]

The Staatsoper had a clientele that was continuously willing and able to pay the highest ticket prices – provided productions were acceptable. 30 per cent of the visitors came to more than twenty evenings per season. Jonas characterised them as 'a knowledgeable, cultured public, but they see all the works as their property'.[41] From their circle came the letters of complaint asking about what Jonas had done to 'my *Magic Flute*'. Of course, he recognised the emotional bond expressed in those words. On the other hand, he criticised the claim to ownership and the insistence on not allowing any aesthetic development. He knew that 'we're too dependent on them to slap them across the face.'[42] However, this is what he did when a line of his found its way into the *Abendzeitung*: 'The women here all look like gilded Christmas trees. I have never seen so much fake jewellery and so much dyed hair in the world.' Their style of dress reminded him of the Rococo, 'a little too much of everything'.[43] He deserved the storm of protest that followed, even though he later denied having made such a statement.

For Jonas, escaping the British system of cultural funding and being able to work not only in Germany, but in Bavaria specifically, meant the greatest freedom imaginable. At that time, the public funding bodies in Germany subsidised almost all theatre companies at a much higher percentage than the British government did with its theatres. Compared to ENO, which had a cap of around 50 per cent, the BSO received 78 per cent of its budget as grants; it was virtually 'papered' with public money, Craig Whitney wrote in the *New York Times*.[44] Article 3 of the Free State's constitution defines Bavaria as a 'Kulturstaat' or cultural state, a fact that Jonas emphasised again and again in order to hold politicians to account.[45]

The Staatsoper, with its approximately seven hundred employees, is a company run by the Free State of Bavaria, administered by the State Ministry for Science, Research and the Arts, as it was then called. The Free State is sole provider of funding. Continuous increases in allowances were common during Jonas's tenure, and the Ministry of Finance took charge of overseeing wage increases for public services.

At that time, Bavaria was an economically prosperous federal state with a stable one-party majority, a favourable state of affairs for cultural funding. The responsibilities at the opera are governed by the 'Grundordnung für die Bayerischen Staatstheater'[46] [Basic Ordinance on Bavarian State Theatre].

Here Jonas experienced his first surprises: 'when you become a theatre manager, you sign a contract in which you undertake, among other things, to adhere to the principles of the theatre you are going to manage.'[47] He had never before encountered such an agreement. For all the artistic freedom that the lavish budget of the Staatsoper offered him, he was shocked at the outset to also have less freedom in certain areas than he had enjoyed in London. While he could negotiate union agreements in London individually, the portion of the budget set aside for wages in Munich was fixed by collective agreements. Only about 5–10 per cent of the budget remained at his disposal.

He was also not allowed to change the ticket prices without the approval of the Staatsministerium. During his tenure, he asked for this approval a total of five times. Only twice were these requests approved.[48] What surprised him most, however, was that successful ticket sales were expected as a matter of course. The occupancy rate was never allowed to fall below 93 or 94 per cent. If that happened, the loss of revenue would be so great and so immediate that the executive director would have to intervene.[49]

When he took office, however, he also had to deal with shortcomings in administration, that could only be explained by previously lax management. The Bavarian Staatsoper in Munich was – and still is – one of the cultural flagships of the Free State. As long as this merely meant that the opera served 'harmless representational purposes'[50] it presented Jonas with no difficulties. He lobbied skilfully and quickly knew who to talk to in order to implement his plans.

Over the years, his predecessors had become too lax with free tickets. The awarding of free tickets at German theatre companies had come to the public eye through an article in the magazine *Der Spiegel*: according to the Bühnenverein (the federal association of theatre and orchestra sponsors), Munich theatres were issuing 77,000 tickets per season. Revenue lost by the Staatsoper in the 1993–94 season through complimentary tickets alone came to around two million Marks. 'The very best seats are always kept free for seven members of the Landtag and four representatives from the Bavarian Senate. Not even the head of department or the ministry's theatrical advisor have to pay a penny',[51] wrote *Der Spiegel*. At the 1993 Opera Festival, around 2,750 free tickets in the most expensive category worth 650,000 Marks were given away. In consultation with the State Ministry, Jonas had reduced the number of 'state free tickets' from 500(!) to 46 at the beginning of his Intendanz.[52]

For the years before Jonas took office, the Supreme Audit Office had criticised the budget management of the Staatsoper several times because deficits had arisen, including 2.2 million Marks in 1991–92.[53] The Staatsministerium had been able to make up for the deficit within its own resources without much noise, probably also because the Bavarian Ministry of Finance was attuned to the concerns of the opera at that time. Many of the decision-makers there were 'always opera-mad', according to Toni Schmid, Ministerial Director for Hans Zehetmair.[54]

In general, hardly anything sensitive about the cooperation between the opera management and ministry was made public. The relationship between Peter Jonas and Minister of State Hans Zehetmair was characterised by great respect and mutual esteem. Zehetmair appreciated Jonas's 'uncommonly multi-layered intellectuality. Talking to him was always enriching, challenging. We had some oddball conversations,' says Zehetmair. 'Peter Jonas was a one-off. As a Greek, I have always said: on the outside he had the Galene, the calm of the sea, he was a soul at rest within himself. And no matter how agitated he was, on the surface he would never let on. I admired him because his personality also included this inner greatness of carrying his illness inwards and not putting it on display.'[55] They dealt with everything internally, especially in relation to the press. 'I was impressed by how strong he was, how energetic and determined he was in tackling the tasks and leading his ensemble. But he also demonstrated inner greatness time and again when he did not put his worries and problems in the foreground, but instead turned towards the potency of his possibilities, the strength that lay in his personality.'

Even during their first conflict over the letter sent to Jonas by his subordinate, Zehetmair had been able to observe the style with which Jonas fought his battles. 'And since he never lost his temper, we both finished every conversation, even the controversial ones, with mutual understanding and respect. I can't really think of any time where I said, "I'm going to smack that guy." Peter Jonas had his own way of thinking, his own style and habitus. All three impressed me. He was entirely a gentleman.'

They also laughed heartily when the British Arts Council made an embarrassing mistake in the spring of 1996 that could have called into question Jonas's loyalty to the Free State: Jonas, aged forty-nine, was on the list of candidates published in the *Guardian* to succeed Jeremy Isaacs at the Royal Opera Covent Garden. He was considered a favourite because of his successful directorship at ENO – 'the most innovative and exciting in British opera history'.[56] The London Commission's letter, however, had been sent to the Bavarian Staatsministerium by mistake. They informed Jonas – and were relieved: Jonas was not interested.

When Zehetmair decided not to run again in 2003, Jonas could understand this decision only too well. He himself had already decided by this time to end his professional career on his sixtieth birthday. Jonas wrote him a farewell letter that visibly moved Zehetmair. Jonas told *Die Zeit* in 2006: 'Alongside the stereotypical beer-brains, there were always people who had culture or instinct or even both. Hans Zehetmair was such a figure.'[57]

David Alden's Tannhäuser

The première at the Opera Festival must be representative of Munich society. Jonas was fully aware of the significance of this event from the very beginning. 'For a state capital, a former royal seat, Munich is relatively small. If you compare it with London or Paris, the number of top institutions and their quality bears no relation to the size of the city.' Jonas described his view of Munich, a city he admired and praised time and again in speeches and articles. 'At all important social events, the same hundred important people meet. The Gesellschaft zur Förderung der Münchner Opernfestspiele [Society of Supporters of the Munich Opera Festival] is – or used to be – the pinnacle of the Munich establishment, although it was always also a sales association for the best tickets.'

Jonas had set his first Festival première on a grand scale: with *Tannhäuser*, he had chosen the work of one of the local gods. Zubin Mehta took over the musical direction of this work for the first time, David Alden the direction. With Waltraud Meier as Venus and René Kollo in the title role, Jonas had chosen a safe cast.

Together with his set designer Roni Toren and his costume designer Buki Shiff, Alden developed a stylised, minimalistic stage world, whose barrenness and coolness symbolised the narrowness of tradition from which Tannhäuser seeks to free himself. Jonas spoke of a 'neo-Pina Bausch interpretation'. However, a sparse stage set did not necessarily mean a technically straightforward one. On the contrary, the stage design for *Tannhäuser* set the highest standards. Once again, it was not clear whether the technology would be able to handle the transitions, especially in the first act.

Controversy was not far away: in the second act, the words 'Germania Nostra' were emblazoned on a wall that filled the back of the stage, and would break in the final scene. It was an allusion to Albert Speer's plans as 'Generalbauinspektor für die Reichshauptstadt [General Building Inspector for the Reich Capital]'. Hitler had considered rebuilding Berlin and renaming it 'Germania'. Alden's interpretation revealed 'that the rift between the artist Tannhäuser and a Wartburg (or Munich?) society that believes itself to be in possession of a "leading culture" is unbridgeable', interpreted *Deutsche Bühne*.[58]

Word of mouth was still the strongest power in theatre. It did its part before the première of the Opera Festival. Rumours spread through the city: the production was going to be 'anti-German' … it would not do justice to Wagner. 'The demand for tickets was enormous. The high expectations!' Jonas said to himself. 'Reports were circulating in the city about scandals that had not taken place.'

Jonas could not have wished for a better *on dit*. At the première on 6 July 1994, 'the audience was boiling,' as Jonas put it. During the second interval, Jonas was summoned to Kollo's dressing room, where Kollo told him that he was unwell. They agreed that Kollo would continue singing, but that Jonas would make an announcement to the audience beforehand, informing them of Kollo's vocal difficulties, but confirming that he would continue to sing for the sake of the première. 'I had to step in front of the audience through one of the doors in front of the wall with the lettering "Germania Nostra". I was met with such a wave of boos … so much hate and anger. I just stood there, inwardly letting all the illnesses I had overcome pass me by and said nothing until it quietened down. After my announcement came polite applause. Kollo's singing was not bad, but not great either.'

During the final applause, the audience celebrated the singers, Mehta and the orchestra. The performance of the directing team, on the other hand, was profoundly rejected. At the state reception following the première of the festival, Jonas was attacked by a former employee of the opera. '"You're a Scheißkerl [bastard], you're anti-German, you don't deserve a place in this house!" she shouted. She was offended to the depths of her soul. At that moment, I myself was feeling unsure about this *Tannhäuser*. I had planned to leave the production in the repertoire, and it ultimately remained there for twenty-four years. Later it became insanely popular with audiences. I was so exhausted. Opera is supposed to be important for society, but *so* important?'

The newspaper commentary was predominantly positive and acknowledged the courage of this interpretation. Gerhard Koch wrote in the *Frankfurter Allgemeine Zeitung* that the new *Tannhäuser* gave an 'impressive account of the company's still-imposing powers'. Alden's direction was 'virtuoso and suggestive', the writing was 'for the national idea, unity of the realm, ascetic virtue and the transfiguration of cant through art. Festival society, the well-to-do, degenerate glitterati, were a perfect fit.' The reaction of the audience: 'Enthusiasm with obligatory resistance to the direction.'[59]

The 'visual upheaval of the last few years' was concluded, Jonas wrote in the *Staatsoper Yearbook* when he took up his post: never again would the visual side of musical theatre be neglected. This diagnosis was certainly true as far as the artists were concerned.[60] But Jonas had underestimated the effort that it would take to make this new visual aesthetic accessible to regular audiences.

This production intensified the conflict that had been looming since the beginning of Jonas's Intendanz: 'The gap between the progressives and the non-progressives in the city had become sharper, also because of the predominantly positive press. My first season had been exciting and new, it had sparked conversation but also started a process that exacerbated the extremes.'

At the end of his first season in Munich, Jonas was deeply exhausted. 'I thought to myself, this profession is not for me. After three years I'll quit and do something else with my life … maybe then I wouldn't have become so ill.' In March 1995, when the first productions of his second season had started relatively quietly, he sat in his office and said to himself: 'Either everything is right or something is really wrong – because everything is too quiet.'

Opera and urban society

When Peter Jonas took up his post as State Director of the Bavarian Staatsoper in Munich, he assumed responsibility for 'a theater that represented a pinnacle of tradition in a city acutely aware of its traditions', as Anne Midgette had it: 'The very building epitomizes traditional values. Destroyed in World War II, it was one of relatively few German theaters to be faithfully restored – graceful neo-Classical facade and all – rather than replaced with a modern building.'[61] The fact that the house was rebuilt at all was due to an initiative by twelve Munich citizens who founded the Verein der Freunde des Nationaltheaters e.V. [Association of Friends of the National Theatre] in 1951 and organised the first of many raffles. The association contributed a total of five million Marks up to the reopening of the house on 21 November 1963.[62] 'The influence of the Munich opera world, the opera crowd in the city, should not be underestimated: Who didn't go to the opera back then!' was how Christine Lemke-Matwey put it. Lemke-Matwey covered the beginning of the Jonas era for the *Süddeutsche Zeitung*. 'It is not comparable with conditions today. The opera was the city's secret heart! The Staatsoper defined the city's cultural identity.'

The appointment of Jonas was a far-sighted and far-reaching decision by Bavarian politicians. But this decision also carried the risk that Munich society would not be able to follow the path Jonas was taking. As late as 1993, Jonas had told the *New York Times* of 'great impatience about the slow progression of visual style here'.[63] In July 1994 he defended himself against the *Financial Times*: 'You are chosen for your competence, I suppose, but also for your taste. That can be my undoing or my glory. Whatever the outcome, I will not change!'[64]

It was not until the second half of the 1990s that people spoke of '*Bildertheater* [theatre of images]' at the opera. It is to his credit that Jonas was one of the first to implement this trend in Germany. However, his programme policy also created uncertainty. 'One asks oneself, what am I actually going to see tonight? The self-evident rituals fell back on themselves, as it were. This was salutary for the audience, but it also required an effort on their part. He also had to fight,' says Lemke-Matwey. 'The Kulturbürgertum – which at that time still represented the middle of society – identified so strongly with the opera that they had to defend themselves when an "outsider" came along who ruined their opera, sent the beloved singers home, and made their the beloved pieces foreign,'

Lemke-Matwey wrote, describing the dynamic that developed in Jonas's first season.

Munich was 'distrustful of outsiders',[65] Jonas told *Time* magazine in 1996. This was also true within the BSO. A birthday party was held for a member of the ensemble in Jonas's office and a certain director of studies attended, highly esteemed within the company for his long years of service, and above all for his musical acumen. He entered the office to hear his colleagues speaking English. Without any consideration for Jonas, or fearing any consequences for himself, he barked in a loud voice that soon *everyone* would have to speak English at work. He could not stand having a British Intendant. 'I can't emphasise enough how different Munich was in 1993,' Jonas stressed. 'The existentialism with which people reacted to all the changes in the opera were the last outpourings of an established Kulturbürgertum: "This is ours, we won't let it be destroyed",' commented Lemke-Matwey. 'Today no one would fight over culture in this way.'

Jonas also recognised that the quality of the theatre and its financial resources provided him with the tools needed to realise the ambitious stage concepts he had in mind.

Each man kills the thing he loves

Together with his wife Lucy, Jonas had moved into a classic Munich flat in Prinz-regentenstraße 72 during the 1993 Festival. He had not been able to find his dinner jacket in the chaos of moving house. But he had been able to find his kilt, neatly folded at the top of a box. He wore it to the première of *Traviata* on 25 July 1993. 'Munich, capital of Tracht [traditional folk costume],' he thought: this should be a great fit.

As in London, Jonas concentrated completely on his responsibilities as general director and, although physically challenged, spent long days working at the BSO. His wife Lucy had given up her job as a music agent and was in the process of setting up their new home. In Munich, she was largely alone. When he came home late in the evening or at night, after having had intense conversations, studied documents and attended a performance, he was completely exhausted. The couple became estranged.

During this time, Jonas was invited to take part in a reading at the Marstall. His choice was Oscar Wilde's *The Ballad of Reading Gaol*. Companions who sensed how things were for the two of them heard the lines in a very personal way:

> Yet each man kills the thing he loves,
> By each let this be heard,
> Some do it with a bitter look,
> Some with a flattering word,
> The coward does it with a kiss,
> The brave man with a sword!

And then, a few stanzas further on:

> And all the woe that moved him so
> That he gave that bitter cry,
> And the wild regrets, and the bloody sweats,
> None knew so well as I:
> For he who lives more lives than one
> More deaths than one must die.

After Lucy and he separated, Jonas moved into a small place on Thierschstraße. Even looking back, he was reluctant to talk about this phase of his life. Although his break-up was neither the first nor the only one at the opera, nor in Munich's high society, 'some people flapped their jaws, but that's always the case,' remarked one companion.

Barbara Burgdorf

During rehearsals for *Giulio Cesare in Egitto*, Jonas had met a young musician whom her colleagues in the orchestra feared they were about to lose. Although this excellently trained violinist had only just won the position of concertmaster at her audition, she had already received a counter-offer. The orchestra Board heard of this, approached the new Intendant Jonas, and asked him to talk to her. It would be a shame, they said, to lose Barbara Burgdorf so quickly. Before she had been offered the post, it had lain vacant for a long time.

Barbara Burgdorf studied at the Hochschule für Musik in Karlsruhe and, as a scholarship holder of the German Academic Exchange Service, with Dorothy DeLay at the Juilliard School in New York. As a soloist and Baroque violinist, she was awarded numerous prizes, including at the Premio Rodolfo Lipizer International Violin Competition. The audition with the Bavarian State Orchestra had been her first.

When Barbara Burgdorf took up her post as concertmaster in May 1992, there had been a lot of chatter about the new Intendant. It was known that he had been seriously ill shortly before. 'Who knows if he'll last long, if he'll even take up the post,' had been the talk of the opera house for weeks. After he took office, Barbara Burgdorf saw him sitting in his box like everyone else in almost every performance. It was only during rehearsals for *Giulio Cesare in Egitto* that they met in person. After rehearsals, the ensemble often went out for a meal and a drink with Ivor Bolton. Jonas was also there a lot. On one of these occasions, Jonas approached Barbara Burgdorf directly. 'I hear you want to leave?' he asked her. 'I found it surprising that the artistic director was so committed to having a female violinist in the orchestra,' Burgdorf said in retrospect. 'I couldn't quite believe that he was serious.' For her, the prospect of working with Zubin Mehta as general music director and with the best artists in the international music world contributed to her decision to stay.

A little while later, they fell in love and became a couple. In 1998 they moved into an attic flat in a new building on Frundsbergstraße in Neuhausen. That district is characterised by magnificent residential and commercial buildings, which date back to the time before the First World War. Their jobs left them little free time, but they spent it together. One of their rituals was a morning walk in Nymphenburg Park. They got up at seven o'clock to cycle to the park, exercise there for three quarters of an hour and then have a hearty breakfast. Around nine o'clock, Jonas was picked up by his driver, so that he was at the opera shortly before ten.

Now and then they met for lunch near the opera or in the Glockenbachviertel. Jonas was wedded to a proper lunch break, which was important for getting through long days at the opera, especially as these were followed by evening visits to performances.

'We were connected by a romantic emotional world and warmth, shaped by our joint work in the theatre. It could not have been deeper,' Burgdorf said. 'We were aware of this unity in every decision and up until the very last medical intervention.' They married in 2012. Before every single performance of an opera, Jonas wished his wife good luck. 'For him, it was always as if that evening were an absolute musical highlight. He wrote me cards with congratulations sent in advance: "Play your heart out!" I often thought: it's only a repertory performance! But it was important to him that the music was really filled with soul, and he couldn't help trying to get everyone involved really committed.'

Pierre Mendell

'If you picked up a programme for an opera at Covent Garden or La Scala in the early 1990s, what you saw was the institution itself represented. Their corporate image was built on this. The particular opera itself played a subordinate role,' Jonas told us. Things had been similar at the BSO.

'It's important to make the Munich house accessible, to change its marketing approach,' Jonas had explained to the international press. He argued to the Staatsministerium that it was not that the occupancy rate necessitated a new marketing strategy, but that it was time for a change of image. Until now, the BSO had stood for the values of the traditional, the elitist, the conservative and the culinary. 'People have to be aware that opera is exciting, theatrical, challenging.'[66]

Jonas also wanted to implement the Felsenstein principle: 'Felsenstein believed that the experience of a visit to the theatre begins with the first glance at a poster. This view triggers a decision-making process and the build-up of expectations. The poster is more than just an invitation. The poster projects the artistic and social outlook of the house and conveys a clear message about the work itself, rather than about its interpretation.'[67]

Jonas wanted to build a powerful, rigorously consistent and easily recognisable image of the Staatsoper that would communicate the importance of the Staatsoper to the people. 'Striving for broad accessibility in the face of intense competition from all possible kinds of media requires powerful, confident and competent marketing, attuned to the ideals of the house in question,'[68] he explained.

For his project, Jonas was looking for a 'free spirit, an artistic soulmate, whose design and direction should interact with what I had planned for this house – and the design should be a union of the artistic, social and economic principles of the house'.[69] Jonas found a congenial partner in the US graphic designer and poster artist Pierre Mendell, who was already known in Munich for his posters for the Neue Sammlung, but also for the Siemens logo. It was Mendell who first took Jonas to the Osteria Italiana in Schellingstraße. The Osteria opened in 1890 as one of the first Italian restaurants in Munich and quickly became a meeting place for artists and intellectuals in Schwabing, although strictly speaking it is located in Maxvorstadt. Franz Marc, Henrik Ibsen, Hans Carossa and Wassily Kandinsky all lived in Schellingstraße. Joachim Ringelnatz, Rainer Maria Rilke and Bertolt Brecht lived nearby. Oskar Maria Graf was a regular, but so was Adolf Hitler, who brought other Nazi leaders such as Heinrich Himmler, Baldur von Schirach and Rudolf Hess.[70] Jonas liked to tell how Hitler's admirer Unity Mitford had sat here for weeks in 1935 waiting for Hitler to finally approach her and for her to gain access to his inner circle.[71] The Osteria became one of Jonas's favourite restaurants in Munich. Here he celebrated his seventieth birthday party, but also his personal farewell party for his friends in November 2019.

But at first, Mendell and Jonas met there every Thursday for lunch and talked 'about God and the world'. Both connected existential themes: Mendell, who was born in Essen in 1929, was in his sixties when Jonas came to Munich. Mendell was the son of a Jewish mother. The family had fled to the Netherlands in 1934, before mother and son were able to emigrate to the USA via France. In 1947 Mendell received American citizenship.[72]

The technical questions were first discussed in Mendell's office at Widenmayerstraße 12 over 'pale, black tea in Chinese cups'. What they developed was the visual expression of what the BSO was to stand for under Jonas's Intendanz. The core of the new corporate image was a leitmotif consisting of the symbols of a heart, mouth, crown and cross. They stood for the existential themes of human life – love, eros, power and death – all dealt with in the operatic canon.

Mendell succeeded in creating a masterpiece with the new visual concept for the Staatsoper, able to convey the spirit of adventure and excitement that Jonas hoped his house could embody. Before each design for an opera poster, Jonas and Mendell discussed in often hours-long conversations what the production was about and their vision. The briefings were a matter for the boss: Jonas did not delegate them to the specialist departments. The posters developed their visual power from the arrangement of forms, lines, surfaces, colours and the typeface, a timeless Bodoni. Mendell used photographs or painted images only as defamiliarised set pieces.[73] As art historian Florian Hufnagl put it, the posters created a 'communication without embellishments' that concentrated on the essential through 'omission, condensation, distillation'.[74] But there was always a second level, 'behind the visible, the inklings of complex sub-contexts flicker'. In this way, the posters could be, just as Felsenstein had envisaged, 'graphic overtures'[75] to one's visit, which was how Karl Michael Armer aptly described the designs.

Gradually, Mendell's designs came to dominate the cityscape. Not only did they catch the eye on advertising pillars and billboards; Jonas and Mendell also insisted on bedecking the National Theatre with flags bearing the designs to mark the season: 'What a fight that was!' exclaimed Jonas. 'People complained in letters to the minister: that's what the Nazis did! And right-wingers wrote to the minister: German flags must hang at the National Theatre!' Today, it is hard to imagine that the National Theatre ever went without flags.'

Pierre Mendell received several awards for corporate design at the BSO. 'There had never been a look like Pierre Mendell's before,' said Christine Lemke-Matwey, underlining its originality. 'Their power lay in the tension between the defiant walls of the National Theatre, rebuilt after the war, and purist aesthetics: it was great!'

Although there can be no question that the design had a great impact, there were two criticisms made: firstly, Mendell found symbols for the essential themes of opera in the leitmotifs of heart, mouth, crown and cross. However, these symbols could also have worked for other theatres in other cities, especially if they had as conservative a history as had Munich: they were not specific to one particular institution. Secondly, although Mendell had indeed created a memorably powerful image, it still gave off an air of elitism. Yes, the images reached groups who had not previously visited the Staatsoper, or had done so only irregularly, but it did not live up to its aim of conveying accessibility to the population as a whole.

But what was a tonic for Jonas was that enough people were ready for the rebrand and forgave him and the house for the images' apparent elitism.

Parsifal

The 1994–95 season started quietly for Jonas. The initial storms triggered by his arrival had subsided. The initial indignation of regular audiences had diminished, and interest in the new programme among new visitors increased. A year before the première of *Parsifal*, on 1 July 1995, the director had not yet been chosen. Jonas wanted a German director, 'but an interesting one!'

Peter Konwitschny was not really known in Munich at the time; since the fall of the Wall, he had worked only in Leipzig, Graz and Basel. Jonas had met him several times, but had kept the meetings secret. Nor had any of his colleagues been aware that Jonas had invited him to a management programming round-table before Konwitschny walked through the door. 'Ladies and gentlemen, in a way this round-table is unnecessary because I have hired a director. Konwitschny would now like to talk to you about his ideas for *Parsifal*.' With that he opened the round-table, to general consternation. 'That was the only time I ever did anything like that!' Jonas defended himself.

After seeing Konwitschny off and returning to the meeting, everyone still seemed in a state of shock. Jonas thought that this was not only because he had made his decision unilaterally. When he met Konwitschny, the scars of the division of Germany were still fresh, and he himself, as a Briton, felt immune. The way Konwitschny had talked about his ideas was alien to his new collaborators.

The planning for Johannes Leiacker's stage concept was elaborate. And the feverish atmosphere during rehearsals was due not only to the hot weather. Konwitschny had worked 'as if possessed by the devil', at one point shouting at the technical team. 'Tomorrow you must buy five cases of beer with your own money as an apology,' Jonas demanded of him. Konwitschny did. Aron Stiehl, who assisted Konwitschny, also got into an argument with Jonas. 'Any other Intendant would have said: 'Punkt [full stop]. That's for me to decide. End of the discussion. but not Jonas,' Stiehl recalled.

In *Parsifal*, as tradition at the BSO decreed, there was to be no clapping after the first act. Konwitschny and Stiehl, 'a devout Wagnerian at the time', as he himself said, were also determined to adhere to this tradition. Jonas, however, wanted people to clap then. 'This is your German madness, don't take yourselves so seriously!' he commanded. '*Parsifal* should not be regarded as sacred. The compromise was that the singers didn't step in front of the curtain, but people could applaud.'

During the dress rehearsal, Jonas realised what a shock he was exposing his audience to. After the first act, no one did clap. Kundry, presented as the Virgin Mary, served communion to the Grail Knights. 'During the première there was indifference,' Stiehl described, 'and after the end of the act there was booing.' Fisticuffs broke out in the stalls. As it was rainy and cool on the day of the première, guests had brought umbrellas. One of the guests booed, another hit him on the head with his umbrella. He reacted violently. The police were called.

In the foyer, Jonas met Minister Zehetmair, who is said to have yelled at him, 'Peter, Peter: that is blasphemy,' even though he otherwise supported the aesthetic line of the house. Jonas is reported to have answered: 'I was brought up strictly Catholic. For me, this is not blasphemy, but redemption.' An audience member attacked Jonas personally in the foyer, holding him by his clothes. Leaflets flew into the stalls during the following performances. 'Through all the years, until the production was finally taken off in 2018, *Parsifal* moved so many audiences, sometimes to tears. The work had a raw emotional power,' Jonas reflected. 'It seemed to embody everything that should happen in theatre and so often does not. It was a sign that it is possible to balance music and dramaturgy to create something of outstanding expressiveness. Munich audiences had always traditionally seen *Parsifal* as something quasi-religious. Here came the East German view: *Parsifal* as a piece of enlightenment.'

A James Bond of the opera

'Even with Everding and Mr. and Mrs. Sawallisch, the Intendant's box was the theatre in front of the theatre – quite different from the general music director's box opposite, which was often deserted or had guests you didn't know sitting in it,' Christine Lemke-Matwey had observed. 'The Intendant's box was was clearly visible from the stalls and one was always looking at it. They wanted to know: who was sitting there? Who had the Intendant brought with him? How were they behaving?'

Mostly Peter Jonas himself sat there, in the early days often with his wife Lucy. He was an Intendant who was always present. The daily dose of adrenaline, the thrill of seeing whether all the small and larger challenges would be overcome in time for the performance, that's what attracted him. Jonas usually went to the ballet only for premières. In opera productions, however, he was at almost every performance for the whole run.

Those who observed his behaviour more closely noticed that Jonas sat ramrod-straight in his box, at least at the beginning of each performance: 'He once told me that he had developed a special technique to "sleep" sitting upright with his eyes open,' Lemke-Matwey revealed. 'He says this is incredibly relaxing for him. Most of the time the music is also beautiful.'

During the Festival season, with its many performances in different venues, all starting at the same time, Jonas had a tactic: he went from performance to performance, first to the National Theatre, in between to the Prinzregententheater, then to the other venues, in order to be back at the Staatsoper at the end of the opera performance to congratulate the singers. 'He sniffed everywhere, felt the pulse and looked to see if a disaster was happening, which he then tried to prevent,' Barbara Burgdorf recalled.

It was of great importance to him that the box be occupied when he could not use it himself. 'He made no stipulations, but he wanted to know who got the seats,' described Katrin Lausberg, who headed his office throughout his Intendanz, then still under the name Fasel. 'As a rule, he knew the people. Mostly they were from around the house, colleagues or friends of colleagues who had been unable to get a ticket. He was very relaxed and generous.'[76]

Fig. 38: Peter Jonas in the Intendant's box

While Jonas could be reasonably sure after two seasons that he would indeed be able to realise his aesthetic vision, he first had to find a public image: his role and its effect in this prominent position of state director, Lemke-Matwey said. 'PJ saw Munich itself as a stage, in the very Baroque sense. There were certainly different Peters, clearly, but could he always tell between them himself? Did he always know who he actually was? It depended on situations and relationships.'

Jonas studied the press kit in full every day. He remembered exactly who had written what and when. If a journalist went too far he intervened directly – or cut the person off from then on. He counted some journalists among his circle of friends, regardless of whether they had reviewed positively or negatively. A hand grenade sat on his desk (it was actually a cigarette lighter), and it was often interpreted by the press as a sign of his readiness to go on the attack. He was happy to let this stand.

Fig. 39: Peter Jonas in a kilt

The image the public has of him from the Munich years was decisively shaped by the photographs of Wilfried Hösl. Jonas had seen Hösl's pictures of the production of *Così fan tutte* by Dieter Dorn and Jürgen Rose at the Cuvilliés-Theater and, without knowing him personally, poached him directly. Hösl not only took the official portraits, but also snapshots of moments when Jonas thought he was unobserved – such as the shot of Jonas in his box, which Hösl took unplanned from a distance of more than twenty metres. The result is a picture that says so much about how Jonas understood himself as an Intendant.

'Peter was a James Bond of opera.'[77] David Alden could not have chosen a better character to describe the image Jonas was trying to project. British understatement, coolness, dry, sometimes black humour, an aura of invulnerability, elegance and nonchalance – all belonged to his image just as much as the Savile-Row suits and ties of his early years. ('Sir was always rather loud with his colourful ties and socks,' commented one ensemble member.)

Fig. 40: Peter Jonas as a fakir

But over the years Jonas increasingly dispensed with the trappings of class that had been indispensable to his position in London. His style of dress became more informal, an expression of his opposition to convention, which was just as important in conservative Munich. As he often suffered with the cold, a scarf became his constant companion and trademark. He let it flutter freely.

After Jonas's kilt had proved such a hit, he brought it out again and again. The kilt, first worn out of necessity, now became an expression of his public role, of his whimsicality. He became his costume. Time and again, newspaper reports mentioned his having a Scottish mother or grandmother. He never corrected such statements, although they were wrong.

There were Scots somewhere in his mother's ancestry, but certainly no family tartan.[78] He had bought his kilt in London because he liked the pattern. Now he wore it to amuse the Munich public, not least with answers to the frequently posed questions regarding what he was wearing underneath. The fact that he also carried the traditional stocking dagger, the 'sgian-dubh', merited a special feature in the *Süddeutsche Zeitung*.[79] It would be unthinkable to go to the Oktoberfest armed like that today. He also used the kilt tactically when he had to make an announcement at the Festival and wanted to distract from its content. When he stepped in front of the curtain in a kilt, he could count on a cheerful reception from the audience.

Jonas loved appearing on stage himself. His performances during the New Year's Eve show enjoyed a cult following. He rehearsed seriously. Footage of rehearsals for his performance in the Maskenball show him warming up and stretching beforehand. He danced the pas de deux with Beate Vollack with an expression of respect and sorrow. His first leap was particularly ungainly, considering he had trained in ballet during his student days. It was great fun for him to be able to show how, thanks to yoga, he was able to fold his long legs. The audience appreciated his commitment on show.

Being the 'James Bond of the opera' did not mean that he was completely emotionally invulnerable. His sense of irony was a way of keeping events and people at one remove. It gave him a better vantage point and helped him defend himself. He did not imitate Ferdinand Leitner: no one ever heard Jonas knocking before entering his office – even though Jonas swore blind that he did. But he had not forgotten Solti's story. Jonas did not assume that success was assured. He did not ever expect to be satisfied with his achievements. He was driven by ambition, by his promise to his sister to find the greatest possible meaning in his life. Jonas bore the weight of an existential insecurity that went far beyond that which most people carry within.

Everyday life at the opera

'Do you think I have learned German? I never had a single lesson. I'm just too lazy for that,' Jonas revealed. 'I can speak German pretty well under pressure. On the very first day, I asked Katrin Fasel and Natalia Ritzkowsky not to speak a word of English to me.' One of his neater bon mots was to describe his Intendanz as the most expensive language course in the world. Observers assumed in his first years in Munich that he spoke much better German than he pretended to.

No one made coffee in his office. At that time, there was still the 'Opera Espresso' restaurant on the other side of the street. When one of his guests asked his office manager if he could get a coffee, Jonas replied: 'Mrs Fasel is not here to make coffee, she has more important things to do!'

He made a point of showing his closest colleagues the esteem in which he held them. When he was looking for assistant directors, he always had the candidates wait ten minutes in his anteroom so that he could later ask Katrin Lausberg and Natalia Ritzkowsky for their impressions. 'It was important to him to get our assessment of whether this person would "fit in",' Ritzkowsky said.[80] Once, an employee of a hotel came into his anteroom and addressed his female staff with a casual 'Now then, girls…' Jonas heard this through the open door and pulled the man up on it: 'How dare you address these ladies as girls?' The man came back two days later with a huge bouquet of flowers to apologise.

Another time, someone from Jonas's wider circle of acquaintances had, through tremendous efforts on the part of Jonas's personal staff, managed to get his desired tickets for a première. At the première party, the gentleman then made disparaging remarks about the production. This stung Jonas, and he did not hold back in giving the gentleman a piece of his mind. The experience clearly affected the man deeply, as two days later he sent Jonas a case of Château Margaux as a peace offering. Jonas accepted, but divided the bottles among his female employees. In a letter of thanks, he wrote that the ladies in his office were pleased with the wine, and 'that it would at least be a small recompense for the trouble they went to over his tickets'.

His inner team grew together quickly. They worked hard, but also enjoyed their work. Jonas had determined that 'real success requires that you enjoy your work.'[81] 'It's all not so serious. It's only opera. If it's no good, then something new will always come along.'[82] They developed acronyms, like DbddhkP for 'Doof bleibt doof, da helfen keine Pillen [stupid stays stupid, no pills can help that]' or sAv for 'selbst Aspirin versagt [even aspirin fails]'. For a while, they did early morning exercises together twice a week in the ballet hall with Ulrike Hessler. 'If he was told not to drink alcohol or eat meat or do yoga every day or this or that because of his health,' says Katrin Lausberg, 'then nothing could get in his way. He adhered to his rules quite strictly, even though they were partly self-imposed. Always.' The 'Via Veneto' in Maximilianstraße was his favourite place for a raucous lunch, because the kitchen was always serving, even when they arrived after four o'clock, when the rehearsals were done.

'Sometimes he was ruthless, but in the end, you always knew what he wanted and where you stood,' says Katrin Lausberg. 'In the beginning, the stagehands found him unapproachable. "He doesn't say hello when he sees us," they complained. I then passed that on. He remembered their names as soon as they had worked together.' Jonas regularly visited the rehearsals, talked to colleagues, no matter what their position was. 'The worst day in a production is always the day of the dress rehearsal. Nerves are always on edge. You've just finished the rehearsal process, there's never enough time,' Natalia Ritzkowsky related. On days like these, Jonas often ran along the corridors past members of the choir and dressers without a word of greeting. Everyone felt the excitement. 'I got excited about that,' Ritzkowsky described: 'I thought he had to at least say hello. It's not the chorus girl's fault that maybe the prima donna is going crazy. In these situations, I did not always find him as confident as I would have liked to see him. I often fought with him about that.' Jonas accepted these hints from her, even though his first response was often: 'Natalia, that's out of line!'

Management round-tables were the ideal podium for 'Sir's performances', which sometimes irritated, but more often entertained. Maurice Lausberg recalled 'the story with the parking permits'.[83] The Intendanz had a pass that allowed the bearer free parking at the airport. If you went on holiday, you could ask to borrow it. 'In one of the weekly management round-tables, Sir came – everyone was already sitting there – and put his cricket bat down the middle of the table. "Has anyone here seen the film *Prizzi's Honor?*" Because few had seen the film, he rambled on about what this black comedy was about.' In one scene, the Don sits at the table with his family and asks: 'Who did this or that?' Everyone is silent, but the Don knows who the culprit is, takes the baseball bat and smashes in the head of one of the people present. 'Sir stood there, the bat was laid on the table and then he revealed: "The airport permit is gone. And I know who didn't bring it back. If the permit isn't back by tomorrow, I'll take my lovely bat here. If you want to know what I'll do with it, just watch the scene from *Prizzi*." The absurd thing was that it was actually me. But I didn't find the permit until a year later, and he didn't know I had it. He was bluffing.'

Whenever the Staatsministerium asked the opera to make savings in the budget, Jonas convened a 'Star Chamber': 'meetings in which everyone had to say what they were giving to the King. Someone who gave too little was executed or hurled out of the window,' says Lausberg. The name was a reference to the sixteenth-century English Star Chamber, which met in a room where the ceiling was studded with gold stars on a blue background. Since then, the term has been used to refer to committees that make arbitrary, secret decisions without due process.

The round-tables to which Toni Schmid, Undersecretary in the Staatsministerium, had to invite the directors of the state theatres were called 'Klingelbeutelrunden [begging-bowl meetings]'. 'In order to prove that savings of the desired magnitude, and especially within the required time frame, were not possible, Sir Peter had his administration draw up its own austerity programmes, which he numbered in Roman numerals: I, II, III et cetera,' Schmid recalled. A total of fourteen plans came into being in this way.

Jonas was a gambler, and communication was his favourite game. If he wanted to avoid unpleasant questions, he simply drifted off-topic. Hardly anyone noticed. His interlocutor had to be quick. Jonas simply turned arguments around. He tested his counterpart's intellectual capabilities: was the other person picking up his thread? Did they even realise it was a thread? 'He liked people who resisted and rebelled against common sense,' Christine Lemke-Matwey said of Jonas. 'He couldn't stand opportunists of any kind.' With his unsparing manner, he alienated his opposite numbers time and again. When his female employees pointed this out to him, he countered: 'Oh, that's typically German of you.'

To the outside world, Jonas always said 'we': 'In a management round-table, he would sometimes say: "I want this or that." It was always "our" success, but he didn't hide behind the "we" when he wanted something himself,' said Katrin Lausberg. In addition to the usual meetings with the staff council and the workplace assemblies, Jonas regularly scheduled a consultation hour in which he made himself available to all colleagues in the building. From time to time, people came to him who were ill themselves and sought his advice. Sometimes he later attended their funerals. Peter Jonas was extremely generous. He didn't care about his money. After main rehearsals, he invited the production ensemble to the 'Schwimmkrabbe', his favourite restaurant in Munich, in spite of its hard chairs and benches, next door to the 'Via Veneto'. Zubin Mehta and stars like Renée Fleming came along. Sometimes a belly dancer performed who reminded him of a young Lesley Garrett. At Christmas, he gave all senior staff a gift, personally chosen and wrapped. He once gave Aron Stiehl a CD with titles from the Berlin Wintergarten of the 1930s. It was named after a song by Otto Reutter: 'In 50 Jahren ist alles vorbei [In 50 years it'll all be over]'. 'Then others will determine life and theatre – that was ultimately his credo,' says Stiehl.

Fig. 41: Caricature by Dieter Hanitzsch

He liked to invite people to have drinks at his table during intervals. He was free with dinner invitations, but that in itself created a difficulty for those closest: they were inhibited from asking Jonas to come to dinner because it was tantamount to inviting themselves.

'He loved arguments,' said Maurice Lausberg, 'crisis and catastrophes'. For Jonas, they were games that allowed him to demonstrate his powers of control. 'If you came running into his office and said it was very urgent and terribly important, he would say: "that's nothing major – please come back tomorrow."' While everyone around him started losing their heads in such moments, he always first looked for his tie. He did this when conductor Fabio Luisi's plane from Dresden was delayed and he could not arrive in time for the start of the performance. The performance was supposed to start at 7pm. At 7:20pm Jonas stepped in front of the curtain, first chatting to the audience for eight long minutes, just to play for time. He then announced: the répétiteur Klaus von Wildemann would conduct the overture, by which time Luisi would have arrived and could take over. For von Wildemann, who was about to retire, it was a wonderful moment, for the audience it was a memorable experience, and for Jonas: just everyday chaos. The following evening it was the counter-tenor who went missing.[84]

Jonas did not lose his cool in the face of disaster, even without an audience looking on. During the pre-sales for the Festival première of Rose's *Don Carlo*, a member of staff from the visitor service department entered his office and confessed to having made a huge mistake. What had happened? 'Someone had forgotten to press a certain button to make sure that the première subscribers also got tickets for the Festival première,' as Katrin Lausberg recounted. In the meantime, the sale had begun. Three hundred and fifty tickets had already been sold for seats that should have been reserved for première subscribers. 'And this was two weeks before the Festival première! Jonas convened a crisis team, but remained quite calm. No outcry. No drama. No hysterical or choleric outbursts, nothing at all.'

It was clear that the mistake had been made, and now the crisis team had to find a solution. They analysed which people were currently booked into which places, and which members of the crisis team knew which people in which group, and arranged to call them. 'Then everyone was given a number of names, and had to make phone calls and try to book the guests into a different performance. That worked.'

When director Herbert Wernicke died in the middle of preparations for the *Ring des Nibelungen*, Jonas called all members of his staff to reassure them. 'He was on top form. "We are making a plan now. What are the options? ... Take Control!" were his favourite sayings,' recalled Maurice Lausberg.

Jonas liked to complain about the German tendency towards obedience, but also about German doom-mongering: in a difficult situation, everyone would always gaze fearfully into the abyss until the one with the greatest authority – that is, Jonas himself – said:

'Yes, this is serious, we have to deal with it.' And then everyone would answer: 'All right, let's do it.'

When there were conflicts, Jonas would sometimes hit the table with the flat of his hand or fist. Or else he would throw his keys, which he always carried with him, into a corner. Then silence fell. No one could drift off, everyone had to remain on the edge of their seat, paying close attention. 'He tried to follow things up with specific questions,' Katrin Lausberg described. 'He could look at people very intensely. That's how you would know that he was serious.'

Sometimes he raised his voice himself, but only rarely. 'He only blew up at me once or twice in decades,' described David Alden, who during a rehearsal was having difficulty deciding how to lead the chorus in a particular scene. He wanted Jonas's permission to allow the choir to perform in the side boxes reserved for the Intendant and the General Music Director.

Alden was pestering Jonas. 'I was probably getting a bit crazy with him,' Alden confessed. 'Jonas answered calmly and with a single sentence: "Don't bite the hand that feeds you!" That hit the mark,' Alden laughed.

Rose, looking back on the time when Jonas took up his post in Munich, comments: 'At the beginning, many people did not trust Jonas with his role and, as an Englishman, he was often met with incomprehension and prejudice. Even if it is no longer conceivable today, some uncertainty was definitely noticeable in him at the beginning.' Jürgen Rose's art has always lain in his knack for keen observation. Many others never noticed these signs in Jonas, or would have dismissed Jonas's statement that he felt ill-equipped for his new role as merely 'fishing for compliments'. 'Jonas had a special ability to protect his artists. He always kept the whole picture in mind. You could feel comfortable with him, trust him, even if there were, naturally, colleagues who were critical and couldn't deal with him. In the case of two or three employees, he made tough decisions: "No, we can't work together." They quickly parted ways.'

'Jonas could be hard on some people, very hard. You wouldn't think so if you experienced him as a typically English, polite person. But he was always right in his decisions.' Jonas was absolutely consistent in his toughness: 'Sir Peter never minced his words when he thought something was wrong. He was not afraid of anyone,' said Toni Schmid from the Staatsministerium. Whenever it was appropriate from his point of view, he also let politicians feel that toughness.

Jonas knew how to hit people at their weakest points: that was part of his darker side. When he wanted to, he could be deliberately hurtful. He had a hard time dealing with people he didn't like, whom he thought were inadequate or too slow. He did not hide his behaviour and sometimes laid into staff members in front of others: stories of these incidents were passed on around the company, but also to the circle around the Staatsoper.

What interested him in these skirmishes was whether the people kowtowed to him, or whether they would fight back and get up again. If they did not, he made things difficult for them.

'Sometimes he said really crass things. For example, he once said to a co-worker: "the only real problem is that your parents didn't use contraception,"' one staff member recalled. In March 1999 Jonas insulted a stagehand, saying, 'You're a negative arsehole!' The stagehands then went on strike for an hour until Jonas asked for their forgiveness.[85] The sometimes-superhuman demands Jonas made on himself he also made on others, sometimes to the point of unfairness: that's how Aron Stiehl saw this side of the man. 'When a colleague who had the 'flu called in sick, he was beside himself. "A producer doesn't get sick." Her contract was not renewed.' He always needed a hate object, too, reported a staff member. 'Once he had set his sights on someone, he wouldn't stop.' One colleague, whom he had decided was not his type, had to put up with 'really quite a lot'. 'Because she came from the former GDR, he always made stupid jokes about East Germany and the GDR. "What would the Stasi have said about that?" That kind of thing happened often.' Peter Jonas was not free of shortcomings, he was definitely not a perfect boss. Some would say that he was appreciated for his edges and corners.

Jonas gathered around him a very close group, his theatre family, who worked together extremely hard, who shared a lot in private and who always had great parties in the wild garden behind the Staatsoper. This did not go unnoticed by those outside this circle. Even the *New York Times* took up the issue with a single, unsubstantiated sentence: 'Within the theatre, Sir Peter is not loved by everyone,'[86] Midgette wrote in 2004. It was a statement that could apply to every director, to every manager. But Peter Jonas was an artistic director who aimed to polarise and who would have only shrugged at Midgette's observation. He wasn't perfect, he wasn't a saint.

His polarising behaviour had a flip side that became valued by many: those who enjoyed his confidence he supported unreservedly. Even years after his retirement he played a decisive role in the appointment of international directors. Jonas was proud of these people who had built a career in the industry out of working with him, whether as artistic directors, singers or in administrative roles. He watched them very closely and knew who had moved on to where.

Aron Stiehl, who would take over as Intendant of the Klagenfurt Stadttheater, saw Jonas as a foster father. 'Since he had not had children himself and could not physically pass on what he wanted to pass on, we ended up being his children,' says Stiehl. 'In us he saw a replacement.'

By 'we' Aron Stiehl meant a select circle of young opera-makers whom Jonas supported professionally and accompanied personally, all based on their talent and potential. When the chemistry was right, Jonas would also help with private matters, without becoming presumptuous or overbearing. After Stiehl handed in his resignation, he found the letter torn up in an envelope at the gate. Jonas had refused to accept it. 'He was of the opinion that if you work so closely together, you don't just write a resignation, you talk to each other first,' Stiehl reported. 'Under labour law, of course, this is not necessarily the case. He asked me how he could keep me at the Staatsoper. "Give me a production!" I said. And so I got the commission for *Dido and Aeneas*. It was the greatest opportunity of my life! He didn't do things like other Intendants, where you stay an assistant forever.'

When Hans Jürgen von Bose's *Schlachthof V* needed someone to make an announcement before a performance, he asked Stiehl to take over. He didn't want to be the focus of audience attention himself: he might provoke a reaction that would damage the work. 'Delegate and trust, that was his motto. He led with loose reins. But the boundaries within which we could move were always clear. Not many Intendants do that!' enthused Stiehl. 'Most of them hem you in and patronise you. "You have to be free as artists", he said, "the fire will be stifled otherwise!" Peter Jonas showed us how to develop as artists. He shaped us in freedom, that was his great art.'

Jonas had an idea of the influence he was having on the younger generation. To break this spell, he adopted an ironic gesture: 'At every farewell, after every conversation, he blessed us like a priest, like a pope of the opera: "It is ended, now go in peace." That was ironic, but there was energy in his gesture, there was a power there.'

During the last months of his life, Natalia Ritzkowsky went with him to Zurich now and again. On these trips, they both talked a lot about the old times, about looking back, but also forward to life, to death. At one point Jonas confessed that he had suffered from not being able to pass something down as a father can to his children. Ritzkowsky told him that he was wrong, that he had. From his Munich years alone, she knew so many people, including herself, whom he had played a decisive role in shaping – admittedly not in the way a biological father would – but these 'children' now carried on his tradition, his 'legacy' into the opera world: 'When I told him that so forcefully, he was very touched to hear it from one of those "children".'

Jonas was also an artistic director who first and foremost made himself available to his artists. 'A former senior employee was frequently attending dress rehearsals, and would criticise his colleagues on stage afterwards,' Jürgen Rose explained. 'There was a point when Jonas was made aware of it, summoned him to his office and really banned him. "As long as I am director, you will not enter the building again." Brutal. It was a shock, but also just right, as protection for the others.'

Right at the beginning of his Intendanz, Jonas had moved the première celebrations to the 'Canteen', a 'yodelling inn, with old glass and fixed tables',[87] as Egbert Tholl described it. He would climb up on a table and gave 'a flaming speech praising everyone involved in the production. It was a statement on the reactionary forces in the house, in the city, in life in general,' says Ritzkowsky.

When a production failed, Jonas defended it to the end. He would employ, not entirely appropriately, the image of the 'faulty child'. After premières that had really 'gone to shit', Jonas took a public roll-call of all staff, starting with the interns and arriving, an hour later, at the leading artistic staff, 'so that every member of the audience felt sure that they had witnessed an incredible moment of musical theatre. When things got really ropey, Sir Peter wore a kilt, so that a good mood was guaranteed in advance, come what may.'[88]

One of the biggest defeats of his era, which had not known many, was the première of the *Abduction from the Seraglio*, Tholl recalled. 'Sir Peter's speech afterwards lasted an hour. When it ended, the wildest première party that the Staatsoper had experienced for a long time broke out.'[89]

Only once did a conflict with a director become public knowledge: Leander Haußmann broke off his work on *Die Fledermaus* at the end of December 1997 and left. What followed was, at least by the otherwise calm standards of Jonas's Intendanz, a mudslinging exchange of at least moderate proportions in the press. The *Süddeutsche Zeitung* had presented Haußmann's point of view in an article that appeared on New Year's Eve, but had not given Jonas's response. The Staatsoper then issued a reply, which Jonas wrote himself.[90]

A year later, he was preoccupied by a scandal surrounding Cheryl Studer's contract, terminated during rehearsals; she had been due to appear as Agathe in the production of *Freischütz* by Thomas

Langhoff, Jürgen Rose and Zubin Mehta. After the dust settled, Jonas pursued a strategy of silence in further talks with the press to ensure the incident was forgotten.[91]

Jonas was rarely absent due to illness during these years. But his illnesses followed him. In 1999, he was diagnosed with an ocular melanoma, which from then on was treated with hyperthermic irradiation at regular intervals. When it grew again despite the radiation treatments, proton radiation was prescribed in 2008. To prepare for the treatment, the eyeball had to be surgically removed from its socket in order to fix a tiny titanium plate to the back of the eyeball, needed to protect the brain from radiation. Jonas suffered terribly from the fear of losing his sight.

In 2004, a precancerous skin lesion was removed in surgery, which was supplemented with several rounds of laser therapy. Jonas suffered from constant stomach and intestinal complaints; he underwent pain therapies and spinal stenosis operations to widen the canal through which the spinal cord runs. Once, when he was really ill, he asked the most important managers and directors to come to the hospital. They discussed how things would go on if he were not there. At the producers' meetings, which he wasn't obliged to attend at all, he sometimes sat leaning against the radiator, shivering because he had chills. Stiehl also vividly recalled the première party of *Don Carlo*, where Jonas asked him: 'Stay close to me, you may have to keep talking because I no longer have a voice.'

Jonas was merciless to himself in his illness, Stiehl said. 'A normal person could never have done that.'

Jürgen Rose

'Jonas was a great leader. He was ten years younger than me, but nevertheless he was someone who protected me, on whom I could completely rely, who was a real boss despite our personal familiarity,' Jürgen Rose said. The two first met, and then only briefly, when Lucia Popp appeared as Sophie in a *Rosenkavalier* in Munich in the 1970s. Otto Schenk directed, Carlos Kleiber conducted and Jürgen Rose was responsible for the stage and costumes.

More than twenty years later, it still felt impossible for Jonas to repeat that production. Too many memories of his with Lucia Popp, and Carlos Kleiber was inseparable from her. Jonas took Rose into his confidence and showed him great appreciation. The younger man had observed with astonishment the role Jürgen Rose played in Munich. Because of his high demands and unconditional insistence on perfection, Rose was a constant challenge to his colleagues. Nevertheless, they did everything possible to implement his ideas. Working hours and budgets were often wildly exceeded in the run-up to the opening night, and the employees were completely overwhelmed. 'But in the end it's all worth it,'[92] said Silvia Strahammer, who as head of the costume workshop was his closest ally at the Staatsoper.

Jonas got to know Rose better when Rose was working with Dieter Dorn on *Così fan tutte*. 'The production was a huge success for Dieter Dorn and Jürgen Rose. It was a sure-fire success and came at just the right moment after *Giulio Cesare in Egitto*. All the Jonas-modern-Handel haters immediately bought tickets,' related Jonas, and he described Rose as a 'real research institute for the theatre… We sometimes forget that he first started out as a costume and set designer and that his ballet costumes for John Neumeier in Stuttgart made him world-famous. Jürgen Rose does not grow old. He has no expiry date.' Jonas was particularly impressed by the fact that Rose had managed to change his aesthetic line several times over the course of his career. Jonas had observed how the strength of Thomas Langhoff's and Dieter Dorn's repertoire grew out of Rose's stage designs, which sometimes themselves formed the starting point for the dramaturges' interpretative innovations. Instinctively, he had developed the idea that Rose had to direct himself. 'Jürgen Rose embodies everything that is good about German theatre. His productions of *The Cunning Little Vixen* and *Don Carlo* were among the most gratifying moments of my life.'

The most important and personal moment of their friendship

was connected with Rose's partner Dieter Mellein, who died of throat cancer in 1997, within a year of diagnosis. In the spring of that year, Rose had worked with Thomas Langhoff on Smetana's *The Bartered Bride*. Mellein had been able to make it to the main rehearsal. The next day, however, he had to undergo a serious operation. Rose had visited him on the day of the première, 16 May 1997, in the hospital Rechts der Isar.

Mellein lay in his room receiving treatment with morphine. He seemed to be doing well. He asked Rose to go to the première party and then tell him about it afterwards. 'He was quite happy and reassured,' Rose recalled. Mellein's doctor, Lieselotte Goedel-Meinen, however, seemed rather worried about this plan. Rose understood why only later.

As planned, Rose went to the première. During the final round of applause, he suddenly collapsed on the stage. He took refuge among the backstage scenery. There was a model village cemetery there. It sheltered him from the audience's gaze. Shielded by a wall, he slumped down on the incline. The technicians looked on with irritation: they had never seen Rose in this state before. Jonas, however, had noted what was happening and had followed. 'He knelt down to me behind the wall and took me in his arms. "Come, come, we can do it," he said. He took me past the technicians into the hallway to the open window. He was with me, alone. This situation was unforgettable.'

Jonas had first offered the direction of *Don Carlo* to Dieter Dorn, and Rose was to be the set and costume designer. Since Dorn refused, the moment had come for Jonas to offer Rose the directing role. Jonas was extremely skilful in his approach. He invited Rose for a talk in his office, where there hung a copy of a painting by Francisco de Zurbarán, an important Baroque painter in Spain's Siglo de Oro.

In passing, the pair spoke about Zurbarán's pictorial worlds and the blossoming of Spanish art and culture under Philip II. Finally, Jonas suggested to Rose that they go to Spain to see the works of art of the time in the museums and the Escorial. 'So,' Rose said, snapping his fingers, 'laying bait, he was very good at that.' But Jonas was also willing to invest in preparing a production. Allowing such a journey, even suggesting it, was far from an obvious move. 'As artistic director, he took responsibility for the decision to offer me, as a newcomer to directing, a big part straight away,' Rose described. 'Jonas could have chosen a smaller one, especially as it was known that I am complicated. His decision initially caused a lot of resistance in the house.'

When Jonas offered him the directorship of Janáček's *The Cunning Little Vixen*, he was certain he was making the right choice. But Rose resisted. His memories of the famous Felsenstein production at the Komischen Oper, which he had seen several times as a student, with its concrete, realistic aesthetics, were too clear in his mind. Jonas insisted, he was sure, and asked him to retire to his house in Murnau and occupy himself with the score. 'He was quite stubborn about it,' Rose said. 'This is also a way of sheltering someone. He could also have said: "No, not interested? Someone else, then."' And Jonas was right. The decisive moment came in Murnau when Rose suddenly found himself very close – 'eye to eye' – with a vixen in the flesh, with her cubs. It had to be a sign, he was sure, and told Jonas.

Jürgen Rose had asked to be given enough time for all the preliminary work on the research and direction, and for auditioning extras. For this, the opera rented rooms in the old Finanzhof behind Maximilianstraße, where Rose and his team spent weeks developing the costumes of the dragonfly, the ant, the badger and the fox, the insects and forest birds, the snails, frogs and chickens from found materials and purchased pieces. For Rose, this freedom gave rise to one of the most important theatrical works of his career. 'Jonas trusted us,' says Rose, 'and that's what I find so exciting, this trust in my imagination, attention to detail, and ambition.'

After *The Cunning Little Vixen*, Jonas demanded that Rose do something classical, a well-known bel canto opera. He had something great in mind that was perhaps alien to Rose: Bellini's *Norma*. Rose hesitated. Jonas had also persuaded Gruberová to take on a role under Jürgen Rose's direction. Until now, she had sung the role only in concert. So this would be her debut playing the part fully. As before, Jonas knew exactly how to arrange things to lure Rose.

But Rose was also a companion who observed Jonas more closely than others. 'Peter Jonas was a person who pays attention, who is curious, who observes, observes very closely. And then sits in his box, behind his curtain, but looks and listens very closely,' Rose described: 'so knowledgeable, so intelligent, so sensitive and yet critical and hard. He worked hard for everything and used his Intendanz as a learning process, not just as a post on which to rest. Because he never rested. In that house, he was always the last resort.'

Zubin Mehta and Sir Georg Solti

Peter Jonas could boast of having brought the best conductors of the time to the Chicago Symphony Orchestra. But he never succeeded in snaring Zubin Mehta. Dorothy Chandler from the Board of the Los Angeles Philharmonic Orchestra was at the heart of this. She had made a momentous mistake that became, in Jonas's words, 'one of the biggest scandals in the music business'.

Shortly before Georg Solti was appointed to the Royal Opera Covent Garden, he had achieved his international breakthrough. He was then *the* big emerging star. Orchestras and opera houses worldwide were interested in him. The Los Angeles Philharmonic Orchestra was not considered the best, but it was surely the best-equipped orchestra in the USA. The Board was led by publisher and arts patron Dorothy Chandler, now looking for a conductor with an outstanding profile. After Solti made his USA debut in Houston under the aegis of Colbert Artist Management, in 1958 Chandler invited him in for talks. The two quickly came to an agreement. Solti left America with a contract as general music director, which gave him plenipotentiary powers and responsibilities. His first season was set to begin in the autumn of 1962. Only a few months after Solti had signed with Chandler, a young and largely unknown Indian conductor won the prestigious International Conducting Competition in Liverpool by a clear margin. Then, in January 1961, this same young man stepped in at short notice to conduct the Los Angeles Philharmonic Orchestra. 'It turned out to be a fantastic concert, full of glitz and glamour! The audience in LA were beside themselves,' Jonas enthused. 'How fine Zubin was then! He was the most handsome man! He was bildhübsch, picture-perfectly handsome, with a charisma that couldn't be matched!'

Dorothy Chandler was also thrilled, and she signed a contract with Mehta as assistant general music director immediately after that concert. Before Mehta signed the contract, he had been told that Solti had agreed to his being taken on.[93] Not so. Solti was on tour at the time, and Chandler had written him a telegram informing him of her plans, but had not waited for Solti's reply before signing up Mehta. The telegram reached Solti two days later. Before he could read it, however, he had already learned from the media that Zubin Mehta was to become his assistant. He did not know Mehta and had nothing against him, but he did not want to accept this breach of his contract. Appointing his assistant ought to have been his decision alone.

Solti submitted his resignation in protest. This dispute dragged on for years. In the meantime, Chandler had moved swiftly to appoint the 24-year-old Mehta as the orchestra's general music director. Mehta's work in Los Angeles became hugely successful.[94] In January 1968, *Time* magazine ran the headline 'The Baton is Passed to Youth' alongside a portrait of Mehta. 'The crowd in Hollywood loved him,' Jonas said. 'Only neither of them was told the truth. It was a bad misunderstanding. In the meantime, Solti was flying high at the CSO.' The best conductors came to Chicago, but not Mehta. Again and again John Edwards and Jonas brought his name into the conversation. Even though all orchestras and opera houses wanted to work with Mehta, Solti rejected the idea completely. His resentment ran too deep.

It was only two years before Jonas moved to London that Solti changed his mind, to general surprise. While he still refused to approach Mehta personally, he gave his consent for Edwards to do so. Edwards was not comfortable with this idea. 'Only P can go to him. P is younger and has nothing to lose,' Edwards is said to have replied. 'He was unworldly at that time, so to speak. He was completely innocent. Send him to Zubin Mehta! No letters!'

The fact that Zubin Mehta, who was really blameless in this conflict, received Jonas as Solti's envoy at all was thanks to Daniel Barenboim. Barenboim and Mehta had known each other since 1956. They were close friends. When Mehta learned that the artistic director of the CSO wanted to visit him, he consulted Barenboim. 'Daniel inoculated Zubin,' was how Jonas put it. Barenboim is said to have told Mehta: 'If they send Peter, talk to him! I know him inside out, worked with him for years. He is straightforward and honest. He tells the truth and knows what he is talking about.'

So Jonas flew to New York, where Mehta was meanwhile engaged as General Music Director of the Philharmonic Orchestra – he worked there with Carlos Moseley, who in turn had been 'music officer' in Bavaria with Georg Solti from 1946 to 1949.

'It was one of the most difficult conversations I have ever had in my life,' Jonas admitted. 'I was deathly nervous.' Mehta received Jonas politely but reservedly. They chatted for a while until Jonas explained that he knew about the conflict, but only second-hand. As far as he was concerned, there was no need to discuss it. But he wanted Mehta to know that the orchestra, Solti and Edwards wanted to invite him to Chicago. Mehta asked why Solti would not come himself. Jonas responded that the breach could not be repaired in a single day. 'I'm already being courted by Vienna and Amsterdam. I may not be there at all when you come, but I can work on it now.' Then they talked about cricket. 'We got on very well.' Finally, Mehta took out his calendar and indicated two weeks in December 1986. They discussed the programme.

Jonas said thank you as he left. 'Don't think it was because of you,' Mehta replied to him. 'Daniel told me I could trust you!'

On 1 December 1986, when Jonas had already started work in London, Mehta performed with the CSO for the first time. He conducted the Brahms piano concertos, and Daniel Barenboim played as soloist.

Zubin Mehta, ideal General Music Director

During his early negotiations with Hans Zehetmair, Jonas had been troubled by the question of who should become the opera's General Music Director. The minister saw the situation as an opportunity; Jonas could calmly start his work and then initiate negotiations. So it was that Zehetmair was able to write in his memoirs that Jonas 'connected me with what was probably the most spectacular staffing coup I have managed in my time in office so far: the appointment of Zubin Mehta as General Music Director.'[95]

However, Mehta turned down an initial offer. He was, however, prepared to take over the musical direction of the first Festival première under the Jonas directorship: the production of *Tannhäuser* directed by David Alden. Already after the first rehearsal, Mehta was taken with the sound of the Munich orrchestra. He had not expected 'this genetically-cultivated tradition of playing Wagner', says Jonas. His cooperation with Alden does not seem to have been entirely smooth. 'Alden's directorial concept was somewhat problematic in its implementation in some places, but I understood what he wanted to say,'[96] was Mehta's tactfully opaque comment on the matter in his memoir.

After the success of *Tannhäuser*, Jonas wanted to make another attempt. He asked Zehetmair for his agreement and a special budget to travel to Chicago for a week in March 1996, where Mehta conducted the *Ring* at the Lyric Opera. His mission was to convince Zubin to become general music director of the BSO from 1998. 'I can get in and out of Zubin's hotel. I know the people who run it,' Jonas told his minister. 'I can be discreet as one can be.' Zehetmair agreed.

The conditions for the renewed negotiations were favourable. Mehta had been obliged to 'take two days off' during the Festival when he conducted *Tannhäuser*, something he thought worth explaining in his memoirs, although both times were for charity events. One day he conducted Mozart's *Requiem* in a concert in the burnt-out library of Sarajevo. 'The hulk of the library, one of the most surreal ruins in this city of twisted steel, pocked walls and shattered glass, must be one of the eeriest venues ever chosen for a performance of the *Requiem*,' wrote the *New York Times*.[97] The second time, Mehta conducted – 'horribile dictu', he commented – the Three Tenors concert on the eve of the football World Cup final. 'I'm sure Jonas didn't take me entirely seriously as a result. But I made a "deal" with him – if he would let me off from this summer performance, then I would come as a substitute in the autumn and conduct *Tannhäuser* once more without pay. That was also accepted,' Mehta wrote.[98] Jonas, on the other hand, did not want to reveal the details of their agreement; he had not been aware that Mehta himself had already done so. Jonas said only that he had done Mehta a personal favour that made them closer friends. For Jonas, it was a good starting position to be able, a little later, in March 1996, to dare offer Mehta the post of General Music Director of the BSO.

Jonas met Mehta in the hotel during rehearsal breaks. 'We worked out a good plan,' Jonas recalled. 'But we had to be careful, because the deal would soon be in the papers.' Finally, Jonas wrote a letter of intent by hand, which they both signed. They saved the question of the level of the salary for later. 'Fortunately, I had so much experience in the American business that I knew what these conductors earned,' commented Jonas, who now had to deal with Mehta's lawyer. The actual salary for his work as General Music Director was set appropriately – 'normal, on the high side', as Jonas put it. That was the sum that would be published. But it wasn't enough for Mehta because of the high income tax he would have to pay in Germany. They got around that problem by offering him a high per-performance fee.

Mehta was to conduct forty performances over around fifteen productions. 'After much, much haggling,' Jonas agreed with Mehta's lawyer. Both sums – salary and performance fee – were enormous, even by Bavarian standards. But at least the Free State would be able to say truthfully that Zubin Mehta was working in Munich. Nevertheless, Zehetmair had to confer with his Minister-President. According to an officially unconfirmed but marvellous Munich story, Zehetmair, showing great tactical nous, is said to have done this during an FC Bayern match. The anecdote goes like this: during a match he attended with Edmund Stoiber, Zehetmair is said to have said to Stoiber: 'You, listen! We're getting a new head of music at the opera.' Stoiber's simple response is said to have been a question: 'And what will it cost?' When Zehetmair then told him the level, Stoiber is said to have exclaimed: 'Are you insane?!' Zehetmair, however, was unfazed: 'Listen here! What does that FC Bayern substitute earn down there?' Stoiber is said to have quickly got things in perspective and agreed to the appointment of Zubin Mehta.

Zehetmair managed to pull off two more coups with regards to Mehta's appointment. Before the media got wind of it, he was able to present Zubin Mehta as the new General Music Director of the BSO to totally unsuspecting media representatives on 18 April 1995, Easter Tuesday. From 1998 to 2006, Mehta would take on forty evening conductorships and two academy concerts annually. But this also meant that Zehetmair won his private race against Christian Ude, who as Mayor of Munich had sought to appoint Mehta as General Music Director of the Munich Philharmonic Orchestra after the unexpected death of Sergiu Celibidache in August 1996: 'That made the headlines in the Munich newspapers,' Jonas stressed. 'It was a tremendous coup.' August Everding, however, had already heard about the appointment. Jonas had told him over the phone: 'August, if you break this story, it's over!'

The appointment came as a surprise even to the State Orchestra. All that was known was that something secret was being negotiated. The orchestra Board had also kept quiet. On the day of the press conference, Peter Jonas came to the assembled orchestra at the end of the rehearsal to inform them about the appointment. Like Mehta, Bolton also took on around forty to fifty performances per season. Almost one hundred of the approximately three hundred and fifty performances that the orchestra played in opera and ballet each season were thus in the hands of two conductors with whom the orchestra had an excellent relationship. The house benefited enormously from this stability.

'The ideal General Music Director is someone who is interested in everything that goes on in the house. A music director must be a working member of the family. Zubin came to the house at nine in the morning, every day. He rehearsed, had lunch and chatted with colleagues. He had meetings in the afternoon and conducted in the evening. He did not go back to the hotel to sleep. He was part of the company. That's how GMDs have to be!' Mehta, too, spoke in his memoirs of feeling 'at home'[99] at the Staatsoper. Like Jonas, he also appreciated firm ties to a house or orchestra. Jonas 'always took a lot of the external things off his hands, like administrative issues or looking for sponsors',[100] Mehta emphasised. 'Peter Jonas was the ideal partner for Zubin Mehta because he relieved Mehta of everything superfluous that he assumed the latter did not need to deal with,' Barenboim said of the collaboration between Jonas and Mehta. 'His outstanding knowledge of the opera repertory did the rest. Besides, Peter admired him! That doesn't qualify anyone, but it helps a conductor immensely.'

The appointment of Zubin Mehta also strengthened the acceptance of Jonas within Munich society.

In Zubin Mehta's seventieth birthday year, Jonas gave around twenty speeches for his friend and partner worldwide, reaching the limits of his physical capacity. He described Mehta as a 'man of natural gifts – of boundless generosity, energy, kindness, humanity; and above all: for a man who, in his life and in his work has never, no matter how sorely provoked, never allowed himself to be carried away by malice – perhaps the rarest of all good qualities… He has a kind of inner peace. This includes two things, his generosity and his greatness of spirit. Which means that he accepts the negative vibrations of others without getting back at them.'[101] He learned from Zubin Mehta: 'resist not evil: but whosoever shall smite thee on thy right cheek, turn to him the other also.' Mehta, he said, was 'the most accessible of all his colleagues', 'a musicians' musician. He needs no armoury of intellectual arrogance; rather, his colleagues in the orchestra simply feel at ease with him because he lets them, and the music, speak with the greatest eloquence.'[102]

His first repertory performance had cost him 'a few more grey hairs, because I suddenly had to be able to conduct an opera with only one rehearsal',[103] Mehta recalled. It was a 'difficult, exciting task', which did not go unnoticed by the orchestra. 'Zubin Mehta's concert performances impressed me most of all,' said Barbara Burgdorf. 'If he had a rehearsal of only two and a half hours for a work of, say, four hours then he became frantic. The prospect of not finishing made him nervous. In the evening he enjoyed the music and with us, as his colleagues, made the performance a living event. With his great ability to span musical arcs, his impeccable conducting technique, gestures and looks, he reached everyone, right to the back of the orchestra pit. This was a lot of fun for everyone involved. Whenever a mistake happened, with him or with us, he would look around and make a gesture that said: it happens to everyone.'

An important factor in Mehta and Jonas's fruitful partnership was the fact they agreed on how fidelity to the original text should be lived out in live opera – as opposed to how the concept might be understood theoretically. Mehta, who had studied with Hans Swarowsky in Vienna, compared fidelity to a work with the varnish that must be removed from a painting so that the basic idea becomes clearer.[104] Music had to be freed from the sometimes centuries-old conventions of conductors.

Jonas, however, understood 'faithfulness to the work as free interpretation. Not faithfulness to the work as a fictitious idea, that is, not as an attempt to understand how the composer might have understood his work.'[105] In his 2001 Queen's Lecture, he even radically rejected the concept of faithfulness to the work and spoke instead of 'objective interpretation'.[106]

Criticism from the Audit Office

At the beginning of his tenure, Jonas had been astonished to discover that his main defined role was to keep the seat occupancy rate at 94 per cent. In a report from the Obersten Rechnungshof [Supreme Audit Office], examining the budgets of the state theatres and state-subsidised theatres and orchestras, payments to Zubin Mehta and the pension scheme for Intendants came in for criticism.

The 'Expenses for the General Music Director of the Staatsoper' received its own sub-chapter. These had increased 'sixfold in seven years'[107] from 1992 to 1999, wrote the Audit Office in its annual report for the year 2000. The report criticised this inflation, noting that the current General Music Director conducted fewer performances than his predecessor, while at the same time had been relieved of some duties as Intendant.[108]

It also demanded an upper limit for conductors' remuneration, as had long been standard practice for vocal soloists in German-speaking countries. Concessions by one institution would quickly affect other cultural institutions and thus jeopardise the financial viability of the public cultural sector in the long term. 'For example, in performances directed by the GMD, around 25 per cent of the total performance income is eaten up by the GMD's fees, even when the Staatsoper is operating at maximum capacity.'[109]

Interestingly, the Audit Office had hit the nail on the head when it addressed growing expenditure on conductors. Reference to the resulting cost spiral, which in the long term endangered the financial viability of such artists, was entirely justified. The fact that the fees for both conductors and vocal soloists were disproportionate to the fees received by others responsible for a performance was not discussed at the time.

But the report did not address the fact that the increase in expenses for the GMD was not only due to adjustments under tax law, but also due to the architecture of the contract itself, which differentiated between a basic salary and fees for evening performances.

The Staatsministerium, to which the Audit Office's criticism was addressed, offered a twofold response. On the one hand, the GMD's remuneration, it said, was in line with international standards. On the other hand, the Staatsministerium tactically invoked the companies' artistic freedom, stating that it was the Staatsoper's prerogative to decide 'on what artistic level' it wanted the house to be led.[110]

The Audit Office's retort was expected: 'In the view of the Audit Office, compliance with the overall budget does not give a cultural institution the authority to disregard the necessary diligence in handling public funds in individual cases.'[111] What followed was customary behaviour for any public body criticised by the Audit Office: as requested, the Staatsministerium reported, in closed session, 'on the reasons for the extension of the contract and the content of the contract for the General Music Director',[112] but still used what leeway it had to defend the interests of the Staatsoper. The Audit Office was ultimately able to offer only commentary: although the Staatsministerium had known that the contractual relationship with the GMD would be dealt with on 8 February, 'a guest performance contract for the seasons 2003 to 2006 was concluded with the GMD dated 8 and 18 February 2001'.[113] This latter contract was not subject to the same administrative obligations, and there was no reduction in the costs per performance.

With this ploy, the Staatsministerium broke free of the Audit Office. The Audit Office recommended that in future the draft contract with conductors of the state theatres should be submitted in advance to the budget committee 'if the annual remuneration exceeds one million euros'.[114]

The fact that Jonas had previously described the auditors at the Supreme Audit Office as 'mousy gentlemen' in the State Ministry's magazine had not helped matters. His quote had put Toni Schmid, in charge of the publication, in something of a bind.

Modern music theatre management

Everyone who takes on a job in the world of publicly subsidised culture in Germany moves between restriction and freedom, between the framework set by the funding bodies and artistic freedom as defined in Article 5 of the Grundgesetz, or Basic Law.

When Jonas took up the post of State Director in Munich, he wanted to treat artistic decisions and management decisions equally, in the spirit of Felsenstein, which meant striking a delicate balance. But in fact, this was a balance that he never really struck. Art always took priority, though he acknowledged his responsibility towards the operational and financial demands of the running of the opera. Jonas shielded artists from the consequences of the conditions set for him by the funding agencies. He never took the support of politicians for granted, nor public interest.

Seemingly insignificant elements of a production could suddenly become the focus of heated public discussion. In his staging of *Siegfried*, for example, David Alden had the hero piss in a urinal. At first the audience reacted in horror. The issue illustrated the balancing act Jonas had to perform: 'As artistic director, I have two little monsters sitting on my shoulders. One cries: "Risk! Risk!" The other warns: "Caution!" Provocation is good, but I must not lose sight of social responsibility, I must not chase people away. For example, the urinal in the first act of David Alden's production of *Siegfried*: we seriously considered removing it at the time, the outrage was so great. We didn't do it because it made sense. Today it is a cult object.'[115] For Jonas, the scene drew its meaning from one of the myths of alchemy: horse urine, apparently, can be used to harden swords, although Alden would not confirm whether this was something they had ever actually seriously discussed.

In the fifth year of Jonas's Intendanz, the critic Wolf-Dieter Peter wrote in *Deutsche Bühne* that the Staatsoper had developed into a much-appreciated place of renewal through demanding directorial concepts, world premières, but also through drastic modernisation in marketing and management, even though most Verdi productions had been a failure.[116] The programme for the 1998 Festival was already on show during the 1997 Festival. Out-of-town guests could book two months in advance using all the usual methods, now even via the internet. The occupancy rate for opera performances was 97 per cent, for ballet 86 per cent. A total of 28 per cent of the total budget of 131 million Marks was generated by ticket sales.

When Peter Jonas met the Munich management consultant Roland Berger over dinner in 1998, his problems with stage technology had still not been solved, although the theatre had reduced its equipment budget from 2.5 million Marks in 1991 to 1.7 million Marks in 1997, despite the demanding stage concepts. Jonas took the opportunity to ask Berger to take on a pro bono project at the Staatsoper. Berger sent him Maurice Lausberg, whom he knew to have an interest in opera. 'It was in the evening, 6 o'clock, when I arrived at the Staatsoper for the first time, with my suit and tie and my big pilot's case,' Lausberg recalled. 'At some point the door opened and Jonas stepped out in his dinner jacket and said, as he was like that, "Pah, finally, salvation has arrived, the man from Berger."' A meeting was already in progress in Jonas's office, and Lausberg was supposed to join him. It was said that Jonas could be extremely charming. But that was the case only when he wanted to, which was not the case that evening. 'The first thing he did was take my pilot case and put it in the middle of the table. "Finally, someone has arrived who knows how to work properly. It's the clever Mr Lausberg from Roland Berger, a real brain. Now everyone: strap in tight." That's how you like to be introduced to new colleagues.'

Jonas wanted to understand the 'People's Republic of Technology' at last. Lausberg's task was to analyse the technical management, its processes and budgets. So he sat down in his tiny cubbyhole in the opera house and began his work.

The fruit of this was that the opera started to implement the fundamentals of project management. In particular, it started to use project plans with milestones, for example stipulating when concepts for stage design and direction had to be handed in or when the models had to be finished; the project team had to know when the final drawings would be delivered by the stage designer and when the construction rehearsal would have to take place so that the workshops would have enough time for production and any changes.

In addition, the Staatsoper introduced budgeting and cost allocation for projects and for the first time it recorded how much time professionals spent on their tasks and how much money was spent on particular tasks. In addition, the role of production manager was created: someone responsible for the project management of the productions.

It is not surprising that Jonas introduced these methods. What is astonishing, however, is that they were not yet a matter of course at the beginning of the 1990s – and that this mammoth operation had previously been able to function at such a high level without them.

When Jonas took over, he had inherited another work-in-progress then infamous among the public: the unfinished reorganisation of ticket sales at the State Theatres. There was an urgent need for action here, too. At the beginning of the 1990s, more than seventy theatres in Germany were selling their tickets via computerised sales systems. In its 1992 annual report, the Bavarian Audit Office quite rightly criticised the General Intendanz for not yet having introduced such a distribution system across the Central Services of the Bavarian State Theatres. The Central Services was the authority that had been responsible for ticket distribution at the Bavarian State Theatres, among others, since September 1993.

In the 1991–92 season, ticket sales for the Staatsoper were still handled manually. There was no central box office, the advance booking period was one week, and the option of ordering by telephone had only just been introduced. The Staatsoper's sales department alone accounted for 22.4 full-time staff positions, an absurdly high number, which was due to the fact that 'for reasons of cash security' two people always had to handle a sales transaction together. Including the Opera Festival, a total of 594,531 tickets were sold in this way during the 1991–92 season. And all that is before any discussion of the quality of customer service. The automation of sales meant that all the houses involved had the potential to achieve significantly higher capacity in the long term, and simply to be able to offer their customers a better service. It meant major savings.[117]

Jonas had a long way to go before he was able to announce an annual increase in the number of tickets sold – and the introduction of online ticketing (prices were now capped at 200 euros per ticket).[118] When *Norma*, starring Edita Gruberová, went on sale, online sales collapsed because within minutes the server was flooded with 30,000 ticket requests: a good problem to have. Offers such as the 99-Mark monthly ticket, tested in 2000, were only a side show.

Returning to his regular consulting business, Maurice Lausberg quickly realised that he would in fact rather work in the opera world. His experience of working with Jonas had him hooked. So Lausberg wrote to Jonas, they met and he was offered the job of production manager.

Queen of Spades, which premièred on 26 July 2002, was the first production in which Lausberg was able to test out the new processes he had been recommending as a consultant. In addition to weekly meetings to check in on the status of the various work processes, he held monthly meetings with Jonas, who was informed about the status of different developments, so he was able to make decisions about cost items that might result in budget overruns.

As these processes got underway, the whole matter quickly became boring for Jonas. 'With Jonas, if you wanted something, you always had to think about what he enjoyed. He was always so eager for new things, always doing crazy stuff. So, he had read somewhere that meetings go better when everyone is standing. So then everyone had to hold meetings standing up, and that was over again after a few weeks. But that's just how he was.'

The topic of sponsorship was of course not new for Jonas. After his successes in London, he might have chosen fundraising as a goal right at the beginning of his Intendanz. That he didn't was probably related to the Staatsoper's comfortable financial situation. Sponsorship? That's all to do with business, Jonas thought, so when the automobile manager Karl-Heinz Rumpf approached with an offer he handed the request over to Lausberg. The two were still in negotiations with the competition, and understood the potential. 'I said to Jonas: "This isn't working badly, why don't we do more of it?" I sat down, wrote a concept and then came back with fancy consultants' charts.'

Together with Bernd Feldmann, the marketing manager at the time, Lausberg researched the fifty largest companies in Munich and began sales work, which immediately bore fruit. In the first year, the Staatsoper concluded contracts amounting to 200,000 euros. 'The goal was to double sponsorship income over one year and triple it after two,'[119] Lausberg said. When the Free State demanded savings of 2.8 million euros in 2004, Jonas offered only 1.5 million euros following a session of his Star Chamber – sponsoring was already going extremely well at that time.

'The most effective way of doing sponsorship is to exercise mild blackmail',[120] Jonas had said before. He saw sponsorship as an element of a company's social responsibility. He made this case compellingly to the companies targeted, from his secure position as a representative of one of the leading cultural institutions in the Free State. What began almost on a whim became an enormous success that extended beyond his Intendanz. In 2018, the Staatsoper raised 4.7 million euros through sponsorship and donations.[121] Despite a prospering Munich economy, the success of the sponsorship programme was no foregone conclusion. A delicate touch was needed, because the Friends of the National Theatre Association, which had raised large sums for the reconstruction of the National Theatre and the programme of the Staatsoper since 1953, and ensured broad support for the opera among the population,[122] could also have seen these efforts as competition. Many members belonged to the circle of 'power brokers in a particular community', as Jonas put it. But in the end, the sponsoring programme was a success because Jonas and Lausberg built sales on the basis of a stringent concept right from the start and understood their activities in terms of what is called 'development' in America: the focus was strictly on establishing a long-term, continuous relationship between a sponsor and the Staatsoper; not the one-off transaction where sponsorship covers an immediate shortfall in funding.

'Our job is to stretch the economic boundaries for art as far as possible – and to go a little beyond those boundaries.'[123] Development was a leadership task for Jonas and successful because of it.

The stolid and the German were shaken off

In the first years of Jonas's Intendanz, a bon mot was doing the rounds in Munich: 'Since Jonas came to Munich, there have been no more unemployed directors in England.' Mocking voices spoke of the Staatsoper as the 'ENO-upon-Isar' or the 'English National Opera South'.[124] This perception even found its way into literature. In his novel *Bildnis eines Unsichtbaren* (Portrait of an Invisible Man), the Munich writer Hans Pleschinski brought to life 'the small miracle' that Munich experienced during this time: 'The stolid and the German were shaken off. It seemed as if Peter Jonas, the artistic director of the Münchner Nationaltheater, had travelled to his English homeland and invited a boisterous boy band: Come to Germany and shake up the theatre for me! There is money there, the stage machinery is first-class, 50,000 Marks for costumes and requisites, more or less … no problem!'[125] Did this image correspond to reality? Naturally, the funding of the Staatsoper was generous, the stage machinery now first class, following mammoth efforts in that area, but what about the British 'Boy Band'?

Looking at the whole period of his Intendanz, Jonas awarded 43 per cent of the directing commissions – thirty-five out of a total of eighty-one – to people from Britain. Note that David Alden, a native New Yorker, also liked to be counted among the British. With his fourteen productions, he had received a total of 17 per cent of the total directing commissions of the Jonas Intendanz – and consequently the title of house director from the press. Alden was followed by Andreas Homoki and the Briton David Pountney, with 6 per cent each. Of the total of seventy-nine commissions for stage designs, 24 per cent went to Britons. British conductors took over 32 per cent of the musical direction work.

Their successes with the Handel operas also brought fame to British singers such as Ann Murray and Christopher Robson. Since Alden and Pountney, as well as Mark Elder, Jonathan Miller, Nicholas Hytner and Richard Jones, had already worked with Jonas at ENO, in contrast to Nigel Lowery and Martin Duncan, there was more than a grain of truth in the wisecrack about 'ENO-upon-Isar'.

As far as the presence of women was concerned, the Staatsoper – with the exception of female singers, choristers and musicians – remained a man's world: Jonas awarded only three directing jobs to women, 8 per cent: Deborah Warner, Francesca Zambello and Doris Dörrie. For stage design, the rate was 12 per cent; for costume design, it rose to 43 per cent. Among the twenty-four people who received commissions for the musical direction of productions, there was only one woman, Simone Young, who was musically responsible for two productions. When asked why, Jonas just shrugged. There was no particular reason. It was the effects of the selection methods common to his generation of managers. Reports that had come to light since 2017 about abuse of power and sexism even in opera houses shocked him deeply. As director, he had never been confronted with such reports or accusations.

The fact that Jonas offered British artists, including singers, an exclusive, international podium was carefully noted in England and perceived as a service to the nation. On 31 December 1999, the Queen knighted Jonas in recognition of his artistic merits – and 'for services as General Director of the Bavarian Staatsoper'. In 1998, she had made him a Fellow of the Royal College of Music. The investiture on 27 April 2000 at Buckingham Palace was conducted by Prince Charles: 'I knelt, the prince struck me on each shoulder and said: "Arise, Sir Peter!"' After a short chat, Jonas was allowed to leave, walking backwards and bowing to the future monarch.[126]

Peter Jonas, the son of immigrant parents and born in south London, was now officially allowed to use the title 'Sir' – an honour that caused some confusion in Munich. He was rightly proud of the honorific. However, many employees found it difficult to address the boss by his first name. For a while he was incorrectly addressed as 'Sir Jonas', until the correct form 'Sir Peter' gained currency. Jonas was only too aware of the extent to which such an honour also implies certain obligations. The Queen's award was a compliment to the Bavarian Staatsoper and the Free State of Bavaria, he commented.

'The British relied on wit and musicality, joy in playing, which should ultimately lead to more happiness,' Pleschinski said, writing of the small miracle that happened in Munich 'with music that otherwise hardly drew crowds'. 'The productions became a crowd-puller and attracted audiences from all over the world. The greyness of the German post-war interpretations was wiped away.'[127] After the outstanding success of the production *Giulio Cesare in Egitto*, the house was under pressure ahead of the première of its second Baroque opera. 'Now everyone is sharpening their knives!' Jonas said to himself. 'If *Xerxes* had not been a success, I might have cancelled the whole Baroque cycle.'[128] But when the curtain fell on 26 February 1996, the audience went 'wild, as is usually the case only after the emotional thrusts of a Wagner or Puccini première'. The production by Martin Duncan and Ultz was 'brilliant', wrote Stephan Mösch in *Opernwelt*.

Many of the people from Munich's Kulturbürgertum who went to the theatre and visited exhibitions had not been attracted by the previous, more orthodox productions at the Staatsoper, Jonas told the *International Herald Tribune* in June 1996. But now they would come precisely because of these works, which were not part of the standard repertoire.[129]

L'incoronazione di Poppea, staged by David Alden, Paul Steinberg and Buki Shiff, was the first opera premièred at the 1997 Festival. A production of *L'Orfeo* by Achim Freyer and Erika Landertinger followed during the 1999 Festival.

When *Rinaldo*, in the production by David Alden, Paul Steinberg and Buki Shiff, premièred during the 2000 Festival, Hans Pleschinski was pleased 'in the sense of an artistic revenge that a composition that had not been considered for almost three hundred years was now attracting people by the thousands'. Tickets to the high-profile spectacles were hard to come by, according to Pleschinski, who did everything he could to get a ticket for the dress rehearsal. 'The crowd outside the gates of the Prinzregententheater was enormous. Five hundred Marks were being offered for admission.' For Pleschinski, the deeper reason for the incredible success of the long-forgotten works was obvious. 'With Baroque music, with its secure structures, the luxurious bel canto, the developments which are always led to a happy conclusion, people today wanted to recover – often perhaps instinctively – from the incessant demands of everyday life, of a world torn apart.' In the second act, Almirena begs King Argante to allow her to weep for her lost freedom. This scene, for which Alden created a breath-taking, oppressive image of suffering, made a deep impression on Pleschinski:

'The singer appeared to be transformed into a white shadow on stage. She seemed to have turned to ice. She floated motionless in space, almost lying down, as if suddenly overtaken by sleep. Her singing slowly melted into the playing of a single violin.

Lascia ch'io pianga,
Mia cruda sorte,
E che sospiri
La libertà

After ten minutes and the end of the quiet, urgent music, after the soft, gradual dissolution of the icy image and 'Lascia ch'io pianga', hardly anyone in the audience dared look away. With great difficulty, they began to break free from the powerful spell and into applause.'[130]

In his novel *Bildnis eines Unsichtbaren,* Hans Pleschinski created a literary monument to the Handel Renaissance created by Peter Jonas and the ensemble of the Bavarian Staatsoper. The single violin that Pleschinski mentioned was played by Barbara Burgdorf. 'It's beautiful, the things that theatre can do,' says Pleschinski's friend in *Bildnis eines Unsichtbaren* as they both leave the dress rehearsal of *Rinaldo* at the Prinzregententheater.

Programme and programme policy

Jonas liked to joke that he had offered the same playbill for thirteen years: in each season, two of the six to eight positions were filled with works by the so-called house gods: Mozart, Richard Strauss or Wagner, plus one Baroque opera and one world première. If one also takes into account the cycles such as the *Ring*, the Verdi and the Bel Canto operas with Edita Gruberová, only a few slots were left for other works. 'My love of underappreciated early-twentieth-century art, for example, didn't come into play at all: Schreker, Korngold, Busoni. Puccini also remained underexamined.'[131] Since Sawallisch had designed an entire season with the works of Richard Strauss, Jonas had to reduce the number of works by this particular house god, but instead included a total of eight Verdi operas in the programme.

Of the eighty-eight new productions of his Intendanz, eight were at the Munich cultural festival Festspiel+, ten were Munich premières and thirteen world premières. A total of fourteen productions were devoted to works of the Baroque period, and twenty-five to works of the twentieth and twentieth-first centuries. Fourteen of these works had first been performed after 1950.

The BSO is associated with important historic premières, especially of works by Wagner and Richard Strauss. Promoting contemporary composers had already been a preoccupation for Jonas during the London years. With just under twenty world premières (including works performed at Festspiel+), including those of works by Eckehard Meyer, Hans-Jürgen von Bose, Hans Werner Henze, Manfred Trojahn, Ruedi Häusermann, Aribert Reimann and Jörg Widmann, Jonas continued this tradition. Five of these premières were commissioned by the Staatsoper.

Jonas commissioned three world premières from the Swiss composer Ruedi Häusermann, with whose work he had become acquainted in 1999. The encounter was an eye-opener for him: Häusermann's work is an answer to the question of how music theatre can be renewed as an art form. Häusermann's first commission for the Munich Staatsoper was *KANON für geschlossene Gesellschaft*, premièred on 28 June 2000 as the opening of the Opera Festival at the Cuvilliés-Theater, 'an important and political statement due to the carefully-considered artistic decision to open established and traditional festivals with a completely new and innovative piece of music theatre.' Jonas saw the work as 'a reference point for Häusermann's brilliant ability to work with seemingly arbitrary improvisational ease in a highly complex and finely tuned, polished and rehearsed formal structure'.[132] This was followed in 2002 by *Väter Unser*, a work by and with Martin Hägler, Ruedi Häusermann, Theodor Huser and Philipp Läng, and in 2006 by *Gewähltes Profil: lautlos*.

In a completely different way, the première of Hans-Jürgen von Bose's work *Schlachthof V* on 1 July 1996 was a stirring experience for Jonas, his personal Solti moment. Von Bose himself had said that the 'martial title' for his 'comic-grotesque opera' was pointing in the wrong direction.[133] The work is named after the autobiographical and stylistically ambitious anti-war novel *Slaughterhouse-Five* by Kurt Vonnegut. As a result of widespread rumours and prejudices, there had already been two serious conflicts in the run-up to the production: the usual publishing house refused to print this opera, and *Schlachthof V* was finally published by Ricordi. Furthermore, an anonymous complaint was received by the Munich public prosecutor's office about Pierre Mendell's poster for the show. The public prosecutor's office failed to find anything criminal in it,[134] but Mendell had indeed created an extremely expressive, haunting poster for the première. A stylised propeller plane in red races towards the ground, on an iridescent black and grey background. The propeller in white forms a swastika.

A terrible row broke out in Munich society, and one that bore no relation to the content of the production itself. Jane Kramer wrote in the *New Yorker* that it was perceived that the word 'slaughterhouse' was a deliberate, subversive, British reference, and even the swastika on the poster constituted a libel against the German people.[135]

The audience reacted with 'orchestrated storms of booing', according to Jonas, who was accused of wanting to 'take revenge on the Germans' as a 'half-Jew'. Right at the beginning of the première, a chorus roared down from the balcony: 'Jonas, go home.' The guests threw leaflets from the stands. Jonas was stung, even though he kept his composure.

In addition to the world premières, Jonas reserved the remaining slots in the programme for rarities, which were often Munich premières. One of the real achievements of Jonas's Intendanz was that he brought these works to a broad audience.

The music of Leoš Janáček was central here: *The Excursions of Mr Brouček*, *Katja Kabanova*, *The Diary of One Who Disappeared*, and *The Cunning Little Vixen*. Jonas had chosen the others according to his personal taste: *The Midsummer Marriage* by Michael Tippett, *The Queen of Spades* by Pyotr Tchaikovsky, *Les Troyens* by Hector Berlioz, *The Rake's Progress* by Igor Stravinsky, *Lulu* by Alban Berg, *Pelléas et Mélisande* by Claude Debussy, as well as *The Rape of Lucretia* and *Billy Budd* by Benjamin Britten.

He prepared two farewell presents for himself and the Munich audience: one of his favourite operas, Humperdinck's *Königskindern*, in a production by Andreas Homoki, and – as the very last production of his Intendanz – Schönberg's *Moses und Aron* in a production by David Pountney, musical direction by Zubin Mehta.

Festspiel+

Munich opera festivals had traditionally been more of an extension of the normal season, with normal repertory performances bolstered with star casts and sold at inflated prices. Jonas, after his first few seasons, began to give the festivals a different profile: 'expansion of the programme, aesthetic intensification, increase in artistic quality and accessibility' were, according to Wolfgang Schreiber, the approaches Jonas took to the Festival. Above all, they were to be popular and affordable.[136] Accordingly, twenty per cent of all seats for the 1997 Festival cost under 25 Marks, and the highest price for a single ticket was 482 Marks.[137]

When advance sales for the Opera Festival began in January 1995, Jonas went to see the queue of customers, some of whom had waited overnight to get the best tickets. He described his conversations with young and old, conservative and adventurous opera-goers, who told him about their experiences in and hopes for the opera house; it was a particularly heart-warming experience. A woman bought bundles of tickets worth 3,600 Marks, not a single one of them for more than 70 Marks. She told Jonas bluntly that she did not approve of everything of his that she saw. But it was so exciting that she didn't want to miss anything.

Something like that meant more to him than official prizes. Jonas thought that the role of festivals could no longer be limited to offering the extraordinary. The music industry had created sufficient alternative outlets for that kind of spectacle. Jonas saw the potential of festivals to take on the function of a research and development department for theatres and opera houses. Audiences wanted to be aesthetically challenged and at the same time to party and indulge in pleasure. This may have been an idealistic image, but Jonas felt such things were worth taking seriously.[138]

Since 1993, Jonas Cornel Franz, who had studied at the Hochschule für Musik und Theater and who headed the directing course at the Bavarian Academy of Music and Theatre, had been working as artistic director of the experimental 'Labor' [laboratory]. From

1998 to 2006 Franz had put on 'Festspiel+' as an adjunct to the main programme. The music-theatrical experiments of this fringe programme took over precisely the research and development function that Jonas had wanted to see the main programme pursue. Festspiel+ was intended to push the 'boundaries of what can be done within the bailiwick of the Staatsoper as an institution,' said Jonas.[139] The three commissioned works by Ruedi Häusermann – *KANON für geschlossene Gesellschaft*, *Väter Unser* and *Gewähltes Profil: lautlos* – fulfilled this function.

At one point, Jonas used Festspiel+ to put up a satirical programme item: '*Vom deutschen Parken*', as Jonas titled the work. The idea was to make fun of the German way of parking. 'At that time, you could still park on Maximilianstraße. Three cars, which had to be repaired anyway, were banged up as part of the performance. Actors posing as passers-by and opera-goers came storming out of the Opern-Espresso café! I loved it. The programme book said: "The artist will be present." But nobody got it.'

Opera for all

The most effective way of organising sponsorship is to exercise mild blackmail, as Jonas had claimed in his article on Bayreuth (see 'Making Speeches').[140] He was talking about commercial enterprises there, which as social actors should feel an obligation to promote culture. Jonas, however, also knew how to use the argument to his advantage vis-à-vis the city administration and politicians.

After Jonas had received a promise from BMW Board member Richard Gaul of 250,000 euros to support a new project, he was able to use corporate assistance as a means of 'blackmailing' local politicians. The project in question lay close to Jonas's heart. 'When I came here, everyone was complaining that you could never get tickets. I thought, what could be nicer than watching an opera together on Max-Joseph-Platz on a summer evening?'

Jonas was inspired in his project by the work of Paul Hamlyn in London. The publisher and philanthropist belonged to a group of Jewish emigrants from Germany who were hugely influential in the British publishing world after the Second World War. Hamlyn financed a programme at the Royal Opera House in which tickets were given for free or sold at an extremely reduced price to people who could not otherwise afford to go to the opera. For several years he also financed the Covent Garden Proms, very popular with the audience. For this purpose, once a year, the seats in the stalls are completely removed. For a whole week, the audience could stand in the stalls or sit on the floor for moderate prices.

'Hamlyn's idea was fantastic,' enthused Jonas, who claimed to have invented the slogan 'Opera for all'. Here, too, he was inspired by his homeland. 'Opera for all' was the name of a British touring company founded in 1949 that performed operas in remote rural parts of the country. Today it is known as the 'English Touring Company'.

However, the only thing it had in common with the idea of transferring opera performances to city squares was the desire to allow as many people as possible to experience opera. 'Theatre for Everybody' was Lilian Baylis's core idea: she was the founder of Sadler's Wells Company, from which ENO emerged. It is only logical that the two monographs published so far on the history of Sadler's Wells and English National Opera should use this formulation. *A Theatre for Everybody* by musicologist Edward Dent appeared in 1945; *Opera for Everybody* by Susie Gilbert in 2009.[141] Jonas did not like these titles. To him, 'Opera for all', was better, because it sounded more comprehensive. By the end of his tenure in London, technological developments would have made live broadcasting to outside spectators possible in principle. But Jonas had not considered it a wise choice at ENO, not only because of the fickle British summer weather, but also because of the Coliseum's location in central London. The obvious place for a crowd to gather would have been Trafalgar Square. Although only a short walk from the Coliseum, even that distance would have proven a technical challenge. 'That was not all. When the performance is over, the singers have to be able to get out in front of the audience as soon as possible, otherwise the whole effect fizzles out,' Jonas explained.

The southern city of Munich, on the other hand, and the Nationaltheater with its façade, were ideal from this point of view. 'We just needed some towels for the cast. Then, barely a minute later, they could stand on the steps outside. That makes a huge difference!' But it wasn't quite that simple after all. 'In 1993–94, Munich was not the city that it is today,' Jonas recalled.

'The Staatskanzlei [state chancellery], the Staatsministerium, the City Council: one after the other they put obstacles in our way, tried to obstruct our project.' They levelled various arguments: they said that the whole project was technically impossible, that traffic would have to be diverted, and tram services too. In addition, more police would have to be deployed for it to work. 'It was a stroke of luck that Richard Gaul, who was a fan of our work, got involved in the project. It was his idea that BMW, as a Munich company, should link itself permanently to the Staatsoper. He wanted to create something that would not make it so easy for our successors to leave that partnership again. When the authorities stonewalled, I could say: "That's BMW's money! How can the city of Munich or the Free State say no when a company that builds cars in this city gives the money to make a popular festival for the whole city!" With this argument, we had won.'

It was mild blackmail: but the end justified the means. For the first public outing, in the summer of 1997, Jonas had not chosen just any old performance. Placido Domingo appeared for the first time as Don José in *Carmen*. For eighty per cent of the guests, it is said to have been their first visit to the opera. Since then, 'Opera for All' has taken place every year, with only one exception: 2016, the year of the Munich mass shooting.

'In the first year, everything was new. The screen was far too small, the quality was not good enough. Over the years, it got better and better. Now, years later, everyone says that an opera season without "Opera for All" is unthinkable!' Jonas was visibly proud. Every year, hours before the performance starts, opera fans start to fill the square. 'There, with their picnic baskets and wine, many an opera novice has turned into a fan. And at the end, when the singers appear in costume and Sir Peter in a kilt on the stairs, the evening becomes a real event and the Opera Festival has become a brand without equal,'[142] wrote Martina Kausch in *Die Welt*. Air mattresses, sun hats and fans are just as much a part of the accessories as, fortunately only rarely, umbrellas and umbrella capes. Dedicated fans don't let bad weather stop them.

At the end, Jonas led the singers onto the steps of the National Theatre 'and cracked jokes that got a few laughs. How many Brits can do that?' asked Tom Sutcliffe. 'The people of Munich love their opera, whatever they may think of some of the performances. They are willing to try anything and are clearly delighted to have a man at the helm of the opera who looks like a star and meets them halfway. Not just opera for everyone. Brilliant, provocative, exciting, moving, famous opera for everyone.'[143]

The concept was quickly copied internationally, including in Hanover, Düsseldorf, Dresden, Zurich, but also in Bayreuth and Berlin. Since 2007, BMW has also been cooperating with the Staatsoper Unter den Linden in Berlin, where it is called 'Staatsoper für alle'. 'At first, I didn't fully realise how important the sponsorship collaboration would become for the company's reputation,' Jonas admitted. The image transfer goes both ways.

Fig. 42: Applause for Diana Damrau at 'Opera for All', Munich, 2005

'I remember Richard Gaul saying to me: "Peter, you are an idiot. You should have registered the slogan as a trademark." I deliberately didn't do that. "Opera for All" was my favourite project. I did it for the opera, for the ensemble and the audience. My reward was to see all the those people in the square.'

When 2017 marked the twentieth 'Opera for All', Jonas's successor, Nikolaus Bachler, invited him to address the audience. 'I was very, very moved. Bachler never needed to do that.'

'"Accessibility", however, struck a nerve,' wrote Jonas in *Die Zeit* in 2013. 'The intoxication of music theatre, without uncomfortable formalities, under the stars and as part of a collective ritual, with all the gladiatorial tension of an arena, was suddenly a sexy alternative and at the same time became a seductive lure.'[144] Thanks to this renewed and exceptional success, Jonas was able to stave off declining attendance figures and arguments over access to culture.

Those would come only after his tenure had ended. As long as the target level of occupancy rate was reached – and that was the case during Jonas's Intendanz, contrary to trends elsewhere – Jonas did not have to concern himself with which part of society his guests came from. Making the Staatsoper accessible? He had achieved that goal: in 2006, the BSO represented the highest quality, both musically and aesthetically; the house was attracting a significantly younger audience; and the occupancy rate in his final season was 97 per cent. Jonas had prepared the company for the twenty-first century. However, accessibility was predominantly understood here as keeping tickets affordable and increasing the proportion of capacity used.

Jonas had never understood the formula 'opera for all' in the sense of Hilmar Hoffmann's cultural-political notion of 'culture for all'. He never engaged with Hoffmann's ideas, although a discussion between the two of them about Hoffmann's remarks on the political potential of opera would have been enlightening.[145] Jonas would have agreed with Hoffmann's idea of civilising a society through culture. But in his work at the Staatsoper, Jonas had not carried out Hoffmann's stated aim of consistently democratising cultural offerings. His efforts to broaden access to opera houses, these 'cathedrals of high culture', were often a problem for the people whose taxes subsidised them, even though he was aware that they lacked the cultural capital to even consider going to the opera.[146] 'Jonas perceived the desideratum and fulfilled it with "opera for all" by not fulfilling it: sitting on a picnic blanket on Max-Joseph-Platz and watching a broadcast on the big screen is completely different from actually stepping over the threshold of the National Theatre,' commented Christine Lemke-Matwey. 'The success of "Opera for All" proved him right. He did not have to go on proving that the Staatsoper was actually having an impact on other social segments of the city. That belief, so self-evident today, was not widely shared back then. At most, people wondered whether the standing-room ticket, for the tier where you can only see the conductor but not the stage, might be too expensive for students. Nobody thought about people from Giesing or Hasenbergl.' Sir Simon Rattle's Zukunft@Bphil programme was one of the first efforts at consistently implementing British-style ideas around cultural education as a means of expanding access in Germany. Rattle began this programme at the beginning of his first season with the Berliner Philharmoniker in 2002–03. We can assume that Jonas would also have had to address these issues had he remained in post, but as it was he merely noted the development. Overall, it passed him by.

Music theatre as social dramaturgy

Jonas rarely addressed the concept of the elite and elitism in his numerous speeches and articles. Where he did, his aim was to hold representatives of the elite, both inside and outside the theatres and opera houses, to account. In his view, 'cultural elitism was not a dirty word.' It was not only 'compatible with democracy, but even its basis'. Its aim was 'to help as many people as possible reach a higher level of understanding. Even if we succeed, we will have to accept that there will always be few who can and will rise to the challenge of Verdi's *Falstaff*, Tchaikovsky's *The Queen of Spades* and Wagner's *Parsifal* (not to mention Beethoven's string quartets and Shakespeare's sonnets), even though these as well as other works represent peaks of human expression.'[147]

The aim of all efforts at the opera houses must be to bring people to a pinnacle, a 'highest point of excellence' in the arts and to open this experience to all and make it accessible, intellectually and economically, to as broad a spectrum of society as possible.

The 'Munich Royal Court and National Theatre' was commissioned by King Maximilian I Joseph in 1810 as the first opera house that aimed to recruit its audience from beyond the ranks of the royal family and the court, and opened its doors to the general public as well. Around 2,000 seats for a population of 54,000 people: that made four per cent, Jonas pointed out.[148] 'Compare this situation to London!' Jonas liked to exclaim in his speeches.

'We who work in theatre also fear the moments of confrontation with the stubbornness of those who refuse to open their elitist opera world to others. They prefer to think of our world as a cosy extension of those old salons of the upper bourgeoisie, which in most cities, however, are quite outdated. They hide their insecurity under the cloak of pseudo-exclusivity.'[149]

In order for this elite, whose access to the offerings of 'high culture' is guaranteed, 'not to remain an exclusive club',[150] Jonas posited that music theatre must see itself as social dramaturgy.[151] Quality, accessibility and the right to fail were the three central components of this approach to reflecting society in music theatre. According to Jonas, opera must challenge our sense of ourselves and the habits and political tendencies in our society. People needed shared ritual, shared experience, either in a religious sense as a dialogue with God or in a profane sense as an inner dialogue with themselves or with others. 'We theatre-makers are obliged to make it clear with our work that culture is just as important for life as education or hospital beds. And when they tell me: "A hospital bed is much more important than a place in the theatre," then I reply: that's right, everyone is able to come to the hospital, but not everyone is sick!'[152] Jonas would often point out that cardiology clinics were used by only about ten per cent of the population, yet no one questioned their utility. Despite his sympathy and curiosity for the tricks of the politician's trade, he considered the world of art more important than 'fights in the boxing ring of politics'. Audience numbers, high revenues, good reviews: he did everything in his power to fulfil these criteria, but he was of the opinion that 'such methods of assessment miss the point of art'. He demanded a deeper, more appropriate understanding of art from politics: 'serious art can stimulate our intelligence, deepen our emotions, expand our vision of the world and open the way to unimagined realms of beauty and tragedy. Art demands attention, concentration and knowledge – qualities that exist only sparsely in our media-dominated epoch.'[153]

He repeated at every opportunity that Bavaria was a Kulturstaat, a 'state of culture', and that this was written in its constitution. He wanted to oblige politicians to make the best and most generous decisions for culture possible, beyond those measures they had settled on so far.

His speech notes for an evening with the Freunden und Förderern des Nationaltheaters [Friends and Patrons of the National Theatre] in November 2002 show how precisely, how meticulously Jonas prepared for performances and how carefully he planned his words. His speaking notes were printed in a size that made for comfortable reading. He marked all words that could be a pitfall for a Brit, especially numbers or words with umlauts, but also transitions between individual pages, using his own system of lines. He started his speech by evoking a sense of fellowship, but then immediately broke through it by obliging his audience to behave in a certain way: 'our opera – your opera – is the forum where we can all confront ourselves and assure ourselves that we have indeed left behind animalism and pure, primitive greed.'[154]

He used his appearances at the Freunden und Förderern des Nationaltheaters to promote his own work and draw attention to awards won by artists from his theatre. When he mentioned that Alden had received the Bavarian Theatre Award for his individual artistic achievements, the notes read: 'Stage direction; wait a moment and face the people!'

He noted he had been invited to attend the Queen's Lecture in Berlin. And that Jane Kramer, in her major article in the *New Yorker* on Chancellor Schröder, had paid tribute to Konwitschny's *Tristan und Isolde*, claiming this production of the Munich Opera Festival 'has more to say to the world about Germany and German consciousness than anything she has found in the words and promises of any politician standing for election, including a Chancellor.'[155] Specifically, she had written that it was a production 'that laughs at itself and at the same time breaks your heart by singing its way out of the deadly entanglements of history that have plagued German opera and politics since the Second World War.'[156]

At another event, Jonas mentioned that Kramer had called the BSO 'one of the best opera houses in the world – and certainly the most interesting'.

In Jonas's speeches, he always argued both politically and intellectually, supporting his words with an emphasis that was unusual to German ears: subsidised theatres, he argued, have the duty 'to prove to the community that a true adventure for hearts and minds can be within everyone's reach'.[157] In a way, he wrote as he spoke. In fact, he directly addressed the effect of his words on the audience when he stated that he was once again on an 'odyssey in a highbrow, "politically correct" art jargon that was full of hot air'.[158]

He liked to break up the argument of his speeches with a reading that excited him. So, in many of his speeches and addresses, such as his Queen's Lecture of 2011, there is an excursus in which he talks about George Steiner's *Grammars of Creation*.

Steiner's magnum opus is a broad investigation of the idea of creation in Western thought, in its literature, religion and history. Steiner recognises that technology and science have replaced art and literature as the driving forces of our culture, and warns that this has not come without significant loss. This is a warning that Jonas took up himself. Or he quoted Pierre Simon Laplace's *Essai philosophique sur les probabilités*.[159]

Sometimes he chose awkward comparisons: 'Even love between two persons is like art: one has to work at it.'[160] And again and again he had facts and figures at the ready, deployed to show his house in the best light – even if 'such methods of assessment miss the point of art': the BSO was the most productive of all opera houses in Germany because it has the highest attendance figures and the lowest subsidies per seat. It received the highest subsidy in absolute terms, but the lowest in terms of tickets sold. Only 60 per cent of the total budget came from public subsidies.

Jonas was also able to be concrete: the BSO managed 350 performances of 51 operas and 22 ballets, ten of which were new productions, in one season. The Opera Festival staged 30 operas in six weeks, generating about a quarter of the annual takings.

By the end of Jonas's Intendanz, the proportion of subscribers had risen from 21 to 26 per cent; the proportion of tickets sold at full price rose by 12 per cent and the number of first-time visitors by around 4 per cent since 2000.[161] 'Under Jonas, the Staatsoper has learned to sing its own praises,' wrote Beate Kayser in *tz*.[162]

So shalt thou feed on death, which feeds on men

'No hope for you, boy, you will be sleeping on a park bench…'[163] was something Jonas had often heard his mother say. He found it hard to be in close contact with her for long. Only when he began to work through his traumatic childhood experiences in analysis was he able to decide to stop resenting his mother for her shortcomings. 'In some ways Peter did not respect his mother. He was very stiff with her,' his cousin Monica Melamid said.

'She had been twisted. When Kathryn died, she lost her mind a little and got stuck in her traumas. When she got older, she was a difficult person.'[164]

Only shortly before Hilda May's death did Jonas manage to re-establish a personal relationship with her. In old age, she lost her short-term memory almost completely and became confused. She refused to pay taxes in the UK and resisted moving into a home. She did not even want to let a care service come to her house in Sanderstead. There she lived like a hermit. The house was visibly falling apart. Jonas had to intervene. 'The only relaxing days in the life of a theatre director are the days after the premières. So I took the day off and flew to London Gatwick at 6.40am,' Jonas said. He rented a small car and shopped at the supermarket. 'I went to her house, cleaned and served her a small lunch. We turned on the television. She loved it, even if she wasn't really watching. When the weather was good, we visited my sister's grave.' And at 5.30pm he flew back to Munich.

In July 2001, Hilda May Jonas died in her son's arms.

Fig. 43: Peter Jonas and his mother Hilda May, c. 2000

With his remarkably precise memory, Jonas had a particular talent for memorising verse. Shakespeare's Sonnet 146 meant a lot to him and he often recited it. In it, the lyrical 'I' addresses his own soul:

> 'Poor soul, the centre of my sinful earth
> Why so large a cost, having so short a lease,
> Dost thou upon thy fading mansion spend?'

With death as a constant companion, Jonas never seemed to be able to get away from how 'short our lease on this earth' is. He returned to this phrase again and again, a legal term worked into Shakespeare's poetry.

The death of his mother was not the only loss for Jonas during these years. Right at the beginning of his Intendanz, on 16 November 1993, Lucia Popp died in Munich from an inoperable brain tumour. For the opera world, this news came as a surprise. Close friends, including Jonas, had been with Popp to the end.

Jonas did not attend the funeral of Antony Costley-White, his friend since student days. He was angry and sought solitude in the mountains. Antony had chosen suicide and met his end on the train tracks near Shrivenham, outside Oxford, on the afternoon of 18 April 1998. His divorce papers had been finalised shortly prior to his death.

Pierre Mendell died on 19 December 2008. Throughout Jonas's entire Intendanz, he was responsible for the Staatsoper's public image. The pair had become close friends over that work. 'I quite like it here, here on this earth,' – that was Mendell's phrase that Jonas was so fond of borrowing. Mendell, terminally ill himself, could not end his own life. 'He waited too long. He had passed that point.' Jonas was with him, too.

'So shalt thou feed on death, that feeds on men,' Shakespeare had written.

Jonas was surrounded by many whom he considered friends. The content of these relationships could vary a great deal. Some had met him during his Munich years, but basically knew nothing about the person he had been before he stepped into the professional limelight. Sometimes purely private matters were not discussed at all.

Donna Leon got to know Jonas as artistic director of the Staatsoper. Like Jonas, the American writer is a connoisseur of the Baroque. After travelling from Venice to Munich for a performance of *Giulio Cesare in Egitto*, she had written a letter of thanks to Jonas, who, as was his habit, answered it personally. Leon had then attended all Baroque productions at Munich, and they became friends.

Even former staff members who had left the BSO, often but not always his protégés, wound up becoming friends. Jonas was not pleased by the thought he could never know for sure whether these friendships were motivated by the career opportunities he could offer. For his part, he saw no conflict of interest, even though he was the one who gave orders, made recommendations and opened doors.

In his life, there were only a handful of people who failed to live up to his trust and esteem. He was very aware of who was no longer in contact in the last phase of his life. Being close to a dying person is not easy, he said, skirting the question of whether their silence hurt him.

Footsteps in the past

In the late 1990s, a request from the BBC opened a door that Jonas had thought closed for good. The BBC asked him to take part in a recording of *This is Your Life* in London. In the show, prominent guests told colourful stories about their lives. The producers tracked down people who had played a role in the celebrities' lives and invited them on as surprise guests. For Jonas, they brought on Lesley Garrett, his former partner and lifelong friend, who had carved out a career in pop and as an entertainer after her time in opera. The show was a lot of fun for them both.

When Jonas flew back to Munich, that seemed to be the end of the story. But Lesley Garrett's neighbour had seen the broadcast and knew that Peter Jonas, with whom she had spent some summer holidays as a child, was in fact her stepbrother. She was Pauline's daughter. Trembling, she stood at Garrett's door. Pauline had only recently died and had left her daughters Walter's documents. Garrett knew that Jonas did not have a single document from his father. 'What a lucky coincidence,' Garrett exclaimed, looking back. 'What were the chances of my neighbour seeing him on the show and making the connection to contact me to get in touch? Peter always seemed to have the good fortune of having things come to him in strange ways. As if his path had been planned out.'[165] Garrett mediated the meeting between the two. Jonas was able to see some key documents: Walter's birth certificate from the Altona registry office, a certificate of competency from the British volunteer Home Guard in the Second World War dated 16 February 1944, an 'Occupational Force Travel Permit' from 1952, the naturalisation certificate from 29 October 1944 and his passports.

But Pauline's daughter also told Jonas about their marriage, about how Walter changed at Pauline's side and how he died. And she handed over letters Jonas had written to his father during his time at Worth School. His father's legacy gave him comfort, but also stirred something. Once again he realised how little he knew of his family's history.

When Peter Jonas took up his post in Munich, he got a letter from Max Sebald. Sebald emphasised the extraordinary importance of Jonas working in Germany: 'Your family is back in Germany.' An intensive correspondence developed between the two. In 2001, Jonas received a small parcel sent to him by the publishing house Hamish Hamilton. It contained Sebald's novel *Austerlitz*. A card was enclosed: 'Max Sebald wants you to have this with his love. He does not want you to miss the following pages…' Now Jonas discovered that Sebald had incorporated his own boarding-school experiences into the character of Austerlitz. Once again, the memory of the boy he had been rose up in him, remembering each day anew 'that I was not at home now, but very far away, in some kind of captivity', as Sebald had Austerlitz put it.[166] 'Since my childhood and youth,' he finally said, looking at me again, 'I have not known who I am in truth. From where I stand now, of course, I see that my name alone and the fact that it was kept from me until my fifteenth year, ought to have put me on the track of my origins, but it has also become clear to me of late why an agency greater or superior to my own capacity for thought, which circumspectly directs operations somewhere in my brain, has always preserved me from my own secret, systematically preventing me from drawing the obvious conclusions and embarking on the inquiries they would have suggested to me.'[167]

Fig. 44: Peter Jonas in Worth rugby team, 1963

Even the photo Jonas had shown him of his rugby XV at Worth had inspired Sebald to use such an image. 'As I approach death, I get sentimental about this. These are very moving moments. Because they are totally by chance. Who was I? Nobody. And Max found me. Or we found each other.' Jonas did not want to hold back his tears. 'But he touched things nobody else could touch.' In his search for his lost memories, 'marks of pain which ... trace countless fine lines through history',[168] Sebald had once again opened up a new path.

Jonas invited Sebald to give the opening speech at the 2001 Opera Festival. He had left the choice of subject entirely open: Jonas would not have been surprised had Sebald spoken about his emigration or the gap between the Germans and the British. Or if Sebald had brought up the bombing of German cities during the Second World War. In 1999, Sebald's collection of essays *On the Natural History of Destruction* was published in German under the title *Luftkrieg und Literatur*. In it, Sebald took the view that a kind of oath of silence had prevented the experience of suffering during the bombing raids from being dealt with in German literature.

Sebald appeared on stage without a script and spoke about Vincenzo Bellini. Sebald had described Bellini's music in his works *Die Ausgewanderten* and *Auf ungeheuer dünnem Eis* as a boon and blessing that made his heart leap every time.

When Jonas gave what he considered to be the most important speech of his life, in 2017, on Wieland Wagner, he too opened with Bellini: 'My own tribute of love for Max. For what he secretly gave me without knowing why. A symbol for my love for Max. For giving me something so valuable.'

After the publication of *Austerlitz*, and even after Sebald's death, Sebald's publishers would send Jonas a copy of every new work. Jonas kept in touch with Ute, who lived in Norwich after Sebald's premature death.

Respect and appreciate artists!

The Free State of Bavaria recognised the achievements of their Staatsintendant a little later than the Queen had done. While another British honour followed in 2000 – he was made a Fellow of the Royal Northern College of Music – nothing from the Germans until the following year. Sir Peter was then awarded the Constitutional Medal of the Free State of Bavaria and the Bavarian Order of Merit in 2001. He clearly preferred the latter, which offered the advantage that the recipient would henceforth have 'free admission to Bavarian museums'.

In 2003, he received the Kulturellen Ehrenpreis [Cultural Award of Honour] of the City of Munich and used the occasion to make an 'incendiary speech':[169] Jonas, who belonged to no party and who no longer felt any 'ambitions for the future', did, however, feel obliged to fulfil the first duty of a citizen: 'distrust of authority. Politicians love to be valorised by cultural institutions and are often mistakenly tempted to believe that their responsibility for these institutions implies ownership.'

Politics, he said, should not 'march in step with the powers of the global consumer market and the mass media to bury art, artists and artistic institutions'. The twenty-seven years of war between Athens and Sparta had been enough to destroy Athens, 'the city at the pinnacle of its age'. The city of Munich, which in his opinion had 'the best and most impressive cultural institutions in the world' – although 'small' – had to at last rally its cultural forces, be they municipal, state or private, and communicate an international image 'that corresponds to its actual importance and its possibilities as a leading location for music, art and literature'. 'I implore you: Respect and appreciate the artists ... and all those who, through honest and hard work at the artistic institutions of this city, contribute to making Munich live up to its nickname of "Athens on the Isar".'[170]

The audience is said to have roared its approval. The fact that Minister of State Goppel, as well as his most important officials, were absent was noticed and criticised by the press: had they 'stayed away because the laureate (Intendant of a state institution!) and his free speech do not fit into the minister's landscape at the moment? A bottomless affront,' raged the tabloid *tz*.

Fig. 45: Awarded the Order of Maximilian, Munich, 2008

When the Munich Faschingsgesellschaft [Carnival Society] awarded Jonas the Order of Karl Valentin in 2006, it seemed like something of a reconciliation between the people of Munich and Jonas's often wry sense of humour. In 2008, the Free State of Bavaria honoured him with its highest award, the Bavarian Order of Maximilian for Science and Art.

Not an opera crisis, a Berlin crisis!

The Deutsche Opernkonferenz [German Opera Conference] had been founded in 1957, but over the years it had never really managed to establish a reputation as an effective lobbyist for the most important German-language opera houses. The focus of their biennial meetings was the exchange of experiences, consultation on current topics, developments and, above all, discussions about the level of fees.

Its role in cultural policy changed abruptly when the representatives of its member theatres were invited to a meeting on 14 October 2000. Jonas remembered the exact date, as it was his fifty-fourth birthday. The Berlin Senator for Culture, Christoph Stölzl, in office since April 2000, presented a proposed new reform programme: 'Measures for Structural Reform of the Stage'. Opera reform lay at the centrepiece. The concept envisaged merging the Staatsoper Unter den Linden and the Deutsche Oper Berlin, drastically reducing the size of their orchestras, especially that of the Staatsoper, and enabling the musicians to be deployed reciprocally by means of a collective in-house agreement.[171] Stölzl then planned to assign content-related programmes to the theatres, which would follow specific repertory boundaries.

Jonas considered this very idea 'most impudent', the paper as a whole 'nonsense', a 'document of contempt' towards the arts, artistic directors and artists.[172] From his point of view, the point of view of a Munich resident, this was not an opera crisis but a Berlin crisis, rooted in the fact that Helmut Kohl's government had already cut the capital's cultural budget at the end of the 1980s. Jonas was not alone in voicing this criticism. Hans-Dietrich Genscher, as chairman of the Friends of the Staatsoper House, and Richard von Weizsäcker also rejected Stölzl's proposals. Representatives of the opera conference also reacted indignantly, especially because Stölzl had not consulted them in advance.[173]

'We were in defensive mode. My heart is always with the left,' Jonas commented. The Opera Conference scheduled a discussion meeting for 27 October 2000. The meeting was moderated by the chairman, Götz Friedrich. During the discussion session, the otherwise-eloquent Stölzl was 'downright dismantled by Jonas and Alexander Pereira from the Zurich Opera House, but was clever enough to invite the critics to write a counter-paper with their own proposals,' reported Jörg Lau.[174] But Götz Friedrich, Jonas and Pereira approached the question in different ways. Friedrich was the epitome of an artist-Intendant; Jonas and Pereira stood for the type of Intendant who concentrated exclusively on the artistic direction, management and financing of their house.

Jonas drew up the agreed counter-opinion jointly with Maurice Lausberg, who was in the process of setting up the new department for development and sponsorship at the Munich Staatsoper.

Little more than a year later, Jonas had the opportunity to revisit the debate with Stölzl at his Queen's Lecture at the Technische Universität Berlin in November 2001. He had been reprimanded by Stölzl, abjured to wake up and understand reality on planet Berlin: 'the non-existence of financial resources on this planet is an incontrovertible fact, doomsday for the arts, especially opera, is inevitable, and rationalisation is only a matter of time.'[175] But Jonas argued that Stölzl had failed to recognise the crucial importance of the identities of the three houses.

Jonas liked to get into such conflicts. 'In this case, he had nothing to lose, but a lot to gain. He brought his experience from his time in London, and his international expertise was trusted,' commented Christine Lemke-Matwey. 'Christoph Stölzl, in particular, fired off some good broadsides, which PJ was able to counter with as much elegance as relish.'

The counter-assessment was available very swiftly. Its core statement was that 'through targeted structural measures, sufficient funds could be saved to escape the debt trap even without a merger, and with a considerably smaller reduction in staff of only 78 jobs.'[176] The Stölzl plan disappeared at the turn of the year 2000–01. On 17 January 2001, Adrienne Goehler succeeded Christoph Stölzl as Senator for Culture. In the meantime, Stölzl's concept had already become 'wastepaper',[177] due to a federal subsidy that implicitly recognised the demands of the houses threatened with merger.

After Götz Friedrich died unexpectedly in December 2000, only two months after the initial meeting, the Opernkonferenz elected Peter Jonas as its first chairman in May 2001. His deputies were Klaus Zehelein from the Stuttgart Staatsoper and Alexander Pereira. This election put into place three 'personalities who can keep their houses on a clearly recognisable line, precisely because they don't ride their hobby horses, but rally the team around a shared goal. All these top cultural managers are not performing artists,' Frederik Hanssen wrote.[178]

International media also took note. In August 2001, the *New Yorker* published an eight-page article by Jane Kramer, which appeared in their successful '*Letter from Europe*' series. The great artistic directors like Zehelein and Jonas 'become powerful cultural personages, not only in the public face of an opera house but in a very real way its identity, and people associate them with a particular style and character, and even a particular take on Germanness.'[179]

Under Jonas's Intendanz, the BSO had developed into one of the most important and best, and sometimes one of the most surprising, opera houses in the Federal Republic of Germany, Kramer attested.[180] Jonas was known for his vision of the BSO as a 'sophisticated and eclectic big-city house', but also for the way he could persuade Bavarian audiences to accept and even expect the BSO to act in this way. Berlin had no director with such a reputation, she argued.[181] Jane Kramer's article in the *New Yorker* was an accolade for Jonas on a global stage. It was the ultimate proof of his success, 'the greatest prize I ever won, more important than the Bavarian Order of Merit or the Order of Maximilian.'

The fact that Jane Kramer had already criticised Christoph Stölzl for his exhibition at the German Historical Museum, which presented Goethe and Weimar Classicism in the foreground but National Socialism in a small, dark room, was a mere footnote.[182]

In the years that followed, Jonas continued to campaign for the preservation of all three Berlin opera houses. The financing of the opera houses in Berlin accounted for only 0.8 per cent of the total budget, so no house should close: that was his position. He called Finance Senator Thilo Sarrazin a 'cultural ignoramus and philistine'.[183]

When the federal government bailed out Berlin's cultural budget in the summer of 2003, the future of all three houses was secured. When the 'Opera in Berlin' foundation was established on 1

January 2004, Jonas became a member of the foundation's board. He was aware of the danger that this solution could become a model for other cultural institutions. He had submitted a paper to the Staatsministerium on behalf of the BSO, a self-owned enterprise, in which he discussed the pros and cons of the legal forms of foundation and limited liability company.[184]

Jonas was a member of the Board of Trustees of the 'Opera in Berlin' Foundation until 2012. This period saw the gruelling search for a general director, a hot seat, as everyone agreed, after Michael Schindhelm resigned after less than two years in February 2007, but also controversial personnel decisions, all of which Jonas supported.

They had also brought him into conflict with his friend Daniel Barenboim. Barenboim was deeply disappointed when Jonas, as chairman of the Opera Conference, advocated the establishment of the Opera Foundation. 'Of course I was absolutely against it, because the independence of each house seemed to me to be of existential importance,' Barenboim explained. 'We talked it out afterwards. Peter said to me: "Daniel, you know how important you are to me, but in the situation where there was a danger that one of the Berlin houses could be closed, I had to fight to keep them all." I finally understood him, but to this day I still don't understand why the foundation had to stay after the danger had passed. It was really very hard. He is a very close friend.'

Being the one that got away

Jonas never regretted retiring at the age of sixty. He had wanted his life back – and he and his wife enjoyed what life had left for them, something he did not take for granted. There were the burdens that came with new treatments, but all the same they enjoyed life to the full. Since his time at boarding school, he had spent his life within institutions. Now he wanted to know if he could do without all that, the structures, the hierarchies, the balance of power.

'I've had a rocky life, not just professionally,' he had told Stephen Moss of the *Guardian*. 'I wanted to be the one who got away.'

In February 2001 Jonas and Zubin Mehta had announced the final extension of their contracts, to the end of the 2005–06 season. When the time came and the final season had begun, to close confidants Jonas seemed a changed man. 'Nothing and no one goes unchanged,' as Randy Crawford had sung.

He wasn't always in the best of moods at this time. The loss of the power that had accompanied him for so many decades must have been most difficult to cope with. Jonas was a powerful person, both inside and outside the Staatsoper, with the most extensive networks. He was deeply anchored in Munich society. Although the people of Munich had not liked him at first, when he left they did not want to let him go. Just like in London, when they had commented that Jonas really cared about the appearance of the foyers, he had been feared in Munich because he saw everything, no matter whether 'the towels in the toilets were replenished, or whether the back stage curtain was really closed and you could no longer see an emergency exit sign. He simply burned for the cause. He shouldered the responsibility,' Natalia Ritzkowsky said. 'You didn't realise how much this responsibility had weighed on him until the last three quarters of the year, when he was suddenly as if liberated, more cheerful and accessible.'

The strike by Länder [state] civil servants against the 42-hour week offered Jonas a final big stage in spring 2006 on which to demonstrate superb crisis management skills. From 13 February, the Staatsoper was affected too, 'but we never lost a performance!' Jonas was proud of that. Some of the operas were performed as concerts, while others had their sets adapted.

Even during his successor's Intendanz, the staff spoke of how Jonas had dealt with this crisis. He had not denounced anyone, but instead positioned himself clearly and confidently and without any arguments. 'Our theatre machinists got 1,600 euros gross, that's what it was all about!' Jonas, who had said many times before that his heart beat on the left, was outraged. 'They were not a special case, they were like the bus drivers and so many others. But in a state like Bavaria, which is really not poor! It was about twenty or thirty euros difference per month. To my innocent mind that doesn't make any sense. Finance Minister Faltlhauser behaved really dishonourably.'

This made Jonas angry. So he stepped up to the ramp before a performance and explained his stance to the audience. The Ministry of Finance, which was officially negotiating with the unions, was of course 'less than happy', Toni Schmid said.

The retaliation came promptly: 'My enemies were the right wing of the CSU,' Jonas said. 'This small group took every opportunity to attack me, including at that moment: he should be dismissed, they said. Because I had criticised the Minister of Finance.' An absurd idea, just a few weeks before the end of his Intendanz. In April 2006 he took advantage of an interview with *Die Zeit* to kick out once more in the press against these 'typical beer-brains'. Zehetmair, he said, had been a person with culture and instinct, 'Goppel too, perhaps. But today, under the Stoibers and Faltlhausers, all that counts is football and balanced budgets and the question of why we don't outsource everything, from orchestras to technology. That depresses me.'[185] He had never experienced so much ignorance, philistinism and haughty condescension.

For his final season, which achieved a fantastic occupancy rate of 98.4 per cent, Jonas decided to present eleven of the fourteen productions from the Baroque repertoire once again, some of them for the last time. With this decision, he also fulfilled what was regarded internationally as his great success: the renaissance of Baroque opera. The BSO's programming policy had emphatically demonstrated that Baroque operas were 'not just fare for early-music aficionados but also compelling music dramas that in contemporary productions could hold the stages of major houses', Anthony Tommasini said, praising Jonas's achievement in his obituary for the *New York Times*.[186] The *New York Times* also ran a critical piece by Anne Midgette. She said, following his departure in 2006, that a certain stagnation had set in, and noted that many of Munich's successful productions dated from the beginning of his tenure, 'when production values seemed to eclipse musical values entirely'. This difference was evened out only when Zubin Mehta took over in 1998.

In the last years of his Intendanz, however, the critics' attention was directed away from Munich and towards such houses as the Stuttgart Staatsoper, which had succeeded in producing 'equally provocative but arguably more thoughtful' performances, Midgette judged.[187] She overlooked the significance of the off-beat elements in the repertoire where Jonas had implemented his personal preferences – especially *A Midsummer Marriage* – with the highest standards of modern directorial theatre.

Bringing these little-known works to the attention of the BSO audience is a merit in itself. 'Jonas has undoubtedly done what he was hired to do – transform the Bavarian Staatsoper from a symbol of reaction into a tone-setting, fashionable house,'[188] wrote Tom Sutcliffe in the *Spectator*. The strength and energy it took for all those involved to transform the Bavarian Staatsoper in Munich from an administration into a modern opera business is surely hard to grasp. 'Sir Peter has found the right way between risk and stereotyping, a path that also fulfils one's obligations towards the institution, which must remain healthy and intact,'[189] said Christian Berner of Zurich Opera.

'The theatre must remain independent, self-willed and a counterweight to everything that seems so secure in society,'[190] Peter Jonas had insisted in July 1994 in a speech at the Cuvilliés-Theater. At the time, he had just taken over the leadership of one of the most prestigious, most traditional and most elitist institutions in the Federal Republic of Germany, the pride of the Bavarian Free State. No other cultural institution could have felt more certain about its work. Jonas was going to work on the very DNA of the Staatsoper.

'Germany has always led developments in theatre, but not in Munich – until Peter came along,' David Alden opined. 'Peter had to somehow get these southern, splendid, rich, well-financed, well-upholstered Munich people to wake up.'

Fig. 46: Sir Peter next to his portrait by Charlotte Harris

Jonas wanted to shift the existential significance that the house had for its guests onto a new footing. His work greatly changed his audience, made them receptive and curious. Intellectually and artistically, but also in terms of management, Peter Jonas adapted the BSO to meet the demands of the twenty-first century. 'Peter Jonas has brought Munich opera into the present day. He left behind a trace of himself which the house still draws on today,' was Christine Lemke-Matwey's verdict. Jonas wanted 'to become a part of the establishment in order to fight the things he dislikes. He manages the balancing act of being part of the establishment without fitting in,' as someone who knew him very well had put it. 'He is admired by many for this, but in doing so he also provokes enmity,'[191] Barenboim observed.

Jonas endured these headwinds, these enmities, even though he too had to realise: nothing and no one goes unchanged. 'I remember his last months at the Bavarian Staatsoper as a great farewell party,' Barbara Burgdorf described. 'That went to the limit of his strength.'

31 July 2006 was the day of the farewell performance, a Monday. It began in the afternoon with a performance of *Meistersinger*

von Nürnberg. The stage entrance was covered with a red carpet: 'Goodbye Sir Peter Jonas, goodbye Zubin Mehta. Thank you very much!' it read in gold. During the first interval, the Friends of the Munich National Theatre unveiled an oil painting they had donated, which would henceforth hang in the portrait gallery of the National Theatre there.

Jonas had chosen Charlotte Harris as the artist. Although she was only twenty-five, the National Portrait Gallery had already commissioned a painting from her. Her portrait of Jonas shows him looking serious and deep in thought, in a turtleneck, dark blue jacket and yellow scarf. Behind him, the red backs of the seats in the stalls can be seen, the beginning of the orchestra pit and the stage no longer visible in the darkness. Harris depicted Jonas in three-quarter and profile view, his left ear hidden, his left hand with the wedding ring captured in the moment of an impulsive movement. Jonas could have chosen anyone for this portrait for the historic gallery. However, the fact that he trusted a representative of the next generation was perhaps symbolic: Jonas had the coming generation on his mind, and he wanted it to succeed.

Aron Stiehl thought that Jonas's greatness could be seen in the way he staged the very last evening of his Intendanz. Although it was to be his and Zubin Mehta's farewell evening, it was also the evening on which the great bass Kurt Moll celebrated his farewell after a 47-year career. 'It was a brilliant idea by Jonas: Moll had made his debut at the Staatsoper with the role of the Night Watchman, and now he would end his career in this role,' Stiehl described. 'Jonas knew that Moll would steal the show from him and Mehta, and he let it happen. Thousands of directors would have given Moll a separate farewell, but not Peter Jonas.'

Even though the role of the Night Watchman – 'Hört, ihr Leut', und laßt euch sagen [Listen, you people, and let me tell you]' – only comprises a few bars, the audience was already gripped after his appearance at the end of the second act. When the final chords had faded away and Jonas – with striped socks under his dinner jacket – and Mehta entered the stage, the audience went wild. Thousands of white handkerchiefs, placed on seats at the start of the third act, fluttered in spectators' hands.

Fig. 47: Sir Peter and Zubin Mehta say goodbye

It was said that the applause could have gone on forever if Minister Goppel had not started his speech. In gratitude for their achievements, he appointed Jonas and Mehta honorary members of the Bavarian Staatsoper.

Theatre is about the moment, Jonas had said. When an Intendanz is over, it lives only in memory. 'You did your best, whether it worked or not. You stimulated people's imagination and seduced them – or not. And then it's over.' In August 2006, this moment had come for Peter Jonas.

Zubin Mehta had asked Jonas at the end of their final season what he would be up to now. 'I am free as a bird. I can do what I want,' was his answer. Once again, Peter Jonas had achieved a key goal: 'I wanted to be the one who got away.'

William Shakespeare Sonnet 146

Poor soul, the centre of my sinful earth,
… these rebel powers that thee array,
Why dost thou pine within and suffer dearth,
Painting thy outward walls so costly gay?
Why so large cost, having so short a lease,
Dost thou upon thy fading mansion spend?
Shall worms, inheritors of this excess,
Eat up thy charge? Is this thy body's end?
Then soul, live thou upon thy servant's loss
And let that pine to aggravate thy store;
Buy terms divine in selling hours of dross;
Within be fed, without be rich no more.
So shalt thou feed on Death, that feeds on men,
And, Death once dead, there's no more dying then.

CODA

'Write quickly,' Peter Jonas told me during a telephone call in August 2018, the day before an operation. 'We need to meet as soon as I'm feeling better.'

By then, we had been working on this book project for just six months. He told me that after a new cancer diagnosis he would now fight a last battle against his lifelong illness.

When we hung up, the images and words of our first working meeting in February 2018 came back to me. Peter Jonas, sitting at his dining table in the Zurich flat, had asked for a week's grace to think before deciding whether he would work with me on the book. For the first time, the recorder was running. He talked about whether he, with all his doubts about himself, could take such work seriously; whether he could muster the desire and the strength, whether he wanted to muster it. He told how he had always reminded his closest colleagues at English National Opera: 'Always go to work and think: today, they will find out. Today, they will realise that actually I know absolutely nothing. Always believe you are going to be fired.' He rapped his knuckles on the table. This was a frequent habit, as I would soon discover.

This self-admonition to evolve constantly expresses a deep truth about how Jonas saw himself in life. But now he knew for sure: in his life, his knocking had always gone unanswered. He had fulfilled his obligations towards his sister. He was described as an 'ideal opera master', as a 'gentle provocateur', as a 'player who won'.[1] In this book I wanted to go in search of the man behind these formulas, to ask what drove all these decades and what made him successful. Hearing this, he looked back, playing chess with death, smiling and amazed at this, his 'God-blessed life' (his words!).

Since that call in August 2018, working on his biography meant accompanying him though his dying days. It meant seeing how he defied his doctors' prognoses for the final time. How he dealt with his pain, the physical pain, but also the emotional pain. How willing he was to suffer, but also how, even as his voice continued to desert him, he claimed authority over the narrative of his own dying.

Even when his body fell into greater and greater disarray, he maintained his dignity. For him, being able to express his feelings, even dark ones, in words was just as much an act of self-assertion as was his insistence on trying new therapies. The conversations and messages through which he maintained intensive contact with his friends, as always in his life, were his way of overcoming the 'loneliness of the dying in our days', in Norbert Elias's phrase.

Peter Jonas did not feel remotely awkward in talking about his fears, his hardships and his disgust. Normative emotional frameworks, which prescribe how a sick person should feel and speak about his experiences, made little impression. He was very aware of the dramatic course of his illness. He determined, until the end, the things that gave meaning to his life and what quality of life meant for him. He knew what gave him hope: to be allowed to continue living on this earth, no matter how wrecked his body, no matter what ordeals he had to endure.

Other people would not have chosen this path, would not have seen any sense in such a painfully prolonged life. Perhaps they would not have had the strength or the support. But Jonas derived such satisfaction from disproving his doctors' final diagnosis once more, and being able to say: 'I am still alive!' He was fully committed to the idea of being able to live, if not forever, at least as long as possible. He endured immense pressure and the most painful situations in furtherance of this hope. Those who have fought for so long cannot stop.

'This is my hand. I can move it, feel the blood pulsing through it. The sun is still high in the sky and I, Antonius Block, am playing chess with Death.' These were the words of Ingmar Bergman's Knight when he had decided to use the reprieve won through playing chess with Death 'for one meaningful deed'.[2]

In early summer 2018, Jonas was diagnosed with thymic carcinoma, a rare, highly aggressive tumour, which was treated with chemotherapy in autumn 2018. His actual disease, Hodgkin's lymphoma, was inoperable and classified at the highest stage of development, 'Stage 4'. 'But no pathos … these are just facts … I am mainly stationary in Munich between Barbara's flat and the university clinic and feel a bit like a prisoner… I miss Scheuchzerstrasse and my pictures…' so Jonas wrote on 6 September 2018, when he had already almost conquered the second cycle of chemo. Another four cycles lay ahead.

He missed Scheuchzerstrasse, his flat in Zurich. For the final time, he had created a perfectly-furnished apartment there, where Busoni had worked on his *Faust*: bright, modern, tidy, with one back room where everything was a mess. He had not wanted to creep through Munich's Maximilianstrasse as a ghost in white sheets and murmur 'Ah, the young people!'[3] Here he also had his Old Masters around him. Jonas spoke of his Zurich apartment as his paradise. 'It was his place of retreat, where he was surrounded by his pictures, the many films, books… Here he could withdraw peacefully,' Natalia Ritzkowsky said.[4] 'In the last few years, he often fled to Zurich to escape his illness, which for him was connected with Munich and his doctors there. In Zurich he was able to catch his breath.'

On 27 September 2018 he revealed: 'I am still fighting, but it's ABSOLUTELY GHASTLY!' The horror was palpable even in such short messages. After he had survived all the cycles, he contacted me on 20 October with an email whose subject line consisted of sixteen exclamation marks:

'I am very ill … and this latest cycle made me much more so. I was OK for a couple of days under Cortisone but then crashed and burned and was incapacitated completely. It takes time to recover from that and the physical damage is great and extensive. I will not bore you with the horrible details but, suffice to say, it is hard to do anything even to read or walk. The tumour is classed as "terminal" meaning that there is no hope of real recovery but the medical team (and I) are fighting hard to win me just more time perhaps even a year if I am lucky and if I am exceptionally lucky maybe a little more but the huge risk is that the treatment could kill me too. Still that is better than if I did nothing ... then it would be a matter of a few months at the most ... and would be very gruesome.'

Together with his wife and the doctors, he decided to take a great risk. As soon as he had recovered from the chemotherapy, he wanted to undergo radiotherapy from November, which consisted of twenty-five sessions over five weeks. As he had already received more than the maximum dose of radiation recommended by doctors for a human lifetime during the treatment of his first cancer in 1976–77, and of his eye in 2008, the outcome was more than uncertain, 'it is a HUGE risk ... but I must try.' In fact, he would live for another sixteen months after completing the radiotherapy. He was 'exceptionally lucky', once again. Barbara Burgdorf and he were able to celebrate a quiet, happy Christmas and look forward with hope to the New Year. His guardian angel was with him.

On 17 January 2019 he called. His voice was no longer the same. It was now forever rough and scratchy. Laughing quietly, he told us that in July last year he had cancelled all his appointments until the end of January, except one. Duty-conscious as always, it was out of the question – 'too embarrassing' – to cancel l'Association des Amis de l'Opéra in Bilbao at such short notice. So he flew there to deliver a lecture.

On 29 January, he was finally able to send good news: 'Big meeting at hospital yesterday. Both oncologists and radiotherapists satisfied with the tests. Tumour has not grown which is good news (nor has it shrunk which was maybe too much to hope for) and is also rather less well delineated so they (and we) are happy with that!' He didn't care that the doctors wanted to do an ultrasound of the lungs every twelve weeks to check whether they were filling up with fluid again. 'Relief ... it is sleeping!'

He immediately wanted to continue working on the book. It was not only his voice that had become weaker. His body clearly bore the signs of treatment. He did not hide this: on the contrary. He talked about it, showed off his fingernails, which, like his hair – he was clearly thrilled about this! – were growing back. He spoke of his encounters in the hospital, of conversations with the nurses, whose robust manner with sick patients he imitated in a raucously entertaining way. He did not like to lie in the room with other patients: it brought back memories of boarding school. He wanted to be alone. Too often, conversations with roommates led him to assume the role of the strongest and to offer comfort, especially when they recognised him. He much preferred to be alone with his thoughts.

In March 2019, his health insurance agreed to prescribe CBD cannabis – 'legal marijuana' – 'so it must be serious', he commented with a laugh. Unlike the usual cannabis, which contains THC, the active ingredient in CBD cannabis does not produce a high and is not addictive. On the contrary, it has many positive effects, including in cancer treatment.

'As the end of your life approaches, some things become very small,' he said as he began on 11 March. We sat with Yorkshire tea in his wife's flat. Snow was falling. He ate a Paris-Brest, very crispy and with lots of cream. He enjoyed it. And for once he ate it all. 'Things suddenly become so unimportant. You realise that your own achievements or failures, everything is much smaller than you think. I think that's good. Because when your successes are minimised that's probably good for your soul, when your failures are minimised it is good for you. The soul is the nobler part,' Jonas philosophised and then laughed.

On 23 April he attended the première of Barrie Kosky's production of *Agrippina*. It turned out to be a happy evening, because of the music, the production, but also because seeing his former opera house was a great treat. During the première celebrations, his successor Nikolaus Bachler announced that the Bavarian Staatsoper had dedicated the production to him. This prompted an article in the *Süddeutsche Zeitung*: 'delicate and slender, he stands there in a black dinner jacket, with sunglasses and a thin woollen cap on his head. But Munich's former Staatsoper director towers above them all with his elegance and almost extravagant cheerfulness.'[5]

Slowly, Barrie Kosky was able to disentangle himself from his various première conversations to approach Peter Jonas. 'He hesitates briefly, then gently embraces the fragile man. But Sir Peter, still overwhelmed by the Handel opera, hugs back with firm pressure. The love of music is something that cannot be lost.'[6] Jonas attended all performances of this production. 'The great thing about it: it was Barrie's most colourful production, but it was dramaturgically pure.' He could not have given higher praise.

On 2 May, we met for the last time in his Zurich flat. He had recently been in Miami for intensive Pilates. He wanted to reclaim his body. 'Yesterday, today was so hard for me. At the end of June 2018, the doctors had told me I would die within the next six months. Now, a year and a half later, I should be dead, but I am not.' He also spoke about friends, companions who no longer contact him. 'I am not angry: some friends cannot cope with a slow death.'

Then he described how, shortly before, he had seen a performance of *Madame Butterfly* at the Bavarian Staatsoper. 'I was feeling a bit sorry for myself. Barbara told me that she would play *Madame Butterfly* twice this week. Then I said to her: "If you're playing up front and it's *Butterfly*, I might have a good cry."' He had to laugh at himself. 'I love *Madame Butterfly* dearly. It is not a technical love, I think the plot is terrible. Puccini was quite unpleasant, today he would be in jail because he was a male chauvinist pig. Cio-Cio-San was twelve years old! Ricordi later changed her age to fifteen, itself bad enough. It's horrible, the American officer with the instincts of a paedophile. But the music is so beautiful! It brings tears to my eyes just thinking about it! Every phrase, even the American anthem, is so beautifully written.'

On 10 April 2019, Antonino Fogliani had taken over conducting *Madame Butterfly*. Jonas was thrilled with his performance.

'Fogliani set off at a crazy speed, with superb conducting. His baton technique is so efficient. He didn't put a foot wrong. I cried the whole evening. At the end, he came up on stage, called the orchestra, but they remained seated and applauded him. They almost never do that with a stranger! It was a great experience. Between my tears, I thought to myself: "My God, what a privilege it was to work at this house, what an honour!"'

At the end of June, Jonas was due another operation, this time on his head. His doctor predicted that he would be able to go home the same evening. 'I am confident!!!!' And rightly so, because just one day later he was able to write: 'It is done … I had been walking around with a ping pong ball in my head!!!!!!!!! getting drunk now!!!'

He could not rest for long. On 6 July he announced: 'I'll be back in Munich from tomorrow and under the knife from Tuesday! Cheerio! P'.

The operation had to be postponed in the end. Before that, he wanted to work on the book again. We met in Munich. The wound from his head operation was barely visible. For the upcoming operation, the hair that had just grown back was to be shaved off, and his wound grafted with skin taken from his scalp and elsewhere. He was in a bad way. 'I'm scared,' he confessed. And 'Barbara is ein Fels in der Brandung [a tower of strength].' He did not talk much more about the next operation.

'The tumour wants to stay with me,' he joked, but he could no longer manage light-hearted irony. In his chess game, he did not have many moves left.

In the summer of 2019, Peter Jonas read a new biography of Michael Tippett by the young Oliver Soden. Jonas was thrilled; he sent several copies with recommendations to acquaintances and journalists. 'Tippett was a great composer, perhaps the greatest composer of the twentieth century! He had a singular, individual voice. Every other composer can be assigned to a tradition, a school. Tippett developed his own traditions,' Jonas enthused, before tracing facets and lines of development from Tippett's life that he had learned about only through Soden's biography.

Jonas had discovered a score of Tippett's *Midsummer Marriage* in a second-hand bookshop and presented it to Ivor Bolton as a sixtieth birthday present. He gave it to the orchestra for its fiftieth birthday and expressed a wish to hear it under his baton. 'I am sad that I will not live to see this opera before I die.' Jonas was silent for quite a while. 'Suddenly I feel so sad. I lost my voice at the moment when I first felt and understood how these operas should be staged. Only now am I beginning to understand … I'm not saying I have the answers, but I understand the questions … the courtesy of a question, that is what interpretation means.'

We walked through the Old South Cemetery in July 2019, and were sitting on a bench when he started talking about his wife. 'Maybe I will be very relieved when it is all over, but I will be very sad for Barbara. What is important is how her hands come into my hands. How can you replace that? I must say, if that wasn't there, I would probably give up. Bye…'

He confessed his love for her beautifully, in words that found their way to her by means other than this book. He laughed with joy. 'Compared with me she is a hero. And she puts up with me and all my neuroses! But I really am unhappy for her now. But she doesn't seem to show it. Goodness knows how I could have lived without her.'

On 8 July, he sent a message with the subject 'Problems!'

> Ugh!!!! OP postponed … in University Hospital (my cancer hospital) as lungs and pericardium full of liquid and gunk so tomorrow instead they will drain pericardium and drain lungs … this will take a day plus two of observation so head tumour postponed till next week (if I am lucky)!!!! SHIT!!!! Best ever P

Everyone was waiting. On 17 July, the news finally came: 'Just woke up after 6 hours general anaesthesia… I am still here and world is still here!!!!!!! only head tumour is gone!!! AMAZING!!! But I am thirsty.' Once again, the prospect of new treatments gave him hope. In August, he started an innovative immunotherapy.

However, the tumour was still producing large amounts of fluid and malignant cells. On 26 August, he reported unpleasant side effects of his immunotherapy. He had to go to hospital regularly for puncture and drainage of his lungs, 'unpleasant and there are limits to what the body can take. In the meantime I can hardly walk … just a few metres … before running out of breath and the simplest tasks now take a very long time! I am also very weak, have to sleep a lot and am still shedding off weight. Everyone is hopeful about the experimental treatment but all seem to know that I am also on the "last lap" so to speak!'

Between a lung-draining procedure and another infusion of immunotherapy, Jonas's doctors gave him five days off. He and his wife spent them in the Deggenhausen valley: 'empty, simple, and beautiful … it might be one of our last chances for a real break.' Just three days later, his wife informed me that he had been admitted to hospital again with respiratory problems. With a complex operation the next day, the doctors hoped to be able to stop the tumour from discharging and to place a catheter in his lung. Since even whispering caused him great pain, his wife asked his circle of friends and acquaintances to refrain from calling. In September, palliative treatment officially began and he was now being given additional oxygen.

But he wanted to work on the book again and had a precise plan of what he wanted to talk about. He asked me to watch Ingmar Bergman's film *The Seventh Seal* again, which now more than ever revealed a lot about his condition. His doctors had given him only one more week, 'but somehow they are keeping me alive … BUT BE WARNED I CAN ONLY WHISPER!!!!!!!! Am dying but it is painfully slow!!!!! Love P'.

What had been a weakened, scratchy voice months before was now just a barely audible huff. He was lying on the sofa with his red and black checked shirt and his Palestinian scarf, the clothes he had worn so often when we worked together. Blankets and a hot water bottle were supposed to keep him warm, but still he felt cold.

Over those weeks he endured dark moments when he doubted

his life's work. 'There is so much to say. The end brings other thoughts into play. I have had moving and tearful visits from Zubin, Daniel, Ivor, David, Mark and Christof Loy, even Barrie Kosky. Zubin came from Naples on a private plane to see me. The next day he had another rehearsal. In the end, we held hands and cried.' He could still swear, though. 'Three days ago, I said to Barbara in the hospital: "What a pity I can't move so well anymore! Otherwise I would take a machine gun or a revolver and just assassinate Trump, Johnson, Orbán and Netanyahu." Okay, this is a childish fantasy, but I'm so angry!'

A tirade followed in which he explained what he was angry about in detail:

'I haven't felt any belief in England for the last three years. Since the evidence of such idiocy, cruelty, lies. I am really beginning to think that we are in a moment so similar to the Weimar republic. Just imagine, in the middle of the Brexit mess, in the middle of Orbán's popularity, the Irish backstop, the re-emergence of violence in Northern Ireland. Tomorrow Merkel drops dead, and AKK [Annegret Kramp-Karrenbauer] has to carry on, the AfD is marching up and down the streets of Chemnitz… Don't tell me you are not afraid!'

It had taken Jonas a long time to recognise that he was the child of emigrants and that he too could not escape this history. For him, being uprooted when he entered boarding school was only the beginning. 'That's why I never really feel at home. I have always felt like a stranger. That's why I'm so deeply touched by the political situation now.' Whenever his condition allowed him, in the last few months of his life, Jonas would drive – or ask friends to drive him – to his paintings and to Zurich. 'Here in this corner of Europe, between Munich, the Allgäu and Zurich, I feel really zu Hause for the first time in my life: at ease, not at home.'

He held a last party on 9 November 2019 at the 'Osteria Italiana', his regular restaurant in Schwabing's Schellingstraße, where he had met Pierre Mendell and so many others. When we sat there for the first time, he ordered one of his favourite dishes: *carpaccio di patate* cooked under the grill with three hard-boiled quails' eggs and black truffle. After a few bites he was full. Like many other cancer patients, he could no longer taste food so intensely, and he had lost the pleasure. From the way Peter Jonas raved and rejoiced, the parties he had held at the 'Osteria' must have been great. Especially for his seventieth birthday. It had been a huge milestone, a boisterous, exuberant celebration that he had indeed turned seventy. This moment was also full of drama because, shortly before, Jonas had seriously injured his head during a hike on the Zürichberg. He wanted to experience such a celebration again, come what may: that was his goal, he put all his strength into it and also expected those closest to him to support him.

On that evening, 9 November, he was extremely weak, fragile, a shadow of his former self. For the last time he wore his kilt, his costume, his armour, a reminder of times gone by. His guests, who had come from all over the world, were able to offer him only a muted greeting. 'No hugs, no kisses' was the rule of the evening, to protect him from pathogens. His friend and doctor Lieselotte Goedel-Meinen sat at his side and banned anyone from touching him. The contrast to previous celebrations could not have been starker.

Many remembered a brilliant and amusing speech – completely improvised because he could not read from the page due to the consequences of the fall. Many of his guests struggled that evening, as Jonas seemed to want to celebrate his passing. As if they were holding a wake for him *before* he had died. He did not see it that way. 'He wanted to say goodbye to all his friends. He wanted to meet death, wine glass in hand, and look it in the eye. He didn't want to slink off the stage, but to face death with his visor open. It was fantastic, so very Peter!' Natalia Ritzkowsky, who had also helped him with the preparations, described his manner, dramatic to the end. 'It was nice to see how many people took on this "imposition", this unbelievable challenge. It was so nice to witness what he meant to people, to feel the significance that he had in their lives.'

At times Jonas nodded off from exhaustion. At some points he seemed close to fainting. He was making inhuman demands of himself. 'That evening, he gave his doctors great power over him without relinquishing his own powers. He completely dispensed with front and back stages. It was deeply touching how he surrendered himself in his fragility to mine and others' gazes,' described Jutta Allmendinger, to whom he had assigned the place of honour at his side. Leaning on his wife and his doctor, who almost seemed to be carrying him, Jonas left the restaurant, waving briefly, not looking back.

After that, the evening drew to a close. No one really wanted to comply with his request to remain seated after he left. Many of his friends saw him for the last time that day. He announced after the party that he wanted to celebrate again the following year. With a mixture of experience, acceptance and repression, he wanted the thought of this new goal to keep him alive.

After the party, it turned out that Jonas was suffering from sepsis. On 20 November 2019 he was still weakened, but also bored: 'I'm still locked up since the party at Rechts der Isar – visit me –! Let us speak tomorrow … just sort of recovering from sepsis!!!' We saw each other a week later, in the evening. He had a date with his oncologist for a beer. But only in the living room. He spoke of death. His voice was no more than a whisper. 'This last week, I nearly died twice. That has happened a few times over the last months. Let's not forget it was a year and three months ago that I was getting this diagnosis: months. I am already far overdrawn. So, the experience of the last week, this sword of Damocles, I am in a bit of an emotional state. The emotion is: one is, I am sorry for Barbara. The other is…' – he broke off, crying – 'I really don't want the party to be over. I would like to see more productions.'

During this time he could not listen to music. It was too demanding. 'I shouldn't go plainly and simply,' he groaned. 'At last, I am here. Although everything hurts and is uncomfortable. I do complain, since it is taking so fucking long. Yet, I don't want the moment to come.' Again he broke off and was silent for a long time. Then he asked for his iPad and sat down: 'I have come to a conclusion about which four pieces I would like for my memorial service. Whether they are possible or not.'

The first piece he requested was the aria *Cara sposa, amante cara* from Handel's first London opera, *Rinaldo*, considered one of Handel's best. Jonas played a version from the dress rehearsal of the Munich production from November 2001, when his mother was dying. Ann Murray sang Rinaldo, Barbara Burgdorf was the concertmaster. He would have liked to see David Daniels in the role, 'if he wasn't in prison', he added maliciously. He asked Daniel Barenboim to perform the second piece, Robert Schumann's *Fantasiestück op. 12, Nummer 1 Des Abend*, 'the most perfect piece of music'. Jonas had not liked Schumann very much until one morning, after a particularly intense dream, he awoke under Daniel Barenboim's Steinway.

'An unforgettable moment in which not a word was spoken and yet everything was said.' That day he played the piece in an arragement by Arthur Rubinstein. Hearing the final bars, he cried again and then remained silent for a long time. 'The third piece is about how much I love it here on earth.' Jonas lifted again. He chose *Zdes' khorosho (How Fair is the Spot)* by Sergei Rachmaninoff, sung by Swedish tenor Nicolai Gedda. The fourth piece was to be the adagio 'Nimrod' from the *Enigma Variations* by Edward Elgar, which he hoped would be conducted by Zubin Mehta and which he heard that day in a performance by the West-Eastern Diwan Orchestra during a performance in Israel. 'Just those four I would love.'

When I said goodbye that evening, I was sure I would never see him again. Then came an experience now familiar to many of his friends. The contrast could hardly have been greater when he wrote, on 4 December, 'Yes! Started new immunotherapy today!!!!!!!'

Then, on 23 December, instead of personal Christmas greetings, Jonas sent out an uncharacteristic circular email whose tone, openness and warmth, but also mercilessness approach towards living and dying, said so much:

18 months ago, as you know, I received a fatal diagnosis and was told that there would be little time left. Like a persistent weed in an untended garden, however, I am still here by virtue of some inner stubbornness and an amazing, inspiring and, at times entertaining medical team in Munich.

The primary tumour in my chest has been stalled: still there spewing forth all sorts of unpleasantness but no larger although no smaller. Further tumours have grown on my scalp, they are 'fast and furious' to quote Hollywood 'C' movies. A year and a half of chemo, radiation, dozens of surgical procedures and even a bout of sepsis have left my frame quite small in size compared to before with a weight of just 56 kilos. Muscle loss is a problem, regaining it is even more so. The days of trekking through Europe with my rucksack are only a memory that I re-live through Barbara's superb photographs.

Barbara is a rock through all this especially on days when I can hardly move and, yet, I still like it here on this weird planet of ours and prefer this route than suddenly being struck down with a heart attack. The latest Immunotherapy (Cemiplimab) is now being tried on my fading mansion of a body and appears to be having some effects, weird though some of them are. It has, however, enabled me to summon up the energy to write this to you and others to wish you:
1) Happy Christmas
2) Guten Rutsch [Happy New Year]
3) That you never have to go through anything like this yourself.
As ever P

Attached was a cartoon that Jonas had probably found in the *New Yorker*. His choice could hardly have been more prophetic: in the foreground, a man is sanitising his hands from a dispenser on the wall. In the background, the Grim Reaper stands in a black robe and says: 'Don't bother.'

Jonas, who had been living with a cancer diagnosis for forty-four years and who could have been an object of study in medical history in his own right, was just witnessing the beginning of a completely new threat. These were 'emerging diseases', highly contagious, hitherto obscure viruses that jump from animals to humans and trigger pandemics, in the face of which medical science is presently largely at a loss.[7]

On 14 March he sent a message with the subject 'Living death': 'Effectively died last weekend … they brought me back twice and I am still alive … just … in Munich rechts der Isar which is closed off… Situation acute maybe few days left…'

On that day, when the closure of public institutions began in Germany as a result of Covid-19, Jonas was still able to make phone calls. What he said was often difficult to understand. He had been in the Rechts der Isar hospital for a week:

'Good of you to call!' He broke off briefly to make a request – 'Schwarzer Tee, bitte, Schwester!' 'I died twice at the weekend, but they brought me back. The short summary is, what with all the cancers, I was in a state of collapse. I got weaker and weaker and then I was unconscious. Self-induced coma. I have been malnourished for years, a psychological story. My body is fighting the cancer.' Again he interrupted himself – 'Vielen Dank, Schwester!' – and continued. 'The nurse is draining my lung right now. My body is slowly breaking down. So far, it has drawn energy from the reserves. My problem is that I can't spit out enough energy. It was only by chance that Lilo was there last weekend and helped me. She fought for me. I only came here to the hospital because of vitamin B. Everything is tight.' And then he said in a firm voice: 'I am not afraid of death.'

Bergman's Knight had said: 'My body is frightened, but I am not.'[8]

I met Peter Jonas for the last time on 5 March 2020.

He spoke of how proud he was of letters from old colleagues, who had let him know what he had meant to them. He was deeply moved by what Aron Stiehl, now Intendant at the Stadttheater Klagenfurt, had written. Stiehl had also sent him an audio file with excerpts from the *Giulio Cesare* première, the moments in which the Roman Empire fell and the the Jonas era began. 'I have a lot to say, much of it is locked away,' Jonas whispered. 'Stiehl's little clip makes me proud. Maybe I did it with some resonance and some enjoyment. Maybe I did something, not just hang around in the theatre.' He snapped his fingers. 'Theatre is just a moment, Julia,' then quoting from *A Midsummer Night's Dream*, the beloved play associated with a wondrous moment in his life. They were the words of Puck's final speech:

> If we shadows have offended,
> Think but this, and all is mended,
> That you have but slumber'd here
> While these visions did appear…
> So, good night unto you all.
> Give me your hands, if we be friends,
> And Robin shall restore amends.[9]

On 20 March, Jonas called again. He was back home. This was the day the Bavarian Chief Minister announced the first lockdown in the Free State of Bavaria. Jonas wanted to report on Daniel Barenboim, who had been calling him every day. Jonas had told his friend how much he missed music. After the memorial concert for Mariss Jansons in January 2020, Jonas was immensely sad that he would never again be able to attend a concert by Zubin Mehta or Daniel Barenboim. Deeply absorbed in himself, he felt a sadness about art during these weeks that he compared to the experience Hanno Buddenbrook had when attending his first performance of *Lohengrin*, of finding music so beautiful that it hurts: when 'the dream became reality. It came over him with all its enchantment and consecration, all its secret revelations and tremors, its sudden inner emotion, its extravagant, unquenchable intoxication.' Mann wrote of how 'he had been overpowered by an attack of the complete despondency which was all too familiar an experience. Again he had learned that beauty can pierce one like a pain, and that it can sink profoundly into shame and a longing despair that utterly consume the courage and energy necessary to the life of every day. His despondency weighed him down like mountains and once more he told himself, as he had done before, that this was more than his own individual burden of weaknesses that rested upon him: that his burden was one which he had borne upon his soul from the beginning of time, and must one day sink under at last.'[10]

From that time on, Jonas would ask Barenboim for a new piano piece every day, and Barenboim would play it for him in the evening. Jonas was deeply grateful for these, the last concerts of his life. Solo piano, that was the repertoire he had come to know through his beloved sister. It was the music with which she had awakened him in his childhood. Once again, the music nourished, gave him comfort. With these last concerts for his friend, Daniel Barenboim accompanied him on his way back to his sister. 'The only thing I have to look forward to is to greet my sister and maybe my mother. To explain what I have been doing in the last fifty-two years since I last saw her. I miss her very much.'

On 2 April 2020, he sent me his last message (we too had been discussing piano pieces): 'BAD DAY today… (there are always some…) so how about the Chopin Etude op 10 nr 6? (My nickname for it is despair)!!!! Only if you have time! Bayer Staatsoper finally completely closed today till 19 April … they are optimists…'

On 20 April Jonas underwent a heart operation at Klinikum Rechts der Isar. He had been aware of the high risk of the procedure, and had made sure he called his closest friends. He woke up after the operation and even made it out of bed. On the evening of 22 April 2020, sitting upright at a table in his room at the clinic, Sir Peter Jonas died of a sudden cardiac arrest.

And, Death once dead, there's no more dying then.

Afterword

Daniel Barenboim

Sir Peter Jonas was one of my closest friends. His death is not only a great loss for me, but also for the international music world, which in him has lost one of its great pioneers.

Even when we met at the Chicago Symphony Orchestra in the early 1980s, I was impressed by his intelligence as well as his ease in dealing with the American mentality. Although the Americans worked quite differently from him, he convinced them all, all of them. His intelligence and humour were the key. Peter had an absurdly good sense of humour. If any tension became apparent in a conversation, he immediately resolved it with humour. At that time, he was already active at an international level, a true European. Over the decades, our friendship became closer and closer. Peter and I knew that we could rely on each other without reservation. That was infinitely valuable to me.

I was also enormously impressed by Peter's musical knowledge: it went much deeper than that of many other people who worked – and still work – in music administration. We could talk about music for hours without either of us bringing up administrative issues. It was so astonishing that a person in a position like his was so interested in music! Peter also had a keen sense for voices and for their development. Once he suggested the British singer John Tomlinson, a bass, to me for an audition as Wotan for the Bayreuth Festival, although the role of Wotan is a baritone. He knew how Tomlinson's voice would develop. The rest is history.

Peter was also an incredibly curious person. To me, curiosity is one of the most important qualities, because without it learning becomes impossible. Curiosity awakens people to action. Few people possess such curiosity, even in old age, as Peter did.

Among Peter Jonas's most important qualities, however, were

his emotional openness and his professionalism. He was a person full of love and devotion to music and the arts, who was highly focused and professional. The combination of these two qualities is extremely rare in people who work in roles like his: many of them either care exclusively about quality and forget about emotional connections, or they lose themselves in their emotions and abandon professionalism.

Peter Jonas was predestined for a leading position in the classical music world because he, who called himself a traditionalist, fought instinctively against the establishment. Peter has always wanted both, that is the key to his personality. He wanted to be a part of the establishment, in order to battle against the things he could not accept. He managed the balancing act of belonging to the establishment without fitting in. He was admired by many for this, but it also provoked hostility. He, who explored Europe on foot, wandered between these worlds and made the transition with apparent ease, great charm and British humour.

He had a real partnership with us conductors. At the Bavarian State Opera, he and Zubin Mehta created a model of how a large, internationally oriented opera house can be managed at the highest level, both musically and aesthetically. Peter and Zubin were united by a common goal that was self-evident for both of them: they wanted to serve art, and they subordinated all other interests to this service.

Peter Jonas was an extremely tough person. In the last weeks of his life, we spoke on the phone every day. There were days when everything was black for him. Days when he thought he could no longer bear his illness. On other days, he had regained his courage. He wasn't playing a part for me: he was absolutely honest. He was not afraid of death. During those weeks, I played him a piano piece every day on the phone, which he had requested from me beforehand. It often moved him to tears, also because he knew he would never attend another concert. Peter had a special strength within himself to continue living despite his illnesses. That is why he fought to the last. For me he lives on in the memory of our friendship, for his audience in the memories of his productions.

This book has now told his story.

– Daniel Barenboim
Berlin, October 2020

Acknowledgements

My first and greatest thanks go to Barbara Burgdorf: for her trust and continued support even after Sir Peter's death.

I would like to express my sincere thanks to Maurice Lausberg, who brought my idea of writing this biography to Sir Peter's attention.

Through working together with Rebekka Göpfert, Agentur Göpfert, I have experienced how much joy the creation of a book can bring when it is conceived of seriously, joyfully and lightly. My heartfelt thanks!

Many of the people who accompanied Peter Jonas have generously and confidentially shared their memories of him in conversations with me. Thank you to:

David Alden, Jutta Allmendinger, Daniel Barenboim, Christian Berner, Barbara Burgdorf, Sir Mark Elder, Lesley Garrett CBE, Martha Gilmer, Wilfried Hösl, Steffen Huck, Katrin Lausberg, Maurice Lausberg, Jane Livingston, Christine Lemke-Matwey, Monica Melamid, John Nickson, Natalia Ritzkowsky, Jürgen Rose, Toni Schmid, Maggie Sedwards, Aron Stiehl and Hans Zehetmair.

Memories, as important as they are, must be verified. Elke Stelle from the library of the Potsdam University of Applied Sciences worked tirelessly to provide me with the necessary literature. I offer her sincere thanks.

Students of cultural work at the Potsdam University of Applied Sciences bore much of the burden of my research.

I would like to thank Ulrike Hentschke, Karl Borowski and Martin Naundorf.

I would like to thank Bianca Döring and Wilfried Hösl of the Bavarian State Opera in Munich for their support.

Even with access to the best literature, some answers can be found only in direct conversation with experts. I would like to thank the following people for their willingness to help:

Birgit Bigler-Marschall, Mary Lou Burge from the Worth

Society, Michael Leitner, David Monod, Ulrike Müller-Harang, Timm Schulze, Hellmut Seemann, Tony Shepping, Michael Strobel, Michael Studemund-Halévy and Frank Villella from the Rosenthal Archives of the Chicago Symphony Orchestra.

A book only becomes a reality if a publisher believes in it. I would like to thank the publishers Suhrkamp/Insel, Rebecca Casati and Elisabeth Honerla.

For Janko Tietzel – in memory of his father Wolfgang.

– Julia Glesner
Potsdam, December 2020

About the Author

Julia Glesner is a theatre scholar. After working at the opera house in Erfurt and the Klassik Stiftung Weimar, she was appointed professor for Cultural Management at the Potsdam University of Applied Sciences, Germany.

Translator

Edward Maltby is a freelance translator working from French and German into English. He is based in Sheffield, in South Yorkshire, and can be reached at maltbytranslation.com

Picture credits

ArenaPAL, London: Fig. 26 (Clive Barda)

Leo Baeck Institute, New York/Berlin: 14, 15

English National Opera, London: 30, 32 (John Stoddart), 33 (Kate Grant/Bolt Agency, with thanks for their generosity), 34, 35 (Bill Rafferty) Julia Glesner, Potsdam: 1, 12, 19

Seventh Seal, Bridgeman.

Dieter Hanitzsch, Munich: 41

Wilfried Hösl, Munich: 6, 37-40, 42, 45, 46 (Charlotte Harris), 47, 48

Nationalarchiv der Richard-Wagner-Stiftung, Bayreuth: 28 (Zustiftung Wolfgang Wagner)

Elizabeth Zeschin, Pulborough: 29

All other illustrations are by Barbara Burgdorf and from private collections.

Endnotes

To portray the best of people

1 Jonas, Peter, quoted from, Täuschel, Annika, 'Porträt. Sir Peter zum 70. Geburtstag', BR Klassik. 14.09.2016, https://www.br.de/mediathek/podcast/klassik-aktuell/portraet-sir-peter-jonas-zum-70-geburtstag/43696.
2 Jonas, Peter, 'Elitäre Kultur für die ganze Öffentlichkeit', in Gräfin Dönhoff, Marion/Markl, Hubert/von Weizsäcker, Richard (eds.), *Eliten und Demokratie. Wirtschaft, Wissenschaft und Politik im Dialog – zu Ehren von Eberhard von Kuenheim*, Berlin 1999, pp. 67-82, p. 81f.
3 Jonas, Peter, 'Kunst – Schlachtfeld der Toleranz. Queen's Lecture', unpublished manuscript, Technische Universität Berlin, 08.11.2001, p. 31.
4 Ibid., p. 23.
5 Jonas, Peter, 'Händel's Steckenpferd. An Anglo-German Dialogue by Steffen Huck and Sir Peter Jonas', unpublished manuscript from the archives of Sir Peter Jonas. Undated.
6 Interview with Daniel Barenboim, 17.03.2020.
7 Clements, Andrew, 'Ten productions that changed British opera', *the Guardian*, 20.08.2011, https://www.theguardian.com/music/2011/aug/20/ten-productions-british-opera.
8 Kynaston, David, *Austerity Britain 1945-51*, London 2007, p. 19.
9 Sutcliffe, Tom, *Believing in Opera*, Princeton 1996, p. 319.
10 Interview with Maggie Sedwards on 30 August 2019.
11 Ranan, David, *In Search of a Magic Flute. The Public Funding of Opera – Dilemmas and Decision Making*, Oxford 2003, p. 62.
12 Jonas, Peter, quoted from unsigned, 'Sir Peter Jonas. Obituary', *The Times*, 28.04.2020.
13 Jonas, Peter, 'Verführte und Verführer', *Der Architekt* No. 3/1995, pp. 149-153, p. 150.
14 Millington, Barry, 'Sir Peter Jonas Obituary', the *Guardian*, 23.04.2020, https://www.theguardian.com/music/2020/apr/23/sir-peter-jonas-obituary.
15 Interview with John Nickson on 29 August 2019.
16 Garrett, Lesley, '#50YearsofOpera'. YouTube, channel: English National Opera, https://www.youtube.com/watch?v=wn8IqPuDH5I.
17 Jonas, Peter, 'Händel's Steckenpferd. An Anglo-German Dialogue by Steffen Huck and Sir Peter Jonas', unpublished manuscript from the archives of Sir Peter Jonas. Undated.
18 Ibid.
19 Jonas, Peter, 'State of the Nations. Peter Jonas gives the German-speaking opera world a check-up', *Opera*, January 2013, pp. 17-27, p. 17.
20 Jonas, Peter, quoted from Tholl, Egbert, 'Guter, alter Kasten', *Süd-*

deutsche Zeitung, 16.11.2013.
21   Ibid.
22   Jonas, Peter, 'Unwinding in Munich', Munich Found, No. 2/1999.
23   Allison, John, 'Three Times Lucky. Interview', *Opera*, June 2006, pp. 655-666, p659.
24   Stiftung Deutsche Krebshilfe, Hodgkin Lymphom. Antworten. Hilfen. Perspektiven, Bonn 2018, pp. 6-9.
25   For all statements on the history of cancer treatment: Hitzer, Bettina, Krebs fühlen. Eine Emotionsgeschichte des 20. Jahrhunderts, Stuttgart 2020, esp. pp. 4-6.
26   Interview with Barbara Burgdorf on 5 March 2020.
27   Interview with Jutta Allmendinger on 18 February 2020.
28   Liu, Lifang et al., 'Cancer in Europe: Death sentence or life sentence', *The European Journal of Cancer*, Vol. 65, issue 9/2016, pp. 150-155, p. 151. Peter Jonas is the only survivor who spoke at the congress and who is also mentioned by name in the article. He comes across as a key witness for the medical profession. The information on his biography is poorly researched: he was not yet 70 years old at the time of the congress, nor had he lived with the disease for 45 years. Cf. Kaulen, Hildegard, 'Wenn der Krebs die Seele auffrisst', *Frankfurter Allgemeine Zeitung*, 24.05.2017.
29   Cf. Hitzer, Bettina, Krebs fühlen. Eine Emotionsgeschichte des 20. Jahrhunderts, Stuttgart 2020, pp. 7, 8.
30   Braunmüller, Robert, 'In meinem Brustkorb ist ein bösartiger Tumor', *Abendzeitung München*, 03.08.2018.
31   Cf. Hitzer, Bettina, Krebs fühlen. Eine Emotionsgeschichte des 20. Jahrhunderts, Stuttgart 2020, p. 420.
32   Original quote: 'visual life histories of nature and humanity in their inevitable but beauteous decline', https://slippedisc.com/208/0/two-gripping-portraits-of-a-great-opera-manager/.
33   Cf. Hitzer, Bettina, Krebs fühlen. Eine Emotionsgeschichte des 20. Jahrhunderts, Stuttgart 2020, p. 385.
34   Sontag, Susan, Krankheit als Metapher, Frankfurt 1996.
35   Cf. Hitzer, Bettina, Krebs fühlen. Eine Emotionsgeschichte des 20. Jahrhunderts, Stuttgart 2020, pp. 19, 21.
36   Másala, Sebastianus, 'Monitum', Acta Apostolica Sedis. Commentarium Officiale, Annus LIV, Series III, Vol. IV. Typis Polyglottis Vaticanus, 30.06.1962, pp. 526, 950, http://www.vatican.va/archive/aas/documents/AAS-54-1962-ocr.pdf.
37   Thaidigsmann, Edgar, '"Religiös unmusikalisch". Aspekte einer hermeneutischen Problematik', *Zeitschrift für Theologie und Kirche*, Vol. 108 (2011), pp. 490-509, p. 494f.
38   Puzicha, Michaela, '…die gemeinsame Regel des Klosters' (RB 7.55). Aufsätze und Vorträge zur Benediktusregel II, Sankt Ottilien 2017, pp. 323, 332.

39   Ibid., p. 146. Cf. pp. 146, 163.
40   Jonas, Peter, 'Kunst, Liebe und Gefahr. Vogue-Gespräch zwischen Donna Leon und Peter Jonas', Vogue Deutschland, August 2003, pp. 228-233, p. 233.
41   Bergman, Ingmar, *The Seventh Seal* Script, Hamburg 1963 (= Cinemathek 7), p. 7.
42   Ibid.
43   Ibid.
44   Siclier, Jacques, 'Nachwort', in Bergman, Ingmar, *The Seventh Seal* Script, Hamburg 1963 (= Cinemathek 7), pp. 75-85, p. 81.
45   Bergman, Ingmar, *The Seventh Seal* Script, Hamburg 1963 (= Cinemathek 7), p. 8.
46   Kiening, Christian, 'Ingmar Bergman: Das siebente Siegel (1957) und Die Jungfrauenquelle (1960)', Kiening, Christian/Adolf, Heinrich (eds.), *Mittelalter im Film*, Berlin 2006, pp. 249-281, p. 250, cf. p. 263.
47   Bergman, Ingmar, *The Seventh Seal* Script, Hamburg 1963 (= Cinemathek 7), p. 22.
48   Steene, Birgitta, quoted in Vassilieva, Ekaterina, 'Schwarz-Weiß als Gestaltungsprinzip in Andrey Rublev und *The Seventh Seal* Eine Schachpartie zwischen Tarkovskij und Bergman', in Franz, Norbert (ed.): Andrej Tarkovskij. Klassiker. Contributions to the First International Tarkovsky Symposium at the University of Potsdam, Vol. 2, Potsdam 2016, pp. 451-469, p. 453.
49   Kiening, Christian, 'Ingmar Bergman: Das siebente Siegel (1957) und Die Jungfrauenquelle (1960)', in Kiening, Christian/Adolf, Heinrich (eds.), *Mittelalter im Film*, Berlin 2006, pp. 249-281, p. 254.
50   Siclier, Jacques, 'Nachwort', in Bergman, Ingmar, *The Seventh Seal* Script, Hamburg 1963 (= Cinemathek 7), pp. 75-85, p. 77f. Jacques Siclier refers to Jean Mambrino with this statement.
51   Jonas, Peter, 'Verweigerung der Bequemlichkeit', in Roers, Georg Maria (ed.), Die ungleichen Brüder. Künstlerreden und Predigten zum Ascher-mittwoch von 1986 bis 2004, Munich 2005, pp. 194-205, p. 194.
52   Ibid., p. 194f.
53   Bergman, Ingmar, *The Seventh Seal* Script, Hamburg 1963 (= Cinemathek 7), p. 22.
54   Jonas, Peter, 'Verweigerung der Bequemlichkeit', in Roers, Georg Maria (ed.), Die ungleichen Brüder. Künstlerreden und Predigten zum Aschermittwoch von 1986 bis 2004, Munich 2005, pp. 194-205, p. 198. Cf. p. 95.
55   Original quote: 'Opera is a very clumsy medium for the expression of political ideologies – its brush is too broad for all those sub-clauses and selective hatreds. Yet political feeling, rather than ideology, is at the heart of all great opera. Its massed forces instinctively address the unspoken areas of emotional politics that are, in the long run, more fundamental. In so doing, it also illuminates the politics of personal relations: the vital fabric of social life that exists in the silence between people – exactly that space which is filled by

music. Janáček described this space precisely: "As the person talked to me in a conventional conversation, I knew, I heard that, inside himself, the person perhaps wept." This reveals exactly the function of music in opera: it is to give expression to that inner voice. Indeed, in Opera, the world is turned inside out for it is the inner voice, the music, which dominates and "conventional conversation" which is the background. The communal act of listening to, and becoming aware of, the "inner voice" in each of us is a crucial social experience.' – Jonas, Peter/Elder, Mark/Pountney, David, *Power House. The English National Opera Experience*, London 1992, p. 12.

56   Jonas, Peter, 'Elitäre Kultur für die ganze Öffentlichkeit', in Gräfin Dönhoff, Marion/Markl, Hubert/von Weizsäcker, Richard (eds.) *Eliten und Demokratie. Wirtschaft, Wissenschaft und Politik im Dialog – zu Ehren von Eberhard von Kuenheim*, Berlin 1999. pp. 67-82, p. 71.

57   Ibid., p. 81.

58   Jonas, Peter, 'Ich goss Farbe über den US-Botschafter'. Sir Peter Jonas interviewed by Johannes Honsell and Oliver Das Gupta. Aquariumsgespräch 4, *Süddeutsche Zeitung*, 29.07.2007.

59   Jonas, Peter, Rede zum Abschied von Andreas Homokis an der Komischen Oper Berlin, unpublished notes, 01.07.2012.

60   Ibid.

61   Jonas, Peter, 'State of the Nations. Peter Jonas gives the German-speaking opera world a check-up', *Opera*, January 2013, pp. 17-27, p. 26.

62   Ibid., p. 20.

63   Jonas, Peter, 'Geleit', in Flierl, Thomas (ed.) *Andreas Homoki. Ein Jahrzehnt Musiktheater an der Komischen Oper Berlin*, Berlin 2012, p. 8f., p. 8.

64   Jonas, Peter, quoted from Midgette, Anne, 'In the Wings in Munich, a Changing of the Avant-Garde', *New York Times*, 20.06.2004.

65   Barenboim, Daniel, 'München und das British Empire', in Hessler, Ulrike/Schirmer, Lothar (eds.) *Wenn Musik der Liebe Nahrung ist, spielt weiter… Wunderbare Jahre: Sir Peter Jonas, Zubin Mehta und die Bayerische Staatsoper 1993-2006*, Munich 2006, pp. 11-15, p. 14.

66   Jonas, Peter, 'Händel's Steckenpferd. An Anglo-German Dialogue by Steffen Huck and Sir Peter Jonas', unpublished manuscript from the archives of Sir Peter Jonas. Undated.

67   Ibid.

68   Jonas, Peter, quoted from Allison, John, 'Three Times Lucky. Interview', *Opera*, June 2006, pp. 655-666, p. 666.

69   Voigt, Thomas, 'As important as a hospital bed. Peter Jonas im Gespräch mit Thomas Voigt', *Opernwelt*, January 1996, pp. 26-28, p. 28.

70   Jonas, Peter, 'Im Gespräch', Presto. *Kulturzeitschrift des Orchesters* der Universität St. Gallen, issue 2, 2003.

71   Lebrecht, Norman, *Covent Garden: The Untold Story: Dispatches from the English Culture War*, London 2000, p. 228.

72   Jonas, Peter, '"Kein Londoner ist Chelsea-Fan". Interview', *Abendzeitung*

München, 18.05.2012.

73   Voigt, Thomas, 'So wichtig wie ein Krankenhausbett. Peter Jonas im Gespräch mit Thomas Voigt', *Opernwelt*, January 1996, pp. 26-28, p. 28.

74   Jonas, Peter, quoted from Allison, John, 'Three Times Lucky. Interview', *Opera*, June 2006, pp. 655-666, p. 658.

75   Jonas, Peter, '"Opernfestspiele müssen populär sein". Interview mit Claus Spahn', *Focus*, No. 27/1997, p. 101.

76   Millington, Barry, 'Sir Peter Jonas Obituary', the *Guardian*, 23.04.2020, https://www.theguardian.com/music/2020/apr/23/sir-peter-jonas-obituary.

77   Amling, Ulrich, 'Mann mit Stil. Zum Tod der Opernlegende Sir Peter Jonas', *Der Tagesspiegel*, 24.04.2020, p. 19.

78   Zehle, Sibylle, 'Große Oper im Kilt', *Die Zeit*, July 1994.

79   Pountney, David, 'Der Wanderer', *Opernwelt*, No. 6/20, p48-50, p48.

80   Crutchfield, Will, 'English Opera Picks Administrator', *New York Times*, 17.07.1984, https://www.nytimes.com/984/07/7/arts/english-opera-picks-administrator.html. Or: Fastl, Christian, 'Art. "Popp, Lucia"' in Österreichisches Musiklexikon, 2001, https://www.musiklexikon.ac.at/ml/musik_P/Popp_Lucia.xml. But also: Pountney, David, 'Der Wanderer', *Opernwelt*, No. 6/20, pp. 48-50, p. 48.

81   These errors are all found in a single obituary, which is also condescendingly entitled: Brug, Manuel, 'Der Brite, der König in Bayern war', *Die Welt*, 23.04.2020.

82   Interview with Steffen Huck on 27 February 2020.

83   Hermanski, Susanne, 'Ein letzter Tanz', *Süddeutsche Zeitung*, 23.04.2020, https://www.sueddeutsche.de/muenchen/stimmen-zum-tode-ein-letzter-tanz-1.4886384?print=true.

84   Tommasini, Anthony, 'Peter Jonas, Innovative Opera Impresario Is Dead at 73', *New York Times*, 02.05.2020.

85   Lederer, Klaus/Vierthaler, Georg, 'Nachruf auf Sir Peter Jonas', Stiftung Oper in Berlin, Berlin 2020.

86   Schreiber, Wolfgang, 'Ein vollendeter Gentleman', *Süddeutsche Zeitung*, 23.04.2020, https://www.sueddeutsche.de/kultur/nachruf-auf-peter-jonas-a-perfect-gentleman-.4886056?print=true.

87   Hermanski, Susanne, 'Ein letzter Tanz', *Süddeutsche Zeitung*, 23.04.2020, https://www.sueddeutsche.de/muenchen/stimmen-zum-tode-ein-letzter-tanz-1.4886384?print=true.

88   Tommasini, Anthony, 'Peter Jonas, Innovative Opera Impresario Is Dead at 73', *New York Times*, 02.05.2020.

89   Original quote: 'He was a very special, amazing, and highly talented man – very disciplined, very dedicated, highly intellectual, and quick witted – as was shown by his incredible career. Peter was a legend and a luminary in the world of international Opera, and no one had a more thorough knowledge of the repertoire and who should be performing it. There was an extraordinary brilliance about him, as an administrator and as a human being, and despite

his health challenges, Peter kept going, never complained, and never gave up.' – Solti, Valerie, quoted from: unsigned, 'Remembering Sir Peter Jonas', Chicago 2020, https://csoarchives.wordpress.com/2020/04/23/remembering-sir-peter-jonas/.
90   Unsigned, 'Sir Peter Jonas', *The Times*, 28.04.2020, p. 49.
91   Allmendinger, Jutta, 'Toodle pip. Erinnerungen an Sir Peter Jonas', WZB Mitteilungen, Issue 168, June 2020, p. 99.
92   Interview with Lesley Garrett CBE on 11 March 2020.
93   Interview with Christine Lemke-Matwey on 15 October 2020.
94   Allmendinger, Jutta, 'Toodle pip. Erinnerungen an Sir Peter Jonas', WZB Mitteilungen, Issue 168, June 2020, p. 99.
95   Barenboim, Daniel, 'München und das British Empire', in Hessler, Ulrike/Schirmer, Lothar (eds.) *Wenn Musik der Liebe Nahrung ist, spielt weiter… Wunderbare Jahre: Sir Peter Jonas, Zubin Mehta und die Bayerische Staatsoper 1993-2006, München* 2006, pp. 11-15, p. 14.
96   Ibid., p.15.
97   Pountney, David, 'Der Wanderer', *Opernwelt*, No. 6/20, p48-50, pp. 49, 50.
98   Tholl, Egbert, 'Der Wanderer. Erinnerungen an Sir Peter Jonas', *Süddeutsche Zeitung*, 24.04.2020, https://www.sueddeutsche.de/muenchen/gedenken-der-wanderer-1.4887636.
99   Pountney, David, 'Der Wanderer', *Opernwelt*, No. 6/20, pp 8-50, p. 50.
100   Lebrecht, Norman, 'Sad News: Sir Peter Jonas is dead', 23.04.2020, https://slippedisc. com/2020/04/sad-news-sir-peter-jonas-is-dead/.
101   Zehetmair, Hans, Kultur bewegt: Kulturpolitik für Bayern, Munich 2001, p. 105.
102   Morreall, John, *Comic Relief. A Comprehensive Philosophy of Humor*, Chichester 2009, p. 145.
103   Midgette, Anne, 'In the Wings in Munich, a Changing of the Avant-Garde', *New York Times*, 20.06.2004.
104   Jonas, Peter, unpublished speech manuscript for the 1998 Fördererabend. Undated.
105   Ibid.
106   Jonas, Peter, unpublished speech manuscript. Address to the press at the Munich Press Club, November 1998.
107   Jonas, Peter, 'Händel's Steckenpferd. An Anglo-German Dialogue by Steffen Huck and Sir Peter Jonas', unpublished manuscript from the archives of Sir Peter Jonas. Undated.
108   Interview with Sir Mark Elder on 11 March 2020.
109   Brug, Manuel, *Opernregisseure heute*, Leipzig 2006, p. 254.
110   Interview with David Alden on 25 September 2020.
111   Interview with Monica Melamid on 6 October 2020.
112   Original quote: 'I've had a rocky life in ways other than professionally, health in particular [he has had recurrent bouts of cancer]. I now have to keep

myself incredibly fit, and I want to do things I know I will not be able to do at 67 or 68. I want to walk across Europe in both directions – from north to south and east to west, Inverness to Palermo and Warsaw to Lisbon – and I'm determined to do it. I also love old-master paintings and I've got an ambition to go to every great collection in Europe and some in the US.' – Moss, Stephen, 'I wanted to be the one who got away', The Guardian, 28.07.2006, p. 10, https://www.theguardian.com/music/2006/jul/28/classicalmusicandopera

113   Jonas, Peter, 'Weitermacher gibt es in diesem Land schon genug', interview with Christine Lemke-Matwey, *Die Zeit*, No. 18, 27.04.2006.

114   Interview with Christian Berner on 8 September 2020.

115   Jonas, Peter, quoted from: unsigned, 'Marc Rothemund erhält den Bernhard-Wicki-Preis', *Süddeutsche Zeitung*, 02.07.2005, www.sz.de/.753376.

116   Jonas, Peter, quoted from dpa report: 'Wicki-Filmpreis für Regisseur Marc Rothemund', *Potsdamer Neueste Nachrichten*, 02.07.2005, https://www.pnn.de/kultur/wicki-filmpreis-fuer-regisseur-marc-rothemund/2236434.html.

117   Unsigned, 'Marc Rothemund erhält den Bernhard-Wicki-Preis', *Süddeutsche Zeitung*, 02.07.2005, www.sz.de/.753376.

118   Original quote: 'Central government does give a tiny sum to Bayreuth, albeit with beancounting strings attached' – Jonas, Peter, 'State of the Nations. Peter Jonas gives the German-speaking opera world a check-up', *Opera*, January 2013, pp. 17-27, p. 17.

119   Jonas, Peter, 'Entschuldigung, das ist doch kein Sommerstaatstheater!', *Frankfurter Allgemeine Zeitung*, 26.07.2011, https://www.faz.net/aktuell/feuilleton/debatten/bayreuther-visionen-peter-jonas-entschuldigung-das-ist-doch-kein-sommerstaatstheater-1548518.html.

120   Tholl, Egbert, 'Der Wanderer. Erinnerungen an Sir Peter Jonas', *Süddeutsche Zeitung*, 24.04.2020, https://www.sueddeutsche.de/muenchen/gedenken-der-wanderer-1.4887636.

121   Jonas, Peter, 'Lieben konnte er. Sir Peter Jonas über Wieland Wagner', *Frankfurter Allgemeine Zeitung*, 24.07.2017. The text printed in the FAZ is a slightly abridged version, the lecture notes are available here: https://wagner-verband-leipzig.de/engl/index.php/wieland-wagner-550/articles/id-31-bericht-2017.html.

122   Tholl, Ebgert, 'Verdi zur Versöhnung. Die Feier zum 100. Geburtstag von Wieland Wagner', *Süddeutsche Zeitung*, 25.07.2017, https://www.sueddeutsche.de/kultur/bayreuther-festspiele-verdi-zur-versoehnung-1.3602370.

123   Chrissochoidis, Ilias/Harmgart, Heike/Huck, Steffen/Müller, Wieland, '"Though this be madness, yet there is method in't." A Counterfactual Analysis of Richard Wagner's Tannhäuser', *Music and Letters*, 2014, DOI: 10.193/ml/gcu081.

124   Jonas, Peter, quoted in Görl, Wolfgang, 'Historisch interessanter vielleicht der Austritt', *Süddeutsche Zeitung*, 22.06.2016, https://www.sueddeutsche.de/muenchen/abstimmung-briten-in-muenchen-sehen-brexit-

als-kollektiven-selbstmord-1.3040761-0#seite-2.
125   Müller, Lothar, 'Im Laboratorium Amerika. Eine Diskussion über die Er – folgsserie Breaking Bad', *Süddeutsche Zeitung*, 28.08.2013, p. 13.
126   Huck, Steffen, 'Vince Gilligan at the WZB – a conversation about economics and morality', YouTube, channel: WZB, August 2013, https://www.youtube.com/watch?v=dLNtlyvQ8Hw

Childhood and Youth

1   Coleman, David, 'Population and Family', in Halsey, Albert Henry/Webb, Josephine, *Twentieth-Century British Social Trends*, Houndmills 2000, pp. 27-93, p. 51. Kynaston, David, *Family Britain 1951-1957*, London 2009, p. 558f.
2   Lebrecht, Norman, *Covent Garden: The Untold Story: Dispatches from the English Culture War*, London 2000, p. 72.
3   Harrison, Brian, *Seeking a Role: The United Kingdom, 1951-70*, Oxford 2009, p. 14f.
4   Kynaston, David, *Austerity Britain 1945-51*, London 2007, p. 260.
5   Original quote: '(T)heir lovingly detailed answer – sherry; tomato soup; sole; roast chicken with coffee – belonged in large part to the realms of fantasy.' – Ibid., p. 246. Cf. p. 95.
6   Ibid., p. 106.
7   Original quote: 'It is more or less the same size as Lebanon, has a similar climate (albeit with no winter), and a geographical echo of his homeland in the lush Caribbean coastline and the magnificent Blue Mountains which divide the island into two.' Campbell, Colin, A *Life Worth Living: The Autobiography of Lady Colin Campbell*, London 1997, p. 4.
8   Tortello, Rebecca, *The Arrival of the Lebanese*, 2003, http://old.jamaica-gleaner.com/pages/history/story0056.htm.
9   Campbell, Colin, *A Life Worth Living: The Autobiography of Lady Colin Campbell*, London 1997, p. 5.
10   His family had no tartan. Cf. e.g. Näger, Doris (2006), 'Alter Ego in Schottenrock', *Süddeutsche Zeitung*, 23.01.2006, p. 51. On the tartan: Brug, Manuel, 'Der Brite, der König in Bayern war', *Die Welt*, 23.04.2020.
11   Studemund-Halévy, Michael, *Im jüdischen Hamburg. Ein Stadtführer von A bis Z*, Hamburg 2011.
12   Unless otherwise stated, the following information comes from an unpublished six-page manuscript by Berndt Wessling, which must have been written around 1997 and bears the title 'Die Geschichte der Familien Wachtel und Jonas' (The History of the Wachtel and Jonas Families). Berndt Wessling has made the manuscript available to Peter Jonas. Not all the information in it could be verified.

13 Eisenberg, Ludwig, *Grosses biographisches Lexikon der deutschen Bühne im XIX. Jahrhundert*, Leipzig 1903, p. 1076f. Digital copy: https://archive.org/stream/ludwigeisenberg00eiseuoft#page/n0/mode/up/search/wachtel.
14 Ibid.
15 Unsigned, 'Gerettet, aber einsam. Elizabeth Melamid', 24.04.208. http://www.bpb.de/geschichte/nationalsozialismus/schicksalsjahr1938/259643/gerettet-aber-einsam-elizabeth-melamid.
16 Jonas, Julius, Begriff und Bedeutung der bona fides bei der Ersitzung und Klagenverjährung, Inaugural-Dissertation, Juristische Fakultät der Friedrich-Alexanders-Universität zu Erlangen, Kiel 1897. The curriculum vitae is on p. 59.
17 Cf. Gewehr, Birgit, Dr Julius Jonas *1874, 2015 http://www.stolpersteine-hamburg.de/index.php?&LANGUAGE=DE&MAIN_ID=7&BIO_ID=2338.
18 Unsigned, 'Gerettet, aber einsam. Elizabeth Melamid', 24.04.2018. http://www.bpb.de/geschichte/nationalsozialismus/schicksalsjahr-1938/259643/gerettet-aber-einsam-elizabeth-melamid.
19 Cf. Gewehr, Birgit, Dr Julius Jonas *1874, 2015. http://www.stolpersteine-hamburg.de/index.php?&LANGUAGE=DE&MAIN_ID=7&BIO_ID=2338.
20 Lorenz, Ina/Berkemann, Jörg, Die Hamburger Juden im NS-Staat 1933 bis 1938/39, Vol. 1 Monographie (=Hamburger Beiträge zur Geschichte der deutschen Juden vol. XLV), Göttingen 2016, p. 288.
21 Morisse, Heiko, Ausgrenzung und Verfolgung der Hamburger Jüdischen Juristen im Nationalsozialismus. Vol. 1 Rechtsanwälte, Wallstein 2003, p. 18. Gewehr, Birgit, Dr Julius Jonas *1874, 2015, http://www.stolpersteine-hamburg.de/index.php?&_LANGUAGE=DE&MAIN_ID=7&BIO_ID=2338.
22 Postcard from Julie to Elizabeth and Margarethe Jonas dated 23 December 1938, http://digifindingaids.cjh.org/?pID=3883838.
23 More information on their lives before emigration: Gewehr, Birgit, Dr Julius Jonas *1874, 2015. http://www.stolpersteine-hamburg.de/index.php?&_LANGUAGE=DE&MAIN_ID=7&BIO_ID=2338 .
24 Unsigned, 'Gerettet, aber einsam. Elizabeth Melamid', 24.04.2018, http://www.bpb.de/geschichte/nationalsozialismus/schicksalsjahr-1938/259643/gerettet-aber-einsam-elizabeth-melamid.
25 Schwarz, first name unknown, quoted from Lorenz, Ina/Berkemann, Jörg, Die Hamburger Juden im NS-Staat 1933 bis 1938/39, Vol. 1 Monographie (= Hamburger Beiträge zur Geschichte der deutschen Juden Vol. XLV), Göttingen 2016, p. 478.
26 http://www.jüdischer-friedhof-altona.de/datenbank.html. The information can be found in the file on the Ohlsdorf Cemetery for the years 1931-1939 in line 2244.
27 Gewehr, Birgit, Dr Julius Jonas *1874, 2015, http://www.stolpersteine-hamburg.de/index.php?&LANGUAGE=DE&MAIN_ID=7&BIO_

ID=2338.
28　Ibid.
29　Möller, Hugo: quoted from Ibid.
30　Ibid.
31　http://www.jüdischer-friedhof-altona.de/datenbank.html, Leisner, Barbara/Fischer, Norbert, Der Friedhofsführer. Spaziergänge zu bekannten und unbekannten Gräbern in Hamburg und Umgebung, Hamburg 1994, p. 72.
32　Lemke-Matwey, Christine/Amend, Christoph, 'Ich ein Deutscher? Ich war geschockt!', *Der Tagesspiegel*, 22.02.2004.
33　Original quote: 'army of servants' – 'For us children, they were also a source of continuous warmth, care and affection. At least we learned at an early age how transient life can be.' – Campbell, Colin, *A Life Worth Living: The Autobiography of Lady Colin Campbell*, London 1997, p. 4.
34　Harrison, Brian, *Seeking a Role: The United Kingdom, 1951-70*, Oxford 2009, p. 3.
35　Rodgers, Lucy/Ahmed, Maryam, 'Windrush: "Who exactly was on board?"', BBC News, 27.04.2018. https://www.bbc.com/news/uk-43808007.
36　No author information, 'Windrush generation: Who are they and why are they facing problems?', BBCNews, 18.04.2018. https://www.bbc.com/news/uk-43782241.
37　Peach, Ceri/Rogers, Alisdair/Chance, Judith/Daley, Patricia, 'Immigration and Ethnicity' in Halsey, Albert Henry/Webb, Josephine, *Twentieth-Century British Social Trends*, Houndmills 2000, pp. 128-175, p. 129.
38　Harrison, Brian, *Seeking a Role: The United Kingdom, 1951-70*, Oxford 2009, p. 4, cf. p. 129.
39　Interview with Monica Melamid on 6 October 2020.
40　Lamb, Mary/Lamb, Charles, 'Preface', in *Tales from Shakespeare*, 1807, quoted in https://en.wikiquote.org/wiki/Tales_from_Shakespeare.
41　Jonas, Peter, 'Warum ich es nicht lassen kann. Peter Jonas' Lieblingsbuch', *Süddeutsche Zeitung*, 31.03.1999.
42　Ibid.
43　Original quote: 'no escape from the tough, tender, purifying embrace of family Britain.' – Kynaston, David, *Austerity Britain 1945-51*, London 2007, p. 633.
44　Kynaston, David, *Family Britain 1951-57*, London 2009, p. 570.
45　Brown, Collum, *The Death of Christian Britain: Understanding Secularisation 1800-2000*, London 2009, p. 9. Kynaston, David, *Family Britain 1951-57*, London 2009, pp. 531-538.
46　Harrison, Brian, *Seeking a Role: The United Kingdom, 1951-70*, Oxford 2009, p. 23.
47　E.g. Allison, John, 'Three Times Lucky. Interview', *Opera*. June 2006, pp. 655-666, p. 658.
48　Harrison, Brian, *Seeking a Role: The United Kingdom, 1951-70*, Oxford

2009, p. 23.
49 http://www.worthschool.org.uk/history.php.
50 https://www.wikitree.com/wiki/Bell-2836.
51 It is possible that this memory does not fall within the period when Jonas was at Worth School, but within the period when he attended St Anne's Convent. The same could apply to his reading skills. This could not be clarified before Jonas's death. But the intensity of his memories was clear nevertheless.
52 Sebald, Winfried Georg, *Austerlitz*, Frankfurt 72015 (1st edition 2001), p. 89.
53 Ibid., p. 90.
54 Ibid., p. 90.
55 Ibid., p. 91f.
56 Winkler, Willi, 'Sir Peter Jonas über die Deutschen', *Süddeutsche Zeitung*, 07.05.2005, pROM8.
57 Reißinger, Marianne, 'Er leidet seit fast 30 Jahren. Münchens Opernchef Sir Peter Jonas: Mein Leben mit dem Krebs', Abendzeitung München, 05.04.2003.
58 The Worth Society, which today looks after alumni matters, was kind enough to search the Abbey's library catalogue for the book that kept Peter Jonas up at night. It could have been *Messiah* by Julian Herbage, 1948.
59 https://www.st-marys-ascot.co.uk/history-of-the-school/.
60 Coleman, David, 'Population and Family', in Halsey, Albert Henry/Webb, Josephine, *Twentieth-Century British Social Trends*, Houndmills 2000, pp. 27-93, p. 63. Cf. Halsey, Albert Henry, 'Introduction: Twentieth-century Britain', in Webb, Josephine, *Twentieth-Century British Social Trends*, Houndmills 2000, pp. 1-23. p. 8.
61 Coleman, David, 'Population and Family', in Halsey, Albert Henry/Webb, Josephine, *Twentieth-Century British Social Trends*, Houndmills 2000, pp. 27-93, p. 61.
62 In the original: 'an important part of marriage', 'physical love-making' and 'intimate love-making'. Kynaston, David, *Family Britain 1951-57*, London 2009, p. 552.
63 Ibid., p. 560.
64 Sebald, Winfried Georg, *Austerlitz*, Frankfurt 72015 (1st edition 2001), p. 92f.

Student Years

1 Briggs, Asa, 'The Plenty Years, 1961-1976', in Blin-Stoyle, Roger (ed.), *The Sussex Opportunity: A New University and the Future*, Brighton 1986, pp. 1-21.

2   https://www.mybrightonandhove.org.uk/places/placeuni/university-of-sussex/university_of_sussex?path=0p115p213p956p.
3   Cf. Daiches, David, 'The Place of English Studies in the Sussex Scheme', in (ed.), *The Idea of a New University: An Experiment in Sussex*, London 1964, pp. 8-99, p. 87.
4   Briggs, Asa, 'The Plenty Years, 1961-1976', in Blin-Stoyle, Roger (ed.), *The Sussex Opportunity: A New University and the Future*, Brighton 1986, pp. 1-21, p. 3. Cf. Blin-Stoyle, Roger, 'Foreword', in *The Sussex Opportunity: A New University and the Future*, Brighton 1986, p. viii-xvi.
5   Briggs, Asa, 'The Plenty Years, 1961-1976', in Blin-Stoyle, Roger (ed.), *The Sussex Opportunity: A New University and the Future*, Brighton 1986, p. 1-21, p.4.
6   Kynaston, David, *Family Britain 1951-57*, London 2009, p. 574.
7   Briggs, Asa, 'The Plenty Years, 1961-1976', in Blin-Stoyle, Roger (ed.), *The Sussex Opportunity: A New University and the Future*, Brighton 1986, p. 1-21, p. 4.
8   Meynell, Esther, *Sussex*, London 1947, p. 240.
9   Cf. McGowan, Margaret, 'A Challenge for the Humanities', in Blin-Stoyle, Roger (ed.), *The Sussex Opportunity: A New University and the Future*, Brighton 1986, pp. 66-78, p. 69. Cf. Briggs, Asa, 'The Plenty Years, 1961-1976', in: Blin-Stoyle, Roger (ed.), *The Sussex Opportunity: A New University and the Future*, Brighton 1986, p. 1-21, p.3.
10 McGowan, Margaret, 'A Challenge for the Humanities', in Blin-Stoyle, Roger (ed.), *The Sussex Opportunity: A New University and the Future*, Brighton 1986, pp. 66-78, p. 69.
11 Gilson, Edwin, 'Memories of Vietnam War Protest at University of Sussex', the *Argus*, 23 February 2018. https://www.theargus.co.uk/news/16043245.we-thought-we-could-change-the-world-memories-of-vietnam-war-protest-at-university-of-sussex/.
12 Daiches, David, 'The Place of English Studies in the Sussex Scheme', in (ed.), *The Idea of a New University: An Experiment in Sussex*, London 1964, pp. 81-99, p. 89.
13 Ibid., p. 90, cf. p. 89.
14 https://en.wikipedia.org/wiki/Buzz_Goodbody.
15 https://archiv.wiener-staatsoper.at/search/person/2268/work/160/role/146.
16 Jolliffe, John, *Glyndebourne: An Operatic Miracle*, London 1999, p. 98.
17 Hughes, Spike, *Glyndebourne: A History of the Festival Opera Founded in 1934 by Audrey and John Christie*, London 1965, p. 231.
18 Jolliffe, John, *Glyndebourne: An Operatic Miracle*, London 1999, p. 99.
19 Norwich, John Julius, *Fifty Years of Glyndebourne: An Illustrated History*, London 1985, p. 94.
20 Jolliffe, John, *Glyndebourne: An Operatic Miracle*, London 1999, p. 122. Cf. Hughes, Spike, *Glyndebourne: A History of the Festival Opera Founded in*

1934 by Audrey and John Christie, London 1965, p. 245f.
21   http://www.whoswho.de/bio/sir-peter-jonas.html.
22   Interview with Sir Mark Elder on 11 March 2020.
23   Jonas, Peter, Festrede zu Ehren von Wieland Wagner. Speech manuscript. Bayreuther Festspiele 24.07.2017, https://wagner-verband-leipzig.de/engl/in dex.php/wieland-wagner-550/articles/id-31-bericht-2017.html.
24   Sandbrook, Dominic, *White Heat: A History of Britain in the Swinging Sixties*, London 2006, p. 246.
25   Quoted from Brown, Mick, 'The Diamond Decades: The 1960s', *Daily Telegraph*, 29.05.2012, from *The Times*, 15.04.1966, https://www.telegraph.co.uk/news/uknews/the_queens_diamond_jubilee/9288411/The-Diamond-Decades-The-1960s.html.
26   Metzger, Rainer, Swinging London, *Kunst und Kultur in der Weltstadt der 60er Jahre*, Munich 2011, p. 339.
27   Cf. Sandbrook, Dominic, *White Heat: A History of Britain in the Swinging Sixties*, London 2006, p. 747f.
28   Greenwood, Walter, *Lancashire*, London 1951, p. 1.
29   Ibid., p. 15.
30   Kennedy, Michael, *Music Enriches All: The Royal Northern College of Music: The First Twenty-One Years*, Manchester 1994, p. 10.
31   Colles, Henry Cope/Cruft, John, *The Royal College of Music: a Centenary Record 1883-1983*, London 1982, p. 69 et seq.
32   Ibid., p. 76f.
33   Falkner, Keith, quoted from ibid., p. 77f.
34   Author unknown, quoted from Bolger Kovnat, Denise, 'Overture', The Rochester Review, 1996, http://www.rochester.edu/pr/Review/V59N2/feature2.html .
35   https://chq.org/about-us/history .
36   https://chq.org/opera-young-artists/young-artist-program .
37   Solti, Valerie, quoted from Lebrecht, Norman, *Covent Garden: The Untold Story: Dispatches from the English Culture War*, London 2000, p. 259.
38   https://slippedisc.com/2015/12/what-to-do-with-a-cougher-in-the-front-row/

Chicago 1974–1984

1   Peck, Donald, *The Right Place, the Right Time! Tales of Chicago Symphony Days*, Bloomington 2007, p. 1.
2   Ibid., p. 6.
3   https://cso.org/about/performers/chicago-symphony-orchestra/chicago-symphony-orchestra1/. Cf. Solti, Georg, *Solti on Solti: A Memoir*, London 1997, p. 173.

4   Morgenstern, Sheldon, *No Vivaldi in the Garage: A Requiem for Classical Music in North America*, Boston 2001, p. 134.
5   Original quote: 'with infinite wisdom to whom I often turned. And his advice, not always what I wanted to hear, was in the long term always right.' https://www.upi.com/Archives/1984/08/10/John-S-Edwards-the-executive-vice-president-and-general/4640460958400/.
6   Interview with Daniel Barenboim on 17 March 2020.
7   Original quote: 'Being in charge of the Chicago Symphony was the fulfilment of my dreams, but at the same time it was a new learning experience for me, a masterclass in musical directorship.' – Solti, Georg, *Solti on Solti: A Memoir*, London 1997, p. 164. Cf. p. 171f.
8   Lebrecht, Norman, *Covent Garden: The Untold Story: Dispatches from the English Culture War*, London 2000, p. 228.
9   *The Right Place, the Right Time! Tales of Chicago Symphony Days,* Bloomington 2007, S. 1.
10 Ibid., p.6.
11 Solti, Georg, *Solti on Solti: A Memoir*, London 1997, p. 172.
12 Ibid., p. 174.
13 Ibid.
14 Rosenthal Archives, Chicago Symphony Orchestra.
15 Ibid.
16 Ibid.
17 Ibid.
18 Ibid.
19 Ibid.
20 Ibid.
21 Ibid.
22 Original quote: 'Chicago at the moment is an endless vision of snow and more snow and "cabin fever" seems to have gripped everybody to an unusual degree.' – Ibid.
23 Original quote: 'I miss Europe so much and only count the days when I can return. I feel like an exile here who goes through a period of oblivion before he can return to his native land, but a talent for oblivion is after all a talent for survival (a Murdoch inspired phrase).' – Ibid.
24 Ibid.
25 Original quote: 'We set off like a circus troupe or medieval army,' Solti described, 'with orchestra members accompanied by their families, from small babies to grandparents, and some of the trustees and supporters.' – Solti, Georg, *Solti on Solti: A Memoir*, London 1997, p. 174.
26 An image of the cover can be found here: https://content.time.com/time/covers/0,16641,19730507,00.html.
27 Lebrecht, Norman, *Covent Garden: The Untold Story: Dispatches from the English Culture War*, London 2000, p. 259.
28 Solti, Georg, *Solti on Solti: A Memoir*, London 1997, p. 166.

29   Ibid., p. 169 et seq.
30   Beckmann, Isabell-Annett, *Hodgkin Lymphom: Antworten. Hilfen. Perspektiven*, Bonn 2018, p. 31f.
31   Solti, Georg, *Solti on Solti: A Memoir*, London 1997, p. 174.
32   Herbort, Heinz Josef, 'Richard Wagner's "Rheingold" in Paris. Weltaus Müll und Plüsch', *Die Zeit*, No. 51/1976, https://www.zeit.de/1976/51/welt-aus-muell-und-pluesch/komplettansicht?print .
33   Ibid.
34   Ibid.
35   Rosenthal Archives, Chicago Symphony Orchestra.
36   Kesting, Jürgen, *Die großen Sänger unseres Jahrhunderts*, Düsseldorf 1993, p. 612f.
37   Matheopolous, Helena, *Great Sopranos and Mezzos Discuss their Art*, Boston 1991, p. 145, cf. p. 154.
38   Heurich, Florian, 'Richard Strauss: Vier letzte Lieder', BR Klassik, 2017, https://www.br-klassik.de/themen/klassik-entdecken/starke-stuecke-richard-strauss-vier-letzte-lieder-06.html.
39   Richard Strauss deleted the word 'both' in the setting.
40   Rosenthal Archives, Chicago Symphony Orchestra.
41   Ibid.
42   Ibid.
43   Ibid.
44   Ibid.
45   Ibid.
46   Ibid.
47   Ibid.
48   Ibid.
49   Ibid.
50   Ibid.
51   Ibid.
52   Ibid.
53   Ibid.
54   Ibid.
55   Ibid.
56   Original quote: 'Harry Zelzer was one of the rare people whose musical "nose" was so extraordinary that it was enough for someone to play the first few notes of a recital for Harry to know the real potential of the artist. His tenacity and courage in presenting young artists contributed greatly to the knowledge of the public and Chicago.' – Zelzer, Sarah, *Impresario: The Zelzer Era 1930-1990*, Chicago 1990, no page given.
57   Ibid., p. 85.
58   Original quote: 'What is a good impresario? Some people say he's an exploiter of other people's talent. I say he's a gambler. If he ends the season in the black, he's a good impresario. One of the most important things for an

impresario to know is the value of an attraction at the box office... I only really enjoy half the concerts I stage, but I'm not in the business to cater to me.' – Ibid., p. 27.
59 Ibid., pp. 26f., 85.
60 Original quote: 'Between seven-thirty and nine a.m. Harry would concentrate on studying box-office intakes, promotional ideas and calls to New York managers at their homes. This was hard on the managers' wives. They pleaded with me to tell my husband not to call so early in the morning. Harry insisted that his best deals were made with the manager before they arrived at their offices.' – Ibid., p. 77.
61 Ibid., p. 80.
62 Ibid., p. 78.
63 Ibid., p. 80
64 Rosenthal Archives, Chicago Symphony Orchestra. Sarah Zelzer must also have had the memorandum when writing her book. Not only does a precise date appear at this point, which is rarely the case, but she also reproduces the contents of the conversation with verbatim quotations.
65 Ibid.
66 Zelzer, Sarah, *Impresario: The Zelzer Era 1930-1990*, Chicago 1990, p. 150.
67 Rosenthal Archives, Chicago Symphony Orchestra.
68 Original quote: 'It all seemed pleasant and reasonable, but I was against it, as I had been from the first moment Harry broached the plan to me. I felt that our organisations were too different in too many ways for the marriage to succeed. I didn't think that the Association would appreciate his gift.' – Zelzer, Sarah, *Impresario: The Zelzer Era 1930-1990*, Chicago 1990, p. 151.
69 Original quote: 'the whole reason Harry gave Allied Arts to the Chicago Symphony to begin with was so that we could get together on fees and block-buying. I turned Serkin down, and so you shouldn't pay him that fee either. It's not right. That damages the purpose of combining Allied Arts with the Orchestral Association.' – Ibid., p. 161f.
70 Ibid., p. 164.
71 Rosenthal Archives, Chicago Symphony Orchestra.
72 Ibid.
73 Ibid.
74 Original quote: 'a tall young actor from England who speaks the connecting lines of Biblical text. His speech is clear, his sense of the story is absolutely compelling, his very presence helps draw us into the drama. He is magnificently a factor in the success of the performance and he doesn't even sing a note.' – Glackin, William, 'Symphony Superb With Vocal Work', *The Sacramento Bee*, 09.04.1978, Page B.
75 Original quote: 'we again realized that both of us had found something which I thought had only existed in the deep recesses of my dream world; a total love, a total trust, a total communication and total identification with

another person without sacrificing one's own sense of freedom and individuality. I have never in fact felt so free in my whole life and at the same time I have never had such inspiration, such total involvement with another person.' – Rosenthal Archives, Chicago Symphony Orchestra.

76   Skinner, David/Belsey, Ronald, *Management of Esophageal Disease*, Philadelphia 1988, pp. v, 146.

77   Southerland, Kevin/d'Amico, Thomas, 'Historical perspectives of The American Association for Thoracic Surgery: Dr David B. Skinner (1935-2003) – a surgeon and something more', *The Journal of Thoracic and Cardiovascular Surgery*, Vol. 151, No. 1/2016, https://www.jtcvs.org/article/S0022-5223(15)01210-6/pdf.

78   Rosenthal Archives, Chicago Symphony Orchestra.
79   Ibid.
80   Ibid.
81   Tamussino, Ursula, *Lucia: Memories of Lucia Popp*, Vienna 1999, p. 119.
82   Rosenthal Archives, Chicago Symphony Orchestra.
83   Ibid.
84   Ibid.
85   Popp, Lucia, quoted in Tamussino, Ursula, *Lucia: Memories of Lucia Popp*, Vienna 1999, p. 104f. Caricature on p. 104.
86   Hintze, Werner/Risi, Clemens/Sollich, Robert (eds.), Realistisches Musiktheater. Walter Felsenstein: Geschichte, Erben, Gegenpositionen, Berlin 2008 (= Recherchen 51), p. 7-12, p. 7f.
87   Mösch, Stephan, '"Der Flieder war's". Wieland Wagner und Die Meistersinger von Nürnberg', in Mösch, Stephan/Friedrich, Sven, 'Es gibt nichts Ewiges', *Wieland Wagner: Ästhetik, Zeitgeschichte, Wirkung*, Würzburg 2019, pp. 175-219, p. 213.
88   Rosenthal Archives, Chicago Symphony Orchestra.
89   Ibid.
90   Miller, Alice, *Das Drama des begabten Kindes und die Suche nach dem wahren Selbst*, Frankfurt 1983.
91   Cf. Ibid., p. 11.
92   Ibid., p. 10.
93   Ibid., p. 11.
94   Ibid., p. 20.
95   Ibid., p. 21.
96   Ibid., p. 17.
97   Ibid., pp. 32, 48, 41, 33.
98   Ibid., p. 23.
99   Miller, Martin, *Das wahre 'Drama des begabten Kindes'. Die Tragödie Alice Millers*, Freiburg 2016.
100 Miller, Alice, *Das Drama des begabten Kindes und die Suche nach dem wahren Selbst*, Frankfurt 1983, p. 12.
101 Interview with Martha Gilmer on 19 August 2020.

102   Original quote: 'He was a force of nature, loving the fight on behalf of the sustenance and the triumph of the arts.' – Gilmer, Martha, 'Remembering Sir Peter Jonas', CSO archives, https://csoarchives.wordpress.com/2020/04/23/remembering-sir-peter-jonas/.
103   Rosenthal Archives, Chicago Symphony Orchestra.
104   Emerick, Laura, 'Daniel Barenboim affirms his deep affection and bond to the CSO', 30.10.2018, https://csosoundsandstories.org/daniel-barenboim-affirms-his-deep-affection-and-bond-to-the-cso/.
105   Rosenthal Archives, Chicago Symphony Orchestra.

Munich 1946–1947

1   Strobel, Michael, 'Die Seele des Ensembles. Erinnerungen an den Dirigenten Ferdinand Leitner (1912-1996)', in Busch-Salmen, Gabriele/Salmen, Walter/Zepf, Michael (eds.), *Musik in Baden-Württemberg*, Jahrbuch 2007, Vol. 14, Munich 2007, pp. 159-171, pp. 162, 159f.
2   Solti, Georg, *Solti on Solti: A Memoir*, London 1997, p. 35f.
3   Ibid., p. 36.
4   Ibid., p. 63.
5   Cf. Weisz, Christoph (ed.), *OMGUS-Handbuch: The American Military Government in Germany 1945-1949* (= Quellen und Darstellungen zur Zeitgeschichte; ed. by the Institut für Zeitgeschichte; Vol. 35), Munich 1994, p. 243; source: Conversation between Edward Kilényi and David Monod from an email from David Monod to JG of 28.08.2018.
6   Solti, Georg, *Solti on Solti: A Memoir*, London 1997, p. 63f.
7   Ibid., p. 65.
8   Thacker, Toby, *Music after Hitler, 1945-1955*, Farnham 2007, p. 44.
9   Strobel, Michael, 'Die Seele des Ensembles. Erinnerungen an den Dirigenten Ferdinand Leitner (1912-1996)', in Busch-Salmen, Gabriele/Salmen, Walter/Zepf, Michael (eds.), *Musik in Baden-Württemberg*, Jahrbuch 2007, Vol. 4, Munich 2007, pp. 159-171, p. 162.
10   Monod, David, *Settling Scores: German Music, Denazification, & the Americans, 1945-1953*, Chapel Hill/London 2005, p. 8.
11   Solti, Georg, *Solti on Solti: A Memoir*, London 1997, p. 69.
12   Thacker, Toby, *Music after Hitler, 1945-1955*, Farnham 2007. Cf. footnote 63, p. 52.
13   Monod, David, 'Internationalism, Regionalism, and National Culture: Music Control in Bavaria, 1945-1948', Central European History, Vol. 33, No. 3 (2000), pp. 339-368, p. 360.
14   Original quote: 'vindication of German art and a condemnation of American philistinism' – Monod, David, *Settling Scores: German Music, Denazification, & the Americans, 1945-1953*, Chapel Hill/London 2005, p.

174.
15   Schläder, Jürgen/Cromme, Rasmus/Frank, Dominik/Frühinsfeld, Katrin, *Wie man wird, was man ist: Die Bayerische Staatsoper vor und nach 1945*, Leipzig 2017, p. 183. Cf. p. 192.
16   Cf. Schläder, Jürgen/Cromme, Rasmus/Frank, Dominik/Frühinsfeld, Katrin, *Wie man wird, was man ist: Die Bayerische Staatsoper vor und nach 1945*, Leipzig 2017, p. 182.
17   Evarts, John, quoted from Solti, Georg, *Solti on Solti: A Memoir*, London 1997, p. 90.
18   Ibid.
19   Solti, Georg, *Solti on Solti: A Memoir*, London 1997, p. 89.
20   Adam, Klaus, 'Kompromissloser Fanatiker', Bayerische Staatszeitung, 14.09.2012, https://www.bayerische-staatszeitung.de/staatszeitung/unser-bayern/detailansicht-unser-bayern/artikel/kompromissloser-fanatiker.html.
21   Cf. Lebrecht, Norman, *Covent Garden: The Untold Story: Dispatches from the English Culture War*, London 2000, p. 230. London 1984–1993.

London 1984–1993

1   Interview with Sir Mark Elder on 11 March 2020.
2   Lebrecht, Norman, *Covent Garden: The Untold Story: Dispatches from the English Culture War*, London 2000, pp. 240-242.
3   Ibid., pp. 245, 246.
4   Interview with Maggie Sedwards on 30 August 2019.
5   Original quote: 'It's easy to sink under the morass of human beings and talent there, and to rise above it you have to be articulate and quick-witted.' – Jonas, Peter, quoted from Allison, John, 'Three Times Lucky. Interview', *Opera*, June 2006, pp. 655-666, p. 659.
6   Cf. Scott, Derek, *German Operetta on Broadway and in the West End, 1900-1950*, Cambridge 2019, p. 108f.
7   Cf. Morley, Sheridan, *Theatre's Strangest Act:. Extraordinary but true tales from theatre's colourful history*, London 2005, p. 42.
8   Garrett, Lesley, *Notes from a Small Soprano*, London 2000, p. 162.
9   Harewood, George, *The Tongs and the Bones: The Memoirs of Lord Harewood*, London 1981, p. 4.
10   Ibid., p. 57, cf. p. 52 et seq.
11   Sutcliffe, Tom, 'The Earl of Harewood obituary', the *Guardian*, 11.07.2011, https://www.theguardian.com/music/2011/jul/11/the-earl-of-harewood.
12   Lebrecht, Norman, *Covent Garden: The Untold Story: Dispatches from the English Culture War*, London 2000, p. 279.
13   Crutchfield, Will, 'English Opera Picks Art Administrator', *New York*

Times, 17.07.1984.
14   Gilbert, Susie, *Opera for Everybody: The Story of English National Opera*, London 2009, p. 307, p. 316.
15   Ibid., p. 323f.
16   Sutcliffe, Tom, *Believing in Opera*, Princeton 1996, p. 339.
17   Ibid.
18   Garrett, Lesley, *Notes from a Small Soprano*, London 2000, p. 175.
19   This GDR television recording shows a performance of *Madame Butterfly* under the musical direction of Mark Elder: YouTube, channel Opernsänger DDR, https://www.youtube.com/watch?v=uJOkTFHiv_s.
20   Sutcliffe, Tom, *Believing in Opera*, Princeton 1996, p. 346.
21   Ibid., p. 347 et seq.
22   Ibid., pp. 181, 436.
23   Ibid., p. 20.
24   Gilbert, Susie, *Opera for Everybody: The Story of English National Opera*, London 2009, p. 38.
25   Ibid., p. 337.
26   Jonas, Peter, quoted in Allison, John, 'Three Times Lucky. Interview', *Opera*, June 2006, pp. 655-666, p. 655.
27   Fay, Stephen, 'A Wilful Determination to Survive', *Sunday Times Magazine*, 08.09.1985.
28   Lebrecht, Norman, *Covent Garden: The Untold Story: Dispatches from the English Culture War*, London 2000, p. 7.
29   Ibid.
30   Ibid., p. 19.
31   Ibid., p. 18.
32   Ibid.
33   Peacock, D. Keith, *Thatcher's Theatre: British Theatre and Drama in the Eighties*, Westport 1999, p. 216.
34   Lebrecht, Norman, *Covent Garden: The Untold Story: Dispatches from the English Culture War*, London 2000, p. 36.
35   Ibid., p. 46.
36   Ibid., p. 41.
37   Peacock, D. Keith, *Thatcher's Theatre: British Theatre and Drama in the Eighties*, Westport 1999, p. 36.
38   Gilbert, Susie, *Opera for Everybody: The Story of English National Opera*, London 2009, p. 314.
39   In German: 'Die Künste müssen, wie die Samen, wachsen, wenn sie blühen sollen. Einige der Samen, die wir im Laufe der Jahre gezüchtet haben, platzen nun auf, um zu wachsen, werden aber durch den Mangel an Platz und Nahrung zurückgehalten. Diese Strategie wird dem Rat helfen, das Saatgutbett auszudünnen und ihnen mehr Raum für ihre Entwicklung und für die Ausplanzung neuen Saatguts zu geben.' – Peacock, D. Keith, *Thatcher's Theatre: British Theatre and Drama in the Eighties*, Westport 1999, p. 42.

40   Ibid., p. 37.
41   Ranan, David, *In Search of a Magic Flute: The Public Funding of Opera – Dilemmas and Decision Making*, Oxford 2003, p. 86.
42   Peacock, D. Keith, *Thatcher's Theatre: British Theatre and Drama in the Eighties*, Westport 1999, pp. 48, 52.
43   Interview with Lesley Garrett CBE on 11 March 2020.
44   Sutcliffe, Tom, 'The Earl of Harewood obituary', the *Guardian*, 11.07.2011, https://www.theguardian.com/music/2011/jul/11/the-earl-of-harewood.
45   Jonas, Peter/Elder, Mark/Pountney, David, *Power House: The English National Opera Experience*, London 1992, p. 15.
46   Ibid.
47   Sutcliffe, Tom, *Believing in Opera*, Princeton 1996, p 171.
48   Gilbert, Susie, *Opera for Everybody: The Story of English National Opera*, London 2009, p. 36.
49   Ibid., p. 360.
50   Sutcliffe, Tom, *Believing in Opera*, Princeton 1996, p. 172.
51   Gilbert, Susie, *Opera for Everybody: The Story of English National Opera*, London 2009, p. 362.
52   Ibid., p. 348.
53   Jonas, Peter/Elder, Mark/Pountney, David, *Power House: The English National Opera Experience*, London 1992, p. 12.
54   Interview with Jane Livingston on 29 August 2019.
55   Sutcliffe, Tom, *Believing in Opera*, Princeton 1996, p. 354.
56   Gerlach-March, Rita, *'Gutes' Theater: Theaterfinanzierung und Theaterangebot in Großbritannien und Deutschland im Vergleich*, Wiesbaden 2011, p. 42.
57   Peacock, D. Keith, *Thatcher's Theatre: British Theatre and Drama in the Eighties*, Westport 1999, p. 39f.
58   Gilbert, Susie, *Opera for Everybody: The Story of English National Opera*, London 2009, p. 326.
59   Ibid., p. 375.
60   Ibid., p. 376.
61   Interview with John Nickson on 29 August 2019.
62   Gilbert, Susie, *Opera for Everybody: The Story of English National Opera*, London 2009, p. 356f.
63   Original quote: 'He was one of the most attractive men I have ever met, with a combination of good looks, power and enormous vulnerability that I found irresistible. PJ as he was known is ridiculously tall and in his youth was built like a rugby prop forward. [...](B)y the time we met he was spare and rangy, which highlighted his striking bone structure and breathtaking blue eyes. The attraction between us was palpable and undeniable, though we spent some time trying to deny it to each other and ourselves.' – Garrett, Lesley, *Notes from a Small Soprano*, London 2000, p. 60f.

64 Ibid., p. 161.
65 Ibid., p. 162.
66 Peters, Pauline, 'Exit Peter Jonas…cheeky to the last', *Evening Standard*, 25.06.1993.
67 Sutcliffe, Tom, *Believing in Opera*, Princeton 1996, p. 321.
68 Ibid., p. 4.
69 Gilbert, Susie, *Opera for Everybody: The Story of English National Opera*, London 2009, p. 421.
70 Bassett, Kate, *In Two Minds: A Biography of Jonathan Miller*, London 2012.
71 Jonathan Miller directs *The Mikado*, YouTube, channel: venompangx, minute 31:30, https://www.youtube.com/watch?v=WfzpePn_9P0.
72 Gilbert, Susie, *Opera for Everybody: The Story of English National Opera*, London 2009, p. 409.
73 Sutcliffe, Tom, *Believing in Opera*, Princeton 1996, p. 350f.
74 Ibid., p. 320.
75 Jonas, Peter/Elder, Mark/Pountney, David, *Power House: The English National Opera Experience*, London 1992, p. 27f.
76 Ibid., p. 44.
77 Snowman, Daniel, *The Gilded Stage: A Social History of Opera*, New York 2009, p. 409.
78 Sutcliffe, Tom, *Believing in Opera*, Princeton 1996, p171.
79 Original quote: 'psycho-historical mysteries whose resonances and implications (submerged in music) invited daringly imaginative amplification and experimental synthesis – so that they merged with the imagery and philosophy of life and art today.' – Ibid., p. 8, cf. pp. 171, 194.
80 Ibid., p. 194.
81 Ibid., p. 174.
82 Ibid., p. 340.
83 Interview with David Alden on 25 September 2020.
84 Original quote: 'Many critics (but not his ENO audience) seemed incapable of looking behind the conscious indecorousness of the productions, the rejection of specific period, the desire to free the *Stage* picture from the weight of extended naturalistic and dramatically irrelevant filling-in.' – Ibid., p. 185.
85 Ibid.
86 Ibid., p. 340.
87 Jonas, Peter, 'Händel's Steckenpferd. An Anglo-German Dialogue by Steffen Huck and Sir Peter Jonas', unpublished manuscript from the archives of Sir Peter Jonas. Undated.
88 Gilbert, Susie, *Opera for Everybody: The Story of English National Opera*, London 2009, p. 410f.
89 Ibid., p. 411.
90 Ibid., p. 417.

91   Thatcher, Margaret, quoted from Sinclair, Andrew, *Arts and Cultures: History of the Years of the Arts Council of Great Britain*, London 1998, p. 60.
92   Gilbert, Susie, *Opera for Everybody: The Story of English National Opera*, London 2009, p. 415.
93   Ibid., p. 314.
94   Ibid., p. 327.
95   Ibid., p. 326.
96   Jonas, Peter/Elder, Mark/Pountney, David, *Power House: The English National Opera Experience*, London 1992, p. 12.
97   Myerson, Jeremy, 'Safe Sex', the *Stage*, 07.09.1989, p. 25.
98   Garrett, Lesley, *Notes from a Small Soprano*, London 2000, p. 187.
99   Milnes, Rodney, 'Editorial. Extremely Naff Opera', *Opera*, 10.1989, p. 1165.
100 Ibid.
101 Pountney, David, quoted from Evans, David, *Phantasmagoria: A Sociology of Opera*, London 2018, p. 144.
102 Gilbert, Susie, *Opera for Everybody: The Story of English National Opera*, London 2009, p. 423.
103 Jackson, Peter, 'The Cultural Politics of Masculinity: Towards a Social Geography', *Transactions of the Institute of British Geographers*, Vol. 16, No. 2 (1991), pp. 199-213, p. 206.
104 Jackson, Peter, 'Towards a Cultural Politics of Consumption', in Bird, Jon et al. (eds.), *Mapping the Futures*, London 1993, pp. 207-228, p. 218.
105 Jackson, Peter/Thrift, Nigel, 'Geographies of Consumption', in Miller, Daniel (ed.), *Acknowledging Consumption: A Review of New Studies*, London 1995, pp. 203-236, p. 406f.
106 Other interpretations of the ad, such as that by David Evans in 2005, clearly fell short. Evans read the ad featuring Karl Phillips exclusively as enacting the stereotype of homosexual opera lovers, precisely because no production was advertised on the poster. Evans, David, 'Speaking Over and Above the Plot. Aural Fixation, Scopophilia, Opera and the Hay Sensibility', *Theory, Culture & Society*, Vol. 22 (2) 99-119, p. 100.
107 Tilden, Imogen, 'How we made it: Ivan Fischer and Tom Randle on ENO's The Magic Flute', the *Guardian*, 08.10.2012, https://www.theguardian.com/music/2012/oct/08/how-we-made-magic-flute-english-national-opera.
108 Anonymous, 'Taking a flyer on publicity', the *Stage*, 21.09.1989, p. 24.
109 Sinclair, Mark, *Trademarks: The Untold Stories Behind 29 Classic Logos*, Grünwald 2015, p. 75 et seq.
110 Gilbert, Susie, *Opera for Everybody: The Story of English National Opera*, London 2009, p. 362.
111 Ibid., p. 426.
112 Griffiths, Paul, 'Hard-Sell of the Century', *The Times*, 26.04.1990, p. 16.
113 Author unknown, 'Radical Reign of a King in the Coliseum', the

Guardian, 23.04.1990.
114   Gilbert, Susie, *Opera for Everybody: The Story of English National Opera*, London 2009, p. 420.
115   Sutcliffe, Tom, *Believing in Opera*, Princeton 1996, p. 171.
116   Ibid., p. 178.
117   Ibid., p. 181, 179.
118   Cf. Gilbert, Susie, *Opera for Everybody: The Story of English National Opera*, London 2009, p. 433.
119   Ibid., p. 431f.
120   Ibid., p. 433.
121   Ibid., p. 456.
122   Sutcliffe, Tom, *Believing in Opera*, Princeton 1996, p. 338.
123   Ibid.
124   Ibid., p. 237.
125   Ibid., p. 239.
126   Ibid., p. 31.
127   Christiansen, Rupert, 'Viennese fancies', the *Spectator*, 14.12.1991, p. 52.
128   Sutcliffe, Tom, *Believing in Opera*, Princeton 1996, p 229.
129   Ibid., p. 237.
130   Burt, Paddy, 'The Lady's not for Squashing OPERA', the *Independent*, 19.02.1995, https://www.independent.co.uk/arts-entertainment/the-lady-s-not-for-squashing-opera-1573920.html.
131   Gilbert, Susie, *Opera for Everybody: The Story of English National Opera*, London 2009, p. 403.
132   Interview with Daniel Barenboim on 17 March 2020.
133   Interview with Hans Zehetmair on 26 November 2019.
134   Ranan, David, *In Search of a Magic Flute: The Public Funding of Opera – Dilemmas and Decision Making*, Oxford 2003, p. 239.
135   Cf. Peattie, Anthony, 'Keeping Up with the Jonas', *Opera Now*, p. 13f., p. 13.
136   Gilbert, Susie, *Opera for Everybody: The Story of English National Opera,* London 2009, p. 450f.
137   Sutcliffe, Tom, *Believing in Opera*, Princeton 1996, p. 338.
138   Cf. Gilbert, Susie, *Opera for Everybody: The Story of English National Opera*, London 2009, p. 452.
139   Quoted from Evans, David, *Phantasmagoria: A Sociology of Opera*, London 2018, p. 144.
140   Jonas, Peter, quoted from Evans, David, *Phantasmagoria: A Sociology of Opera*, London 2018, p. 144.
141   Author unknown, 'Nicholas John, dramaturge and editor (1952-1996)', in Kahn, Gary (ed.), *Die Meistersinger von Nürnberg (Overture Opera Guides)*, London 2015, pp. 338-340, p. 339.
142   Gilbert, Susie, *Opera for Everybody: The Story of English National*

Opera, London 2009, p. 35.

143   Original quote: 'If you ask what is the aim of an opera company, the straight answer must be "to perform opera to as high a standard as lies within the company's possibilities – and then to raise the standards a bit higher". All other considerations – of place, specialization, casting, tradition and so on – are secondary.' Harewood, George, 'Introduction' in Jonas, Peter/Elder, Mark/Pountney, David, *Power House: The English National Opera Experience*, London 1992, p. 6f., p. 6.

144   Original quote: 'A manager is responsible for the work of a company as a whole, and, while it might theoretically be possible for individual productions to flourish in spite of him, a company style could hardly develop without his enthusiasm.' – Ibid., p. 6f.

145   Jonas, Peter/Elder, Mark/Pountney, David, *Power House: The English National Opera Experience*, London 1992, p. 9.

146   James, Barry, 'Notes, Words and Stage in the Peter Jonas Mix', *International Herald Tribune*, 09.05.1991.

147   Sutcliffe, Tom, *Believing in Opera*, Princeton 1996, p. 338.

148   Original quote: 'a period of astonishing zest, drive and creativity, with 1985-7 marking its high point, with a succession of extraordinary and exciting productions that challenged traditional and complacent attitudes to opera as an art form, as well as making the Coliseum one of the most dynamic theatres in Europe' – Gilbert, Susie, *Opera for Everybody: The Story of English National Opera*, London 2009, p. 462.

149   Original quote: 'catapulted the ENO into the international limelight, far outstripping the troubled Royal Opera at Covent Garden through a combination of big and bold theatrical ideas, an unswerving commitment to high musical standards, and long-term artistic goals which have broadly survived the financial constraints imposed by dwindling subsidy.' – Ibid., p. 460.

150   Original quote: 'ENO's powerhouse had run out of steam and Peter Jonas was on his way to run the Bavarian State Opera in Munich, leaving a large deficit and leaking roofs to Dennis Marks, a BBC producer with no previous experience of running a theatre. His music director, equally innocent, was to be Sian Edwards. ENO, in disarray' – Lebrecht, Norman, *Covent Garden: The Untold Story: Dispatches from the English Culture War*, London 2000, p. 380.

151   Gilbert, Susie, *Opera for Everybody: The Story of English National Opera*, London 2009, p. 463. See Whitney, Craig, 'London Opera Is Losing Its Leaders; Lack of Government Aid Is Blamed', in *New York Times*, 29.04.1991, Section C, p. 14.

152   Gilbert, Susie, *Opera for Everybody: The Story of English National Opera*, London 2009, p. 463f.

153   Ibid., p. 474.

Munich 1993–2006

1   Koch, Gerhard, 'Verschlafene Ballnacht', *Frankfurter Allgemeine Zeitung*, 02.02.1994, p. 29 – Midgette, Anne, Berlioz, 'La Damnation de Faust', *Opera News*, Vol. 58, No. 12, 05.03.1994, pp. 48f., 48. Gale Academic OneFile, https://link.gale.com/apps/doc/A14842070/AONE?u=sbbpk&sid=AONE&xid=6b9734fc.
2   Clark, Andrew, 'Firebrand or Fashion Victim?', *Financial Times*, 04.07.1994, D 85.
3   Koch, Gerhard, 'Verschlafene Ballnacht', *Frankfurter Allgemeine Zeitung*, 02.02.1994, p. 29.
4   Jonas, Peter, '21 March 1730 – 21 March 1994', Liner notes to the CD Box Set Georg Friedrich Händel, *Giulio Cesare in Egitto*. Live-Produktion aus der Bayerischen Staatsoper, 2002, Munich: Farao Classics 2012, pp. 11-18, p. 14.
5   Ibid.
6   Ibid., p. 5.
7   Ibid.
8   Interview with Barbara Burgdorf on 5 March 2020.
9   In the original: 'a hearty, albeit not very baroque reading out of the orchestra' – Midgette, Anne, 'Handel: Giulio Cesare', *Financial Times*, Vol. 59, No. 2, August 1994, p. 42. Gale Academic OneFile, https://link.gale.com/apps/doc/A15627478/AONE?u=sbbpk&sid=AONE&xid=6620e029.
10   Jonas, Peter, '21 March 1730 – 21 March 1994', Liner notes to the CD Box Set Georg Friedrich Händel, *Giulio Cesare in Egitto*. Live-Produktion aus der Bayerischen Staatsoper, 2002, Munich: Farao Classics 2012, pp. 11-18, p. 15f.
11   Mehta, Zubin, *Die Partitur meines Lebens: Erinnerung*, Munich 2006, p. 279.
12   Bayerischer Oberster Rechnungshof, Jahresbericht, Munich 1995, p. 169, https://www.orh.bayern.de/images/files/Jahresberichte/1983-996/Jahresbericht_1995.pdf.
13   Original quote: 'The Bavarian State Opera is a fine example of a wealthy West German house realizing it's time to do something about its image. It's also a fine example of how much money a theater can swallow. Internationally, the house has attracted much attention recently by having had to close for two full seasons in the last five years for renovations to its hydraulic stage machinery, each time at a cost of about $24 million over and above the annual operating budget. The failure of the hydraulic system could be a metaphor for many productions in wealthy West German theaters: lots of money poured in, little quality control.' Cf. Midgette, Anne, 'Reunification Blues', *Opera News*, Vol. 57, No. 17, June 1993, p. 10f. Gale Academic OneFile, https://link.gale.com/apps/doc/A3784354/AONE?u=sbbpk&sid=AONE&xid=6bcd4d6.

14   Rockwell, John (1993): 'For Opera in Munich, Optimism seems Forced', *New York Times*, 13.07.1993, Section C, p. 13.
15   Interview with Jürgen Rose on 3 March 2020.
16   Interview with Wilfried Hösl on 26 November 2019.
17   Interview with Aron Stiehl on 12 June 2020.
18   Jonas, Peter, '21 March 1730 – 21 March 1994', Liner notes to the CD Box Set Georg Friedrich Händel, *Giulio Cesare in Egitto*, Live-Produktion aus der Bayerischen Staatsoper, 2002, Munich: Farao Classics 2012, pp. 11-18, p. 13.
19   Jonas, Peter, 'Backstage. Interview', *Wall Street Journal Europe*, 07.02.2003.
20   Tholl, Egbert, 'Sieg der Respektlosigkeit', *Süddeutsche Zeitung*, 20.12.2012.
21   Those who interpret this basic programmatic line as having existed from the beginning are wrong. Cf. Schreiber, Wolfgang, 'Macht der Bilder im Haus der Gefühle' in Hessler, Ulrike/Schirmer, Lothar (eds.), *Wenn Musik der Liebe Nahrung ist, spielt weiter... Wunderbare Jahre: Sir Peter Jonas, Zubin Mehta und die Bayerische Staatsoper 1993-2006*, Munich 2006, pp. 27-46, p. 39.
22   Tholl, Egbert, 'Sieg der Respektlosigkeit', *Süddeutsche Zeitung*, 20.12.2012.
23   Abbate, Carolyn/Parker, Roger, *Eine Geschichte der Oper*, Munich 2013. First picture section, Fig. 5.
24   Interview with Daniel Barenboim on 7 March 2020.
25   In the original: 'interpretative arts is still part of the core of the society's arguments, that is means something' – Kramer, Jane, 'Opera Wars. How German should German music be?', *New Yorker*, 20.08.2001, pp. 38-45, p. 45.
26   Interview with Christine Lemke-Matwey on 15 October 2020.
27   Original quote: 'presence, intellect, and a kind of infectious and highly articulate imperviousness to the claims of stupid or offensive people, which gave him a moral high ground often described by his admirers as "the British confidence", and by Jonas himself as "ten years' training" with the monks.' Kramer, Jane, 'Opera Wars. How German should German music be?', *New Yorker*, 20.08.2001, pp. 138-145, p. 144.
28   Sutcliffe, Tom, *Believing in Opera*, Princeton 1996, p. 20.
29   Jonas, Peter, 'Sir Peter Jonas und die Deutschen. Interview with Willi Winkler', *Süddeutsche Zeitung*, 07.05.2005.
30   Ibid.
31   Original quote: 'that the city that had nurtured Hitler in the country that his father had fled because of Hitler was now nurturing him' – Kramer, Jane, 'Opera Wars: How German should German music be?', *New Yorker*, 20.08.2001, pp. 38-45, p 45.
32   Rockwell, John, 'For Opera in Munich, Optimism seems Forced', *New York Times*, 13.07.1993, Section C, p13.

33 Cf. Peter, Wolf-Dieter, 'Ein Sir an der Isar', *Deutsche Bühne*, No. 6, 2006, pp. 20-23, p. 20.
34 Zehetmair, Hans, *Kultur Bewegt: Kulturpolitik für Bayern*, Munich 2001, p. 104.
35 Peter, Wolf-Dieter, 'Ein Sir an der Isar', *Deutsche Bühne*, No. 6, 2006, pp. 20-23, p. 20.
36 Midgette, Anne, 'In the Wings in Munich, a Changing of the Avant-Garde', *New York Times*, 20.06.2004.
37 Schreiber, Wolfgang, 'Ein vollendeter Gentleman', *Süddeutsche Zeitung*, 23.04.2020. https://www.sueddeutsche.de/kultur/nachruf-auf-peter-jonas-a-perfect-gentleman.4886056?print=true.
38 Original quote: 'He can praise his predecessors and still talk of radical changes by using the theater's yearlong closing as an excuse. And by stressing Munich's progressive artistic past (which in truth was only periodic and was rarely reflected in its opera), he can postulate an ideal audience that may not yet exist. Mr. Jonas is no naif; he recognizes that despite his all-embracing manifestos, he may have trouble pleasing both the conservatives and the progressives.' – Rockwell, John, 'For Opera in Munich, Optimism seems Forced', *New York Times*, 13.07.1993, Section C, p. 13.
39 Cf. Midgette, Anne, 'Reunification Blues', *Opera News*, Vol. 57, No. 17. June 1993. p 10f. Gale Academic OneFile, https://link.gale.com/apps/doc/A13784354/AONE?u=sbbpk&sid=AONE&xid=6bcd41d6.
40 Cf. Schreiber, Wolfgang, 'Macht der Bilder im Haus der Gefühle', in Hessler, Ulrike/Schirmer, Lothar (eds.), *Wenn Musik der Liebe Nahrung ist, spielt weiter... Wunderbare Jahre: Sir Peter Jonas, Zubin Mehta und die Bayerische Staatsoper 1993-2006*, Munich 2006, pp. 27-46, p. 31.
41 Jonas, Peter quoted from Fabian, Imre, 'Weltoffenes Musiktheater', *Opernwelt*, June 1993, pp. 12-14, p. 13.
42 Clark, Andrew, 'Firebrand or Fashion Victim?', *Financial Times*, 04.07.1994, D 85.
43 Jonas, Peter, quoted from Reisch, Ulrike, 'Opernchef: Münchenerinnen behängt wie Tannenbäume', Abendzeitung München, 19/20.02.1994, p. 26.
44 Cf. Whitney, Craig, 'London Opera Is Losing Its Leaders; Lack of Government Aid Is Blamed', *New York Times*, 29.04.1991, Section C, p. 14.
45 Constitution of the Free State of Bavaria as per the announcement of 15.12.1998 (GVBl. p. 991, 992, BayRS 100-1-I), last amended by the Act of 11 November 2013 (GVBl. P. 638, 639, 640, 64, 642), https://www.gesetze-bayern.de/Content/Document/BayVerf.
46 Announcement by the Bavarian State Ministry of Science and the Arts on the revision of the Basic Regulations for the Bavarian State Theatres on 26 April 2014. 09. 2018 (KWMBl. S. 387) https://www.gesetze-bayern.de/Content/Document/BayVV_2246_WK_1022 – Ranan, David, *In Search of a Magic Flute: The Public Funding of Opera – Dilemmas and Decision Making*, Oxford 2003, p. 232.

47   Jonas, Peter, quoted from Ranan, David, *In Search of a Magic Flute: The Public Funding of Opera – Dilemmas and Decision Making*, Oxford 2003, p. 239.
48   Cf. Allison, John, 'Three Times Lucky. Interview', *Opera*, June 2006, pp. 655-666, p. 665.
49   Jonas, Peter, 'Händel's Steckenpferd. An Anglo-German Dialogue by Steffen Huck and Sir Peter Jonas'. Unpublished manuscript from the archives of Sir Peter Jonas.
50   Jonas, Peter, quoted from Voigt, Thomas, 'So wichtig wie ein Krankenhausbett. Peter Jonas im Gespräch mit Thomas Voigt', *Opernwelt*, January 1996, pp. 26-28, p. 26.
51   Unsigned, 'Erlauchter Teil', *Der Spiegel*, No. 50, 13.12.1993, p. 63f., p.63, https://www.spiegel.de/spiegel/print/d-3693235.html.
52   Cf. Schreiber, Wolfgang, 'Macht der Bilder im Haus der Gefühle', in Hessler, Ulrike/Schirmer, Lothar (eds.), *Wenn Musik der Liebe Nahrung ist, spielt weiter... Wunderbare Jahre: Sir Peter Jonas, Zubin Mehta und die Bayerische Staatsoper 1993-2006, Munich 2006*, pp. 27-46, p. 34.
53   Bayerischer Oberster Rechnungshof, Jahresbericht 1995, Munich 1995 p. 163. https://www.orh.bayern.de/images/files/Jahresberichte/1983-1996/Jahresbericht_1995.pdf.
54   Interview with Toni Schmid on 4 March 2020.
55   Interview with Hans Zehetmair on 26 November 2019.
56   Unsigned, 'The Wanted List', the *Guardian*, 25.03.1996.
57   Jonas, Peter, 'Weitermacher gibt es in diesem Land schon genug. Interview with Christine Lemke-Matwey', *Die Zeit*, No. 18, 27.04.2006.
58   Peter, Wolf-Dieter, 'Ein Sir an der Isar', *Deutsche Bühne*, No. 6, 2006, pp. 20-23, p. 21.
59   Koch, Gerhard, 'Ein wunderböser Traum', *Frankfurter Allgemeine Zeitung*, No. 156, 08.07.1994, p. 31.
60   Jonas, Peter, 'Musiktheater als Dramaturgie der Gesellschaft', *Opernwelt*, October 1993, p. 11f., p. 11.
61   Original quote: 'a theater that represented a pinnacle of tradition in a city acutely aware of its traditions… The very building epitomizes traditional values. Destroyed in World War II, it was one of relatively few German theatres to be faithfully restored – graceful neo-Classical facade and all – rather than replaced with a modern house.' – Midgette, Anne, 'In the Wings in Munich, a Changing of the Avant-Garde', *New York Times*, 20.06.2004.
62   The Verein der Freunde des Nationaltheaters e.V. shows the historical film Ein Bürgersieg by Rudolf Reißner on its website, which is an impressive document of this citizens' initiative: https://www.freunde-des-nationaltheaters.de.
63   Jonas, Peter, quoted from Rockwell, John, 'For Opera in Munich, Optimism seems Forced', *New York Times*, 13.07.1993, Section C, p. 13.
64   Clark, Andrew, 'Firebrand or Fashion Victim?' *Financial Times*,

04.07.1994, D 85.
65   Walsh, Michael, 'Kilt vs. Lederhosen', *Time* magazine, 29.01.1996, p. 55.
66   Midgette, Anne, 'Reunification Blues', *Opera News*, Vol. 57, No. 17, June 1993. P. 10f. Gale Academic OneFile, https://link.gale.com/apps/doc/A13784354/AONE?u=sbbpk&sid=AONE&xid=6bcd41d6.
67   Jonas, Peter, 'Palamon und Arcitas heute', in Mendell, Pierre, *Plakate für die Bayerische Staatsoper*, Baden 2006, pp. 7-12, p. 7.
68   Jonas, Peter, unpublished speech manuscript for the film première on 05.07.1994 at the Cuvilliés-Theater.
69   Jonas, Peter, 'Palamon und Arcitas heute', in Mendell, Pierre, *Plakate für die Bayerische Staatsoper*, Baden 2006, pp. 7-12, p. 8.
70   Cf. de Michielis, Stefano, *Osteria Italiana: Wo die Liebe zur italienischen Küche begann*, Munich 1998, pp. 9, 10, 12f.
71   Schad, Martha, '"Das Auge war vor allen Dingen ungeheuer anziehend". Freundinnen und Verehrerinnen', in Leutheusser, Ulrike (ed.), *Hitler und die Frauen*, Stuttgart/Munich 2001, pp. 2-27, p. 97.
72   Beinert, Wolfgang, Mendell, Pierre, https://www.typolexikon.de/mendell-pierre/ .
73   Sample posters can be seen here: http://www.mendell-design.de/staatsoper.htm.
74   Hufnagl, Florian, 'Das Bild der Stadt', in Mendell, Pierre, *Plakate für die Bayerische Staatsoper*, Baden 2006, pp. 13-17, p. 15f.
75   Armer, Karl Michael, 'Grafische Ouvertüren', in Mendell, Pierre, *Plakate für die Bayerische Staatsoper*, Baden 2006, pp. 25-30, pp. 25, 27.
76   Interview with Katrin Lausberg on 12 July 2018.
77   Interview with David Alden on 25 September 2020.
78   See for example Näger, Doris, 'Alter Ego in Schottenrock', *Süddeutsche Zeitung*, 23.01.2006, p. 51. On the tartan: Brug, Manuel, 'Der Brite, der König in Bayern war', *Die Welt*, 23.04.2020.
79   No author given, 'Streiflicht', *Süddeutsche Zeitung*, 24.09.1997, p. 1.
80   Interview with Natalia Ritzkowsky on 19 June 2020.
81   Jonas, Peter, quoted from Voigt, Thomas, 'So wichtig wie ein Krankenhausbett. Peter Jonas im Gespräch mit Thomas Voigt', *Opernwelt*, January 1996, pp. 26-28, p. 27.
82   Jonas, Peter, quoted in Tholl, Egbert, 'Sieg der Respektlosigkeit', *Süddeutsche Zeitung*, 20.12.2012.
83   Interview with Maurice Lausberg on 4 March 2020.
84   Cf. Moss, Stephen: 'I wanted to be the one who got away', the *Guardian*, 28.07.2006, p. 10, https://www.theguardian.com/music/2006/jul/28/classicalmusicandopera.
85   Hubert, Rudolf, 'Intendant Jonas verpatzt die Probe', *Münchner Abendzeitung*, 05.03.1999.
86   Midgette, Anne, 'In the Wings in Munich, a Changing of the

Avant-Garde', *New York Times*, 20.06.2004.
87   Tholl, Egbert, 'Der Dompteur der Dinosaurier', *Süddeutsche Zeitung*, 14.10.2016.
88   Tholl, Egbert, 'Guter, alter Kasten', *Süddeutsche Zeitung*, 16.11.2013.
89   Tholl, Egbert, 'Der Wanderer. Erinnerungen an Sir Peter Jonas', *Süddeutsche Zeitung*, 24.04.2020. https://www.sueddeutsche.de/muenchen/gedenken-der-wanderer-1.4887636.
90   For Leander Haußmann's point of view, cf. Mauro, Helmut, 'Einmal Fledermaus, nie mehr Opernregie', *Süddeutsche Zeitung*, 03.02.1998. Jonas then issued a counterstatement, which he had written himself: Jonas, Peter, 'Zuviel Champagner?', *Süddeutsche Zeitung*, 04.01.1999.
91   Cf. Umbach, Klaus, 'Vom Thron gestoßen', *Der Spiegel*, 02.11.1998, https://www.spiegel.de/spiegel/print/d-8029104.html, Jonas, Peter, 'Schottenrock, Götterdämmerung', *Deutsche Bühne*, No. 2/94, pp..8-11, 62.
92   Strahammer, Silvia, 'Jürgen Rose und die Kostümwerkstätten der Bayerischen Staatsoper', in Pargner, Birgit/Deutsches Theatermuseum München (ed.), Jürgen Rose, *Nichts ist so lebensfüllend wie das Theater*, Leipzig 2015, p. 132.
93   Unsigned, 'Six Decades of Zubin Mehta', 2018, https://www.laphil.com/about/watch-and-listen/six-decades-of-zubin-mehta.
94   The LA Phil offers an informative film with many historical recordings, https://www.laphil.com/about/watch-and-listen/six-decades-of-zubin-mehta.
95   Zehetmair, Hans, *Kultur bewegt: Kulturpolitik für Bayern*, Munich 2001.
96   Mehta, Zubin, *Die Partitur meines Lebens: Erinnerung*, Munich 2006, p. 272.
97   Original quote: 'The hulk of the library, one of the most surreal ruins in this city of twisted steel, pocked walls and shattered glass, must be one of the eeriest venues ever chosen for a performance of the Requiem.' – Sudetic, Chuck, 'Sarajevo Journal: In the Very Ashes of War, a Requiem for 10,000', *New York Times*, 20.06.1994, Section 1, p. 4.
98   Mehta, Zubin, *Die Partitur meines Lebens: Erinnerung*, Munich 2006, p. 273.
99   Ibid., p. 277.
100   Ibid., p. 275.
101   Jonas, Peter, quoted in Schreiber, Wolfgang, 'Muttersprache Mozart', in *Süddeutsche Zeitung*, 29.04.2016.
102   Jonas, Peter, 'Laudatio auf Zubin Mehta anlässlich der Verleihung des Wilhelm-Furtwängler-Preises beim Beethovenfest Bonn am 11.29.2011', unpublished manuscript.
103   Mehta, Zubin, *Die Partitur meines Lebens: Erinnerung*, Munich 2006, p. 276.
104   Ibid., p. 247.
105   Jonas, Peter, 'Festspiele für Fanatiker. Interview mit Sir Peter Jonas. Sonderbeilage Opernfestspiele München', *Süddeutsche Zeitung*, 23.06.2005.

106 Jonas, Peter, 'Kunst – Schlachtfeld der Toleranz. Queen's Lecture', 08.11.2001, Technische Universität Berlin, unpublished manuscript, p. 22.
107 Bayerischer Oberster Rechnungshof, Jahresbericht, Munich 2000, p. 181, https://www.orh.bayern.de/media/comform2content/documents/c6/a331/f36/Jahresbericht2000.pdf.
108 Cf. Ibid.
109 Bayerischer Oberster Rechnungshof, Jahresbericht, Munich 2000, p. 182. https://www.orh.bayern.de/media/com_form2content/documents/c6/a331/f36/Jahresbericht2000.pdf.
110 Ibid.
111 ORH-Bericht, 'Staatstheater und staatlich geförderte Theater und Orchester', TNr 40, Munich 2000, https://www.orh.bayern.de/images/files/Jahresberichte/2000/Ergebnisse/00-40.pdf
112 Ibid.
113 Ibid.
114 Ibid.
115 Jonas, Peter, 'Weitermacher gibt es in diesem Land schon genug. Interview with Christine Lemke-Matwey', *Die Zeit*, No. 18, 27.04.2006.
116 Peter, Wolf-Dieter, 'Neue Ansichten, neue Aussichten', in *Deutsche Bühne*, 12.12.1997, p. 18f.
117 Oberster Rechnungshof Bayern, Jahresbericht 1992, Munich 1992, pp. 195-200. https://www.orh.bayern.de/images/files/Jahresberichte/1983-1996/Jahresbericht_1992.pdf.
118 Peter, Wolf-Dieter, 'Ein Sir an der Isar', *Deutsche Bühne*, No. 6, 2006, pp. 20-23, p. 23.
119 Lausberg, Maurice, quoted in Kausch, Martina: 'Staatsoper vervierfacht Fundraising-Erlöse', *Welt am Sonntag*, 20.06.2004. https://www.welt.de/print-wams/article111942/Staatsoper-vervierfacht-Fundraising-Erloese.html.
120 Jonas, Peter, 'Entschuldigung, das ist doch kein Sommerstaatstheater', *Frankfurter Allgemeine Zeitung*, 05.06.2008, p. 37.
121 Bayerische Staatsoper München, Jahresbericht, Munich 2019, p. 26f., https://www.staatsoper.de/media/content/PDFs/Publikationen/JAHRESBERICHT_18_INNEN_DRUCKPRODUKTION_Innen.pdf.
122 Etscheit, Georg, '50 Jahre neue alte Staatsoper – Musentempel statt Schuhschachtel', dpa report of 14.11.2013.
123 Jonas, Peter, 'Entschuldigung, das ist Nonsens', interview, *Münchner Merkur*, 28/29.10.2000. His recognition of the achievement of sponsors did not stop him from calling them, from a less prominent platform, 'wealthy airheads' who 'feast on the flesh of our artistic integrity'. In Jonas, Peter, 'Verführte und Verführer', *Der Architekt* No. 3/1995, pp. 149-153, p. 149.
124 Allison, John, 'Three Times Lucky. Interview', *Opera*, June 2006, pp. 655-666, p. 663.
125 Pleschinski, Hans, *Bildnis eines Unsichtbaren*, Munich 2002, p. 262.
126 Jonas, Peter, 'Königliches Kompliment', Abendzeitung München,

18.05.2000.
127   Pleschinski, Hans, *Bildnis eines Unsichtbaren*, Munich 2002, p. 262.
128   Jonas, Peter, 'Weitermacher gibt es in diesem Land schon genug. Interview with Christine Lemke-Matwey', *Die Zeit*, No. 18, 27.04.2006.
129   Mösch, Stephan, 'Kunst und Klamauk', in *Opernwelt* No. 4/1996, pp. 4-6, p. 6. Cf. Jonas, Peter, quoted in Morris, Roderick C., 'A British Dash of Verve', in *International Herald Tribune*, 26.06.1996.
130   Pleschinski, Hans, *Bildnis eines Unsichtbaren*, Munich 2002, pp. 263, 264.
131   Jonas, Peter, 'Weitermacher gibt es in diesem Land schon genug. Interview with Christine Lemke-Matwey', *Die Zeit*, No. 18, 27.04.2006.
132   Jonas, Peter, 'Neue Wege des Musiktheaters', in Gerstenberg, Judith (ed.), *Umwege zum Konzert. Ruedi Häusermann – eine Werkschau*, Berlin 2015, pp. 236-239, pp. 237, 238.
133   Von Bose, Jürgen, 'Ich will, daß man meine Musik versteht. Gespräch mit Claus Spahn', in *Süddeutsche Zeitung*, No. 47, 28.06.1996, p. 13.
134   Jonas, Peter, 'Die Augen sperren die Ohren auf', *Süddeutsche Zeitung*, 28.06.2006, p. 13.
135   Original quote: 'that the word "slaughterhouse" was a deliberate, subversive, British reference to them, and even that the swastika formed by a bomber propeller on the poster designed for the festival constituted a libel against the German people.' – Kramer, Jane, 'Opera Wars: How German should German music be?', *New Yorker*, 20.08.2001, pp. 138-145, p. 143f.
136   Schreiber, Wolfgang, 'Macht der Bilder im Haus der Gefühle', in Hessler, Ulrike/Schirmer, Lothar (eds.), *Wenn Musik der Liebe Nahrung ist, spielt weiter... Wunderbare Jahre: Sir Peter Jonas, Zubin Mehta und die Bayerische Staatsoper 1993-2006*, Munich 2006, pp. 27-46, p. 45.
137   Jonas, Peter, '"Opernfestspiele müssen populär sein". Interview mit Claus Spahn', *Focus*, No. 27/1997, p. 101.
138   Jonas, Peter, 'Festivals All Over the World', Applaus No. 9/1991, no page reference.
139   Jonas, Peter, 'Opera Festivals – Why?', *Opera Festivals*, pp. 11-17, p. 17.
140   Jonas, Peter, 'Entschuldigung, das ist doch kein Sommerstaatstheater', *Frankfurter Allgemeine Zeitung*, 05.06.2008, p. 37.
141   See Dent, Edward, *A Theatre for Everybody: The Story of The Old Vic and Sadler's Wells*, London 1945, and Gilbert, Susie, *Opera for Everybody: The Story of English National Opera*, London 2009.
142   Kausch, Martina, 'Staatsoper vervierfacht Fundraising-Erlöse', *Welt am Sonntag*, 20.06.2004, https://www.welt.de/print-wams/article111942/Staatsoper-vervierfacht-Fundraising-Erloese.html.
143   Sutcliffe, Tom, 'Catching the seasonal spirit', the *Spectator*, 03.08.2002, p 38f., p 39.
144   Jonas, Peter, 'Oper im Internet: Unter Quarantäne', *Die Zeit*, No. 40,

26.09.2013.
145   Hoffmann, Hilmar, *Kultur für alle: Perspektiven und Modelle*, Frankfurt 1979, pp. 59-96, p. 66.
146   Jonas, Peter, 'Elitäre Kultur für die ganze Öffentlichkeit', in Gräfin Dönhoff, Marion/Markl, Hubert/von Weizsäcker, Richard (eds.), *Eliten und Demokratie: Wirtschaft, Wissenschaft und Politik im Dialog – zu Ehren von Eberhard von Kuenheim*, Berlin 1999, pp. 67-82, p. 68.
147   Ibid., pp. 67-82, p. 71.
148   Jonas, Peter, 'Opera Festivals – Why?', in *Opera Festivals*, pp. 11-17, p. 17, p. 12.
149   Jonas, Peter, 'Elitäre Kultur für die ganze Öffentlichkeit', in Gräfin Dönhoff, Marion/Markl, Hubert/von Weizsäcker, Richard (eds.), *Eliten und Demokratie: Wirtschaft, Wissenschaft und Politik im Dialog – zu Ehren von Eberhard von Kuenheim*, Berlin 1999, pp. 67-82, p. 81, p. 80. Cf. p. 69, p. 71.
150   Ibid., p. 80.
151   Jonas, Peter, 'Musiktheater als Dramaturgie der Gesellschaft', *Opernwelt*, October 1993, p. 11f., p. 11.
152   Jonas, Peter, quoted in Voigt, Thomas, 'So wichtig wie ein Krankenhausbett. Peter Jonas im Gespräch mit Thomas Voigt', *Opernwelt*, January 1996, pp. 26-28, p. 26.
153   Jonas, Peter, unpublished speech manuscript for the sponsors' evening 1998, undated.
154   Jonas, Peter, unpublished speech manuscript for the supporters' evening, 8 November 2002.
155   Jonas, Peter, unpublished speech manuscript for the sponsors' evening 1998, undated.
156   Kramer, Jane, 'The Once and Future Chancellor: Letter from Europe', *New Yorker*, 14.09.1998, pp. 58-71, p. 58.
157   Jonas, Peter, 'Verführte und Verführer', in *Der Architekt* No. 3/1995, pp. 149-153, p. 152.
158   Jonas, Peter, unpublished speech manuscript for the film première on 5 July 1993 at the Cuvilliés-Theatre.
159   Jonas, Peter, 'Verführte und Verführer', in *Der Architekt* No. 3/1995, pp. 149-153, p. 149.
160   Jonas, Peter, '"Art is not necessary, art is indispensable!", Interview with Sir Peter Jonas', *Startmagazin*, University of St Gallen, No. 4, 17.10.2004, p. 4.
161   Cf. Schläder, Jürgen, 'So sieht modernes Musiktheater aus. Sir Peter Jonas, das Opernmanagement und die Dramaturgie der Gesellschaft', in Bayerische Staatsoper (ed.), *Münchner Opernfestspiel*, Munich 2006, pp. 26-41, p. 26.
162   Kayser, Beate, 'Können wir nur noch Barock?', *tz*, 02/03.08.1997.
163   Lemke-Matwey, Christine/Amend, Christoph, 'Ich ein Deutscher? Ich war geschockt!', *Der Tagesspiegel*, 22.02.2004.

164   Interview with Monica Melamid on 6 October 2020.
165   Interview with Lesley Garrett CBE on 11 March 2020.
166   Sebald, Winfried Georg, *Austerlitz*, Frankfurt 72015 (1st edition 2001), p. 70.
167   Ibid., p. 68f.
168   Ibid., p. 24.
169   Kayser, Beate, 'Und wo blieb der Staat?', *tz*, 24/25.01.2004.
170   Jonas, Peter, 'Glanz der Würde', *Süddeutsche Zeitung*, 24.01.2004.
171   Lau, Jörg, 'Berlin, letzter Akt?', *Die Zeit*, 11.01.2001.
172   Jonas, Peter, 'Entschuldigung, das ist Nonsens', interview *Münchner Merkur*, 28/29.10.2000.
173   Kramer, Jane, 'Opera Wars: How German should German music be?', *New Yorker*, 20.08.2001, pp. 138-145, p. 142.
174   Lau, Jörg, 'Berlin, letzter Akt?', *Die Zeit*, 11.01.2001.
175   Jonas, Peter, 'Kunst – Schlachtfeld der Toleranz. Queen's Lecture', 08.11.2001, Technische Universität Berlin, unpublished manuscript p. 12.
176   Lau, Jörg, 'Berlin, letzter Akt?', *Die Zeit*, 11.01.2001.
177   Ibid.
178   Hanssen, Frederik, 'Wo das Musiktheater zur Spielwiese der Autokraten wird', *Der Tagesspiegel*, 29.04.2001.
179   Kramer, Jane, 'Opera Wars: How German should German music be?', *New Yorker*, 20.08.2001, pp. 138-145, p. 142.
180   Ibid., p. 139f.
181   Ibid., p. 142.
182   Ibid., p. 142.
183   Jonas, Peter, quoted from Lautenschläger, Rolf, 'Weiss mit Flierl im Opernduett', *tz*, 27.01.2003.
184   Dolak, Gregor, 'Ich wollt, ich wär ein Huhn', *Focus*, 01.03.2003.
185   Jonas, Peter, 'Weitermacher gibt es in diesem Land schon genug', Interview with Christine Lemke-Matwey, *Die Zeit*, No. 18, 27.04.2006.
186   Original quote: 'Yet he also made the case that Baroque operas were not just fare for early-music aficionados but also compelling music dramas that in contemporary productions could hold the stages of major houses.' – Tommasini, Anthony, 'Peter Jonas, 73, Opera Impresario with Daring Vision', *New York Times*, 05.05.2020, Section A, p. 24.
187   Original quote: 'Many of the Munich productions cited as Jonas successes date from the beginning of Sir Peter's tenure, a time when production values seemed to eclipse musical values entirely. Musical stability arrived in 1998 with Mr. Mehta, who seems to be enjoying his tenure as music director. But critical acclaim has gravitated in recent years towards theatres like the Stuttgart Opera, where productions are equally provocative but arguably more thoughtful.' – Midgette, Anne, 'In the Wings in Munich, a Changing of the Avant-Garde', *New York Times*, 20.06.2004.
188   Sutcliffe, Tom, 'Catching the seasonal spirit', the *Spectator*, 03.08.2002,

p. 38f., p. 38.
189   Interview with Christian Berner on 8 September 2020.
190   Jonas, Peter, unpublished speech manuscript for the film première on July 1993 at the Cuvilliés-Theatre.
191   Barenboim, Daniel, 'Munchen und das British Empire', in Hessler, Ulrike/Schirmer, Lothar (eds.), *Wenn Musik der Liebe Nahrung ist, spielt weiter... Wunderbare Jahre: Sir Peter Jonas, Zubin Mehta und die Bayerische Staatsoper 1993-2006*, München 2006, pp. 11-15, p. 14.

Coda

1   Büning, Eleonore, 'Der ideale Opernherr', *Frankfurter Allgemeine Zeitung*, 14.10.2016, p. 11, author unknown, 'Die Strategie eines sanften Provokateurs', *Süddeutsche Zeitung*, 02.08.1994, p. 4. – Sucher, C. Bernd, 'von einem, der ausog, das wundern zu lehren', No. 8/2006, pp. 6-10.
2   Bergman, Ingmar, *The Seventh Seal* Script, Hamburg 1963 (= Cinemathek 7), p. 23.
3   Cf. Winkler, Willi, 'Sir Peter Jonas über die Deutschen', *Süddeutsche Zeitung*, 07.05.2005, p. 8.
4   Interview with Natalia Ritzkowsky on 19 June 2020.
5   Czeguhn, Jutta, 'Ein Abend für Sir Peter', *Süddeutsche Zeitung*, 24.07.2019, https://www.sueddeutsche.de/muenchen/szenario-ein-evening-for-sir-peter-jonas-.4538694.
6   Ibid.
7   Hitzer, Bettina, *Krebs Fühlen: Eine Emotionsgeschichte des 20 Jahrhunderts*, Stuttgart 2020, p. 7.
8   Bergman, Ingmar, *The Seventh Seal* Script, Hamburg 1963 (= Cinemathek 7).
9   In Schlegel's translation: 'Wenn wir Schatten euch beleidigt, / O so glaubt – und wohl verteidigt / Sind wir dann –: ihr alle schier / Habet nur geschlummert hier / Und geschaut in Nachtgesichten / Eures eignen Hirnes Dichten./.../ Nun gute Nacht! Das Spiel zu enden, / Begrüßt uns mit gewognen Händen!'
10   Mann, Thomas, *Buddenbrooks: Verfall einer Familie*, Frankfurt 1974 (1903), p. 702.

Printed in Great Britain
by Amazon